CHRISTIAN THEOLOG

SERIES EDITO₁

Timothy Gorringe   Gr

CHRISTIAN THEOLOGY IN CONTEXT

Any inspection of recent theological monographs makes plain that it is still thought possible to understand a text independently of its context. Work in the sociology of knowledge and in cultural studies has, however, increasingly made obvious that such a divorce is impossible. On the one hand, as Marx put it, 'life determines consciousness'. All texts have to be understood in their life situation, related to questions of power, class, and modes of production. No texts exist in intellectual innocence. On the other hand texts are also forms of cultural power, expressing and modifying the dominant ideologies through which we understand the world. This dialectical understanding of texts demands an interdisciplinary approach if they are to be properly understood: theology needs to be read alongside economics, politics, and social studies, as well as philosophy, with which it has traditionally been linked. The cultural situatedness of any text demands, both in its own time and in the time of its rereading, a radically interdisciplinary analysis.

The aim of this series is to provide such an analysis, culturally situating texts by Christian theologians and theological movements. Only by doing this, we believe, will people of the fourth, sixteenth or nineteenth centuries be able to speak to those of the twenty-first. Only by doing this will we be able to understand how theologies are themselves cultural products—projects deeply resonant with their particular cultural contexts and yet nevertheless exceeding those contexts by being received into our own today. In doing this, the series should advance both our understanding of those theologies and our understanding of theology as a discipline. We also hope that it will contribute to the fast developing interdisciplinary debates of the present.

Karl Barth

AGAINST HEGEMONY

Timothy Gorringe

OXFORD
UNIVERSITY PRESS

*This book has been printed digitally and produced in a standard specification
in order to ensure its continuing availability*

OXFORD
UNIVERSITY PRESS

Great Clarendon Street, Oxford OX2 6DP

Oxford University Press is a department of the University of Oxford.
It furthers the University's objective of excellence in research, scholarship,
and education by publishing worldwide in

Oxford New York

Auckland   Cape Town Dar es Salaam Hong Kong   Karachi
Kuala Lumpur Madrid Melbourne Mexico City   Nairobi
New Delhi Shanghai Taipei Toronto
With offices in
Argentina Austria Brazil Chile Czech Republic France Greece
Guatemala Hungary Italy Japan South Korea Poland Portugal
Singapore Switzerland Thailand Turkey Ukraine Vietnam

Oxford is a registered trade mark of Oxford University Press
in the UK and in certain other countries

Published in the United States
by Oxford University Press Inc., New York

Oxford is a registered trade mark of Oxford University Press
in the UK and in certain other countries

Published in the United States
by Oxford University Press Inc., New York

ISBN 0-19-875247-4

To

Chris Rowland

companheiro na espera do Reino por vir

He was a man of the world, who was occupied with the questions of public life, the question as to the right or wrong of anarchy, for instance, or the question about the best form of the State, or of the allowability or otherwise of revolution or the assassination of tyrants, before he was occupied with the question of the content of the New Testament.

Karl Barth on Calvin, 1922

Barth's theology is no timeless theology but speaks emphatically to its concrete period, and in the same way is stamped by that concrete period.

Michael Weinrich

Preface

Possidius, Augustine's biographer, remarked that anyone who claimed to have read everything Augustine wrote was certainly lying. How much more likely to be true is this of Barth, whose *Church Dogmatics* is almost twice as long as the *Summa Theologiae*, and who alongside that published well over one hundred books and articles in his lifetime, many of them major works in their own right. The *Gesamtausgabe* is meanwhile adding texts of work which remained unpublished, like the Göttingen Dogmatics and the lectures on Calvin, which likewise take their place as major works. If we add the secondary literature, which comprises many thousands of books and articles in many languages, then reading everything relevant becomes an impossibility. Life is short and there are many calls on one's time apart from writing on Barth. Nevertheless I think I can truthfully say that all the major items in his bibliography have been consulted, and in most cases lived with over many years.

Acquaintance with the secondary literature is necessarily much more selective. I have learned greatly from the work of F. W. Marquardt, Peter Winzeler and Sabine Plonz, as will be obvious. Likewise I, along with all other students of Barth, am in debt to the brilliant work of Bruce McCormack, whose treatment of Barth's early period is unlikely to be superseded for many years. The onus on those who differ from him, as I do in some respects on Barth's position in Weimar, is to make an equally compelling case.

As a student I recall being wearied by the many tedious paraphrases Barth has attracted, and I have written with Hans Frei's warning, about the way any attempt to summarize Barth turns the material to dust, constantly in my ears. Rereading the central expository chapters of this book I fear the same fate. Yet I hope I have made clear that, as Gollwitzer insisted, 'This man's spirit cannot be reduced to a simple or single formula.' And with others who have attempted to read Barth 'from the left' the study is undertaken not primarily because of the intrinsic fascination and beauty of his theology, which I do not deny, but because, like Barth, I hope one day for a society which has escaped from capitalist hegemony. The Christian gospel is a vision of a society beyond all hegemony. Perhaps the situation where it is from each according to their ability to each according to their need is the kingdom, and we all know that no political programme is identical with that. Neverthless, Barth insisted vehemently that provisional political goals, in which hegemony is resisted and overcome, were essential. And the great theme of his theology, from start to finish, is that the reality of God, and faith as response to that reality, is not a prop for the infirm, an opiate for the masses, nor an optional extra in the culture of contentment, but an essential aspect of human liberation, that without which human liberation cannot be achieved. As the most consummately imaginative elucidation of the gospel in the twentieth century I believe that his theology, despite some of its reactionary features, remains a potent contribution to human liberation, and it is in the interests of arguing that case that this study is offered.

T.G.

Exeter
October 1998

Contents

Abbreviations

B–B	*Karl Barth–Rudolf Bultmann Briefwechsel 1911–1966*
B–B (ET)	*Karl Barth–Rudolf Bultmann Letters 1922–1966*
B–R	*Karl Barth–Martin Rade: Ein Briefwechsel*
B–Th I	*Barth–Thurneysen Briefwechsel 1913–1921*
B–Th II	*Barth–Thurneysen Briefwechsel 1921–1930*
CD	*Church Dogmatics*
EvT	*Evangelische Theologie*
ET	English translation
KD	*Kirchliche Dogmatik*
R1	*Der Römerbriefe*, 1st edn
R2	*Der Römerbriefe*, 2nd edn
SJT	*Scottish Journal of Theology*
TEH	*Theologische Existenz Heute*
ZTK	*Zeitschrift für Theologie und Kirche*

1

Theology as Struggle against Hegemony

If only the Church had been compelled before Marx to show in word
and action, and had been able to show, that it is just the knowledge
of God which automatically and inevitably includes within itself
liberation from all hypostases and idols, which of itself can achieve
liberation!

Karl Barth, 1926[1]

THE PROBLEM OF HEGEMONY

The most cursory acquaintance with Barth's work makes it obvious that
there is something perverse in including the word 'against' in the title of a
book about him. Despite what many of his critics alleged he was not an
'eternal Nay sayer'. On the contrary, he was adamant throughout his life
that, whilst it was often important to say 'No' it was still more important to
say 'Yes', and that the 'No' only existed for the sake of the 'Yes'. 'Against
Hegemony' then, catches only one moment, and that not the crucial one, of
his theological effort. On the other hand it does characterize an important
aspect of his work which links all stages of his theology, from his 1911 article
on 'Jesus Christ and the Movement for Social Justice' to the last, posthu-
mously published, fragments of the *Dogmatics* on the 'lordless powers'.
From first to last his work is 'against hegemony'.[2] It is this above all which
distinguishes his work as a contextual theology, as a response to his context.
This book as a whole attempts to substantiate that claim but I need first to
clarify its terms, beginning with the concept of 'hegemony'.

Whilst the Weimar Republic ran its tragic course, Barth's contemporary
Gramsci (he was born five years later than Barth, in 1891) was struggling
with the same kind of problems with which Barth was wrestling in Romans,
though in a very different way, in outlining a theory of hegemony. How was

[1] 'Ludwig Feuerbach', in *Theology and Church*, tr. L. Pettibone Smith, London, SCM, 1962,
234.
[2] Another way of putting this is to say that an important aspect of the unity of Barth's theology is its relatedness to its context. F. W. Marquardt, *Theologie und Sozialismus: Das Beispiel
Karl Barths*, 3rd edn, Munich, Kaiser, 1985, 337.

it that the mass of people could be taken in by a charlatan like Mussolini? Imprisoned by this former friend and co-worker from 1926 until his death in 1937 Gramsci speaks of hegemony in his *Prison Notebooks* as 'a conception of the world that is implicitly manifest in art, in law, in economic activity and in all manifestations of individual and collective life'.[3] What he was trying to get at was the way in which ideas and practices 'come to be taken-for-granted as the natural and received shape of the world and everything that inhabits it'.[4] Thirty years after Gramsci, in the draft for paragraph 78 of the *Church Dogmatics*, Barth described 'the lordless powers' as 'not just the supports but the motors of society':

They are the hidden wirepullers in man's great and small enterprises, movements, achievements and revolutions. They are not just the potencies but the real factors and agents of human progress, regress, and stagnation in politics, economics, scholarship, technology and art, and also of the evolutions and retardations in all the personal life of the individual. It is not really people who do things, whether leaders or the masses. Through mankind's fault, things are invisibly done without and above man . . .[5]

Barth is concerned here with the same problem as Gramsci, the way in which we lose our freedom in the face of societal forces. This is not a problem identified in 1960, when this piece was written, but in 1916, as he reflected on the complicity of the European churches with the war effort. The question was the same: how is it that people are so deceived? And the further question: What are we to do about it?

Hegemony is a cultural reality which is bound up with the existence of ideologies. As Gramsci described it 'culture' refers to the values, norms, beliefs, and institutions which, reflected in language, express a common conception of the world and are embodied in a cultural-social unity.[6] The 'Kultur Protestantismus' which Barth attacked was the common conception of the bourgeois world into which he was born. It provided the sacred canopy for a particular vision of cultural-social unity. Its enemies—people like Karl Liebknecht and Rosa Luxemburg, but also Karl Barth—saw that it required an ideological analysis. Ideology, said Barth, in his 1960 reflections, was the assignment of permanent normativity to the ideas and conceptions through which we try to make sense of the world. Of course we need the-

---

[3] A. Gramsci, *Selections from the Prison Notebooks*, New York, International Publishers, 1971, 328.

[4] J. and J. Comaroff, in *Of Revelation and Revolution: Christianity, Colonialism and Consciousness in South Africa*, Chicago, University of Chicago Press, 1991, 23. I take the subheading of this section of the chapter from their work.

[5] Barth, *Das christliche Leben*, Zürich, Theologischer, Verlag, 1976, 378/9; ET *The Christian Life*, tr. G. W. Bromiley, Edinburgh, T. & T. Clark, 1981, 216.

[6] Gramsci, *Prison Notebooks*, 21.

oretical and practical ideas more or less cogently worked out, but when we absolutize them we lose our freedom. We are taken over by the party line. We think we possess the ideology but in reality it possesses us. The person bound to an ideology 'no longer has anything of his own to say. He can only mouth the piece dictated to him as intelligibly as he can'.[7]

Barth has rightly been described as a 'theologian of freedom'.[8] From one point of view the *Church Dogmatics* is a gigantic exploration of the meaning, presuppositions, and actualization of human freedom. The negative, critical, mode of this exploration is the attack on hegemony, on world views which take over the freedom of the gospel. Further, to a very significant extent Barth believes that God frees us by liberating us from hegemony. The centrality of revelation in Barth's thought, not just in the early work, or in the first two volumes of the *Dogmatics*, but also in IV/3, means that the negative attack is also positive liberation. How do human beings take up their vocation of freedom? An important part of Barth's answer is: Through the saving knowledge of Jesus Christ. But this means that the issue of ideology is inescapable, and it does in fact recur again and again in the *Dogmatics* in the form of the attack on world views.

It should be clear that culture, ideology, and the struggle against hegemony were all key issues for Barth throughout his life. On the one hand Barth was always keenly aware of the necessity for conversations with the contemporary world, 'whatever the means'. 'Retreats behind Chinese Walls never served theology well.'[9] On the other hand, from the moment when, as a young pastor, he encountered the Genevan poor and began to read socialist literature, to his last years, Barth saw plainly how theology and church could be colonized, and theologians become the pious spokemen of the powers that be. He himself sought strenuously to avoid this fate. From his time in Göttingen on he frequently described himself as 'swimming against the stream', the title he gave to a collection of his post-World War II political writings. Of course there is the question, raised by critics very early on, as to whether Barth was self deceived.[10] Was he really swimming against the stream, or was he the voice of just another ideology—contemporary critics would say in particular, patriarchal ideology? A verdict on that question hangs on our understanding of his entire

---

[7] *Christliche Leben*, 384; ET, 225. In a sense my understanding of Barth as struggling against hegemony is parallel to John Macken's account of Barth's wrestling with autonomy only, since I read this in an ideological-critical, and therefore political sense, I am more disposed to understand it positively. J. Macken, *The Autonomy Theme in the Church Dogmatics: Karl Barth and his Critics*, Cambridge, Cambridge University Press, 1990.

[8] C. Green, *Karl Barth: Theologian of Freedom*, London, Collins, 1989.

[9] Barth, 'Evangelical Theology in the Nineteenth Century' in *The Humanity of God*, tr. J. N. Thomas and T. Wieser, London, Collins, 1967, 17.

[10] M. Jacob, '. . . noch einmal mit dem Anfang anfangen' *EvT* 32 (1972), 606–24.

theology, but that his two Romans commentaries were conceived in a profoundly anti-hegemonic spirit is unlikely to be denied, as was shown with
crystal clarity by the exchange it provoked with his former teacher Adolf
von Harnack in 1923.

Harnack was the epitome of the culturally assimilated theologian, a close
friend of the Kaiser (and ennobled by him), and leading signatory of the
petition in favour of the First World War. Shocked by Barth's *Romans*, and
his Aarau lecture, he insisted that God must be understood on the basis of
culture, on the basis of knowledge gathered by culture, and on the basis of
ethics, if culture and one's own existence were to be protected against
atheism.[11] Barth replied savagely that such statements may,

> as expressions of special 'experiences of God' (e.g. the experiences of the War) have
> their significance and value in comparison with the experiences of primitive peoples
> who do not yet know such great treasures. (Consider, for example, the signific-
> ance and value of the statements of the War-theologians of all countries.) *These*
> statements can definitely not be considered as the 'preaching of the gospel'.
> Whether they *protect* culture and the individual 'against atheism' or whether they
> *sow* atheism, since they come out of polytheism, would remain an *open* question in
> each case.[12]

In the two Romans commentaries the assault on hegemony took the form
of the attack on religion, a movement which receives its mature expression
in CD I/2 (1935) but which was never abandoned. At this time this was
Barth's clearest form of ideology critique. The overt paganism of the Nazi
movement, the enthusiastic embracing of a theology of the German *Volk* by
his Göttingen colleague Emmanuel Hirsch, the dangerous dalliance with
völkisch ideas by former allies like Gogarten, put the question of idolatry
squarely in the centre. Barth countered this with his majestic exposition of
the doctrine of God. His account of 'the God who loves in freedom', the
triune God who freely elects Israel and Church, is his most fundamental
response to the new form of hegemony.

When the post-war settlement valorized the capitalist liberal state, and
McCarthyite hysteria provoked theological echoes from the likes of Reinhold Niebuhr, Barth again challenged this religio-political settlement at the
most fundamental level in his threefold account of reconciliation and of
human sin. From his denial of the sovereignty of accepted scientific method
in CD I/1, to his opposition to 'natural theology', to his refusal to condemn
communist regimes as he had condemned National Socialism, to his about
turn on baptism, all this was a refusal of hegemony, a refusal of what was

---

[11] *Revelation and Theology: An Analysis of the Barth–Harnack Correspondence of 1923*, ed. H. M.
Rumscheidt, London, Cambridge University Press, 1972, 30.
[12] Ibid., 33.

self evident to most of his contemporaries. Over against all self evident and 'natural' theologies he sets the reality of the God who loves in freedom—the One who can in no circumstances ever be colonized or be the subject of any hegemony. The insistence that theology cannot be wedded to any ideology is found at every stage of his work. In the last revised fragment of the *Dogmatics*, with one eye on his critics, he insists that God is not a first or last principle (like communism or anti-communism). 'God is not identical with any ideology, and is not to be confused with such. Hence conversion to Him is not to be confused with any human decision for rearmament or disarmament in orientation to any ideology.'[13]

It is because Barth's theology, from first to last, is an attempt to witness to *this* God that it resists all attempts to find interpretive master keys, which would again bring it under theological-cultural hegemony. Theology which is against all hegemonies, *Widerstehende Theologie* in Peter Winzeler's fine phrase, is a theology of grace and freedom. Only the sourest of Barth's critics would disallow that. It is also, however, from first to last, a *political* theology or, to use the term which became current shortly after Barth's death, a contextual theology. To claim that for Barth is a far more contentious issue.

BARTH BETWEEN IDEALISM AND HISTORICAL MATERIALISM

In 1972 F. W. Marquardt dropped a bomb in the playground of Barth scholarship with his claim that Barth was a lifelong socialist, and that socialist praxis was the interpretive key to Barth's theological output.[14] Scholarly uproar followed.[15] At that time all were agreed that Barth's book on Anselm, and his recognition that he had a made a 'false start' with the *Christliche Dogmatik* of 1927, signalled his final break with idealism—but what did this mean? Many of those who rubbished Marquardt's thesis agreed that Barth turned against Cartesianism, the priority of the thinking subject, but still presented us with an emphatically idealist Barth—that is, a Barth primarily given to working out the implications of his *ideas*, his theological system. Even Helmut Gollwitzer, Barth's former student, and one of his closest allies, his preferred candidate for the Basle chair, noted that Barth's trust in the power of the sermon 'forces us to raise the question whether a vestige

---

[13] CD IV/4, 140.

[14] Marquardt, *Theologie*.

[15] The Habilitation thesis from which the book emerged was not accepted at the Theologische Hochschule in Berlin and Jüngel refused to be external examiner for it. Gollwitzer resigned his Chair in protest.

of idealism is not at work in Barth here, a vestige of the idealist faith in the power of ideas, namely, that on the basis of the right theology, the right praxis will be created'.[16] Barth always hoped, he notes, that the Church would be renewed and liberated through a renewed sermon. He failed to emphasize that comprehensive work for structural change in church and society was also necessary. Does this mean that we must go along with the dominant idealist way of reading Barth?

To what extent was Barth influenced by idealism? He certainly took from his education, and from what he learned from his brother Heinrich, a real enthusiasm for Plato and Kant. He understood the virtues of epistemological idealism, as a critique of naive realism but, just as he found it necessary to critique revolution more sharply than reaction because it stood nearer to the truth, so he saw the dangers of idealism.[17] The danger of idealism is that the overweening human subject can easily forget that it is not our access to God but God's access to us which is theology's concern.[18] Similarly in ethics: 'The law of faith is distinguished from the law of Idealism by the fact that it is established [*aufgerichtet*]. We must understand that in the strong sense the knowledge of faith is ac-knowledgement.'[19] The emphasis on God's inalienable subjectivity and the priority of God's Word was deeply hostile to the German Idealist tradition. It was Feuerbach above all who showed how fragile and easily reversible that tradition was. Moreover, Barth was at one with Feuerbach in his 'anti-spiritualism' which had 'the oldest Christian tradition on his side'. In an echo of the opening paragraphs of the *German Ideology* Barth insists that Feuerbach worked 'as an honest man . . . as a zealous opponent of all specifically academic theology which begins with some kind of abstraction and runs out into some kind of ideology, which stands in no sort of relation to the real life of men in their cities and villages, their taverns and inns'.[20] Barth, too, worked as such an 'honest man', though naturally he was no vulgar materialist. He had a certain sympathy for historical materialism.[21] Distinguishing it from the metaphysical materialism of Haekel he notes that Marxism lives 'from that which, in historical materialism, is not only a forceful construction but historically undoubtedly true and real'.[22] This is its capturing of what was actually happening in the nine-

---

[16] H. Gollwitzer, 'The Kingdom of God and Socialism' in G. Hunsinger (ed.), *Karl Barth and Radical Politics*, Philadelphia, Westminster, 1976, 111.

[17] His critique of epistemological idealism is worked out most clearly in 'Schicksal und Idee in Theologie' in *Vorträge 1925–30*, 344 ff., and in *Ethik* II, 98 ff.; ET, 294 ff.

[18] 'Schicksal und Idee', 369.

[19] *Ethik* II, 101; ET, 312.

[20] Barth, 'Feuerbach' in *Theology and Church*, 231–2.

[21] He discusses it in the course of his exposition of 'Soul and Body in their Interconnection' in CD III/2. KD III/2, 464–8; CD, 387–90.

[22] KD III/2, 466; CD, 387.

teenth century, in which the Church, with its support of the ruling class and tacit indifference to questions of the body and of economics, contributed to a soulless human existence. In its preaching of the resurrection it ought to have signified that 'the judgement and promise of God compass the whole man, and therefore cannot be affirmed and believed apart from material and economic reality, or be denied or pushed aside as ideology in contrast to material and economic reality'.[23] This, too, was a concern of his theology, though when it comes to either idealism or materialism as philosophical principles his final word, repeated in many contexts, was that 'The Christian hope first deserves its name when with *one* stroke it makes materialism *and* idealism impossible.'[24]

Gollwitzer's question relates to historical idealism, which 'locates the primary or sole motor of historical change in agency, ideas or consciousness'.[25] Is this inevitable for a 'theologian of the Word', someone who roots theology in revelation, which means for those of us 'between the times', in Scripture? Or does his opposition to other forms of idealism not also carry over into this sphere?

Barth sharply rejects economic determinism, the view that the ideological 'superstructure' is merely an epiphenomenon of the social and economic 'base'. In this he is at one with Marx and Engels themselves.[26] Nevertheless in his own historical work he recognized the reality of what was later to be called 'overdetermination'.[27] In his lectures on 'Nineteenth-Century Protestant Theology', delivered first in Münster and then in Bonn, Barth advised his students to 'make a synchronous chart for every single year of the period . . . It should have five columns: the first for entering the most important dates of world history in general; the second for the most noteworthy events in the history of culture, art and literature; the third for church history in general; the fourth for the dates of birth and death of the most prominent theologians of the period; and the fifth for the years in which their most important books were published. Anyone who does this

---

[23] KD III/2, 467; CD, 390.

[24] Barth, 'Feuerbach' in *Theology and Church*, 232 n. 1.

[25] Roy Bhaskar, 'Idealism' in *A Dictionary of Marxist Thought*, ed. T. Bottomore et al., Oxford, Blackwell, 1983, 218.

[26] Cf. the letter of Engels to J. Bloch, 21 September 1890. K. Marx and F. Engels, *Correspondence 1846–1895*, London, Lawrence, 1934, 475.

[27] Althusser took this concept from Freud's idea of 'overdetermination' to spell out the causal complexity in the relation of economic, cultural, and social factors. It is 'an attempt to avoid the isolation of autonomous categories but at the same time to emphasize relatively autonomous yet of course interactive practices'. Raymond Williams, *Marxism and Literature*, Oxford, Oxford University Press, 1977, 88. To recognize 'determination' is not equivalent to a belief in determinism. As Williams notes, to be determined has an active as well as a passive sense, it invokes human agency—and in Barth's case, divine and human agency.

, mass of connexions.'[28] The 'mass of connexions' Barth refers to is
ning of Althusser's 'overdetermination'. We see it at work in an illu-
ng way in both the Calvin lectures and the lectures on the nineteenth
c.. y.[29] In outlining the problem of theology in the eighteenth century,
Barth draws attention to the way the Church was determined by the state,
to the way its ethics were caught up in middle class moralizing ('typical
middle class ideology'), a consequent subjection of the themes of theology
to a naturalistic science, and the growth of individualism. Marquardt is
surely right that we have here a 'model example' of historical materialist
interpretation.[30] The purpose of the present essay is to try and follow
Barth's advice in respect of his own theology. It is perhaps to take up the suggestion made long ago by Jean Louis Leuba, that Barth must be read
'prophetically' rather than 'systematically', as a theologian who is above all
concerned with the way in which God's Word shapes history, rather than in
setting out an account of the divine essence.[31]

It cannot be strongly enough insisted that this is not done with reductive
intent, with the claim that Barth's doctrine *emerged* purely as a response to
contemporary events. On the other hand, Barth was someone who took the
need of the theologian to respond to his or her context with absolute seriousness, and we can therefore expect to learn something from the process.
This implies a very qualified assent to Geoffrey Bromiley's claim that in
Barth's Schleiermacher lectures we find evidence of Barth's predominant
concern 'not for background, influences and historical development, but for
subject matter'.[32] It is quite true that Barth is from first to last concerned
with *die Sache*, the heart of the matter, God's revelation in Christ. Precisely
for that reason a dualism between 'background' and 'ideas', material and
spiritual, is utterly foreign to him, as his lectures on Protestant theology
indicate. To read Barth as first and foremost a person of ideas is to do him a
profound injustice. The very structure of the *Dogmatics*, the integration of
theology and ethics, the refusal to separate law and gospel, is a sign of his

---

[28] Barth, *Protestant Theology in the Nineteenth Century: Its Background and History*, tr. B. Cozens
and J. Bowden, London, SCM, 1972, 17, 25–6. For my own attempt to follow Barth's advice, see
the Appendix. In view of Barth's method here I cannot agree with Schellong that Barth 'did not
know the method which questions the contents of dogmatics about sociopolitical origins,
influences and tendencies; he would hardly have considered it to be appropriate theologically'.
'On Reading Barth from the Left' in Hunsinger (ed.), *Karl Barth and Radical Politics*, Philadelphia, Westminster, 1976, 144. Barth's own studies show that he knew more about this than
Schellong allows.
[29] Barth called his method 'genetic'. For comments on the genetic method see Barth, *Die
Theologie Schleiermachers*, 8; ET, p. xvii. Bruce McCormack offers a genetic reading of Barth
which is a historical material reading in all but name.
[30] Marquardt, *Theologie*, 317. I draw on the whole discussion of Barth's 'historical materialism' but formulate more cautious conclusions.
[31] J. L. Leuba, 'Le problème de l'église chez Karl Barth', *Verbum Caro* 1 / 1 (1947), 4–24.
[32] Barth, *The Theology of Schleiermacher*, tr G. Bromiley, Edinburgh, T. & T. Clark, 1982, p. vii.

determination not to allow so much as a knife blade between theory and praxis.[33] In his furious response to the Prussian churchman Otto Dibelius, Barth wrote:

Dibelius characterizes the difference between us as if he was the representative of the Church, i.e. of praxis and love, and I the representative of theology, i.e. of a Christian theory. According to my view any serious undertaking makes that kind of opposition impossible. Praxis and theory, Church and theology, love and knowledge, simply cannot be set over against one another in this kind of abstract way.[34]

Barth had already made this clear in *Romans*, where he warns us that we do not have a dogmatic section (Romans 1–11) followed by 'ethics' (Romans 11–16), but that the first section is 'theory of praxis'.[35] Similarly, the very first page of the *Dogmatics* defines theology as critical reflection on the action (*Handeln*) of the Church.[36] The task of theology is to clarify the presuppositions of church praxis. Praxis comes first precisely because God is 'No fifth wheel on the wagon, but the wheel that drives all wheels.'[37] The engagement of God with the uttermost depth of all reality makes dualism impossible. Barth reiterated this position in the *Dogmatics* describing any distinction between 'theoretical' and 'practical' as 'a primal lie, which has to be resisted in principle'.[38] Barth was not an idealist any more than he was a vulgar materialist. Rather, as a Christocentric thinker, he took spirit and matter, soul and body, ideas and their socio-historical outworking, together. It is true to say that Barth's theology was never a predicate of his politics, but also true that politics is never simply a predicate of his theology. Either extreme misses the dialectical unity of theory and praxis at the heart of Barth's whole theology.[39] 'Is there a Christian praxis which is not formed by Christian theory?' he asks. 'Or conversely, a Christian theory which does not also have an element of Christian praxis?' The understanding of Christ as the light of life can be understood *only* as 'a theory which has its origin and goal in praxis'.[40]

---

[33] This is the mistake Macken makes in finding 'Much of the evidence that . . . Barth is modern and . . . committed to the characteristically modern quest for freedom lies outside his theology—in his biography, in his political and cultural interests.' Macken, *Autonomy*, 176. Barth lived his opposition to dualism. Biographical concerns, in his case, are reflected in his theology.

[34] Nachwort to *Quousque tandem*, cited in Marquardt, *Theologie*, 285.

[35] R2, 412; ET, 426–7.

[36] KD I/1, 1; CD, 3.

[37] R1, 102.

[38] KD I/2, 880; CD, 787.

[39] E. Jüngel, *Karl Barth: A Theological Legacy*, Philadelphia, Westminster, 1986, 41, 104, rightly protests against making Barth's theology the predicate of his politics, but to my mind inverts this formula too easily. He notes earlier the need to determine the relation between theory and practice in *Barth*, 27.

[40] KD IV/3, 86; CD, 79.

It is precisely this dialectical unity which led him, very early on, to break with Christian socialism. In his Tambach lecture on 'The Christian's Place in Society' Barth expressed his preference for Dostoevsky over Tolstoy, because in the former we find 'the free survey and understanding of the actual life of society', whilst in the latter we are 'preached to'.[41] One of the reasons Barth had to break with religious socialism was similar to Marx's well known hostility to socialist literature: ultimately it is reductive and lacks the depth to do the job required of it. The hegemony of world capitalism cannot be challenged simply by moral critique. Barth shared this view. For him it is the living God, active in history, who challenges the lordless powers. Just as polemical literature was an insufficient response for Marx, who saw that the massive work of analysis in *Das Kapital* was a necessary part of the project of revolution, so Barth's great work, likewise an unfinished project, is his contribution to what, in *Romans*, he called 'God's revolution'. Helmut Gollwitzer implies as much in making precisely this comparison between Barth and Marx. Barth was, he says, like Marx, 'a man of solidity, a funda-mental thinker and worker. The rambling talk of the world improvers who were then posing as socialists was just as foreign to him as the theological liberalism which called itself Christian . . . A theologian's socialism without a solid theological foundation was to him a way of losing everything through a lack of substance. A church so instructed would fail to provide both the world and socialism with the very substance which the church and only the church was supposed to bring to them.'[42]

It cannot be said that the dust has yet settled on Marquardt's reading of Barth but what is by now clear is that Barth was throughout his life vividly and intensely engaged at all sorts of levels with the society in which he lived. Failure to recognize that, to treat him as a person for whom ideas alone were important, is the reason that, as Hans Frei noted, if one attempts to sum-marize Barth 'the material dies in one's hands'.[43] The inadequacy of the 'neo-orthodox' label as applied to Barth lies in the fact that it represents an idealist, atemporal abstraction, a divorce of Barth's theology from its living

[41] 'Der Christ in der Gesellschaft' in *Das Wort Gottes und die Theologie*, 55; ET *The Word of God and the Word of Man*, tr. D. Horton, London, Hodder & Stoughton, 1935, 305.
    Barth shared with Marx an enthusiasm for Balzac, on account of his 'stupendous knowledge of the world and man'. E. Busch, *Karl Barth: His Life from Letters and Autobiographical Texts*, tr. J. Bowden, London, SCM, 1976, 209.
[42] H. Gollwitzer, 'The Kingdom of God and Socialism' in Hunsinger, *Barth and Radical Pol-itics*, 81. Sabine Plonz makes a similar point when she argues that it was not direct political action, but Marx's attempt to gain understanding of the entire field of social praxis which pro-vides the point of comparison between Barth and Marx. *Die herrenlosen Gewalten: Eine Relektüre Karl Barths in befreiungstheologischer Perspektive*, Mainz, Grünewald, 1995, 347.
[43] H. Frei, 'Eberhard Busch's Biography of Karl Barth' in H. M. Rumscheidt (ed.), *Karl Barth in Re-View*, Pittsburgh, Pickwick, 1981, 109.

context. Without that living context it is indeed, in Bradley's words, 'an abstract ballet of bloodless categories'. But what is meant by context needs careful definition.

BARTH'S CONTEXT

Given Barth's practice in lecturing on doctrine we must take it as a minimum requirement that we try to apply the same measures in seeking to understand his own theology. The task is, as Dieter Schellong has put it, to show 'why, to what end, and how Barth's theology is formed and situated among the social conditions, developments and tasks of its time'.[44] Barth was a person of extraordinary vitality: he kept up to date with contemporary literature and philosophy, loved music, and read the newspaper assiduously. At the same time he was, more than most other great theologians, a profoundly political animal. Barth was not a world historical figure like Luther—his name does not appear in the standard histories of the time—but he constantly responded to his political context *as a theologian*. George Hunsinger notes that Barth's three theological 'breaks' were all related to crucial historical circumstances: his break with liberalism to the First War, his break with religious socialism with the failure of revolution in Germany and Switzerland, and his break with dialectical theology with the rise of Nazism.[45]

Barth's first significant theological publication appeared in 1909, and he was still writing in the year of his death, 1968. We can venture the following rough periodization for these years:

- The collapse of the *Belle époque* (–1918)
- Weimar (1919–33)
- The dominance of German Fascism (1933–45)
- The Cold War (1946–62)
- Thaw and *Aggiornamento* (1962–8)

The first two of these periods correspond fairly closely to periods of Barth's development and the last corresponds to the period of his retirement. I have chosen to treat the thirty years during which the *Church Dogmatics* emerged in three chapters, which necessarily fit somewhat roughly into this historical framework.

Born in 1886 Barth grew up and went to university in the heyday of the *Belle époque*. Amidst profound underlying tensions, and prophetic

---

[44] D. Schellong, On Reading Karl Barth from the Left' in Hunsinger, *Barth and Radical Politics*, 150.

[45] Hunsinger, *Barth and Radical Politics*, 224.

anticipations of colossal disorder from writers like Nietzsche and artists like Munch or Picasso, the middle class, to which Barth belonged, enjoyed general prosperity and the foundations of civilization seemed solid. In hindsight we understand where the arms race between Britain and Germany was leading but for Barth's generation of university students it seemed, in Golo Mann's words, 'a harmless and carefree age'.[46] Harnack's *What is Christianity?*, with its 'simple gospel' of the Fatherhood of God and the brotherhood of man, was its theological manifesto. This world went more or less gaily to war in 1914. By 1918 it lay in ruins, though figures like Hindenburg and Harnack never recognized that. To this period belongs all Barth's early work.

After an abortive socialist revolution, and the murders of Liebknecht and Rosa Luxemburg, the Weimar republic came into being in the chaos of postwar Germany. Barth's first commentary on Romans, finished during the heady days of the previous year, when it looked as if socialist revolution might sweep the whole of Europe, quickly needed revision. In 1921 he was called to Göttingen and worked in Germany until finally expelled by the National Socialists in 1935. All of his early dogmatic work, including *Church Dogmatics* I/1, was done within the context of Weimar. In hindsight Weimar is indeed a period 'between the times' but there are indications that people at the time so understood it. Golo Mann comments that 'The Weimar state was ... more an appendage of the Empire of William II or of Bismarck than it was a distinct historic epoch; it was an interregnum between two eras, the second of which was ... infinitely worse.'[47] A number of commentators have done detailed work in situating Barth's work in the rich political and cultural life of the doomed republic.[48]

From 1935 to his death in 1968 Barth lived and worked in Basle. This period, however, witnessed at least two shifts which bore on Barth's work. Once Barth was in Switzerland he was freer to intervene politically than he had been in Germany. To the consternation of the Swiss authorities he urged the struggle against Fascism as obedience to the divine command. The first four volumes of the *Dogmatics* run from 1932 to 1942, and this struggle is always in the background.

Earlier than many others Barth was convinced of eventual Allied victory, and the moment war ended he addressed himself to Germans as a friend. His great theology of creation, written between 1942 and 1951, must be read as a tremendous affirmation of the goodness of the created order in the face of Auschwitz and the destruction of the war years, just as the music of

---

[46] G. Mann, *The History of Germany since 1789*, tr. M. Jackson, London, Chatto & Windus, 1968, 280.

[47] Mann, *Germany*, 416.

[48] See for example the work of B. McCormack, S. Webb and P. Winzeler.

Mozart, famously apostrophized in CD III/3, had been in the face of the Lisbon earthquake.

The McCarthyism which affected Europe, as well as the United States, led to critical, sometimes hysterical, attacks on Barth for his steady support of Christians under communism which continued to the end of the 1950s. At the same time, American capitalism, under the banner of 'freedom', became the major global power. The doctrine of reconciliation engages critically throughout with these vaunted claims for 'freedom', and with the pride, lies, and inaction of self confident Western human beings.

This framework determines the shape of the book, as an attempt to follow Barth's response to his context. As noted, developments in Barth's thought do not correspond neatly with these historical epochs. From 1931 until 1962 Barth was working on the *Dogmatics* and there is not only development but also profound continuity in this work. Rather than take the *Dogmatics* volume by volume I have chosen, rather, to take it in three great blocks, respecting Barth's attempt to address the great *loci* of the creed. Although the struggle against Fascism did not come to an end until 1945 Barth, and increasingly the Swiss government, was clear about the outcome from 1942 onwards. I deal with the first four volumes of the *Dogmatics* primarily in the context of Fascism. The doctrine of creation is more difficult: it covers the end of the war and the beginning of the Cold War. Rather than split the exposition of this doctrine I have tried to read it consistently as a response to the horrors of the period. I have then, finally, read the four parts of volume IV together, although there are also important internal developments within them.

Reading Barth's theology in context in this way does not contradict the affirmation of a remarkable unity in his theological output from 1916 to 1968, a unity Barth himself insisted on.[49] This might be expected in a span of fifty years. We read Anselm or Aquinas as men of the eleventh or thirteenth centuries, not decade by decade, and we can expect historians of doctrine in 500 years' time to read Barth, in the same way, as a person of the twentieth century.[50] Further, one or other phase of global capitalism characterized all of the eras Barth lived through, and he was always aware of that, as we shall see. A reading of Barth which ignored that not only would make no sense of his ethics, but would not be able to understand his doctrine of God or

---

[49] In 1947 Barth denied any break between the theology of *Romans* and the *Dogmatics*. 'In *Romans* I drew the bow and let the arrow fly . . . and the target moved, and therefore seems different.' 'Brechen und Bauen' in *Der Götze Wakkelt*, 112. John Webster speaks of 'a massively consistent argument, each part of which builds upon and interprets the other parts'. *Barth's Ethics of Reconciliation*, Cambridge, Cambridge University Press, 1995, 13.

[50] Having said that, Peter Brown's great biography of Augustine is an obvious exception, which does indeed chart Augustine's course 'decade by decade'.

Christology either. So there are good reasons for continuity as well as for change and development even within the period we are looking at.

More important still is the role of the wider context in which Barth situated himself. He often commented that he might, in other circumstances, have been a historian, and he had a profound historical knowledge which ranged from local history to that of the American civil war. What makes Barth different from other historians, however, is his vivid sense of the communion of saints:

Augustine, Thomas Aquinas, Luther, Schleiermacher and all the rest are not dead, but living. They still speak and demand a hearing as living voices, as surely as we know that they and we belong together in the Church . . . we cannot play our part today without allowing them to play theirs. Our responsibility is not only to God, to ourselves, to the men of today, to other living theologians, but to them. There is no past in the Church, so there is no past in theology. 'In him they all live.'[51]

We cannot sufficiently emphasize this aspect of Barth's understanding of 'context'. Luther and Schleiermacher, in particular, were both theological and political figures not only for Barth but for many of his contemporaries, as the difficulties between Lutheran and Reformed in the church struggle make clear. Similarly, just as Bismarck loomed behind much which happened in twentieth century Germany so it was impossible to ignore those Barth identified as his theological spokesmen. This accounts for the particular asperity directed at Ritschl.

THE SWISS VOICE

Another vital aspect of Barth's context is the fact that Barth was Swiss. Criticizing Marquardt, Dieter Schellong speaks of 'the slightly offensive tone of a biographical revelation' in his book.[52] The implication is that there is something reductionist in reading Barth through his biography. The point, however, is not to claim that once we understand what moved Barth in a particular direction we have understood the doctrine, but that these circumstances illuminate our understanding of what is going on. That Barth was a Swiss whose family roots lay in Basle has real significance in the formation of what McCormack has called, alluding to Peter Gay, 'the making of an outsider'. Culturally, Basle is a border zone. Part of the deeply rooted tradition of Swiss democracy it nevertheless looks in both anxiety and admiration to its German neighbour. Thus Barth recalled that Bismarck was a

---

[51] Barth, *Protestant Theology*, 17.

[52] D. Schellong, 'On Reading Karl Barth from the Left' in Hunsinger, *Barth and Radical Politics*, 150.

family hero of his childhood; he recalled the excitement of his first journey into Germany as a young student; and his years teaching in Germany clearly meant engagement with a much broader and more vigorous field of action and culture than he could find in parochial Basle. Reporting on John Mott's visit to Switzerland in the *Basler Nachrichten* in 1911 he echoes the then conventional view of German cultural destiny noting that, in contrast to Anglo-Saxon pragmatism and indifference to dogma, 'the Germans have always had the role of exploring the inner depths and deepening positions and questions, especially with regard to the highest matters'. The disinclination we feel towards Mott, he observes, 'puts our German way of doing things in a remarkable light' (namely that Mott comes out as more of a socialist than Kutter and Ragaz!).[53] This shared cultural inheritance between Germany and German Switzerland also extends, in Gerhard Sauter's view, to spirituality. The Blumhardts came from Württemburg and Ragaz and Barth from German Switzerland, he comments, but they were all at home in the same spiritual atmosphere.[54]

At the same time, when his former teachers supported Germany's occupation of Belgium and France he could write to Martin Rade that 'Something of the deep respect which I felt within myself for the German character is forever destroyed.'[55]

This identity yet difference with German culture is characteristic of Swiss German thought, but especially of Barth. He valued his Swiss identity, and obtained permission to have dual nationality after his promotion to Münster in 1925 conferred German citizenship on him. On the one hand Barth was 'painfully aware' of how deeply at home he felt in Germany, and how much he belonged to the Germans, as he confessed to Thurneysen when faced with the offer of a Chair in Bern.[56] There is little doubt that, without the Nazi catastrophe, he would have 'buried his bones beside the (German) Rhine', as he told his Bonn students on leaving. On the other hand any stepping out of line on strictly national issues saw the accusation 'Swiss! Foreigner! Disturber of the peace!' flying round his head, as Barth reported to Thurneysen in January 1923, when the issue was whether or not to respond to a friendly greeting of French theological students.[57] Barth's old friend and former mentor Martin Rade, the editor of the *Christliche Welt*, warned him to be extremely restrained, as a Swiss, and it was partly for this reason that during the 1920s he was shy to intervene politically.

---

[53] Barth, *Vorträge und kleinere Arbeiten 1909–1914*, ed. H. Drewes and H. Stoevesandt, 1993, 283, 279.
[54] G. Sauter, 'Nachwort' to E. Buess and M. Mattmüller, Freiburg, Exodus, *Prophetischer Sozialismus: Blumhardt–Ragaz–Barth*, 1986.
[55] Barth to Rade, 1 October 1914, B–R, 101.
[56] B–Th II, 536.   [57] B–Th II,131.

In fact, during both world wars Switzerland's principal linguistic divide led to sharply opposing attitudes to Germany within the country, and Barth's Swiss identity certainly had a critical significance in giving him complete immunity to the *völkisch* ideas so prevalent in Germany in 1918. His Swiss background also meant that he read the German political scene as an outsider, with all the attendant advantages and disadvantages.

BARTH AS CONTEXTUAL THEOLOGIAN

To put a theology in context is one thing. Contextual theology—in which a theologian actively seeks to respond to the events of the day—is another.[58] Barth himself felt that his ideas had emerged precisely in and through such a response. In a letter written in 1957 Barth denied that he had ever had any kind of overall plan for his work: 'I used what I thought I had learned and understood so far to cope with this or that situation, with some complex of biblical or historical or doctrinal questions, often with some subject presented to me from outside, often in fact by a topical subject, e.g. a political issue. It was always something new that got hold of me, rather than the other way round . . . My thinking, writing and speaking developed from reacting to people, events and circumstances with which I was involved, with their questions and riddles . . . I did not *want* to be, do or say this or that; I was, did and said it when the time had come. That is what working on the *Church Dogmatics* was like for twenty five years.'[59] Marquardt summarizes this in a lapidary way in his thesis that Barth's methodology is his theological biography.[60] A theology which emerges in this way represents a response to the culture of which it is a part but is also, as Barth acknowledges, a political theology. 'Wherever there is theological talk, it is always implicitly or explicitly political talk also,' Barth told students in Leiden in 1939.[61]

That the first *Romans* represents a profoundly contextual theology in this

---

[58] The best account of Barth as a contextual theologian is the collection of essays edited by C. Villa-Vicencio, *On Reading Barth in South Africa*, Grand Rapids, Eerdmans, 1988.

[59] Letter to T. A. Gill, 10 August 1957. Cited in Busch, *Barth*, 420–1.

[60] Marquardt, *Theologie*, 230. More fully: 'As Barth thought through christologically Jesus' person through the work, nature through history . . . so he was unable to divorce theology from theologians, ethics from ethicists, Christianity from faith—nor theory from praxis. His methodology is in this sense his biography, and one simply cannot get round this to understand Barth's teaching from the standpoint of his authority.' Ibid., 291.

[61] Busch, *Barth*, 292. The inextricability of theology and politics is a theme to which Barth often returns. So, for example in 1946: 'This gospel which proclaims the King and the Kingdom . . . is political from the very outset, and if it is preached to real (Christian and non Christian) men . . . will necessarily be prophetically political . . . It is a bad sign when Christians are frightened by 'political' sermons.' 'The Christian Community and the Civil Community' in *Against the Stream*, 47.

sense is universally acknowledged but, in the view of many scholars, it was a stance Barth quickly abandoned. Criticizing Marquardt's 'confused' book, Klaus Scholder expressed the view that, 'With the turn to biblical theology Barth effectively gave up political engagement. The political world in the narrower sense, the world of political ideas and decisions, no longer formed any fundamental part of his theological thinking.'[62] One of the editors of Barth's complete works, Gerhard Sauter, protested against Marquardt that Barth had no political theology 'in any plausible sense of the term'.[63] They could appeal to one of the members of the dialectical theology movement, Friedrich Gogarten, who, in the Preface to his counterblast against Barth, *Gericht oder Skepsis*, in 1937, which justified his own flirtation with the German Christians, argued that Barth's engagement with specifically theological questions pushed political concerns entirely to one side. 'I saw the danger of Barth developing a timeless, self satisfied, theology which, despite all the emphasis on the Church, actually lost all connection with church life.'[64] One of Barth's sternest Anglo-Saxon critics, R. H. Roberts, takes such a critique further still. The *Dogmatics* stands before us, he says, 'as a warning as to what may happen if the God of the orthodox Christian gospel is prized apart from the structures of contemporary human life'. In Barth's theology the incarnation loses its roots in the shared and public reality of the world in which we live and his theology as a whole is a perfect illustration of religion as alienation![65] From quite a different angle other scholars, and especially T. F. Torrance, have characterized Barth as above all concerned to do justice to theological 'science', to elaborate a new and better theology. Torrance recognizes only an 'intellectual' context for Barth's work, and what that means is the development of liberal theology since the Enlightenment, with its valorization of human autonomy.[66]

Some of those who knew Barth best, such as Helmut Gollwitzer and Georges Casalis, protested in support of Marquardt that throughout his life Barth remained a committed socialist.[67] Savagely, but with some justice, Casalis commented in 1970 that 'The gleaners have developed a Barthian scholasticism more or less condemned to death whilst the free amongst his pupils follow dubious and difficult paths leading we know not

---

[62] K. Scholder. *Die Kirchen und das Dritten Reich*, i, Berlin, Verlag Ullstein, 1977, 56; ET, *The Churches and the Third Reich*, i: *1918–1934*, tr. J. Bowden, London, SCM, 1989, 45.

[63] G. Sauter, 'Soziologische oder politische Barth-Interpretation?' *EvT* 35 (1975), 176 f.

[64] F. Gogarten, *Gericht oder Skepsis*, Jena, Diedrichs, 1937, 8.

[65] R. H. Roberts, 'Barth's Doctrine of Time' in S. W. Sykes (ed.), *Karl Barth: Studies of his Theological Methods*, Oxford, Clarendon, 1979, 145.

[66] See for example T. F. Torrance, *Karl Barth, Biblical and Evangelical Theologian*, Edinburgh, T. & T. Clark, 1990.

[67] E.g. H. Gollwitzer, 'Reich Gottes und Sozialismus bei K. Barth', *TEH* 169 (Munich 1972); G. Casalis in R. Gegenheimer (ed.), *Porträt eines Theologen*, Stuttgart, Radius, 1970.

where.'[68] He recalls how, in the open evenings on political themes held at Barth's house in the winter of 1937/8, Barth had insisted that whoever does not think politically on the right lines, and act accordingly, cannot be a genuine theologian.[69] In a similar vein Barth told Gollwitzer, in connection with the peace movement in the 1950s, that anyone who did not understand him politically could not understand him theologically either.[70] In the radio interview recorded shortly before his death he observed that the church struggle stood in 'the closest connection' with his whole theological undertaking.

The theology which I tried to fashion out of Scripture was never a private affair, foreign to the world and humanity. Its object is: God for the world, God for human beings, heaven for the earth. It followed that my whole theology always had a strong political component, explicit or implicit . . . this interest in politics accompanies me to the present day.[71]

Barth mentioned in this interview his engagement in unionization whilst Pastor in Safenwil, his leading role in the formation of the Confessing Church, his unpopular stand in Switzerland during the Second World War, and his still more unpopular refusal, after the war, to howl with the wolves in condemning communism.

The inevitability and necessity of contextualization received the strongest affirmation in the *Dogmatics* themselves. If identification with a current world view is one of the deadly errors of the Church, Barth warned, the other is that the gospel becomes perverted 'into an impartation of general, timeless and irrelevant Christian truth'. We have to recognize that the gospel will be 'radically, totally and at bottom irresistibly influenced by all the presuppositions which it inevitably brings from its relationship with the world around'. There are no philosophical, historical, national, cultural, political or economic factors which do not help to shape the Church's presentation of the gospel.[72] Because this is true 'the *Dogmatics* is *also* a commentary on contemporary history'.[73]

---

[68] Casalis in Gegenheimer, *Porträt*, 47.

[69] Gollwitzer similarly recalls that the open evenings in the winter semester of 1930/1 were devoted to a discussion of the political parties. Meeting Gollwitzer in 1933 Barth remarked: 'Herr Gollwitzer, someone told me you joined me at a meeting last night. You're making great progress!' in *Stimme der Gemeinde* 18 (1966), 285–6.

[70] Cited in P. Winzeler, *Widerstehende Theologie: Karl Barth 1920–35*, Stuttgart, Alektor, 1982, 27.

[71] Barth, *Letzte Zeugnisse*, Zürich, Evangelischer Verlag, 1969, 21.

[72] KD IV/3, 936, 940; CD 817, 821. Apart from Marquardt there are a small group of scholars who have championed the view that Barth was a contextual theologian: Peter Winzeler, Peter Eicher, Dieter Schellong, Sabine Plonz and Michael Weinrich, whom I cite as an epigraph to the whole book: P. Eicher and M. Weinrich, *Der gute Widerspruch: Das unbegriffene Zeugnis von Karl Barth*, Neukirchener, Patmos, 1986, 119.

[73] Marquardt, *Theologie*, 299.

Given Barth's uncompromising insistence here, how do we account for what appears to be an Olympian stance, above the fray, in the development of the themes of the *Church Dogmatics* from 1931 onwards?

THEOLOGY 'WITHOUT DIRECT ALLUSIONS'

Those who oppose a historical materialist reading of Barth can appeal to what often seems to be the silence of the text regarding political matters. Here, however, we have to note that it is characteristic of Barth's approach from the very beginning that his most fundamental critiques are often unspoken. Thus his exposition of the second chapter of Romans in the first commentary offers us a critique of Ragaz; in his Feuerbach lecture he had Gogarten in mind; and he advises us in the Preface to *Church Dogmatics* IV/1 that a sustained engagement with Bultmann is going on, though Bultmann is rarely mentioned. In his final radio interview he notes the political content both of the first Romans commentary and of the Barmen confession although in the latter case there was nothing explicitly political in the text.[74] In the same way he insists, in 1932, that I/1 has political implications:

I am firmly convinced that, especially in the broad field of politics, we cannot reach the clarifications which are necessary today, and on which theology might have a word to say, as indeed it ought to have, without first reaching the comprehensive clarifications in and about theology which are our present concern . . . I believe . . . that, quite apart from its ethical applications, a better Church dogmatics might well be finally a more significant and solid contribution even to such questions and tasks as that of German liberation than most of the well meant stuff which even so many theologians think in dilettante fashion that they can and should supply in relation to these questions and tasks.[75]

Hans Urs von Balthasar, who cannot be accused of reading Barth from the left, observed that Barth's dogmatics 'is capable from the beginning of generating practical and political consequences'. He goes on, 'The more deeply one becomes acquainted with Barth's thought, the more evident become such connections—in both directions, so that one is both the effect and the cause of the other.' Barth's earliest political positions, he noted in 1951, had been maintained unchanged through all the transformations of his thought, and in this he remained true to himself.[76] More strongly, Peter Winzeler speaks of Barth's theology as his first line of political struggle. As he puts it,

---

[74] *Letzte Zeugnisse*, 21.
[75] KD I/1, p. xii; CD, p. xvi.
[76] Hans Urs von Balthasar, *The Theology of Karl Barth*, tr. E. Oakes, San Francisco, Ignatius, 1992, 45.

arth formulated the theological conditions under which the Church could engage in free political struggle.[77]

Of course, Barth's belief that one could move from theology to politics might have been a misjudgement, and Barth's revision of his view of Ragaz, late on in life, at least raises that question.[78] What cannot be doubted is that Barth *believed* that, *precisely as a theologian*, he was making a contribution to the struggle against Hitler. This is very clear in his 1933 pamphlet, *Theologische Existenz Heute!*

As soon as Hitler became dictator, on 23 March 1933, a policy of *Gleichschaltung* (assimilation) was instituted, which involved the taming of the civil service, the party system, state governments, the unions—and the Church. At the end of April 1933 the naval chaplain Ludwig Müller was appointed plenipotentiary in Protestant church affairs. At the prompting of many friends and students Barth drew up a pamphlet in response, finally written on 24 and 25 June. It was most probably the (shortlived) appointment of August Jäger as State Commissar for the Prussian Church, the largest of the Landeskirchen, which prompted Barth to have it printed. According to Helmut Traub the first draft contained 'unnecessary aggravations, goads [*Reizworte*]' which branded the whole Hitler regime as ruthless and corrosive, though it was not an explicitly political manifesto. Barth read it to Traub and Charlotte von Kirschbaum who advised him that it would land him, the publisher and the printer in jail at once. Barth rewrote it describing it ironically (on Stoevesandt's account of events) as 'Your assimilated [*gleichgeschaltete*] text', though Traub emphasizes that it remained the same 'in intention and substance'.[79]

The document is indeed in many places quite oblique, which is not surprising given the atmosphere of the time—many left intellectuals were already in gaol, and the SA were engaged in daily violence. The overriding call in the pamphlet is for the Church to be faithful to its witness. 'The decisive thing which I seek to bring to these problems today', wrote Barth, is 'to carry on theology, and only theology, now as previously, and as if nothing had happened. Perhaps there is a slightly increased tone, but without direct allusions [*Bezugnahmen*]: something like the chanting of the hours by the Benedictines nearby in Maria Laach, which goes on undoubtedly without break or interruption, pursuing the even tenor of its way even in the Third Reich.'[80]

---

[77] Winzeler, *Widerstehende Theologie*, 150.

[78] See Barth's remarks to M. Mattmüller in P. Bock, *Signs of the Kingdom: A Ragaz Reader*, Grand Rapids, Eerdmans, 1984, p. xix.

[79] H. Stoevesandt, ' "Von Kirchenpolitik zur Kirche!" Zur Entstehunggeschichte von K. Barths Schrift "Theologische Existenz Heute!" ' *ZTK* 76 (1979), 118–38.

[80] I use the text in Barth, *Gottes Freiheit für den Menschen*, Berlin, Evangelischer Verlag, 1970,

Pursuing theology, 'as if nothing had happened'. This remark is often misinterpreted to mean that the important business is theology, no matter what is going on in the world around: *Fiat theologia et pereat mundum*. When Brunner taxed him at the end of the Second World War with having abandoned fifteen years of theologically political activism to return to the 'passive unconcern' he had recommended in 1933, Barth replied: 'It is a legend without foundation that in 1933 I recommended a "passive unconcern" to the German people when I urged that preaching should go on "as if nothing had happened", i.e. in face of the so called revelation in Adolf Hitler. Had that advice been thoroughly pursued then, National Socialism would have come up against a political opposition of the first order.'[81] Barth's view was that 'there is no more urgent demand in the whole world than that which the Word of God makes, viz. that the Word be preached and heard'.[82] Looking back in 1938 Barth observed that what he said in the pamphlet was what he was always trying to say—'but now, suddenly, I had to say the same thing in a situation where it could no longer have the slightest vestige of an academic theory. Without my wanting it, or doing anything to facilitate it, this had of necessity to take on the character of a summons, a challenge, a battle cry, a confession.'[83]

What the Word taught was, even if nowhere nearly as clearly spelled out as at the beginning of the war in Switzerland, still courageous considering that a copy of the pamphlet was sent to Hitler. 'The German Evangelical Church, through her responsible representatives, has not comported herself as the Church which *possesses* her Leader [*Führer*] . . . He possesses her . . . When it is recognised that He, and He alone, is the Leader, there is the possibility of theological existence.'[84] This stand is reminiscent of the stand of the early Church which emphasized the responsible citizenship of Christians and undertook to pray for Caesar, but refused to offer incense to his 'genius', in other words refused to recognize his absolute lordship. Moreover, the eight reasons for Barth's refusal to go along with the German church in fact spell out his political principles sufficiently clearly:

It is not the Church's function to help the German people to recognise and fulfil any one 'vocation' different from the 'calling' from and to Christ . . . The Church

---

147–76; ET by R. Birch Hoyle, *Theological Existence To-day!*, London, Hodder & Stoughton, 1933. Here p. 147.

[81] '"Theologische Existenz' heute'": Antwort an Emil Brunner' in *Christliche Gemeinde im Wechsel der Staatsordnungen: Dokumente eine Ungarreise, 1948*, Zürich, 1948, Evangelischer Verlag, 66–70; ET in *Against the Stream*, 106–18.

[82] Ibid., 148.

[83] Barth, *How I Changed my Mind*, ed. J. Godsey, Edinburgh, St Andrew Press, 1969, 46.

[84] Ibid., 161.

believes in the Divine institution of the State as the guardian and administrator of public law and order. But she does not believe in any state, therefore not even in the German one, and therefore not even in the form of the National Socialist State. The Church preaches the Gospel in all the kingdoms of this world. She preaches it also *in* the Third Reich, but not *under* it, nor in its spirit.[85]

Along with others who joined the Confessing Church, Barth denounced the 'Aryan clause':

The fellowship of those belonging to the Church is not determined by blood, therefore, not by race, but by the Holy Spirit and Baptism. If the German Evangelical Church excludes Jewish-Christians, or treats them as of a lower grade, she ceases to be a Christian church.[86]

Because of the Church's existence under the Word, 'no moratorium and no *Gleichschaltung* can befall them. They are the natural frontiers of everything, even of the "Totalitarian State" . . . They are this for the salvation of the people: *that* salvation which neither the State nor yet the Church can create, but which the Church is called upon to proclaim.'[87]

As was clear from the first Romans commentary onward, and as he reiterated in CD I/1, which had appeared in 1932, Barth took with total seriousness the claim that 'the Word of God makes history'. In that volume Barth had quoted Luther: 'On the last day God will say to me . . . Hast thou heard that? and thou shalt say, Yea, and He saith further, Why then hast thou not believed? and thou then sayest, Oh, I held it for a word of man since some poor chaplain or village parson said it . . . none considereth that beneath lies the divine majesty . . . it is not a preacher's word but God's Word.'[88] The German Christians clamour for a leader, says Barth, but we have one in Christ, who is known to us in preaching, and where the Word of God is witnessed to there, 'even if one be but an ever so insignificant theologian, or the obscure village pastor, or even not a pastor or theologian at all, but "merely" somebody like a lay elder, then one is *himself* the genuine Bishop, if he only knows his Bible and his Catechism.'[89] Not just in 1933, though critically then, Barth believed that a Church obedient to the Word *made a difference*.

Was this just wishful thinking? Secular historians are divided in their view. Gordon Craig is dismissive. The resistance of the left, he writes, produced no impressive result, but still it compared favourably with the churches. Neither Protestant nor Catholic churches took a stand against the crimes of the regime. 'The authoritarian tradition of both Churches blunted their critical capacities and their collective conscience.'[90] Golo Mann, however,

---

[85] Barth, *How I Changed my Mind*, ed. J. Godsey, Edinburgh, St Andrew Press, 1969, 163–4.
[86] Ibid., 165.   [87] Ibid., 176.   [88] KD I/1, 96.
[89] *Theologische Existenz Heute*, 161.   [90] Craig, *Germany 1866–1945*, 666.

believes that the policy of *Gleichschaltung* did not succeed with the churches. 'The fortress of the faith stood at the centre of the German state, from the jubilant beginning to the bitter end, unconquered and virtually unassailable.'[91] Against that reading we should perhaps set Adenauer's devastating judgement in a letter to a Bonn pastor in 1946: 'I believe that if all the bishops had together made public statements from the pulpits on a particular day, they could have prevented a great deal. That did not happen, and there is no excuse for it. It would have been no bad thing if the bishops had all been put in prison or in concentration camps as a result. Quite the contrary. But none of that happened and therefore it is best to keep quiet.'[92] If we bear in mind what Barth said in 1933 about every Christian being a leader or bishop the question becomes even sharper. Pondering the impact of Schleiermacher's theology, in 1924, Barth noted that it raised very serious questions both about the truth of Protestantism and about the divine guidance of the Church. 'The more we ponder them, the more serious the situation becomes.'[93] These questions apply to the very substance of Christian faith. It is because they are raised so passionately, urgently, intelligently, and with such imagination by Barth that his theology, in its whole sweep, continues to demand our attention.

[91] Mann, *Germany*, 427.
[92] K. Scholder, *A Requiem for Hitler*, tr. J. Bowden, London, SCM, 1989, 139.
[93] Barth, *Die Theologie Schleiermachers*, 462; ET *The Theology of Schleiermacher*, tr. G. W. Bromiley, Edinburgh, T. & T. Clark, 1982, 259.

2

God's Revolution

1909–October 1921

> This western front business couldn't be done again, not for a long time
> . . . They could fight the first Marne again, but not this. This took
> religion and years of plenty and tremendous sureties and the exact
> relation that existed between the classes . . . You had to have a whole-
> souled sentimental equipment going back further than you could
> remember.
>
> F. Scott-Fitzgerald, *Tender is the Night*

A LIBERAL EDUCATION

Barth came from a well established middle class family, with many notable
nineteenth century preachers and theologians amongst his ancestors. University, for him, was a matter of course. From 1904 to 1906 Barth studied at
Bern, and then went for a year to Berlin, where he studied under Harnack
and Gunkel. A short sojourn in Tübingen was followed in 1908 by three
semesters at Marburg, where he was a committed student of Herrmann and
also inevitably influenced by the reigning neo-Kantianism of Natorp and
Cohen.[1]

These were exciting years to be a student in Germany, which understood itself, with some justice, to stand in the forefront of cultural progress. Einstein formulated the Special Theory of Relativity in 1905, and
Nils Bohr outlined Quantum Theory in 1914. Bruckner, Mahler, and
Richard Strauss were expressing musically what expressionists were
attempting to say in art. Max Reinhardt was the leading director in Berlin,
and in the year Barth went there Rilke published one of his most famous

---

[1] Simon Fisher offers us an indispensable study of the Marburg background, and makes
clear that Barth had studied not only Herrmann but Cohen carefully. In my view his argument
that Barth was influenced by neo-Kantian epistemology right into the *Dogmatics* has to be
treated with caution as Barth was seeking a specifically theological methodology, in principle
unsystematic in its borrowings from philosophy, from 1916 on. S. Fisher, *Revelatory Positivism?:
Barth's Earliest Theology and the Marburg School*, Oxford, Oxford University Press, 1988.

works.[2] The *Die Brücke* movement of expressionism began in Dresden in 1905. Kandinsky was working in Munich and the Blue Rider school was established in 1912. Modernist architecture was first being executed in the studio of Paul Behrens in Darmstadt, where Walter Gropius, Mies van de Rohe, and le Corbusier were all pupils. The slogan of this movement, 'less is more', we also find on the lips of the early Barth.

For the student there was a tension, visible in Barth's own writings, between the idea of *Bildung*, which produced cultivated people familiar with 'the best which has been thought and known' on the one hand, and a radical anti-bourgeois critique on the other. Barth was a profoundly *gebildeter Mensch*, deeply read in German literature, and especially in Goethe and Schiller, as the first Romans commentary shows. (Jülicher remarked ironically in his review of this commentary that Schiller was quoted 'somewhat more often than the interest of the Pauline text seems to require'!)[3]

On the other side was the critique of this whole vision of culture which had been gaining force for half a century, and whose most powerful spokesman was Nietszche, who was, in the words of Gottfried Benn, 'the earthquake' of that generation of students.[4] Amongst the avant garde it was fashionable to be anti-bourgeois. The plays of Wedekind were on at Berlin whilst Barth was studying there, calling into question the hypocrisy of bourgeois sexual morality. The satirical weekly *Simplicissimus* lampooned the court and the ruling classes. Above all German expressionism, followed closely by Kandinsky and Klee, sought a radical break with realist and bourgeois convention. This art stressed 'the grotesqueness and mendacity' of bourgeois culture. Dadaism, which began in 1916 in Switzerland, very much as a protest against the war, demanded 'the complete destruction of the current and exhausted means of expression'.[5] In point of fact the war marked the final collapse of a cultural epoch whose demise the writers, musicians, and artists had been announcing for many decades. Drawing on Barth's autobiographical reminiscenses all commentators note the complicity of liberal theology with the war effort in bringing about Barth's new start but equally the two Romans commentaries may be seen as the theological equivalent of the attempt of the art of Beckmann or Kandinsky to break with bourgeois convention. This has

---

[2] Barth may very likely have seen his famous production of *A Midsummer Night's Dream*, whose 'Well roared lion!' he liked to quote ironically later in life. Rilke's *Die Weise von Liebe und Tod des Cornets Christoph Rilke* was published in 1907.

[3] J. Moltmann (ed.), *Anfänge der dialektischen Theologie*, i, Munich, Kaiser, 1977, 88.

[4] See H. M. Pachter, *Modern Germany: A Social, Cultural and Political History*, Boulder, Col., Westview, 1978, 39.

[5] A. Hauser, *The Social History of Art*, iv, London, Routledge, 1962, 218–19.

been seen not just by theologians, but also by art historians, who find
the early texts of Barth illuminating for the art of the second decade of the
century.[6]

Though Barth was able to throw himself into student life with the
passion which characterized everything he did, he was also, and especially
during his time in Germany, a serious student. He said later of his time in
Berlin that Harnack's attempt to bring religion and culture into harmony
scientifically 'impressed him so much that he wholly neglected the rich cultural opportunities Berlin afforded . . . He was chained to Harnack . . . in a
kind of stupor so that even the Berlin Philharmonic could not lure him from
his studies.'[7] It was, however, Herrmann, in Marburg, who was '*the* theological teacher of my student years'.[8] Barth knew him as 'an articulate independent thinker' with 'the ring of prophetic utterance' in his voice.
Rebellious students, repudiating all authority, 'listened gladly when traditionalism on the right, rationalism on the left, mysticism in the rear were
thrown to the refuse dump, and when finally "positive and liberal dogmatics" were together hurled into the same pit'.[9] Herrmann it was who
gave Barth that thorough knowledge of Schleiermacher which kept him
wrestling with him for the rest of his life. For Herrmann, Schleiermacher's
Speeches were the most important piece of Christian writing after the New
Testament. Like Schleiermacher a religion of experience is at the heart of
his theology. God is known to us through revelation, but this is not doctrine
but personal experience mediated through the inner life of Jesus. As in
Schleiermacher, the power of this inner life is passed down through the gen-
erations of believers to the present day. The power and self evidence of this
experience means that we are from the start fortified against the attacks of
historical criticism. Herrmann evidences the same kind of ambiguity about
history as Schleiermacher. On the one hand this is a profoundly historical
theology, in that historical process—spiritual history in Herrmann's
terms—is central to it, but on the other hand it sits light to the kind of empirical work which Ranke above all made the touchstone of historical
study. Learning from him one can understand why Barth infuriated historical critics throughout his life!

Barth made waves at once with his first serious publication: 'Modern Theology and Work for the Kingdom of God', which provoked two professor-

---

[6]   So Matthias Eberle, *World War I and the Weimar Artists*, New Haven and London, Yale University Press, 1985. More on this below.

[7]   B. A. Willems, *Karl Barth*, cited in *Revelation and Theology*, ed. H. M. Rumscheidt, London,
Cambridge University Press, 1972, 4.

[8]   'The Principles of Dogmatics according to Wilhelm Herrmann' in *Theology and Church*,
238–71.

[9]   Ibid., 257, 267.

ial responses.[10] Asked to account for the fact that so few young people were offering themselves for mission work Barth replied that theological training these days, with its emphasis on religious individualism and historical relativism, left one wondering not only about mission but about the pastorate! The modern student is unable to take over his faith from the Christian tradition, even though he recognizes that the 'power and peace of his inner life' is owing to the New Testament. At the same time his integrity as a student forces him to treat the documents of the New Testament as documents like any other. The modern theologian (and Barth acknowledges his debt to Herrmann) lives with this ambiguity, reconciling critical study and personal faith. Barth concludes (the irony is delicious when we set this alongside the 1923 exchange with Harnack): 'Religion is for us a strongly individual experience, and we consider it a duty to work out our position, clearly and positively, in regard to the general human cultural consciousness on its scientific side.'[11]

Another example of his Herrmannian stance is provided by the long scholarly paper on 'The Christian Faith and History' which he gave to a gathering of pastors in 1910.[12] The relation of faith and history was, he said, *the* problem for Christian theology at present. Faith he defined as 'experience of God, unmediated consciousness of the presence and reality of the trans-human, trans-worldly and therefore simply superior power of life'.[13] It is not opposed to history but is itself the 'historical Moment par excellence', which actualizes and makes historical our cultural consciousness (*Kulturbewußtsein*). 'Faith and the historicity of culture become synonyms.'[14] It can be seen that from this perspective faith cannot be threatened by the findings of historical research. In his review of the meaning of faith from New Testament times to the present it is the Schleiermacher of the *Speeches* who is the hero, revealing how faith is born in the individual. He it is who makes clear to us Luther's meaning(!): it is in and through Schleiermacher's intuition (*Anschauung*) that justification and election become fact, 'in the feeling brought about by God'.[15] Faith rests on Jesus' own consciousness of God which can be mediated to us through the New Testament but also through the work of artists and composers such as Michelangelo, Bach, Mozart, and Beethoven, but also from the numberless 'little ones' who are 'bearers of Christ's reality'. Whichever way, Christ needs to be born in us, as Angelus Silesius says.[16] As for Herrmann, it is the power of Jesus' inner life which is

---

[10] The article appeared in *Zeitschrift für Theologie und Kirche*, 1909. It can now be found in Barth, *Vorträge und Kleinere Arbeiten, 1905–1909*, 341–7. One of its critics was Arthur Drews, whose two volume work on 'The Christ Myth' had just appeared. In reply Barth insisted that faith gave the believer greater certainty than historical research.
[11] Ibid., 347.   [12] Barth, *Vorträge 1909–1914*, 149–212.   [13] Ibid., 161.
[14] Ibid., 163.   [15] Ibid., 186.   [16] Barth, *Vorträge 1909–1914*, 191.

redemptive, which cannot be mediated to us through historical science. Barth concludes by pointing out that the one account of the relation of faith and history which is impossible is that of Troeltsch.[17]

Though Barth turned decisively against liberal theology, its two principal teachers, Kant and Schleiermacher, always remained important to him. Five or six years after this paper Schleiermacher was identified as the source of much that was wrong in contemporary theology, but Barth felt Brunner's later dismissal of him (in *Das Mystik und Das Wort*) was too hasty, and he himself kept up the engagement until the end of his life.[18] Kant too, whom he studied intensively both at university and in the pastorate, provided much of the philosophical orientation for his later thinking.

PROPHETIC SOCIALISM

Apart from the liberal theology and critical philosophy he imbibed as a student Barth was also deeply influenced by what has been called the tradition of 'prophetic socialism'.[19] All over Europe, in the second half of the nineteenth century, socialism gained ground, and from the start there were Christians who felt that this was the practice of which Christianity was the theory. Whilst some Christian socialism, such as Friedrich Naumann's in Germany, quickly ran aground and became nothing but a support for nationalism, other forms were much deeper and more interesting. This was preeminently true of Christoph Blumhardt. His father, Johann Christoph, had a ministry of healing and exorcism in Bad Boll which began with the recognition, 'Jesus is the Victor'. Exorcism was not understood as a fringe activity but as related to the whole world of forces which oppress human beings, including the political. Developing this sense Christoph took the step into active Social Democratic politics. Unlike Naumann, however, this did not represent an abandonment of specifically Christian concern. On the contrary, the practical activities of both Blumhardts were rooted in faith in the power of the living God. Christoph Blumhardt's election to the regional parliament was, said Barth, 'a completely unpolitical, simple, and obvious

---

[17] Barth sent Troeltsch a copy of the paper. Troeltsch replied with lofty irony that 'he could bear it'.

[18] 'Although certainly "against" Schleiermacher in my own way, I for my part was neither so certain nor so completely finished with him as Brunner undoubtedly was after he had completed that book.' Barth, *The Theology of Schleiermacher*, tr. G. W. Bromiley, Edinburgh, T. & T. Clark, 1982, 266. The *Nachwort* to this edition of his Schleiermacher lectures gives a vivid picture of Barth's early years, and his intellectual development.

[19] The term is used by Buess and Mattmüller in *Prophetischer Sozialismus*, on which I draw in what follows.

confession before God and man of his living belief in the future'.[20] Hope was the dominant feature of his message: 'hope for a visible and tangible appearing of the lordship of God over the world (in contrast to the simple, and so often blasphemous, talking about God's omnipotence); hope for radical help and deliverance from the former state of the world (in opposition to the soothing and appeasing attitude which must everywhere come to a halt before unalterable "relationships"); hope for all, for mankind (in contrast to the selfish concern for one's own salvation . . .); hope for the physical side of life as well as for the spiritual'.[21] Blumhardt exercised a powerful influence on the Swiss church, which led to the growth of a religious socialist movement in Switzerland quite unlike that in Germany. In fact it was, in Barth's view, 'a characteristically Swiss movement'.[22] Its leading figures, Hermann Kutter and Leonhard Ragaz, both learned from him and there is a real lineage from Blumhardt, through them, to Barth.[23]

This movement was just under way when Barth began university at the age of eighteen in 1904. Ragaz had preached in Basle Münster the previous year in connection with the building workers' strike, seeking to give a 'salvation historical reading' of the events. In December 1903 Kutter published *Sie Müssen*. The living God as witnessed to by Scripture is its theme and it aimed to waken middle class congregations to a sense of what God was doing in history, not least in Social Democracy. Social Democrats were dismissed as atheists, said Kutter, but in fact it was they who exemplified the Beatitudes, who hungered and thirsted after righteousness. 'They do what God has done from the beginning through his witnesses: they take the side of the poor and oppressed in a thoroughgoing way—and are supposedly godless!'[24] Through these socialists God is teaching the church what needs to be done.

In September 1906 Ragaz published *The Gospel and Today's Social Struggle* and the following month the first religious socialist convention was held in Switzerland. Ragaz gave the opening address, arguing that the capitalist economic order contradicted the gospel in all principal points. No Christian could defend it. At the very least they could have no interest in its continuance. The Christian socialist journal *Neue Wege* was founded to keep up the

[20] Barth, 'Past and Future' in *The Beginnings of Dialectical Theology*, ed. J. Smart, Richmond, John Knox Press, 1968, 44.

[21] Ibid., 41–2.

[22] K. Barth, 'Reformierte Theologie in der Schweiz', in *Ex auditu verbi: theologische opstellen aangeboden aan Prof. Dr. G. C. Berkouwer ter gelegenheid van zijn vijfentwintigjarig ambstjubileum als hooglerar in de Faculteit der Godgeleerdheid van der Vrije Universiteit te Amsterdam*, Kampen, J. H. Kok, 1965, 36.

[23] M. Mattmüller, 'Der Einfluss Christoph Blumhardts auf schweizerische Theologen des 20 Jahrhunderts', *Zeitschrift für evangelische Ethik* 12 (1968), 233–46.

[24] H. Kutter, *Sie Müssen*, Jena, 1910, 5.

concerns of the conference, and Ragaz soon became its sole editor. Barth was amongst its readers and contributors. Six years later Basle Münster was filled with red flags, and a huge gathering of socialists was addressed by Jaures, Keir Hardie and August Bebel. These were stirring times and it is hardly surprising that, as Barth later recalled, 'Every young Swiss pastor who was not asleep or living somehow behind the moon . . . was at that time in the narrower or wider sense a "Religious Socialist".'[25]

Barth had cited Ragaz in one of his earliest talks on 'Zofingia and the Social Question', given to a Bern student association in January 1906. Ragaz, from a working class background himself, was keenly aware of the reality of class conflict and Barth acknowledged the truth of his claims. 'We have to agree', he said 'that the rift between Capital and Labour, Mammonism and pauperism, rich and poor . . . grows continually larger.'[26] The problem, he said, could not be solved by force, or treating the poor like caged animals. The social question was part of the human problem which Jesus responded to, and which found in the Reformation its religious, and in the French revolution its political, solution. These do not bring in the kingdom of God but are its necessary premisses. As far as the student society (Zofingia) went he argued that it was important to take a positive line on the question. Better understanding of the working classes was called for. Since student action was primarily a matter of learning, let us learn the ins and outs of the social question both theoretically and practically. We must strengthen our sense of responsibility. He closed with various practical proposals, including watchfulness on the alchohol problem. There is little social analysis here to be sure, but Barth shows himself keenly aware of political realities, and especially sensitive to the question of class.

THE 'RED' PASTOR

Barth was ordained in September 1909 and served a two year curacy with the German speaking congregation in Geneva before becoming pastor of Safenwil, a rural area rapidly becoming industrialized. Given the strength of the religious socialist movement it is not surprising that Barth's encounter with real poverty during his curacy in Geneva, and then with poorly paid workers in Safenwil, should lead him both to a study of socialist literature and even more to action. 'In the class conflict which I saw concretely before me in my congregation', he wrote in 1927, 'I was touched for the first time by the real problems of real life. The result was that for some time . . . my only theological work consisted of the careful preparation of sermons and

[25] Barth, 'Ruckblick', in *Offene Briefe*, ed. D. Koch, 1984, 189.
[26] Barth, *Vorträge 1905–1909*, 74.

classes. What I really studied were factory acts, safety laws and trade union-ism, and my attention was claimed by violent local and cantonal struggles on behalf of the workers.'[27] He was 'passionately involved with socialism and especially with the trade union movement' and studied Sombart and Herkner, the Swiss trade union newspaper and the *Textilarbeiter*.[28] He gradu ally compiled several thick notebooks full of facts and figures about the industrial situation.

The 'situation' Barth mentions worsened after 1914. Though Switzerland hastened to reaffirm her neutrality she nevertheless called up her armed forces, 250,000 men. As in the combatant countries, the call up generated political demands for a new order. The British blockade, followed in 1917 by the U-boat war, made the import of food and necessary supplies extremely difficult. Food and other essentials were rationed, and increased taxes were necessary to pay for the war economy. There was sharp inflation, whilst wages were sometimes reduced. The working classes bore the brunt of what was happening. Under these conditions anti-militarism and union militancy grew. The Swiss Social Democratic Party, which Barth joined in 1915, was radicalized, committed to class war and the dictatorship of the proletariat. When the Party proposed to celebrate the anniversary of the Russian Revolution in 1918 Zürich was occupied by the military. The SPD there-upon called a general strike demanding proportional repre-sentation and a 48-hour week. The strike only lasted 24 hours, as many of the workers' demands were met, but the strike leaders were imprisoned for periods of up to six months. The Soviet delegation, still committed to world revolution, and influential in the action, was expelled. Barth was keenly involved in all these events at local and regional levels, attending not only religious socialist but Social Democratic congresses. Twice people tried to persuade him to go full time into politics, and he himself delivered forty-three lectures and talks on socialist themes during the Safenwil years.

Barth's thorough acquaintance with socialist theory is already clear in the lecture (described by the local entrepreneur as 'a long rabble rousing speech') he gave shortly after his move to Safenwil on 'Jesus Christ and the Movement for Social Justice'. Both the gospel and socialism represent move-ments 'from below to above', rooted in partisanship for the poor, and soli-darity is at the core of both. Poverty and need cannot be spiritualized because for Jesus 'there are not two worlds, but the one reality of the kingdom of God'. Jesus rejected private property and believed in common ownership. His dismissal of the idea that 'what is mine is mine' marks him out as 'more socialist than the socialists'. From the gospel one learns that

[27] From the faculty album at Münster, reprinted in K. Barth–R. Bultmann, *Letters 1922–1966*, tr. G. W. Bromiley, Grand Rapids, Eerdmans, 1981, 154.

[28] Barth, *Theology of Schleiermacher*, 263.

'one must become a communal person, a comrade, in order to be a person at all'.[29] '*Real* socialism is real Christianity in our time.' True Christians needed to be socialists, but true socialists had to be Christians if they wished to reform socialism.

A more nuanced affirmation of socialism is found in the lecture on 'Religion and Socialism' which he gave four years later, in 1915, shortly after he had joined the SPD. Here socialism is acclaimed as a sign that the kingdom of God is not standing still, and that God is at work in the world. In socialism, as opposed to in religion, 'God is taken seriously politically'.[30] Socialism in itself is not the kingdom but a 'reflection' or 'signpost' of it.

Apart from his many socialist addresses Barth ran evening classes for workers helping them understand their situation. He worked hard and systematically on socialist theory and social analysis. Practically he was involved in the formation of three local unions, was sent as delegate to many socialist conferences, and was finally asked if he would stand as a representative for the Aargau General Council. Like Ragaz he was against joining the Third International, and was present in 1920 when the decision was taken against it. Barth's commitment to socialism was undoubted but it was essentially a practical rather than an ideological matter. He was, he said at the end of his life, 'only marginally interested in socialist principles and ideology'.[31] In Marquardt's terms, Barth was from the beginning a 'questioning member of the movement'. Barth and Thurneysen 'set up their "drilling machine", as they once said, against everything, put all in question, and experienced themselves as radically put in question'. This questioning attitude made Barth in particular 'a Religious Socialist *sui generis*'.[32]

QUESTIONS ABOUT RELIGIOUS SOCIALISM

The correspondence between Barth and Thurneysen, which began in earnest in 1914, shows how large a part religious socialism played in their lives in the first two years of the war. For a while Barth clearly understood himself as a religious socialist: in the volume of sermons he and Thurneysen published in 1917 he talks of the questions Blumhardt puts to 'We socialist theologians'.[33] The two leaders of the movement were, however, drifting

---

[29] G. Hunsinger, in Hunsinger, *Barth and Radical Politics*, 35–6.
[30] Cited in Jüngel, *Barth*, 93.   [31] *Letzte Zengnisse*, 44.
[32] Marquardt, *Theologie*, 84.
[33] K. Barth and E. Thurneysen, *Suchet Gott, so werdet ihr leben!*, Munich, Kaiser, 1928, 176.

apart. Kutter increasingly distanced himself from religious socialism after 1910, urging the gospel as a critique of all ideologies. His refusal to affiliate with any party left him free to criticize all, a position Barth found too easy.[34] Late on in life Barth acknowledged that it was from Kutter, whom the Barth–Thurneysen circle knew as 'Papa', that he learned 'to speak the great word "God" seriously, responsibly and with a sense of its importance'.[35] He grew wary of him after Kutter published a book supporting the German war effort, but this did not mean the lessons he had learned from him were lost. On the contrary, engagement with him continued long into the next decade.

Unlike Kutter, Ragaz was a committed political activist. He joined the Social Democratic Party in 1913, but the failure of European socialism in 1914 led him increasingly to pacifism. His passionate critique of religion must have influenced Barth's own movement in this direction. The kingdom of God, he said, represented the abolition of all religion. Christ 'does not want a religion, but rather a Kingdom, a new creation, a new world'.[36] Suspicion of theology was part of the legacy of Blumhardt and he grew increasingly disenchanted with both theology and church. Called to a Chair of practical theology in Zürich in 1908 he resigned this in 1922 and went to live in the Zürich slums, earning his living thereafter as editor, preacher and through adult education, and continuing his theology through Bible studies in which he sought to reflect on contemporary events.

From the start Barth felt closer to Kutter than to Ragaz and an unusual strain of animosity runs through many of his references to the latter. By 1915 Thurneysen is complaining that *Neue Wege* is leading them up blind alleys. There is a feeling that Ragaz is somewhat shallow.[37] The two men took different sides during the First World War, Kutter supporting Germany and Ragaz the Entente. In the face of this rift Barth saw value in both positions, praising Kutter's call to 'wait' and reflect but acknowledging the need for action. 'Ragaz's endeavour to put principles into practice', he wrote to Thurneysen, 'is an indispensable, though secondary, element, in spite of its evident "danger".'[38] Many years later Barth felt that Ragaz had tried to turn religious socialism into a system and that he had 'never wrestled carefully or profoundly' with the attempt to understand socialism as a prophetic call for the Church to be herself, to pursue her own proper task.[39]

[34] B–Th I, 32.
[35] Barth, *Theology of Schleiermacher*, 263.
[36] Bock, *Signs of the Kingdom*, 28 f.
[37] B–Th I, 70.
[38] B–Th I, 79.
[39] KD 1/1, 76; CD, 74.

In the light of a talk by Hans Bader at a religious socialist conference in 1915 Barth defined the differences between the two men thus:

Ragaz: Experience of social needs and problems. Ethical demand. Belief in development. Optimistic evaluation of Social Democracy. Opposition to the church. Religious-socialist party with conferences and 'new ways'. Emphasis upon sympathy with workers and other laymen. 'They talk about us'. Martyrdom hoped for and sought. Protest against war.

Kutter: Experience of God. God's Kingdom as promise. Insight into the enslaved condition of human beings without God. The Social Democrats can never understand us! Religious responsibility *in* the church in continuity with the pietistic tradition. Circles of friends for *spiritual* deepening and for work. Concentration primarily on pastors. Building dams for a much later future.

What followed was what was significant:

Conclusion: The religious socialist thing (*Sache*) is out, taking God seriously begins . . . [40]

More than either of these Swiss religious socialists, by whom he was unavoidably influenced, Barth was impressed by Christoph Blumhardt, whom he met in 1915. He was also strongly influenced by Zündel's book on the elder Blumhardt, which he read after the meeting, and he later included a chapter on him in his lectures on nineteenth century theology. Christoph Blumhardt's passion for the new, wrote Barth after Blumhardt's death, grew out of his faith in God's reality. His attack on the bases of present-day society, culture, and church arose from his understanding of God's forgiving, redeeming love. Unlike the Church, which began with human wickedness and thought religion could ease it a little, Blumhardt felt there was much that was good and hopeful in the world but 'as a whole it needs and awaits a thoroughgoing redemption and renewal, not through religion, but through the real power of God'.[41] The impact of the Blumhardts on Barth can hardly be overestimated. Neither were theologians, but they *lived* the affirmation 'God is God' which was at the heart of Barth's early theology, and they did so *in the midst of society* without ever giving politics priority over faith.

We have seen that between 1911 and 1915 Barth became markedly more cautious about identifying socialism and the kingdom. Even before his meeting with Blumhardt his self confessedly naive faith in socialism was shaken by the failure of the Socialist International to resist the war. 'I had

[40] B–Th I, 78–9. Marquardt comments on the difference between Kutter and Ragaz that Kutter's 'living God' was philosophically rather than biblically grounded, whilst Ragaz's 'kingdom of God' arose from political principles rather than from Scripture. Marquardt, *Theologie*, 94. This would help to understand Barth's need to move beyond them.
[41] Barth, 'Vergangenheit und Zukunft', in Moltmann, *Anfänge*, i, 45; ET, 41.

credulously enough expected socialism, more than I had the Christian church, to avoid the ideology of war, but to my horror I saw it doing the very opposite in every land.'[42] In Germany the SPD became, in Naumann's words, 'a patriotic workers' movement'. 'It approves the war expenditures and joins in our common task without any difference.'[43] This failure, together with the impact of Blumhardt's critical stance, made it impossible for Barth to be a conventional religious socialist in the Ragaz mould.

DISCOVERING A NEW WORLD

When the first World War broke out Harnack headed a petition of ninety-three German intellectuals to the Kaiser expressing support for the German war effort. The Court Preacher Ernst von Dryander expressed the mood of virtually the entire Church in telling his Berlin congregation, on 4 August, that they were going into battle 'for our culture against the uncultured, for German civilisation against barbarism, for the free German personality bound to God against the instincts of the undisciplined masses'.[44] At the end of his life Barth recalled that at this point 'An entire world of theological exegesis, ethics, dogmatics, and preaching, which up to that point I had accepted as basically credible, was thereby shaken to the foundations.' Liberal theology, beginning with Schleiermacher, had 'unmasked itself'.[45]

As it emerges in the correspondence with Thurneysen, however, not even the need for an alternative presented itself immediately. Rather, a critical correspondence with Rade about the religious justification of the war, the meeting with Christoph Blumhardt, and a growing dissatisfaction with Ragaz's ethicism gradually led to the perception of this need.[46] 'More reflectively than ever before we began reading and expounding the writings of the Old and New Testaments. And behold, they began to speak to us—very differently than we had supposed we were obliged to hear them speak in the school of what was then called "modern" theology.'[47]

[42] B–B (ET) 154.

[43] Cited by Jüngel, *Barth*, 88.

[44] K. Scholder, *The Churches and the Third Reich*, i: *1918–1934*, tr. J. Bowden, London, SCM, 1987, 6.

[45] Barth, *Theology of Schleiermacher*, 264.

[46] Marquardt points out that the betrayal of socialism by the social democratic parties also played a large part in Barth and Thurneysen's disillusionment. Marquardt, *Theologie*, 121.

[47] Barth, *Theology of Schleiermacher*, 264. Gollwitzer points out that in the theology of Herrmann theology and ethics were separate. The unity of dogmatics and ethics which became a hallmark of Barth's theology 'is nothing but the theological programme for the knowledge practised in Safenwil . . . this he had not heard from Herrmann. This was the deepest break with Marburg.' Not only did his teachers ratify the war but also their separation of dogmatics and ethics. 'The Kingdom of God and Socialism' in Hunsinger, *Barth and Radical Politics*, 85.

ıe determination to take God seriously is already evident in a talk given
ɛ town church in Aarau in January 1916 in which we seem to see Barth's
thought on the move before us. The lecture begins with a solid Kantian
appeal to the conscience. Conscience is 'the only place between heaven
and earth in which God's righteousness is manifest'.[48] In face of the great
atrocities of life, such as capitalism and the war, we reach out, like drown-
ing men grasping at straws, for the certainty which conscience gives.
The trumpet blast of conscience awakens our need for the righteousness
of God, but it is then dulled by our reforming and religious efforts. In point
of fact the European conflict reveals the god we worship to be an idol:
'He cannot stop those who believe in him—all those excellent American and
European representatives of culture, welfare and progress, all those upright,
zealous citizens and pious Christians from falling on one another with fire
and murder to the amazement and derision of the poor heathen in India
and Africa.'[49] Where then do we turn? We have to turn to the God who does
not simply underwrite the moral codes our consciences so easily approve:
'To do God's will means to begin with God anew. God's will is not an
improved continuation of ours. It stands over against ours as a Wholly
Other.'[50] Instead of attempting to improve things ourselves we have to allow
'the only real thing' to happen, namely for God to take his own work
in hand. We have to learn to wait on God, to do God's will, and then, and
only then, do morality, state, culture, religion, and church become possible—for the first time!'[51] We begin with conscience and end with faith in
God's new and powerful act. And this act renews morality, state, and culture
as well as religion and church. 'The Bible, as it was here discovered, was a
political discovery.'[52]

It was Thurneysen who suggested during a shared holiday in June that
what was needed was a 'wholly other' foundation, and they both realized
that for them the theology which began with Schleiermacher was finished.
Barth set to work on Romans almost at once, but shared his excitement
over 'The New World in the Bible' with Thurneysen's parishioners in the
autumn. If we do not begin with religious experience, where should we
begin? We have not gone to Scripture because we have reduced it to a hand-
book of ethics or doctrine. But, 'It is not right human thoughts about God
which form the content of the Bible, but right divine thoughts about human
beings.'[53] What we find in Scripture is not religion, piety, human history, but

---

[48] 'Die Gerechtigkeit Gottes' in *Das Wort Gottes und die Theologie*, Munich, Kaiser, 1925, 6; ET
by D. Horton, *The Word of God and the Word of Man*, London, Hodder & Stoughton, 1935, 10.
[49] *Das Wort Gottes*, 14; ET, 22.
[50] Ibid., 15; ET, 24.   [51] Ibid., 16; ET, 26.
[52] Marquardt, *Theologie*, 95.
[53] 'Die neue Welt in der Bibel', in *Das Wort Gottes*, 28; ET, 43.

God, God's lordship, God's honour, God's ungraspable love—not uɪᴄ human standpoint, but the standpoint of God. We have to learn to understand this afresh: 'God is the content of the Bible. But what is the content of the content? A new thing breaks in! But what is the nature of this new thing?'[54] It is known in the creation of a new *world*, which is what God is establishing through the Spirit in believers.[55] Marquardt does not exaggerate when he describes the 'new world' as entailing 'the revolutionary overthrow of existing middle class society'. The rediscovery of God was not the result of philosophical labours but part of a movement of vehement social involvement. Thus the 'wholly other' was 'no metaphysical-distancing but rather a social-qualifying concept'.[56]

GOD IN REVOLUTION: THE FIRST ROMANS COMMENTARY

It is in the first Romans commentary, which was completed in August 1918 and published the following year, that these insights are for the first time fully worked out. Barth said it was written in 'the joy of discovery'. Certainly it is characterized in places by what can only be described as wild excitement. After his holiday with Thurneysen Barth had sat down under the apple tree in his garden with the commentary of Tobias Beck which his father had used. He learned from him and the other older commentators like Bengel and Tholuck not simply to reproduce the historical critical works which by then were the hallmark of serious New Testament work. Fortunately, Barth wrote in his preface, he was not forced to choose between the historical critical method and the old doctrine of inspiration, but were he to do so he would unhesitatingly choose the latter. The task of the exegete is to see through the historical into the spirit of the Bible, which is the eternal Spirit and to hear Paul, the 'prophet and apostle of the kingdom of God to all people in all ages'. What was it that Barth heard?

The Theme of the Letter

Perhaps the most marked feature of the new theology is the vivid sense of the reality of God, engaging with the world, which Barth is struggling to bring to speech, and which was to become the hallmark of his entire theology. 'Our theme in this letter', he writes, 'is our knowledge of God realised

---

[54] Ibid., 29; ET, 44. This is a question put to Kutter, where Barth is striving to go beyond his account of the actuality of God. Marquardt, *Theologie*, 150.

[55] *Das Wort Gottes*, 32; ET, 50.   [56] Marquardt, *Theologie*, 111.

in Christ, in which God draws near not objectively but creatively and immediately, in which we not only see, but are seen, not only understand, but are
understood, not only grasp, but are grasped.'[57] That God grasps us means
that we share in the immediacy of the knowledge with which God knows
Godself.[58] Indeed, 'The concept of God is given us as immediately as our
own Being.'[59]

This emphasis on the immediacy of our knowledge of God recalls the
theology of his earlier addresses, but there is here an inversion of the liberal
problematic: not our search for God, but God's grasping of us is what is at
stake. We think not from the grounds of human God consciousness but *'von
Gott aus'*, as Kutter had described it.[60] For Barth it is precisely a strategy of
the principalities and powers to characterize God ever more abstractly so
that the idea of God becomes 'an ever more faded "religious" master
concept for all sorts of inner worldly lordships and significant things'.[61] Over
against this, Barth insists time and again that God is God, and that the
meaning of history is God's meaning.[62]

The Victory of God

Human beings are estranged from their Origin (*Ursprung*), God, who can
also be characterized Platonically as 'the Good'.[63] To speak of God as the
'Origin' did not imply pantheism but was, rather, a way of talking about the
immediate relation human beings enjoyed with God before the Fall.[64] In our
present, post Fall, state 'The seed of the immediate knowledge of God is
trodden down before it comes to harvest.' This happens in two ways. First,
we make of God an Idea, an empty abstraction, out of the source of Life one
life factor amongst others. But secondly, we deny God the thanks which are
God's due, refuse to acknowledge our absolute dependence, and in our
moralism place ourselves autonomously alongside God.[65] 'There is only *one*
sin: the desire to be autonomous over against God.' The desire to be as God
bore fruit in vaunted 'knowledge of humankind', 'experience', psychology,

---

[57] R1, 19.   [58] R1, 158.   [59] R1, 28.
[60] R1, 71.   [61] R1, 36.   [62] R1, 71.   [63] R1, 20, 375.
[64] Von Balthasar reads it as a sign of pantheism. *The Theology of Karl Barth: Exposition and
Interpretation*, tr. E. Oakes, San Francisco, Ignatius, 1992, 71 ff. Barth had already used the
concept in his lecture on 'Faith in the Personal God', and used it still at Tambach. Marquardt
shows that Barth learned it from the critical idealism of his brother Heinrich and that it functioned as a mediating term between immediacy and objectivity. He concludes: 'Barth's interest
in critical idealism was not dominated by epistemological or ontological questions (*Daseins-
frage*), not the dialectic of thought, nor of Being, History and nature, but the concrete dialectic
of society, its thesis and antithesis, its origin (*Ursprung*) in God, its analogical relation to God.'
Theologie, 219. See the discussion at 207–19.
[65] R1, 30.

'historical' thinking.[66] This analysis of sin, McCormack points out, had profound political overtones. The Enlightenment project was bound up with our 'taking charge of our own destiny'. 'To place the conception of a self-constituted, self-centred, and self-relating subjectivity under the sign: Sin! was at the same time to strip the bourgeois preoccupation with self-realization through acquisition of money and power of any possible ideological justification.'[67]

Because sin is bound up with autonomy, redemption is return to the Origin, which is what Christ accomplishes both for us and for the whole cosmos.[68] Eschewing a forensic account of Christ's death, Barth finds the establishment of redemption in the reversal of our pride. Through his obedience Christ fulfilled the true destiny of human life. His death was 'the fulfilment of a human life in the immediacy with God which had once again been found'. As such it introduced 'something new into world history, the fundamental overcoming of the old'.[69] In him the Origin 'reappears'.[70]

The note of Blumhardt's 'Christ is Victor' is also sounded. 'In the death of Christ the struggle, and in his resurrection the victory, of divine reality over the powers of sin and death have been consummated.'[71] The cross is not our salvation as suffering and struggle, but *through* the cross the glory of the Father, the resurrection, is inserted between us and our sin.[72] The resurrection is 'a revelation of unmistakeable clarity' which reveals the meaning of the cross to us.[73] Anticipating what he was later to develop in the *Church Dogmatics* Barth speaks of the resurrection as the divine verdict on Christ's obedience.[74]

Again astonishingly anticipating later developments, Barth speaks of the victory of God as accomplished 'in heaven' before it is realized on earth. This age is not the final one. There is 'not only a truth which is beyond this world [*jenseitige Wahrheit*] but there are also events beyond this world, a world history in heaven, an inner movement in God'. What we call 'history' and 'events' are but the confused reflection of turns that happen there. The cross is one such 'turn'. God's faithfulness breaks through the inescapable necessity of God's wrath against humans, and creates righteousness on earth and the possibility of eternal life.[75] In Christ 'God's reality [*Sache*] becomes our reality.'[76]

The metaphor of 'breakthrough' is one Barth particularly favours. It

---

[66] R1, 177–8.

[67] B. L. McCormack, *Karl Barth's Critically Realistic Dialectical Theology: Its Genesis and Development 1909–1936*, Oxford, Clarendon, 1995, 167. He points out that this also constituted a critique of political liberalism to the extent that this made an end in itself of the freedom of the individual.

[68] R1, 200.   [69] R1, 225.   [70] R1, 53, 65.   [71] R1, 98.   [72] R1, 215.

[73] R1, 98.   [74] R1, 197–8.   [75] R1, 161.   [76] R1, 313.

presupposes his distinction between 'so called' history, history 'in Adam', which human beings make for themselves, and 'actual' history, the history God makes, history 'in Christ'.[77] God's history breaks through into so called history, and when this happens time is fulfilled by eternity in its deepest sense, in an 'eternal Now'.[78] That this happens means that in the stream of so called history the new element of actual history which swims against this stream is visible.[79] 'Breakthrough' moments are the moments when real history becomes visible, in which the kingdom (actual history) is established in the midst of so called history. The breakthrough of God's power in Christ is not a 'historical' event, in the sense of an event which can be understood and assessed by the canons of Rankean historiography, but the 'uncovering of the never still, necessary reality in the cross section of time'.[80]

Is the relation of divine history and human history, then, to be conceived simply in terms of a series of 'moments', of 'breakthroughs' which are not otherwise related? No, because complementing this imagery are metaphors of continuity: 'way', 'movement', 'development', process, above all 'organic' and 'organism'.

The organic metaphor is obviously partly a protest against Protestant individualism. When Christ's resurrection inserts us into the stream of organic life, then 'We simply stand within this process . . . we want to be nothing other than an organic particle of the creation, bound up with the whole, which is now reconciled with God.'[81] We must live and grow in the organism which stems from Christ.[82] Return to the Origin, through participation in the organism or movement, is what constitutes the 'process eschatology' of this commentary.[83]

Without endorsing liberal ideas of progress, however, Barth also wishes to emphasize the sense of real movement and change in both human and cosmic history.[84] The germcell of life has once again been planted in history and nature so that divine history grows within human world history.[85] Both God and human beings are involved in a movement and follow a way. Adam-Christ marks 'the way of God in world history. A *way* of God. No stasis [*Zustand*] . . . no stable 'reality'. That you only find in hell. Where we are

---

[77] R1, 66–7, 223–5.   [78] R1, 86–7.   [79] R1, 66–7, 85.

[80] R1, 106. The force of this, McCormack comments, was to secure the reality of God against the constructivist epistemology which governs all historical study'. McCormack, *Barth's Theology*, 147.

[81] R1, 171.   [82] R1, 227.

[83] The term 'process eschatology' is Michael Beintker's, 'Der Römerbrief von 1919', in G. Sauter (ed.), *Verkündigung und Forschung: Beihefte zu 'Evangelische Theologie'*, ii, Munich, Kaiser, 1985, 24.

[84] Marquardt points out that Barth developed these ideas at the same time as Bloch's *Spirit of Utopia*, with its categories of possibility and of latency-immanence. Marquardt, *Theologie*, 92.

[85] R1, 24.

dealing with *God*, it goes forward, in the face of victorious decisions.'[86] We live and suffer not outside, but inside God's movement.[87] God is with us not as an alien Stranger but as our nearest most intimate acquaintance, his will not a ' "strange rule which lies athwart our free feelings, but as the pulse of our own organism" [Kutter], our own deepest, truest, freedom'.[88] We live in a 'messianic present', inaugurated by the decisive turn in heaven, in which a life process is opened up on earth, in the psychological-historical side of our being. 'We are no longer the same. We are inserted in the process which carries forward from the beyond into the present.'[89]

Picking up the language of Durkheim, and using it with characteristic freedom, Barth contrasts organic growth with 'mechanical' change, change that is man made: 'The divine grows organically, and so needs no more mechanical building up.'[90] This means in the first instance that, over against the insistence of the Christian socialists, we do not have to 'build' the kingdom. It does not come through our efforts. 'There is life, which is grounded through the fullness, the outpouring, the breakthrough of the grace of God . . . and now organically unfolds itself.'[91] In this 'unfolding' the true striving of idealism is finally honoured, so that Plato, Kant, and Fichte stand in a line with Moses as prophets of recovered immediacy. 'Where else than in Christ can idealism be *more* than idealism?'[92]

To have faith is to be caught up in God's movement.[93] It is to say 'Yes' to the divine 'Yes' in Christ, to give an answer of faithfulness to the faithfulness of God. This note of affirmation and victory is the decisive mark of the book. Its counterpart, however, is an equally decisive series of negatives: to individualism, moralism, pietism, and—religious socialism!

Against Religion and Individualism

Over against the victorious work of Christ stands the ambiguity of religion and church. 'Round about 1909', Barth remarks, with an eye ironically on his own studies and entry into the pastorate, religion had become such a palpably powerful force that a special counter blow against its 'history and presence' was urgently needed.[94] 'Restless world committees were at work. In Basle the socialists were triumphant, in Edinburgh the Christians looked

---

[86] R1, 189.   [87] R1, 155.   [88] R1, 207.   [89] R1, 166.

[90] R1, 90. 'The coming world comes not mechanically, but organically' R1, 21. In *The Division of Labour in Society*, which was published in 1893, Durkheim had distinguished between mechanical and organic solidarity, the former representing the taken for granted solidarity of pre-industrial society, and the latter the solidarity industrial communities needed to work at and construct.

[91] R1, 195.   [92] R1, 104–5.   [93] R1, 475.

[94] An allusion to the great theological encyclopaedia, *Religion in Geschichte und Gegenwart*, the first edition of which appeared between 1909 and 1913.

forward to the arrival of the kingdom of God . . . but whether the concern of all this was really God's concern, whether God wanted all this—no one seriously asked that question!'[95] This was not strictly true. Barth had learned from Blumhardt that religion was opposed to the kingdom of God. 'The unhappy word "religion" was not heard at Möttlingen and Bad Boll' he wrote in his article on the younger Blumhardt.[96]

Barth's critique was directed especially at the Church which, as Goethe noted, 'has a good stomach':

She receives Moses, and turns his inheritance into a codex of letters . . . she receives the letter to the Romans, and carefully dismembers the living whole into individual dead pieces, reshapes the Truth in the truths into 'doctrine and ethics', and praises 'her' Paul. She receives Francis and elevates him to head of the Order and Saint, and later to the darling of all aesthetes . . . she receives Luther, and makes him patron of 'inwardness', 'Germanness', 'evangelical freedom', as they call these empty nothings . . . finally they make the cross in a million ways the symbol of highest humanity . . . they *sing* the suffering Christ . . . in all this the Church—not the world!—once again crucifies him.[97]

Barth took from his exegesis of chapter 4 a critique of the religious hero. In faith there are no heroes but only fellow sinners and the fellow redeemed.[98] Religious hero worship is part of a false piety and religiosity which 'leads to nihilism'.[99] Barth had been plagued by a pietist mission in the course of writing the commentary, and it is hardly surprising that pietism attracts fire. Grace is not 'experience' (both *Erlebnis* and *Erfahrung*). 'That is a prejudice of Pietism . . . primarily (grace) is the divine presupposition, the new order under which we are placed, the altered world context to which we are led.'[100] When we are truly redeemed we do not need any hot house piety. 'The method of pietism is only possible, in its presuppositions and effects, under the wrath of God.'[101] One of the things from which Christ redeems us is the 'Inferno of Pietism' which occludes the real work of God in history.[102]

Near the heart of religious experience is the priority of the individual, but 'God cannot be honoured simply in a "personal" life. Truth is not for the individual.'[103] In place of the individual is the organism of God's kingdom, in which we are rooted and need to grow.[104] 'The faith of the individual is nothing before God, insofar as she wants to be more than a momentary expression of the movement. But the movement is not borne by the individual but by the Christian community.'[105] 'The theme of world history is

[95] R1, 400–1.   [96] Barth, 'Vergangenheit und Zukunft', in Moltmann, *Anfänge*, i, 45.
[97] R1, 421–2.   [98] R1, 117.   [99] R1, 33.
[100] R1, 206–7.   [101] R1, 288.   [102] R1, 293.
[103] R1, 272. For a different account of the two meanings of 'organic' see McCormack, *Barth's Theology*, 153–4.
[104] R1, 255.   [105] R1, 475.

not the single person with their conscience, but the set to of the great objective powers: Sin and Righteousness, under whose lordship all Being, and therefore also the being of the individual, turns either to life or death.'[106] McCormack notes that we have here an incisive critique of the bourgeois assimilated Church. Barth's emphasis is 'an assault on a central feature of late bourgeois culture: the understanding of the human individual as the creative subject of culture and history . . . Against the divisive individualism which had given rise to class warfare and world war, Barth posited a diviner "universalism".'[107]

We can say, then, of religious realities and experiences that they are consequences of a cause, signs of a reality, forms of a content—but no more than that. They are not there to be celebrated in themselves. 'God's decisive deed goes before them, and God's purpose way beyond them. They are means, no more, and woe betide us if we forget that.'[108]

Grace Versus Ethics

Just as the reality of grace calls into question the individualism and human security of religion so it challenges our understanding of morality. ' "What shall I do?" Answer: Above all stop asking that question! Every word of it is ambiguous and confused.'[109] This is because, when we are part of the organic life of the new community, every 'ought' flows 'organically' from our new being in the Spirit. As opposed to the 1916 lecture on the righteousness of God, conscience in this commentary has a merely negative function, which can only make clear the gulf between God and human beings. In fact, 'From the last standpoint, which we have to take in Christ, there are no ethics. There is only the movement of God which demands each moment a quite specific knowledge of the situation and to which a necessary deed corresponds.'[110] The answer to the moral question is not ethics but grace.[111] All 'interim ethics' or monastic ethics are done away with. They are against grace because against the freedom we have been given. This does not mean passively 'leaving all to God'. Living in the kingdom of grace means serious, candid knowledge of unredeemed reality, clear consciousness of the responsibility of each individual, openness to the changing command of the hour, and readiness to take the next step which will bring the movement towards its goal.[112] Our behaviour as Christians is shaped by mutual exhortation: 'Exhortation is not a law or an ideal, an establishing of how it ought to be but the reality of a life in which the ideal is engaged in fulfilment, step by step.' It is an expression of the whole community on the move.[113]

---

[106] R1, 236. [107] McCormack, *Barth's Theology*, 141. [108] R1, 121.
[109] R1, 263. [110] R1, 524. [111] R1, 203. [112] R1, 241. [113] R1, 463.

Part of the attack on conventional ethics is an attack on religious socialism, and in particular Ragaz, for whom the book was a 'stab in the back'.[114]
Without being named, Ragaz was attacked in the exegesis of both chapter 2
and 13, and he recognized the critique only too well. 'Inspired by Kutter,
misusing Blumhardt, full of poison, spite and pride' he wrote in his diary.[115]
In the exegesis of the second chapter he appears as the 'Pharisee', the religiously righteous man. 'Pacifism and social democracy do not represent the
kingdom of God', wrote Barth, 'but the old human kingdom in a new
guise'.[116] Those who develop critiques of the existing order can be prophets,
but they can also be Pharisees.

They treat God's reality as if it were a human reality, to be met with other human
realities. Instead of teaching about the goodness of God, which is over them, crying
out and sighing with all people that they should be friends, they place themselves in
a partisan way over against most other people, more proud than the Godless. They
enjoy themselves in their special situation and pose of struggle. And because they are
not worried by the progress of *actual* history they feel that much more secure in the
exceptional religious-ethical situation within *so called* history. They forget how relative this situation is.[117]

Although they stand theoretically on God's side, practically speaking they
are God's 'worst hindrance'.[118] They turn the gospel into a new law. It is
hardly surprising that Ragaz felt wounded and misunderstood by this!

The Christian in the Midst of Revolution

And what of the political vocation which was at the heart of Ragaz's religious socialism? Barth reads the passage from Romans 12.16 to 13.10
together under the heading of 'Superiority': what he has in mind is what is
at stake in *truly* overcoming the world. 'Your method is solidarity with the
enemy. Not the feeblespirited indifference, friendliness and tolerance over
against his impossible way of doing things, not the false community of fire
and water, but the mercy of God'.[119] What this means for political responsibility is spelled out in twelve steps, the keynotes of which are Paul's 'Be subordinate!' on the one hand, but an absolute refusal of legitimacy to the state
on the other.

The State as we know it is characterized by naked power, the 'devilish art
of the majority'.[120] Christians can have nothing to do with this, because
'their State is in heaven'. Their stance over against the State is 'in principle

[114] Buess and Mattmüller, *Prophetischer Sozialismus*, 148. Ragaz disliked R1 also because he
thought it smacked of quietism(!) and accused it of being a 'theology of the waiting room'. K.
Blaser, *Combats- Idées- Reprises: Karl Barth 1886–1986*, Freiburg, Lang, 1987.
[115] Cited in F. W. Marquardt, *Der Christ in der Gesellschaft*, Chr Kaiser Munich 1980 p. 12.
[116] R1 42.   [117] R1, 46.   [118] R1, 47.   [119] R1, 498.   [120] R1, 501–3.

revolutionary' in that they deny its fundamental principle of the use of power.[121] Christians must be prepared to engage in political duties, but without absolute seriousness. On the contrary, their concern is with the 'absolute revolution of God' which 'revolutionises revolution'.[122] Christianity 'does not agree with the State, it negates it—both its presupposition and its essence'.

It is *more* than Leninism! As far as Christianity is concerned it is 'all or nothing' in the sense that the fulfilment it expects is not . . . the goal or result of a development or a gradual 'ascent of man' but the discovery of a new creation or the substance of a new knowledge. *This* programme cannot be the object of any ethics.[123]

To be subject to the authorities, as Paul recommends, means not to take them seriously, to deny them ideological legitimation (to 'starve them religiously').

Barth takes it for granted that a Christian can have nothing to do with 'Monarchy, Capitalism, Militarism, Patriotism and Liberalism'. Anticipating his Tambach lecture, he writes: 'The divine may not be politicised nor the human theologised—not even for the benefit of democracy and social democracy.' We must not confuse divine renewal with human progress. Whatever is done against the present state can in no way represent the victory of God's kingdom.[124] Revolt against the ruling powers leads to the region of God's wrath.[125] If the worst comes to the worst we may, however, find ourselves in 'confused situations' in which evil cannot be overcome by good. We may then act with 'ethical determination' but this is outside the sphere of the Christian ethic: 'As regards the ethic of the confused situation, the New Testament has nothing to say.'[126]

None of us can avoid complicity in the guilt of political realities. We need therefore to take part in state and party life knowing that God will forgive 'even our political sins'.[127] Even 'fundamentally dirty' political realities 'work together for good, with those who love God'. So long as the Christian remains true to her ways the mine is laid which will blow the idols sky high.[128] We must be careful, however, not to be untrue to God by marching into the political arena flying God's flag. It is certainly not God's spirit which drives a person to heroic political deeds. 'The Spirit does not knock at the hard shell of politics. It bursts it from inside!'[129] The important thing is to

---

[121] R1, 503–5.   [122] R1, 234.
[123] R1, 505–7.   [124] R1, 507–9.   [125] R1, 509–10.
[126] R1, 495. McCormack argues that in this commentary Barth recognizes a twofold ethic, namely, an ethic of God's command and, in the 'confused situation', a retreat to Kantian ethics. I find the evidence for this less than convincing. Is Barth here not struggling with what happens to our 'immediacy' and exhortation when we are on the barricades? Admittedly, this is a desperate solution!.
[127] R1, 510.   [128] R1, 511–12.   [129] R1, 512–16.

deny the state the pathos, seriousness and importance of the divine.[130] In
that we are all part of the fallen order of things we have no choice but to live
ethically and politically but 'we struggle against the State fundamentally and
radically and—pay taxes . . . join the Party, fulfil the functions . . . which fall
to us'. Respect to whom respect, honour to whom honour—'but not one
step further!'

Fulfil your duties without illusion, but no compromising of God! Payment of tax,
but no incense to Caesar! Citizens initiative and obedience but no combination of
throne and altar, no Christian Patriotism, no democratic crusading. Strike and
general strike, and streetfighting if needs be, but *no* religious justification and
glorification of it! Military service as soldier or officer if needs be but under *no* circumstances army chaplain! Socialdemocratic but *not* religious socialist! The betrayal
of the gospel is *not* part of your political duty.[131]

'Only love builds the new world.' The state might not worry that we withold
only this final honour to it, but if it realized the danger of these revolutionary methods, then martyrdom might become a real possibility.[132]

Marquardt believes that what we have here is Leninist subversive tactics—
'the absolute opposite of anarchism, not utopian dialectic, but dialectical
materialism in which the most radical anarchist denial of the State runs
together with a highly political participation in the State'.[133] He believes that
Barth offers us a theological reflection on Lenin's *State and Revolution*.[134]
However that may be, Barth echoes Marx's call for permanent revolution,
over against petty bourgeois haste to bring everything to a conclusion.[135]
The love of Christ remains faithful to 'the hope, the unquiet, the longing,
the radical and permanent revolution'.[136] At the present moment (1918!)
Spirit can be nothing other than revolution—'precisely what we call revolution at the moment!'[137] Amidst the disappointments of contemporary
socialism we look forward to the hour when the embers of Marxist dogma
are newly kindled and 'the socialist Church will be resurrected in a socialist
world'.[138] In terms which anticipate liberation theology he insists that the
movement of the kingdom is 'fundamentally and one sidely a movement
from below'. Whilst I can be a Jew to the Jews and a Greek to the Greeks I

---

[130] R1, 516–17.   [131] R1, 517–21.   [132] R1, 522.

[133] Marquardt, *Theologie*, 135.

[134] Bas Wielenga drew attention to parallels between Lenin's *State and Revolution* and Barth's
exegesis of Romans 13. 1–7, noting especially Barth's comment, 'The Christian's state and
revolution is in heaven'. R1, 507; Lenin's *Weg zur Revolution*, Munich, 1971, 433–6. Marquardt
argues that the first edition of Lenin's pamphlet appeared in 1918 in three different versions and
Barth could have seen it. Jüngel counters that Lenin's pamphlet only appeared on 20 November 1918. Jüngel, *Barth*, 159.

[135] Lenin's article appeared in German on 20 November 1918, and Barth's MS went to the
printers in December. Cf Jüngel, *Barth*, 101, 159.

[136] R1, 353 and the Marx citation there.   [137] R1, 316.   [138] R1, 444.

cannot be lord to the lords or an aesthete to the aesthetes. 'Over against everything which wants to be great I must take the standpoint of the small people, with whom God begins, not because they are virtuous but because *their* righteousness does not stand in the way, or at least, does less so.'[139] The belief in God's revolution is quite clearly not meant to be the disarming of 'real' revolution (which is part of 'so called' history), but part of actual (i.e. divine) history, which has concrete effects in the present.

The excitement of this writing is palpable. Given the seriousness with which religious socialism was taken in Switzerland, given the events of the General Strike, the debates within his party about tactics, this is burning advice about what constitutes the true revolution. Critics have noted the continuities with liberal theology within this commentary: the emphasis on evolutionary process, the immanence of the kingdom of God in history even, it is alleged, a speculative identity of divine and human activity.[140] It is the differences, however, which are overwhelming, in particular the return to an actualist theology of grace which was almost lost without trace in the theology Barth learned. The attack on the bourgeois religious and political world was by no means new—we find it in both Kutter and Ragaz—but the radical depth of the questioning was quite unmistakable to contemporaries. It was *this* book, and not the second commentary, which earned Barth his Chair, a profoundly paradoxical response to it!

Reviews and Reactions

Amongst reviewers Jülicher was offended by the 'presumptuous' Foreword, in which Barth had said that if the book were not at once taken up it could wait its time. The book brought home to him, he said patronizingly, 'the significance of practical exegesis as compared to strictly scientific exegesis'. The claim to hear the voice of the eternal Spirit seemed to him to be gnosticism. Correctly seeing the attack on cultural optimism he believed, rather more astonishingly, that Barth taught that 'there is no more progress in history, that development is forever at an end'.[141] Brunner much more accurately found the heart of the book in the principled break with 'the optimistic concept of evolution which rules almost undisputed over our religious, moral and scientific thought'.[142] Barth has withstood the temptation to psychologize, and instead brought the timeless, 'absolute' nature of faith to light. On the other hand he, along with other reviewers, misread the language of organism and immediacy to mean that human beings retained

---

[139] R1, 490.
[140] H. Kirsch, cited in Winzeler, *Widerstehende Theologie*, 155.
[141] Moltmann, *Anfänge*, 95; ET, 79.
[142] Ibid., 81; ET, 65.

'an undisturbed reservoir for the voice of God'! Thirty years later von Balthasar endorsed such readings in speaking of 'a radical philosophical mysticism which takes seriously the historicity of the world'.[143] In his view the book primarily gives expression to a mysticism of identity 'tinged with the unique accents of religious socialism'. However much we may disagree with Marquardt in detail, however, he compels us to read the commentary in the light of Barth's vehement and practical involvement in Safenwil. Read in this light it is certainly not the announcement that there is no more progress in history, nor a philosophical mysticism of a Platonic-Hegelian type (a creation of the study if ever there was one!) but an attempt to hear the word of Paul as the Word of God in the midst of absolutely concrete political realities.

FAREWELL TO REVOLUTION?

'The Christian in Society', Tambach, September 1919

As the first commentary went to press the First World War ended and the General Strike took place in Switzerland. In the next year Barth, along with Ragaz, campaigned against the Swiss Social Democrats joining the Third International. His arguments are exactly those spelled out in *Romans*. The violence of a revolution like that in Russia merely replicates the old society. Socialism must produce something better than that! He is also critical of the compromises of Weimar.[144] Meanwhile, German religious socialists seeking direction in the immense confusion of post-war Germany had arranged a conference at Tambach, in Thuringia. By a nice irony Barth originally turned down an invitation to go to Tambach, and was only invited at the last moment—to take Ragaz's place! Little known in Germany, he was thought to be one of Ragaz's disciples. Ragaz felt he had to stay in Switzerland to further the campaign against the Third International.

From the very start there were those who thought that the lecture under-cut everything Christian Socialism stood for. Barth himself later described it that way in his angry farewell article for *Zwischen den Zeiten*.[145] It is quite clear, however, that it represents no retreat into quietism, but rather a further radicalization, a deepening of the understanding of God's revolution. From Blumhardt Barth has taken a strong affirmation of worldly reality, and like him wants to find God at work there. To those who come,

---

[143] Balthasar, *Theology of Barth*, 67.

[144] In the article, 'Das was nicht geschehen soll', in the *Social Democrat Daily*, 15 August 1919. See McCormack, *Barth's Theology*, 193–4.

[145] Moltmann, *Anfänge*, ii, 419. For this assessment see also J. Cort, *Christian Socialism*, New York, Orbis, 1988, 207 ff.

not yet a year after the war, the key question is the way life h
into question through mass death.[146] The message is: we can
involved in side shows! The God who is the revolution be·
tions is at work in all reality. Our task is to share in *this* m...
lecture has five sections.

Where are we to turn for guidance in the midst of the confusion surrounding us? Only 'the Christian' has something to offer, but the Christian
is—'The Christ', the Christ of Colossians in whom and for whom are all
things, and who is therefore 'in us'. That Christ is the lord of all reality
means that the two seemingly dissimilar 'magnitudes', the Christian and
society, cannot be torn apart. We cannot erect fences between the elect and
the rest: as Marquardt has put it, one of the key messages of the lecture is
that there should be 'no apartheid', no erecting of fences between the
politically correct and the others. *All* are in Christ.[147] But neither can we
accept the destructive 'autonomy' of culture, state, and economic life which
amounts to idolatry, the recognition of 'a whole row of godlike hypostases
and powers'.[148] That Christ is one with God rules this out. 'The Divine is
something whole, complete in itself, a kind of new and different something
over against the world . . . It is complete or it is nothing.'[149] We must neither
secularize Christ nor clericalize society.

The problem with religious socialism, says Barth, is that it behaves as if
God belongs in a special religious domain. We know where this leads: to
Friedrich Naumann, who had come to accept a radical two kingdoms theology with the pronouncement that 'Jesus has nothing to say about the arms
race'(*Flottenpolitik*).[150] Instead, we need to learn to perceive the living God
building a new world. On the one hand there is the promise of God's reality,
and on the other the impossible and deadly separation of the religious and
the secular. As Christians we are called to a 'priestly stirring' (*Bewegen*) of the
hope and need in which we stand through which the solution which is in
God can find a freer way to us.

In his second section Barth spells out his presuppositions: not a 'standpoint', but an attempt to 'catch the bird in flight'. As it was for Barth in
Romans so for all those at Tambach the word 'movement' was crucial—all
were involved in the socialist movement, or the religious movement. Over
against these what is truly important is the movement *senkrecht von oben*,
cutting through all these movements as their hidden sense and motor, the

---

[146] So Plonz, *Herrenlosen Gewalten*, 168.

[147] Marquardt, *Der Christ*, 54.

[148] Barth, 'Der Christ in der Gesellschaft' in *Das Wort Gottes*, 38; ET, 279.

[149] Barth, *Das Wort Gottes*, 36; ET, 277.

[150] Fr. Naumann, 'Briefe über Religion' in *Werke*, i, Westdeutscher Verlag, 1964, 626. Cited
in Plonz, *Herrenlosen Gewalten*, 164.

movement of God's history, the movement whose power and significance is revealed in the resurrection of Jesus.[151] This movement is not to be identified with religion. It is God with whom we have to do. 'The Wholly Other in God—itself resisting all secularization, all mere being put to use and hyphenated—drives us with compelling power to look for a basic, ultimate, original correlation between our life and that wholly other life.'[152] But precisely the point is to look for the *connection* between our life and that wholly other life. Barth speaks to those who have the mass murder of the First World War written on their hearts. What we are gripped by, in the movement of God, is 'the revolution of life against the unbounded power of death'.[153] The power of death rests in the claim to self-sufficiency and autonomy, the valorization of authority, the family, art, religion *for their own sake*. These abstractions are 'the power of death'.[154] But, an echo of Blumhardt: 'It is the light of victory into which our hope and need have entered. The hope rather than the need is the decisive, the supreme moment . . . God applies the lever to lift the world, and the world is being lifted . . . God in history is a priori victory in history.'[155]

Barth presupposes in the lecture above all 'the great syntheses of the Epistle to the Colossians'. The situation in which we are placed *vis-à-vis* the world by the resurrection is so radical that we dare not identify our hopes for social change and revolution with the kingdom of God. Of course our protests are integral moments in the kingdom of God but the kingdom of God does not begin with them, as it is the revolution which precedes all revolutions and all established societies. Beyond, and comprising the divine negation, which our protests echo, is the divine affirmation, and it is only by affirming the world as it is—and not by chasing a dream world—that our protests can be fruitful. Theologically this affirmation rests in the fact that God is the creator. For this reason the *regnum naturae* belongs to the kingdom, and the affirmation of it, which is crucial to any desire to change things, is found in the glorious everydayness of Jesus' parables. From this affirmation follows the need to take our determinate place in the course of events, the stance of responsible solidarity.[156] We have a 'joyful freedom' to go in and out of the house of mammon and of the state without becoming servants of idols, cheerfully recognizing the state as 'the beast from the bottomless pit'. In all this: 'we affirm life'.

Barth now turns to the *regnum gratiae*. In words which are repeated in the second *Romans* (at 12.16), Barth acknowledges that 'We live more deeply in the No than in the Yes, more deeply in criticism and protest than in naiveté, more deeply in longing for the future than in participation in the present.'

[151] Barth, *Das Wort Gottes*, 40; ET, 283.   [152] Ibid., 43; ET, 288.
[153] Ibid., 45; ET, 291.   [154] Ibid., 47; ET, 293.
[155] Ibid., 49; ET, 297.   [156] Ibid., 57; ET, 312.

There certainly is a critical attack on society, echoed by Kierkegaard, Tolstoy, Nietzsche, Dostoevsky, and socialism. There is no option but to be part of this attack. And yet 'That No is not the last and highest truth but is the call from home which comes in answer to our asking for God in the world.'[157] How then should we act? Once again we are warned to avoid all abstractions.[158] We have to enter fully into the subversion and conversion of this present and of every conceivable world, but practically this means being 'hope sharing and guilt sharing comrades' within democracy. Not *religious* socialists then, but critical party members, supporters of the frail Weimar republic with all its compromises.[159]

Finally: whence is the source of our involvement? Not, as Emmanuel Hirsch had suggested, 'within' ourselves, but beyond, 'perpendicularly from above'. 'We throw our energies into the most humdrum tasks, into the business nearest at hand, and also into the making of a new Switzerland and a new Germany, *for the reason* that we look forward to the new Jerusalem coming down from God out of heaven.'[160] Our eschatological faith guides our political action, following attentively what is done by God. Precisely this keeps us at sober, revolutionary, disturbing action, pulled neither into an empty Yes like Naumann, nor an empty No like Tolstoy, but living in the dialectical tension in which God becomes real for us.

This lecture, it should be clear, is anything but a retreat from revolution. In it, as Sabine Plonz has argued, the kingdom of God functions as the origin of all historical movement, as its goal, and as its critique.[161] God's engagement imparts a dynamic character to all reality so that the 'movements' in which all Barth's hearers were caught up are now radically 'transfigured' (to use Paul Lehmann's term) and which Barth's theology glimpses 'like a bird on the wing'. 'Movement' then 'is the structural principle of the Tambach lecture'.[162] Its deadly opposites are autonomy and abstraction, both of which lead us away from the positive, joyful affirmation of life, and cheerful political action, to which we are called. Far from being a retreat this is the talk of someone for whom religious socialism now seems superficial, insufficiently radical, just as Lenin regarded much revolutionary activism as an 'infantile disease'. Barth believes heart and soul that *reality can be changed* because *God* is at work in reality. The task is to learn the meaning of true revolution, to join in the revolution of the kingdom which is before all revolutions.

---

[157] Ibid., 59; ET, 312.   [158] Ibid., 60; ET, 313.

[159] The joy and affirmation so characteristic of this lecture makes Barth more than a *Vernunftrepublikaner*, as McCormack describes him. McCormack, *Barth's Theology*, 201.

[160] Barth, *Das Wort Gottes*, 67; ET, 323.   [161] Plonz, *Herrenlosen Gewalten*, 150.

[162] Ibid., 156.

Von Balthasar described Barth's second *Romans* as 'theological expressionism'.[163] Though Germany's most famous artist, Max Beckmann, disliked being classed as an expressionist it is noteworthy that the art historian
Matthias Eberle finds powerful similarities and shared assumptions between
this lecture and Max Beckmann's *Confessions*, written just before the end
of the war.[164] Both Barth and Beckmann agree that it is impossible to withdraw from life in society. Barth writes: 'One cannot turn away from life,
from society. Life surrounds us on all sides; it poses questions to us . . .
we have to stand up to it.' Beckmann writes: 'Absenting onself completely
in order to get one's share of that famous personal purity and communion
with God seems to me bloodless and also wanting in human charity.
We should first do what there is to be done, and our work is painting.'[165]
Barth speaks of regaining the 'great objectivity with which Paul meets
the prophets and Plato'. Beckmann writes: 'Out of thoughtless imitation
of appearances, and feeble, archaistic degeneration into empty decoration,
and out of a false and sentimentally morbid mysticism, we will hopefully
arrive at a transcendental objectivity that might emerge from a deeper
love of nature and mankind.'[166] Where Barth saw 'Christ within our
selves'as a symbol of promise in the night of cataclysm and revolution,
Beckmann assumed the role of 'Christ within himself', though without
hope of redemption. Beckmann wrote: 'My religion is pride before God,
defiance of God. Defiance because he created us such that we cannot
love ourselves.' 'In my paintings I blame God for everything he did
wrong.'[167] Eberle's case for real correspondences here is a strong one.
It is not impossible that Barth read Beckmann's *Confessions*, but even if he did
not it is clear that Barth is responding to the mood he represents, not moral-
istically, and not by an empty preaching of 'hope' but at the most fundamental level by attempting to create a theology which is utterly engaged,
and free of the clichés which Beckmann and thousands like him had
rejected.

Biblical Insights

In the spring of the next year Barth addressed the Aarau Student Conference, ten years after he had himself listened to Troeltsch at the same event
with 'dark foreboding' as he described how the social significance of Christianity would gradually dwindle away. Now Barth himself began with the
question of what the Bible offered toward an understanding of the meaning

[163] Balthasar, *Theology of Barth*, 83.
[164] Stephen Webb first drew attention to this work: *Re-Figuring Theology: The Rhetoric of Karl Barth*, Albany, State University of New York Press, 1991.
[165] Eberle, *World War I*, 89.   [166] Cited in ibid., 90.   [167] Ibid., 91.

of the world. Barth finds a critique of religion and religious exp～
Scripture.[168] 'The polemic of the Bible, unlike that of the religions till tou～,
is directed not against the godless world but against the religious world,
whether it worships under the auspices of Baal or Yahweh.'[169] 'Jesus simply
had nothing to do with religion.'[170] Why? Because religion falsifies our
experience of the world: Barth's critique of religion is ideology critique.[171]
Only the wholly other God can give us life out of death. What we find
in Scripture is, in Overbeck's words, the 'wisdom of death', that is, the
wisdom which knows that life is only through Christ's death. From the life
out of death comes the 'warning against Mammon (which is truly
not meant in a social ethical sense)—that God alongside God who, as the
penultimate one, wants to hide the reality of life from us in death dealing
reification'.[172] Life comes out of death, and death out of life, but we cannot
preach this cheaply:

Let us not deceive ourselves: all our contemporaries stand in angst and need before
the closed wall of death, hardly aware of the new thing which waits behind it, and
we do not help with our speculative constructions and evangelistic or social busyness
. . . For the sake of the suffering of millions, for the sake of the forgotten blood of
many, for the sake of fear of the Lord, not that! If any word needs substantiation,
attestation and realisation through corresponding ethical, social and political action
it is the biblical saying that death is swallowed up in victory.[173]

Only this attestation and realization is the true naming of the Easter
message, the movement in which its truth is known. By contrast there is

---

[168] *Das Wort Gottes*, 80; ET, 66. There is a fascinating exchange on the significance of religious
experience in the Barth–Brunner correspondence. Brunner, who was close to Kutter, confessed
that he had little 'experience' of God, and this made him miserable. He signed off as Barth's
zurückgebliebener Weggenosse. Barth replied that his experience was identical, but: 'It really
becomes clearer and clearer to me that this religious labyrinth has no exit . . . It is a question of
God, and why do we marvel if he is not found in the psychological labyrinth of our religious
experience? "Why seek ye the living among the dead?" . . . We are not Pietists; we can know
and really know that faith in no ways consists (neither positively nor negatively, neither opti-
mistically nor pessimistically) in taking this whole psychological reality as serious and important. Rather, with our eyes closed, as it were, we hold on to God.' Letter of 9 July 1916, quoted
in J. Hart, *Karl Barth Versus Emil Brunner: The Formation and Dissolution of a Theological Alliance
1916–1936*, unpublished D. Phil thesis, Oxford, 1993, 12.

[169] *Das Wort Gottes*, 82; ET, 70.

[170] Ibid., 94; ET, 88.

[171] So Marquardt: 'The transcendentalism of Barth and Thurneysen's thinking is not metaphysical but . . . ideology critical. Under ideology critique must be understood both bourgeois
and religious system building.' *Theologie*, 117.

[172] *Das Wort Gottes*, 89: 'dem Tode täuschend ähnliche Dinglichkeit die Realität des Lebens
uns verhullen will'. The phrase is difficult to translate, but the English version (ET, 81) certainly
conveys the exact opposite of what Barth means. Marquardt's paraphrase is: 'Capitalism as a
system is the power of death, which oppresses life.' *Theologie*, 113.

[173] *Das Wort Gottes*, 92. Once again the translation turns Barth's politics into pietism. ET, 86.

'religion's blind and vicious habit of eternally maintaining that it possessess something, feasting on it'. The resurrection brings a new *world* in which the forgiveness of sins bears on the sphere of moral and political reality by reconstituting the moral subject.[174] Barth emphasizes both that the concern of God goes far beyond the religious, to the reconstruction of the world, and that the renewal of the world is accomplished 'beyond nations, parties and classes' in the God fearing individual.[175]

Overbeck

These insights were complemented by Barth's reading of a posthumous collection of the writings of the Basle church historian, and atheist, Franz Overbeck. In 1920 Barth published his response to this collection in an article entitled 'Unsettled questions for theology today', which is most certainly full of 'the joy of discovery'! It is, he writes, 'a dangerous book, a book filled with the apocalyptic air of judgement'.[176] The judgement was on a church which Overbeck saw had sold out to the dominant culture, and in particular on Harnack, for whom he reserved a particular venom. For Overbeck humanity and human history stood between *Urgeschichte* and death. True Christianity existed only in the *Urgeschichte*; it is above time. Along with Weiss and Schweitzer, Overbeck believed in the radically eschatological character of early Christianity. As soon as the Church lost that, he argued, the degeneration of church history began. In particular, the attempt to reconcile faith to knowledge marks out any theology as irreligious. Liberal theology was deeply committed to such a project by attempting to provide historical grounds for faith. Barth agreed. Modern Christianity is 'denatured', the loss of eschatological tension spells its coruption. Without it its claim to advise human beings is 'the wisdom which brings death'. Overbeck and Blumhardt stand back to back, the one backward looking and critical, the other forward looking and hopeful. Using Overbeck against himself Barth took up a sarcastic reference to the need for theology to be based on daring, and made it into a statement of theological intent. 'Daring' meant developing a theology which took eschatology seriously, which disowned the concordat with bourgeois culture, which did not try to prove its credentials by historical means (something which Barth had in any case learned from Herrmann). This was the agenda of the second Romans commentary.

---

[174] Ibid., 96; ET, 92.   [175] Ibid., 98; ET, 94.
[176] 'Unsettled Questions for Theology Today' in *Theology and Church* tr. L. Pettibone Smith, London, SCM, 1962, 57.

GOD'S REVOLUTION: THE SECOND COMMENTARY
ON ROMANS

Along with Overbeck, and further study of Paul, Barth mentioned closer acquaintance with Plato and Kant, which came from attending his brother Heinrich's lectures, and the writings of Kierkegaard and Dostoevsky as key influences for the new edition. He also emphasized that this commentary, like the first, arose in response to events: 'The present situation in its complete concreteness is our starting point.'[177] 'A wide reading of contemporary secular literature, above all of the newspapers, is urgently recommended to anyone who wants to understand Romans.'[178] The importance of this to Barth is evident from the letter he wrote to Thurneysen on armistice day 1918, recovering from flu and thankful not to have had to preach because of the difficulty of making any connection between newspaper and New Testament. 'What can we say about all this? One stands astonished . . . as the face of the world changes visibly: on this side of things. But the other side: the meaning and content, the actual trend of it all, the movements in the spiritual realm which now take place . . . If we had turned to the Bible *sooner* we might have had firm ground under our feet!'[179] The second *Romans* is the continuation of the attempt to relate the 'new world' of the Bible and turmoil of contemporary events which is made in the first.[180]

Far and away the most significant of these events were the failure of the revolution in Germany and the brutal success of the Russian revolution. Many on the left regarded the German revolution as 'a great swindle'. It was referred to as the 'so-called revolution'.[181] As far as Barth was concerned all this raised questions of theological substance. Those who consider these questions idle can go their way, says Barth. 'Others of us find the question of what theology has to say important, precisely at the moment when apparently all are pressing to cry out on the streets.'[182] The pressure of the revolutionary crowd, in other words, was real, where for the first *Romans* it was far more status quo positions which were being opposed. The need to come to terms with revolution was a major priority for the German church, and Romans 13 was the central text under discussion.[183] We may suspect that one of the reasons Barth could not simply reprint the first edition was because some of his central themes such as the priority of community,

---

[177] R2, 413; ET, 427.   [178] R2, 411; ET, 425.   [179] B–Th I, 299–300.

[180] So Marquardt: 'Barth sought in the Bible contemporary political orientations for action in the revolutionary situation of 1918.' *Theologie*, 95.

[181] P. Gay, *Weimar Culture: The Outsider as Insider*, Harmondsworth, Penguin, 1974, 10–11.

[182] R2, p. viii; ET, 4.

[183] Scholder, *The Churches 1918–1934*, 8.

expressed in the language of organism, were now co-opted by the right.[184] At the same time Barth's own drastic assertion in the Preface to the second edition that 'not one stone remains unturned' needs to be taken with a pinch of salt. Rather, as Peter Winzeler has put it, the first commentary is *aufgehoben*, taken up and subsumed, in this one.[185]

A striking illustration of the depth to which Barth responds to his context are the correspondences between Max Beckmann's shocking *Die Nacht*, painted shortly after Barth's first *Romans* appeared, and Barth's exegesis of Romans 1.18–32 in the second commentary, which had the same title. Drawing on his experiences as a medical orderly during the war Beckmann depicted the human condition in images of imprisonment, rape, and torture. Stephen Webb has compellingly illustrated these correspondences. Barth, says Webb, 'forces humanity into the very same room that Beckmann has painted . . . our vision, like the numbed stares of the villains in Beckmann's painting, is too darkened for us even to begin to see our true situation . . . The night is the time of God's wrath, and Barth portrays it with the same relentless courage combined with the same lack of sympathy that can be found in Beckmann.'[186] For Beckmann the hope of resurrection was destroyed by the war. He painted an as it were liberal Protestant 'Resurrection' in 1909, full of conventional imagery, replaced in 1917 by another 'Resurrection', this time a vision of desolation and emptiness. These paintings are the appropriate commentary on Barth's journey from optimistic liberal Protestantism to the thoroughgoing eschatology of the second commentary, in which he sought to respond theologically to terror and chaos.

The reviews of the first edition, the positive more than the negative, had also taught him what he had to avoid. When people thought he was talking about the immanence of God in the soul, or a particular kind of religious experience, sharp reworking was required! In its views of ongoing process, of the immediacy of our knowledge of God, and its affirmation of the Western cultural tradition from Plato to Fichte, the first commentary still manifested many affinities with liberalism. The notion of dialectic played an altogether minor role within it. Barth now approached the whole text as a witness not to organic growth but to the dialectic of God and the creature, time and eternity.

When a Swiss reviewer of the first commentary remarked that Barth's attempt to discern the 'inner dialectic' of Romans amounted merely to his imposing his own system on it he replied famously that 'if I have a system it is limited to a recognition of what Kierkegaard called the "infinite qualitative distinction" between time and eternity . . . "God is in heaven, thou art

---

[184] Gay, *Weimar Culture*, 89, 100, 110.   [185] Winzeler, *Widerstehende Theologie*, 155.
[186] Webb, *Re-figuring Theology*, 15.

on earth." The relation between such a God and such a man, and the relation between such a man and such a God, is for me the theme of the Bible and the essence of philosophy.'[187] The dialectic between time and eternity which made this commentary famous, and which eventually led to the description of the theology of Barth, Brunner, Gogarten, and even Bultmann for a while, as 'dialectical theology', was from the start a way of dynamiting the concordat between culture and theology but it was also, as the exegesis of chapter 13 makes clear, a stern warning against political titanism. The *point* of the infinite qualitative distinction, almost universally misunderstood in Anglo-Saxon circles as a typically Calvinist attack on human sin, is political.

Jülicher's review also forced him to clarify his method, and the preface to the second edition sketched out what amounts to a hermeneutical manifesto, which remains one of the landmarks of hermeneutic discussion in the twentieth century. The question of the nature of interpretation, says Barth, is 'the supreme question'. Why? Barth found the entire question of the Church's *raison d'être* bound up with it. As he read the New Testament he found material which 'urgently and finally concerns the very marrow of human civilization'.[188] He found a revolutionary attack on the way the world was at present constituted. When he turned to the standard commentaries of Jülicher or Lietzmann, however, he found that they contained 'no more than a reconstruction of the text, a rendering of the Greek words and phrases by their precise equivalents, a number of additional notes in which archaeological and philological material is gathered together, and a more or less plausible arrangement of the subject matter'.[189] They reduce the text to runes. The effect of this was to defuse its dangerous subversive effect and to render it harmless. These commentaries, and this way of handling the text, were a sign of the subordination of the Church to the bourgeois cultural norms expressed in the Prussian Academy. He contrasted them with the creative energy with which Luther or Calvin approached the task, so that 'Paul speaks, and the person of the sixteenth century hears.' How, then, to remedy the situation? The key thing, Barth believes, is to measure words and phrases by 'that about which the documents are speaking'. 'The Word ought to be exposed in the words. Intelligent comment means that I am driven on till I stand with nothing before me but the enigma of the matter . . . till I know the author so well that I allow him to speak in my name and am even able to speak in his name

---

[187] Barth, *Der Römerbrief*, 12th unaltered edition, Zürich, Theologischer Verlag, 1978, p. xiii; ET, 10. The translations are my own, but I include page references to the translation by E. Hoskyns, *The Epistle to the Romans*, London, Oxford University Press, 1933.

[188] R2, p. xii; ET, 9.   [189] R2, p. x; ET, 6.

[190] The exegete must learn to 'attentively think after' (*nachdenken*) ~ncepts of the Apostle.[191] As we do so, and the Word in the words ~mes clear, this has practical, indeed explosive, consequences, which ~kes the practice of appending a homiletic commentary to the 'scientific, scholarly' one impossible.

The Theme of the Letter[192]

Under this heading the first edition spoke of the immediate knowledge of God, but now Barth has learned from Kierkegaard that 'to be known directly is the characteristic mark of an idol'. The hidden God 'is not to be found in Romans, can neither be brought to speech nor written about, nor, indeed, "done", because God absolutely cannot be an object of human striving'. If God is known, it is the result only of miracle.[193] The name of this miracle is Jesus Christ. 'The content of the letter to the Romans is that the hidden God as such is the revealed God in Jesus Christ.' The letter's substance, theology, God's Word on human lips, is only possible on the grounds that this subject, the hidden God, has as its predicate—the revealed God.[194] That God is revealed does not, however, mean that we can count on such knowledge, make it our possession. On the contrary, precisely in Jesus 'God becomes truly secret, makes Godself known as the Unknown, speaks as the eternally Silent One. In Jesus God fends off all importunate intimacy, all religious impertinence.'[195] We have here the dialectic of veiling and unveiling which Barth was to develop to such effect in the *Church Dogmatics*.

In the first letter the key words were 'organic', and 'organism'. Here these have disappeared. Those metaphors emphasized God's interiority to all reality. Now 'God is, in the last event, outside of this world.'[196] God is *Ursprung* (Origin) but not *Ursache* (First Cause)—in other words, not the first of a chain of causes.[197] God is to be identified with neither heaven nor earth, because God is Wholly Other, not a member of any universe. The affirmations of classical Christian theism are insufficiently radical. To underline God's reality as 'Wholly Other' Barth uses the geometrical and algebraic analogies for which this commentary is famous—the 'tangent touching the circle', the minus sign outside the brackets of all human constructions—

---

[190] R2, p. xii; ET, 8. Once again the Anglo-Saxon discussion of Barth's hermeneutics, on the whole hostile, would benefit from an appreciation of its political significance.

[191] R2, p. xiii; ET, 11.

[192] Both Romans commentaries begin with a section entitled '*Die Sache*'. It is interesting that in Beckmann's second 'Resurrection' the inscription *Zur Sache* (Get to the point) appears. Both Beckmann and Barth were concerned to focus on 'the real issue' and not to be deflected by half truths and evasions.

[193] R2, 408; ET, 422.   [194] Ibid.   [195] R2, 73; ET, 98.

[196] R2, 301–2; ET, 318.   [197] R2, 342; ET, 357.

which convinced some critics for ever that according to Barth the gospel was 'thrown at the world like a stone'.[198] His point was that, as Kierkegaard had argued, a Christianity which had lost its ability to shock, and become a direct communication, becomes 'a tiny superficial thing, capable neither of inflicting deep wounds nor of healing them; by discovering an unreal and merely human compassion, it forgets the qualitative distinction between man and God'.[199] Instead of organic connection we now have *krisis*—Barth uses the Greek form—the judgement of God on all that we do, which stands over all history and all earthly existence.[200]

The qualitative distinction finds its expression in eschatology, no longer 'organic' but 'consistent'.[201] In one of the most famous sentences in the book he declares that 'A Christianity which is not absolutely and totally eschatology has absolutely and totally nothing to do with Christ.'[202] This eschatology is the crisis which the death and resurrection of Christ faces us with, which makes any idea of 'progress' or normal movement impossible. Another key word of the first commentary was 'the way'. Now we learn that this way is defined almost entirely in negatives. To the extent that we can call it a 'way' we must understand it as the shadow cast by the cross on all 'healthy' humanity, where our most secure standing place is shattered, set ablaze and finally dissolved.[203]

What, then, is the content of the 'miracle' through which God is known? It is revelation in Christ. The truth of God is not that of necessary reason.

God's eternity is not the non-dangerous, non paradoxical, easily affirmed constancy of general ideas (the idea of God, of Christ, of mediation). His power is not the necessity of a logical mathematical function. God is Personality, the unparalleled, the only, the particular . . . and the human historical Jesus bears witness to God. Jesus is the Christ. God's particularity shines through his existentiality. Therefore in spite of all believing and unbelieving historicism and psychologism we have the scandal of an eternal revelation in Jesus . . . God is no 'contingent truth of history'. God's deed goes beyond all mythologising, all pragmatising, all historical narration with an abrupt 'Never!' and 'Always'.[204]

Again in language which was later taken up in the *Dogmatics*, Barth maintains that God is 'unveiled' only as God is veiled. The revealed God remains

---

[198] R2, 6; ET, 29. The criticism is Tillich's. Barth complained in 1958 that Tillich and Niebuhr insisted on interpreting him 'as though I had been asleep since 1920'. Busch, *Barth*, 457.

[199] R2, 6; ET, 29. Hoskyn's translation. This is reminiscent of E. M. Forster's jibe at 'poor little talkative Christianity' in *A Passage to India* written in 1924.

[200] R2, 22; ET, 46.

[201] McCormack rightly emphasizes that this is one of the key differences between the two editions. *Barth's Theology*, 231 ff.

[202] R2, 298; ET, 314. This remark was anticipated in R1, but not stated so forcibly. R1, 241, 246, 250.

[203] R2, 221; ET, 239.   [204] R2, 260; ET, 277.

the hidden God. The human historical Jesus bears witness to God, but is not himself revelation. The unveiling which remains a veiling is our knowledge of Christ in cross and resurrection. Barth here rejects the Reformation *munus triplex*, which was to be the foundation of his great doctrine of reconciliation. With an eye on the Jesus of liberal theology he denies that the personality of Jesus, the Sermon on the Mount, the miracles, all the details of Christ's life, neither the immediate nor the eschatological side of the gospel, exist in their own right. 'All is illuminated by the light which proceeds from his death.'[205] Of course the crucifixion cannot be understood without the resurrection, but this is not 'an event amongst other events'. It is the 'unhistorical relation of Christ's whole historical life to his Origin in God'.[206] Christ's life, which can be understood solely in terms of passive obedience, is known only through the resurrection, this 'non historical historical event'.[207] The concept of resurrection emerges with the concept of death, that is, with the concept of the end of all historical things as such. The bodily resurrection of Christ stands ever and again over against his bodily crucifixion and nowhere else.[208]

The critical, highly dialectical character of this knowledge of God is reflected in the faith which responds to it. If it aspires to be anything more than an empty space faith becomes unbelief. Anything at all which might make faith the adoption of a point of view or method, whether it be paradox, brokenness, waiting on God—all this is nothing but works righteousness.[209] The characteristic marks of Christianity are 'deprivation and hope' rather than having and being.[210] The gospel is not there to give comfort but to witness to the power of God who raises the dead. 'It is the alarm cry, the fire bell, of a coming new world.'[211] 'The gospel is not a truth amongst other truths. It places all truths in question.'[212] This Word is so new, so unheard of, so unexpected that it appears, is understood and taken on only as contradiction.[213] Jesus comes 'not to change anything, not to improve the flesh through morality, to transfigure it through art, to rationalize it through science, to overcome it through the Fata Morgana of religion, but to proclaim the resurrection of the flesh, the new human being who recognizes herself in God, because she is made in God's image (*Ebenbild*), and in whom God recognizes Godself since God is her pattern (*Urbild*)'.[214] The response to this proclamation is faith. Faith is 'respect before the divine incognito, love of God which is conscious of the qualitative distinction between God and human beings, God and the world, affirmation of

---

[205] R2, 136; ET, 159.   [206] R2, 175; ET, 195.   [207] R2, 136, 184; ET, 159, 204.
[208] R2, 185; ET, 205.   [209] R2, 31–2; ET, 56–7.   [210] R2, 12; ET, 36.
[211] R2, 13; ET, 38.   [212] R2, 11; ET, 35.   [213] R2, 14; ET, 38.
[214] R2, 260; ET, 277.

the resurrection as the turning point of the world, affirmation of the divine No! which brings us to a shuddering halt before God'.[215] Faith itself is an 'impossible possibility', a phrase intended to contradict what liberal theology regarded as only too self evident a human possibility.[216] This is the faith which corresponds to the faithfulness of God and this is the theme of the letter.[217]

Faith runs together with hope. 'Whatever is not hope is stupid, a block, a chain, difficult and awkward, like the word "reality". It does not liberate us but takes us prisoner. It is not grace but judgement and ruin. It is not divine leading, but fate. It is not God but a mirror image of unredeemed human beings.'[218]

The Critique of Religion

'The critique of religion is the beginning of all critique.'[219] This word of Marx is a fair description of the purpose of the devastating critique of religion which, present in the first commentary, is given a central place here. Only when the 'criminal arrogance of religion' has been done away can we learn to think *von Gott aus*, in other words, not from a starting point in human subjectivity or religious experience.[220] Why? Because religion functions as opiate, underwriting human illusions.[221] In religion human beings seek to master their world, and make themselves finally secure, but God cannot become the prisoner of any human programme. God's Wholly Otherness is what resists all attempts at hegemony whether those of the establishment or, what Barth obviously found more offensive, of religious socialism. God can only be spoken of through paradox. If, in speaking of God's revelation in Christ, 'we have not trodden on the toes of every single human method of investigation and grievously annoyed it, we have spoken of something else'.[222]

Religion is precisely where human beings bolt and bar themselves against God. Just where people believe they are raising themselves above common lusts and failings, precisely there, in religion, do they find themselves on 'the highest summit in the kingdom of sin'.[223] It is no chance that 'the odour of death' hangs over these summits. Religion does not liberate us, 'indeed it

---

[215] R2, 14; ET, 39.   [216] R2, 114; ET, 138.   [217] R2, 17; ET, 42.

[218] R2, 298; ET, 314. As Marquardt remarks, this is not so far from *The Principle of Hope*—hope as the principle of all reality. *Theologie*, 191.

[219] K. Marx, 'Contribution to the Critique of Hegel's Philosophy of Law', K. Marx and F. Engels, *Collected Works*, iii, Moscow, Progress, 1975, 175.

[220] R2, 13; ET, 37.   [221] R2, 218; ET, 236.

[222] R2, 261; ET, 278.   [223] R2, 224; ET, 242.

s us more surely than anything else'.[224] It is the 'working capital'
The boundary of religion is 'the line of death which cuts
n what is possible with human beings and what is possible with
between flesh and Spirit, time and eternity'. An irrepressible bourgeois reality, it refuses to die. 'Enough, it must die, and in God we are free
of it.'[225]

This is one side of the dialectic. On the other side we have no option but
to be religious. 'What else can we honestly do than be—religious people,
repenting in dust and ashes, wrestling with fear and trembling that we might
be blessed and, if we have to take a position, taking that of adoration.'[226] We
have no option but to cultivate religion, to reform and revolutionize it. But:
'the more consistently we are involved in religion the deeper the shadow of
death which lies over us'.[227] Why? Because it is religion which faces us with
the reality of sin, death, and the knowledge that we do not know God, of
our radical otherness with respect to the Creator.[228] It is the worst enemy we
have—apart from God. Precisely for this reason we have to stay with it, to
remain in solidarity with the Church, fully aware of the antithesis between
church and gospel.[229]

This dialectical critique is, of course, directed against the Church, but also
against those like Ragaz who had come to believe the Church was impossible. Such a position Barth scornfully dismissed as 'pseudo radicalism'. We
do not escape from sin by removing ourselves from religion.[230] Barth's 'decision for the Church' is already apparent in this commentary where the
rather general account of 'Need', 'Guilt', and 'Hope' of the first commentary are replaced by an account of the tribulation, guilt, and hope of the
Church in the exegesis of chapters 9–11 and where his commitment to
staying in the Church is made clear.[231]

At the same time, doubtless through the influence of Kierkegaard, Barth
consciously contradicts what he said in the first commentary about the individual. Human beings do not stand before the God question via the detour
of 'the whole' but 'in their own need and hope'. The individual is not 'part'
of anything, but herself 'the whole'. Each individual is met by the eternal
distinctness (*Ungleich*) of God.[232] At the same time we note the corrective:
'We announce the right of the individual, the eternal worth of each person
[Kierkegaard!] in that we announce that their soul is *lost* before God and
in God taken up [*aufgehoben*] and redeeemed.'[233] In a word which strikingly
anticipates Levinas, Barth speaks of the neighbour as 'the uplifted finger

---

[224] R2, 259; ET, 276. [225] R2, 220–1; ET, 238.
[226] R2, 234; ET, 252. [227] R2, 237; ET, 255.
[228] R2, 232; ET, 250. [229] R2, 317; ET, 333.
[230] R2, 223; ET, 241. [231] R2, 355; ET, 371.
[232] R2, 427; ET, 441–2. [233] R2, 91; ET, 116.

which by its "otherness" reminds us of the Wholly Other'.[234] The individual of the second commentary is 'identical with the new man . . . characterised by individuality without arbitrariness and community without division into hierarchies'.[235]

Loss of the organic language, and the increased sharpness of the note of crisis, bears on what is meant by salvation. Where we were caught up into the organic stream of Christ's life we now have to understand that properly understood there are no Christians. 'There is only the opportunity for all alike at once accessible and inaccessible—to become Christians.' The actualistic strain, God's reality breaking through or becoming real ever and again, already pronounced in the first commentary, is far greater here.

The attack on religious socialism is continued. 'Religion is not the Kingdom of God, even if it is the kingdom of God religion of Blumhardt's epigones, but human work.'[236] The Church is not set over against the world; it is the world conscious of its need, the place where the sickness of the world comes to a head and therefore hope for all is included in hope for the Church.[237]

The Great Disturbance

The letter to the Romans is 'theory of a praxis'. Nowhere are we concerned with abstract thought.[238] Anticipating later developments Barth insists that doctrine and ethics belong together. As in the Tambach lecture, ethics follows from our knowledge of Christ. 'The primary ethical deed is the knowledge of God whose concrete intuitability [*Anschaulichkeit*] is given in the death of Christ and his parable: the concrete Other.'[239] Ethics is not 'criticism from high places' but mutual admonition (*Ermahnung*) by those who share solidarity in sin. This mutual admonition is devoid of human justification, but rests on grace, on forgiveness. Grace is the secret of ethics. Grace is 'divine impatience, discontent, dissatisfaction'. It is the enemy of every ethic, even of the essential 'interim ethic'. It is the axe laid to the root of the good conscience which the well to do citizen so enjoys in the civil service, in his vocation, or in politics. 'There is no more underhand means of defence than when concerned moral people . . . treat ethics as an account of innerworldly purpose, rather than as the critical negation of all purpose and seek to ground it on goods and ideals rather than on the forgiveness of sins.'[240]

---

[234] R2, 427, 429; ET, 441, 444.   [235] Plonz, *Herrenlosen Gewalten*, 187.

[236] R2, 350; ET, 366.   [237] R2, 393; ET, 407.   [238] R2, 412–13; ET, 427.

[239] Plonz, *Herrenlosen Gewalten*, 189.   [240] R2, 416; ET, 430.

Once again, the anti-bourgeois thrust of this thinking on ethics is clear.[241] Grace is the theory which as such is practice, the indicative which has the force of the categorical imperative, knowledge of the will of God, the knowledge that we are known of God, the power of the resurrection.[242] In relation to salvation the note of victory in the first commentary is here replaced by the somewhat different 'knowledge' which grace, or faith, imparts.

Barth distinguishes between primary and secondary ethical action. 'Primary ethical action' is repentance which follows from giving the glory to God, from worship. It is 'offering our bodies as a living sacrifice'. 'Secondary ethical action'—the way we behave to our neighbour and in community—follows from this.[243]

We may understand ethics in terms of negative and positive possibilities. The positive possibility is agape rather than eros where Barth anticipates Nygren in many of the main lines of argument. Negative possibilities are those actions in which we find parables of the kingdom in weakness rather than strength, folly rather than wisdom. Christianity 'is always there where there are no apparent solutions, but not there where people have come to terms with things. It has a certain partisan preference for the oppressed, for those falling short, for the immature, for the sullen, those ready for revolution—and to this extent the Socialists in large measure win approval.'[244] The twofold possibility is 'either (positive) a demonstration for life in the hope of the resurrection, and as such includes a protest against the many sided evidences of the world's addiction to death. Or (negatively), the dialectical reverse side, a demonstration against all idolatry and for the "exalting" of the lowly.'[245] Christianity is purely and simply the protest against all the high places which human beings build for themselves, and 'as such it is the absolute Ethic, and as such proclaims the coming world'.[246]

God's Revolution

In the second edition, according to Marquardt, Barth carries out 'a sensational anti-revolutionary turn'.[247] This much quoted remark is less often taken together with the detailed qualifications which follow: 'talk of

---

[241] McCormack cites Ruschke: 'This ethic escapes from bourgeois utilitarian and goal-oriented thinking.' *Barth's Theology*, 276.

[242] R2, 188; ET, 207.   [243] R2, 416–17; ET, 431.

[244] R2, 448; ET, 463.   [245] Plonz, *Herrenlosen Gewalten*, 189.

[246] R2, 451; ET, 467.   [247] Marquardt, *Theologie*, 142.

the "revolution" of God is turned into talk of "God's" revolution'.[248]
from this abandoning us to the status quo what it actually sets up is the principle of permanent revolution.

In the second commentary, as in the first, Barth insists that the attitude of
the letter is 'unmistakeably revolutionary'.[249] However, where in the first
commentary the target was principally legitimism and principled religious
reform, here the target is revolution. Barth's change was made in response
to 'a certain stratum of readers of his first commentary who read out of that
a "principle of revolution" and expected more of the same from him'.[250] In
a heavily ironical rhetorical move, well aware of the reactionary use made
of *Romans* over the centuries, Barth observes that 'It is highly unlikely
that anyone will become a reactionary on the grounds of having read
Romans!'[251] Barth makes plain beyond a peradventure that there is no
defence of legitimism in chapter 13. 'There is here no word of approval of
the existing order.' But *Romans* does not endorse the revolution going on in
Russia, a 'Titanism of revolt and upheaval and renovation'. The problem is
that 'Revolutionary Titanism is far more dangerous and godless than the
reactionary kind because in its origin it is so much closer to the truth.'[252] As
in the first commentary, Barth insists that evil is never the answer to evil.
Before Hannah Arendt he was well aware that revolutions devour their own
children. The true revolution is forgiveness of sins and resurrection of the
dead, but the revolutionary chooses hatred and insubordination instead.
This choice is worse than the legitimist option for satisfaction, security, and
usurpation because 'by it God is far better understood, but so much the
worse abused'.[253] What then? An endorsement of the status quo, a 'thorough depoliticization of the concept of revolution'?[254] To put it this way suggests a turn away from political action and involvement to 'the conversion
of the individual' so beloved by right wing Christians. But Barth intends no
such thing. 'No revolution is the best preparation for the true revolution',
he writes 'but even no revolution is no safe recipe'.[255] We need a 'devastating undermining of the existing order' which comes by depriving State,
Church, Society, Positive Right, Family, Organized Research—but also,
of course, revolutionary action—of their pathos. These things 'live off the
credulity of those who have been nurtured upon vigorous sermons-
delivered-on-the-field-of-battle, and solemn humbug of all sorts'. If you stir

---

[248] Ibid., 149; cf. 158: 'Barth is thinking of a revolution *sui generis*, an apocalyptic revolution
of God happening of its own accord, which can no longer be accomplished in the antirevolu-
tionary demonstration of revolutionaries but which can only be witnessed to.'
[249] R2, 468; ET, 484.   [250] Marquardt, *Theologie*, 160; R2, 460; ET, 476.
[251] R2, 461; ET, 478.   [252] R2, 462; ET, 478.   [253] R2, 465; ET, 481.
[254] Jüngel, *Barth*, 102.   [255] R2, 467; ET, 483.

up revolution against them their pathos is provided with fresh fodder. Depriving them of their pathos starves them out.[256] This is the negative, critical, attacking moment which must be supplemented by the truly revolutionary action of love, 'the great positive possibility'.

> Not a single act but the bringing together of all positive (protesting!) ethical possibilities . . . We define love as the 'Great Positive Possibility', because in it the revolutionary aspect of all ethics comes to light, because it is actually concerned with the denial and breaking up of the status quo [*das Bestehende*] . . . insofar as we love one another we cannot wish to uphold the present order as such, because in love we do the new thing which brings the old crashing down.[257]

Love is the denial and demolition of the existing order which no revolt can bring about, the destruction of everything which is—'like God'.[258]

But is the act of love possible? Barth drew on what he had learned from his brother Heinrich to affirm this possibility, exegeting Paul's words that we must act, 'knowing the time'. Plato had solved a famous difficulty about the move from rest to motion with his notion of the *exaiphnes*, the 'moment'.[259] Barth appropriates the idea of a 'moment not in time' to explain how the act of love becomes possible. This 'Moment' is 'the eternal moment, the *Now*—when the past and future stand still'.[260] The Now of revelation takes the place of Plato's *exaiphnes*, and it is here there is the opportunity for the occurrence of love. This is not only an account of an 'impossible possibility' but a way of insisting on permanent revolution. 'Love enters the realm of evil, in order to leave it again at once. Love builds no tabernacles, for it seeks to create nothing that abides, nothing that "exists" in time. Love does what it does only in the knowledge of the eternal "Moment". Love is therefore the essentially revolutionary action.'[261]

Where, then, does this leave political action? 'A political career . . . becomes possible only when it is seen to be essentially a game; that is to say, when we are unable to speak of absolute political right, when the note of "absoluteness" has vanished from both thesis and antithesis.'[262] What is

---

[256] R2, 467; ET, 483. Marquardt argues that Barth 'thinks and argues with the radicalness of the anarchists'. *Theologie*, 165. 'Theological radicalism of eschatological thinking and later of christological exclusiveness has, in social-political undertakings, anarchist consequences'. Ibid., 307. I agree with respect to this stage of Barth's thought but believe he took a different line when it was needed, namely in Weimar.

[257] R2, 476–7; ET, 493. As in the Tambach lecture I find the emphasis in this commentary on affirmation, and cannot agree with McCormack that anger is its distinctive tone (McCormack, *Barth's Theology*, 243). Barth was capable of writing with searing anger, as in the farewell to *Zwischen den Zeiten*, or *Nein!*, but the mood is quite different here.

[258] R2, 480; ET, 496.   [259] For this Platonic idea see Jüngel, *Barth*, 67–8.
[260] R2, 481; ET, 497.   [261] R2, 482; ET, 498.   [262] R2, 472; ET, 489.

stated here is something like the 'eschatological proviso' which liberation theology has insisted on as a way of saying that human projects are not identical with God's kingdom. But we also have to ask where Barth's exegesis leaves God, and the answer is that 'from now on the word "God" can no longer be thought without thinking of his revolution'.[263]

Revolutionary Theology

At the end of the commentary Barth turned to the task of theology in what is clearly a response to Overbeck, from whom he takes the description of the 'fatal prattle of systematic theology'.[264] Of course our language cannot break through to the Absolute, but nevertheless alongside and indeed, tragicomically, *in* all orderly, regular, bourgeois possibilities of reflection, there exists the revolutionary possibility of theology, which is an out and out onslaught on kitsch![265] Yes, theology is a totally unpractical and non-religious undertaking, but only because it is concerned with the most practical of all human desires. It represents an unheard of attack on the human being who seeks security because it is aware that every human venture can be no more than a demonstration or parable. It attacks the nerve centre of the self confidence of those who find their security in 'science' (a claim which obviously angered Harnack). Its witness to the gospel constitutes this revolutionary attack. Only as it makes this attack does it deserve its place in the academy. Theology is, in essence, an abnormal, irregular, dangerous revolutionary *attack* on the things the secure human being takes for granted. Why? Because this is what follows from taking its object seriously. 'To be scientific means fidelity to the object. Fidelity to the object in theology is unconditional respect before the uniqueness of the theme . . . humanity in its ultimate distress and hope, humanity before God.'[266] 'Theology today can be based on nothing but daring', is what Barth had taken from Overbeck. This venture or dare (*Wagnis*) becomes a whole manifesto: it is theology which is responsible for setting a question mark at the outermost edge of the university and of all civilization, and this is why its place within the *universitas litterarum* is vital.

Reviews and Reactions

Announcing his sympathy with Barth's work Bultmann solemnly (and so far as one can see without irony) put it in the line of Schleiermacher's *Speeches* or Otto's *The Idea of the Holy* as an attempt 'to prove the independence and

[263] Marquardt, *Theologie*, 159.   [264] R2, 317; ET, 333.   [265] R2, 514; ET, 529.
[266] R2, 515; ET, 531.

the absolute nature of religion'![267] For him it establishes the miracle of faith
in a way that proves Barth a true disciple of Herrmann, 'with whom Barth
is in complete agreement'. Significantly, his criticisms regarded Christology
and hermeneutics. Bultmann felt that to talk about the intersection of vertical and horizontal planes in Christ implied a lapse in the direction of liberal
lives of Jesus. Part of the dogmatic task Barth undertook in Göttingen was
to show why that was not necessarily the case. As for hermeneutics: whilst
Bultmann agreed that words and sentences had to be measured by the
subject matter he did not feel Barth had actually done this, because he was
far too uncritical of Paul. 'It is impossible to assume that everywhere in the
Letter to the Romans the subject matter must have found adequate expression, unless one intends to establish a modern dogma of inspiration.'[268]
Other spirits may speak through Paul as well as the Spirit of Christ. Barth
responded in the preface to the next edition that Bultmann was not radical
enough. There are *no* words in the letter which are not words of other
spirits. The exegete cannot sort out some passages which are of Christ, and
others which are not. The whole is placed under the *krisis* of the Spirit of
Christ. 'The whole is litera, that is, the voice of those other spirits. The
problem is whether the whole must not be understood in relation to the true
subject matter which is the Spirit of Christ.'[269]

   Von Balthasar is amongst those who take Barth's statement of a total revision between the commentaries with a pinch of salt. His sense of the continuities rests on his claim that the first commentary is predicated on a notion
of our original identity with God, which remains essential to the dialectic
of the second. In the second commentary, according to him, nature is
identified both with sin and grace, and the radicalization of this contradiction destroys the relative continuity of the socialist world view.[270] The
problem with von Balthasar's reading of both commentaries is their focus
on the German idealist background. Barth himself, of course, later talked of
the 'strange crust of Platonic and Kantian thought' in the commentary, but
on the other hand, he wrote to Bultmann in 1928 that 'In Romans and now
in the *Dogmatics* my path has in fact been that . . . I have reached out on the
right hand and the left for terms and concepts that I found to be the most
appropriate without considering the problem of a pre-established harmony
between the matter itself and these particular concepts.' There was, he
cheerfully admitted, 'something gypsylike' in this procedure. Any reading
which shackles Barth too closely to German idealism runs the risk of
missing this cavalier quality.[271] In this case von Balthasar misses Barth's
avowed intention to open up 'the dangerous element in Christianity'. It is

[267] *Anfänge*, 119; ET, 100.   [268] *Anfänge*, 141; ET, 119.   [269] R2, p. xx; ET, 17.
[270] Balthasar, 70–1.   [271] B–B (ET), 41.

strange, Barth notes, 'how utterly harmless and unexceptionable commentaries on the Epistle to the Romans and most books about Paul are'.[272] The second *Romans* is still a dangerous book, perhaps too anarchist for comfort. Any reading which misses that misses the whole.

Bruce McCormack argues that 'almost the sole purpose' of the second edition was 'the work of clearing away debris' (Barth himself later referred to it ironically as 'bomb theology'!).[273] Masterly as his detailed reading is, this seems to me an impossibly negative reading of a work which, precisely in its critique, is mapping out new territory in ethics, and especially of political ethics, in our understanding of religion, of theology, and of hermeneutics.[274] To take an architectural analogy, what we have here is not so much a clearing of ground as a coherent brilliant sketch of a new theological world. The sheer bafflement of Harnack in the face of this theology is like the bafflement of those who listened first to Schoenberg or tried to make sense of expressionist art. It is not the pain simply of confronting ruins. Barth liked to emphasize later on the extent to which he changed his mind. What is astonishing, rather, is the extent to which major turning points and decisions in his later work are anticipated in both of these early manifestos.

UNDERSTANDING GOD IN THE WORLD

Though part of no movement Barth is profoundly at one with the spirit of the age both in the vehemence and in the broad lines of his attack. There is a shaking of the foundations in science, art, music, and philosophy at this time—but also in theology.[275] Those who link this theology to the general crisis of the times are right to the extent that Barth seeks quite explicitly to 'speak to the moment'. In no sense is this ivory tower theology, but theology emerging from profound engagement in social and political realities. Unlike most of the other radical movements of the time, however, Barth works by rediscovering the radicality of the tradition of which he is a part.

---

[272] R2, p. xvi; ET, 13.

[273] McCormack, *Barth's Theology*, 245. Barth's remark is in 'Brechen und Bauen' in *Der Götze Wakkelt*, 113.

[274] In particular, the insight that Christian ethics have to be understood in terms of grace, a specifically Reformation insight which was largely lost sight of under the impact of Kant, is seminal for all of Barth's later explorations in ethics.

[275] Schellong points out that the early work of left intellectuals like Lukacs, Bloch, and Korsch was all published at this time and cites Adorno's view that it was this decade, rather than that of the 1920s, which represented a real intellectual and artistic turning point. Schellong, 'On Reading Karl Barth from the left' in Hunsinger, *Barth and Radical Politics*, 147.

The tremendous journey Barth undertakes in these five or six years travels via the attempt to radicalize Kutter's vivid sense of the reality of God. Barth is grasping at, and speaking of, God at the heart of all reality (and this meant above all, political reality) which is what he means by God's 'objectivity'. 'Does not the entire misery of our situation', wrote Barth to Brunner in 1916, 'simply exist in that, again and again, we turn back to ourselves, instead of stretching out to the Objective? Don't we fail . . . to give our obedience and trust to God as *God*, God above all in his objectivity?'[276] 'Don't you see the sighing after the real, living God which is the core of our theology as well as of yours?' Thurneysen asked Kutter, in response to criticism. The compulsive dialectic of *Romans* is nothing but a 'uniquely great sighing after God in Godself'.[277] The need of this dialectic arose from the attempt really to understand God in the midst of 'the suffering of millions'. This attempt forced broken speech upon him.

We see from the Tambach lecture that the move from the first to the second *Romans* was prompted by Barth's realization that he was simply repeating the religious socialist mistake—identifying God too closely with a particular political movement. This meant that in many ways it remained caught within the existing cultural hegemony. In the second commentary therefore, as at Tambach, he swung the tiller sharply the other way, at the same time insisting that the concern of the gospel was the *whole* world, the whole of reality, and not just the religious part of it. For Barth, Social Democrats like Naumann had betrayed their trust and lost sight of the fact that the God of the New Testament demands not the conversion of some things but of 'all things, the renewal of the whole world, a permanent change of this life . . . indeed the most radical Social Democrats are not radical enough'.[278] Those critics who read Barth's eschatological language of diastasis in a sceptical way, and who thought thereafter that Barth was interested only in God and not in human history, could not have been more mistaken.[279] Whatever Barth learned was set to work with the utmost freedom to try and bring to speech his great theme—God's reality, as it bears on ours. This reality, as we have seen, was from 1916 onwards understood

---

[276] Hart, *Barth versus Brunner*, 12.   [277] B–Th II, 315–16.

[278] 'Vergangenheit und Zukunft' in *Anfänge*, i, 41; ET, 38. This demand for a *Veränderung des Lebens* anticipates the *Real Verändernde Tatsache, dass Gott ist* of KD IV/1.

[279] This seems to me to apply also to Macken's view that in his early theology Barth was interested in 'the polemical assertion of the claims of the divine subject in opposition to a theology that had reduced itself in the wake of Idealism to a concern with the subjectivity of man'. Macken, *Autonomy*, 24. This is to put it far too abstractly. Barth was not interested in opposing anthropocentricism as such. The question is why, and in the interests of what, did he proclaim the revolution of God?.

as truly revolutionary.[280] This was expressed in different ways: in the first commentary through metaphors of continuity, in a 'process' eschatology in which 'world history and the history of Spirit is interpreted as organ of the process of resurrection';[281] in the second commentary through metaphors of diastasis, especially designed to ward off the error of confusing human revolution with God's revolution. The 'consistent eschatology' of this commentary came to function as what Käsemann, and later liberation theology, came to call the eschatological proviso. In both, the resurrection of Christ is what provides the theological dynamic, but Bultmann had some cause to ask whether 'Christ' were not merely a symbol for Barth at this stage. The move to truly Christological thinking only happens in Göttingen.

Barth's attack on religion was a form of ideology critique which exploded the world of plenty and sureties and religious sentimentalities which, as Scott Fitzgerald observed, made the Somme possible. Like many of his contemporaries Barth saw that with the war that world, the world of his student days, was over and that the debris needed clearing away. Buess and Mattmüller are right to include Barth in the tradition of prophetic socialism not only because both Ragaz and Kutter, in spite of all criticism, wanted Barth as their successor in Zürich and Neumünster respectively but, more profoundly, because the urgent note of prophecy, the compulsion to speak, the incomparably vivid sense of *God* in the midst of human affairs, all this is characteristic of everything that Barth wrote between 1916 and the second commentary. The wild energy of the first commentary, the way in which the second was written, 'stumbling between breakfast table, desk and bed' for eleven months, is evidence of a man possessed—but possessed in the way he speaks of the biblical figures in 'The New World' lecture. These figures are aware of something going on; they look up, and others follow their gaze. Or, in the image which stayed with him for the rest of his life, the biblical commentator or theologian has the role of the 'pointing finger of John the Baptist'. What is so remarkable and refreshing about this is the record of an intense experience entirely unconcerned about the experience in itself, but only about the central theme, *die Sache*, as he entitled the opening sections of both commentaries. Whether or not Barth drew on Lenin, what is gripping is that this theology is theory of quite clearly revolutionary practice, a bringing together of what had quite wrongly been put asunder—action and reflection, dogmatics and ethics—in the interests of a new world. For this reason the need to respond to day to day social and

---

[280] Marquardt, *Theologie*, 168.   [281] Ibid., 259.

political reality must also be given *methodological* significance for Barth, who emerges as a thoroughly contextual theologian.[282] The question, raised by friends as well as critics, is whether this remains true when the theologian is no longer 'the red pastor' but 'Herr Professor'.

---

[282] So also Plonz, *Herrenlosen Gewalten*, 162 n. 67.

3

Between the Times

October 1921–March 1930

Had we returned home in 1916, out of the suffering and the strength
of our experiences we might have unleashed a storm. Now if we go
back we will be weary, broken, burnt out, rootless, and without hope.
We will not be able to find our way any more.

Erich Maria Remarque, Im Westen nichts Neues

WEIMAR

Barth had already begun rewriting *Romans* when he was sounded out on
the possibility of a Chair at Göttingen in January 1921, a possibility finally
confirmed in May. The family moved at the beginning of October. The
Weimar Republic was nearly two years under way, and Barth's stay in
Germany was almost coincident with its existence: he was expelled eighteen
months after its demise.

'The Republic was born in defeat, lived in turmoil, and died in disaster.'[1]
With Allied tanks pushing German forces back pell mell, General Ludendorff, the initiator of the spring offensive of 1918, which had been intended
as the German *coup de grâce*, finally told the Kaiser at the end of September
of that year that it was essential to sue for peace. The chancellor, Hertling,
who had been thoroughly identified with Ludendorff's policies, resigned
and his place was taken by Prince Max von Baden. His attempt to retain a
liberalized monarchy was quickly overtaken by events. When the German
admiralty decided to put to sea for a final death or glory battle with the
British fleet the sailors mutinied. All over Germany there were strikes and
mutinies, and on 8 November Kurt Eisner proclaimed a socialist republic in
Munich. That day von Baden told the Kaiser he had to go. The new German
republic was proclaimed the next day.

Faced with the threat of communist revolution the first chancellor of the
republic, and head of the Social Democratic Party, Friedrich Ebert, called in

---

[1] Gay, *Weimar Culture*, 1.

the army. Whilst the rank and file were by and large disillusioned with the war the army leadership were still possessed by a vision of German glory, convinced they were only defeated by the 'stab in the back' of Allied duplicity and civilian political cowardice, and stung to fury by the conditions of the Versailles Treaty. When the Communists took over Berlin in January 1919 so called 'Free Corps' units put them down, and were responsible for the murders of Liebknecht and Rosa Luxemburg that month, and of Eisner in February. A strike in Berlin in March was put down with the loss of 1,500 lives. These actions were condoned by a judiciary which had continued unchanged, and which punished answering left wing violence with extreme severity.

The new democracy was thus fragile from the start, lacking as it did any deep roots, with the authoritarianism of the Kaiser, and Bismarck before him, as its immediate precedents. It put a touching faith in the *Bildung* which for many had been destroyed by the war. The first national assembly convened in Goethe's theatre in Weimar because, as Ebert put it, 'The idealism of our great poets and thinkers must fill the life of our new Republic.'[2] Its new constitution, ratified in August 1919, guaranteed freedom of speech and assembly, and rested on the principle that 'State power emanates from the people', but nevertheless vested great emergency powers in the president, who was free to choose and dismiss the Chancellor. The adoption of proportional representation meant that there was always significant support for right wing nationalist, Catholic centre, and independent socialist parties as well as for the SPD, which in 1919 had 38 per cent of the vote and remained the biggest single party until 1932. This lack of a clear majority party undermined the possibilities of stability, profoundly threatened by the murder of leading politicians, such as Erzberger and Rathenau, who were identified with 'shameful' appeasement policies.

Since the war had been financed by loans the new government found itself bankrupt, a situation immeasurably worsened by the war reparations imposed by the Allies. The value of the Mark slowly depreciated until January 1922, when it began to spiral out of control. The French and Belgian occupation of the Ruhr the following January, in response to failure to keep up with reparations, pushed this to truly astronomical proportions. By November 1923 one US dollar was worth 4,200,000,000,000 Deutschmarks. Whilst the big industrialists made fortunes the poor and the middle classes suffered.[3] Inflation hit the middle classes harder than the war and Barth himself was the recipient of aid from Dutch well-wishers. Gustav

---

[2] Cited by Pachter, *Modern Germany*, 90. Thomas Mann had similar views, cf. K. Bullivant, 'Thomas Mann and the Politics of the Weimar Republic' in K. Bullivant (ed.), *Culture and Society in the Weimar Republic*, Manchester, Manchester University Press 1977.

[3] Craig, *Germany 1866–1945*, 450 ff.

Stresemann, the leader of the moderate right wing People's Party, finally managed to bring this under control towards the end of 1923, new currency was issued, and a few years of relative stability followed until Germany was caught up in the world wide economic crisis of 1929. Though Hitler did not finally come to power until 1933 it was this which effectively marked the end of Weimar.

The Ruhr occupation provoked intense German indignation, which Barth shared.[4] Dissatisfaction with what was perceived to be Stresemann's conciliatory policy with the French provoked the Munich *putsch* of Hitler, Göring, and Ludendorff in November 1923 but this failed even more ludicrously than the earlier attempted right wing coup led by Kapp. Although there were six governments between December 1923 and June 1928, here too there was stability, symbolized by the fact that Stresemann was foreign minister of all of them. He negotiated French withdrawal from the Ruhr by 1925 and, following the Treaty of Locarno in October of that year, enabled Germany's entry into the League of Nations in 1926. In the following two years there was not only peace but also prosperity.

Against this political background Weimar culture acquired, even in its own time, an almost legendary status. Following the political scene it had three major phases. As in other combatant countries the immediate post war period was a time when conventions were flouted and the only rule was that 'anything goes'. Stability at the end of 1923 ushered in the *neue Sachlichkeit*, cynically read by the left as the return to bourgeois values.[5] As the situation deteriorated after 1930 popular culture was to a large extent captured by the propagandists, and the intellectuals either fled or retreated into internal emigration.

Weimar was first a popular culture. It was coincident with the first great period of the cinema, of the gramophone record, later of the radio, the period when sport first became a mass spectator interest. Jazz and new dances like the Charleston caught on all over Europe and all the combatant nations reacted to the horrors of war with a culture of frivolity and sexual cynicism.[6] Berlin was known not only as the cultural but also as the vice capital of Europe. 'Amid a general collapse of values,' wrote Stefan Zweig, 'insanity seized middle class people who so far had been orderly and rigid . . . To be suspected of virginity would have been considered a disgrace in

---

[4] B–Th II, 130.

[5] See the articles by J. Hermand in Bullivant, *Culture and Society*, and now 'Neue Sachlichkeit: Ideology, Lifestyle, or Artistic Movement?' in T. Kniesche and S. Brockmann (eds), *Dancing on the Volcano: Essays on the Culture of the Weimar Republic*, Columbia, Camden, 1994.

[6] See Brockmann, 'Weimar Sexual Cynicism' in Kniesche and Brockmann, *Dancing*. He traces it to the cold blooded government provision of brothels for both officers and rank and file during the war.

any Berlin girl's high school.'[7] Joseph von Sternberg's play *The Blue Angel*, based on a novel by Heinrich Mann, and Brecht's *The Rise and Fall of the City of Mahagonny* have made this side of Weimar famous. The reverse side to this, of course, was a retreat from defeat and horror into convention and sentimentality which generated the kitsch for which Weimar is equally famous. At the same time, alongside all this there was also strident idealism, especially in the youth movement. On the right this centred on the exaltation of the German *völk*, but on the left there was a thriving, often pacifist, idealism. Working class communists remembered Weimar as a hopeful time, when it was self evident to be socialist.[8] Both the hope and the faith in German *Volkstüm* were shared by the Church.[9]

At the same time 'high culture', building on the astonishing advances of the pre-war years, was exceptionally vigorous. The iconoclastic post-war mood made the expressionist and modernist paths easier. These were by no means the same. Surveying the ruins of the old culture the founder of the Bauhaus, Walter Gropius, sought 'a radical solution to our problems'. Architecture, sculpture, and painting should come together 'in a single shape, rising to heaven from the hands of millions of craftsmen as a crystal symbol of a new emerging faith'.[10] 'What Gropius taught', comments Peter Gay, 'was the lesson of Bacon and Descartes and the Enlightenment: that one must confront the world and dominate it, that the cure for the ills of modernity is more, and the right kind of modernity.'[11] The dazzling achievements of the physical sciences in mid-war Germany were part of this faith—not in progress, but in modernity, a faith in which theology was part of an irrational past. The pressure which led to Bultmann's *Scope of Demythologizing* essay in 1941 came from here.

Equally as famous was the Germany of post-expressionist artists and of great writers. The phrase *Neue Sachlichkeit* was coined by the director of the Mannheim art gallery, G. F. Hartlaub, in 1925 for an exhibition which would bring together the work of artists who had neither been too impressionistically relaxed nor expressionistically abstract but who had 'remained unswervingly faithful to positive palpable reality, or who have become faithful to it once more'.[12] On the right these included the neo-classicists, but on the left Otto Dix, Georg Grosz, and Max Beckmann. Hartlaub saw in the new realism, of which Remarque was the best known literary example, both

[7]   S. Zweig, *Die Welt von Gestern*, Frankfurt, Fischer, 1970, 287.
[8]   See K.-M. Bogdal, 'Weimar from the Perspective of Oral History' in Kniesche and Brockmann, *Dancing*; also Gay, *Weimar Culture*, 82 ff.
[9]   See Scholder, *The Churches 1918–1934*, 35 ff, 100 ff.
[10]   Quoted by Gay, *Weimar Culture*, 103.
[11]   Ibid., 106.
[12]   Cited in P. Selz, *Beckmann*, London, Abbeville, 1996, 34.

resignation and cynicism on the one side and enthusiasm for observed reality on the other. *Neue Sachlichkeit* was opposed to the emotional indulgence of expressionism. Emotional states, Beckmann told his pupils, have to be transmuted into a rational, formal structure.[13] The artists of Weimar were committed to a search for reality behind appearance, and sentimental realism was anathema to them.[14]

A whole series of great novels appeared in this period: Hermann Hesse's *Demian* was published in 1919 and *Steppenwolf* in 1927; Kafka's *The Castle* in 1920 and *The Trial* in 1925; Thomas Mann published *The Magic Mountain* in 1924, and *Joseph and his Brothers* ten years later. The most significant event in poetry was the publication of Rilke's *Duino Elegies* in 1923. In the opera, 1925 saw the première of Alban Berg's *Wozzeck*, and 1928 of Brecht's *Threepenny Opera*.

Throughout his years in Germany Barth kept open evenings for his students where politics and current cultural events were discussed. During Weimar he and his students looked at a string of political biographies: Tirpitz, Liebknecht, the Kaiser, Scheidemann, and Ludendorff amongst them. 'So far so good,' Barth commented to Thurneysen. 'Elimination of the political *as such*, pursuit of the question of the motives of their actions and their relations to one another.'[15] Amongst literary works were books by Shaw (whose *Major Barbara* impressed Barth greatly), Raabe, Jacobsen, Thomas Mann, and Fontane.[16] This was the formal side of Barth's lively engagement with the culture of his time, which remained intense to the end of his life.

In his letters Barth made caustic observations about German academic life at the time, about the German professors, 'donkeys', standing round in top hats honouring Ritschl, 'masters at finding ingenious, ethical, and Christian bases for brutalities'.[17] However, he also found colleagues, like Heinrich Scholz, or the Jesuit Eric Pryzwara, of the highest calibre, who tested his mettle and forced him to modify his thinking. This was to be expected, for in the wider fields of intellectual life, especially in the Institutes and on the fringes, there was a brilliant flowering. We have only to think of the work of the Warburg Institute, led by Cassirer and Panofsky, of Horkheimer and Adorno at the Frankfurt Institute, of Karen Horney, Melanie Klein, and Wilhelm Reich at the Psychoanalytical Institute in Berlin, and of Walter Benjamin—whose doctoral thesis on German tragic drama was turned down by Frankfurt University. Heidegger's *Sein und Zeit*, which Bultmann treated as a *praeparatio evangelica*, appeared in 1927. There was in Weimar, writes Peter Gay, 'a real community of reason devoted to radical inquiry,

---

[13] Cited in P. Selz, *Beckmann*, London, Abbeville, 1996, 34.
[14] Gay, *Weimar Culture*, 113.   [15] B–Th II, 252.   [16] B–Th II, 329.
[17] B–Th II, 60, 131.

open to ideas impossible or scandalous to traditional practitioners'.[18] The work of the Warburg Institute in particular, Gay notes, was marked by an austere empiricism and scholarly imagination which was the antithesis of the brutal anti-intellectualism and vulgar mysticism which threatened to barbarize German culture in the 1920s.

It is clear that Barth's theology has to be located against this whole cultural and intellectual background, as well as against political events. In June 1919 Karl von Ossietzky noted that Germany had a right to expect an absolute break in old methods, and reconstruction, in the political, economic, and spiritual-ethical area.[19] There was no lack of movements which attempted to provide the lead in this latter area. In an article in the *Frankfurter Zeitung* in 1922 Siegfried Kracauer picked out the anthroposophical teaching of Rudolf Steiner, the messianic communism of Ernst Bloch, the belief in structure held by the George circle, and the renewed sense of community in both the Church and Judaism as a reaction to the 'metaphysical suffering from the lack of deep meaning in the world'.[20] He could have added the Patmos group, around Rosenzweig and Buber, whom Barth met but could make no sense of, and also the movement of dialectical theology.[21]

The founding of the journal *Zwischen den Zeiten* by Barth, Thurneysen, and Gogarten in August 1922 was the theological counterpart to other famous Weimar journals and its aim was precisely what Ossietzky had in view. Barth had already spoken of living 'between the times' in *Romans* but it was Gogarten who put the phrase on the map, in a young man's angry rejection of all he had been taught, in an article for *Christliche Welt*:

It is the destiny of our generation to stand between the times. We never belonged to the period presently coming to an end; it is doubtful whether we shall ever belong to the period which is to come . . . Where we heard you, we heard the best and truest of intentions, but they sounded hollow to our ears . . . The tormenting question never left us, the question of whether we, who were supposed to give everything with the Word, could have anything at all to give. Indeed, we received nothing. We received much that was scholarly, much that was interesting, but nothing that would have been worthy of this Word.[22]

---

[18] Gay, *Weimar Culture*, 32. This rules out Schellong's suggestion that *Sehnsucht* (longing) was the dominant structure of feeling of the Weimar intellectual. 'On Reading Karl Barth from the Left' in Hunsinger, *Barth and Radical Politics*, 148.

[19] Cited in Gay, *Weimar Culture*, 18.

[20] Cited in R. Wiggershaus, *The Frankfurt School*, tr. M. Robertson, Cambridge, Polity, 1994, 69.

[21] Barth's correspondence with the Dutch theologian Miskotte is a record of his complete incomprehension of what Rosenzweig was trying to do, perhaps the most palpable evidence we have of Barth's complete lack of antennae for what contemporary Judaism was about. K. Barth–H. Miskotte, *Briefwechsel 1924–1968*, Zürich, Theologischer Verlag, 1991.

[22] *Die Christliche Welt*, 34/24 (1920), cols. 374–8 tr. in *The Beginnings of Dialectical Theology*, ed. J. M. Robinson, John Knox Press (1968) 277.

The new journal was to oppose the hitherto dominant liberal theology, and promote a theology of the Word (though Barth was aghast at
Gogarten's proposal that it should be called *Das Wort*: 'unbearably preten-
tious . . . better to call it 'The Ship of Fools' than burden it with this sacred
millstone, which doubtless corresponds only too well to Gogarten's intentions and delusions of grandeur').[23] The remarks about Gogarten here indicate an unease which Barth felt also about Brunner, and about Bultmann,
who was lumped together with them in the popular mind. 'If only one could
persuade Emil to be more focussed instead of listening to everything
so recklessly,' he said in 1924. 'I have a feeling that Emil, with his 'Law
and Gospel' is rushing headlong to destruction—into the arms of Althaus
and Holl. He should watch out.'[24] Much of the problem with Gogarten was
a sense that there were things simply not shared with the Lutherans. The
controversies between Lutheran and Reformed were never resolved, he
wrote to Bultmann. They will perhaps come to a head 'in a great explosion
within ZZ', a prophecy which was fulfilled in 1933.[25] For their part,
Gogarten also proposed separating from the group at least once, Brunner
felt misunderstood by Barth from the beginning, and Bultmann was never
really on board. Nevertheless this journal, which was more or less cotermi-
nous with Weimar, was a forum for much of the most creative and challenging theology in Germany during its 11 year span. Barth published in it
frequently, but insisted from the start that he was not interested in founding
a school.[26]

Barth's years in Germany were a period of extraordinary productivity. By
the time Barth reached Göttingen he was already a celebrity, though he felt
completely unprepared for his job as 'Professor of Reformed Dogmatics'.
He was to hold three Chairs in rapid succession during his time in Germany:
at Göttingen between 1921 and 1925, Münster from October 1925 to 1930,
and Bonn from March 1930 to his expulsion in June 1935. He developed
his work on four fronts. In the first place his work at Göttingen, where
the faculty was strongly Lutheran, involved his teaching Reformation doctrine. He taught courses, therefore, on the Heidelberg Catechism, the
theology of Calvin, Zwingli, the theology of the Reformed Confessions,
and on Schleiermacher. When he announced lectures in dogmatics the
faculty objected and he had to settle for 'Instruction in the Christian
Religion'. At Münster, a Catholic heartland, he began his series on
Protestant theology in the nineteenth century, adding the larger and even
more significant material on the eighteenth century in Bonn. These courses
involved him in intensive work not only on the periods in question, but

---

[23] B–Th II, 110.   [24] B–Th II, 293.   [25] B–B (ET), 32.
[26] B–Th II, 234. Reporting on a discussion in Leipzig: 'Conclusion: No repeating of catch-
words! No forming a school! . . . Think for yourselves!

also on patristic and scholastic theology. Here the necessity for engagement with Catholicism became urgent, and he gave seminars on Anselm and Aquinas, as well as engaging in important debates with Eric Pryzwara. This, then, was his first sphere of scholarly activity. At the same time, as someone who took Scripture as God's Word with absolute seriousness, he lectured each semester on different New Testament books, on Ephesians, James, 1 Corinthians, 1 John, Philippians, Colossians, the Sermon on the Mount, and John. Only the work on 1 Corinthians and Philippians was actually published at the time. This work in history of doctrine and Scripture was the basis for his own original dogmatic work. A complete dogmatics was offered at Göttingen, whilst a greatly expanded course was offered at Münster, the Prolegomena of which was published as *Christliche Dogmatik* in 1927. Out of this work then emerged his ground-breaking *Ethics* of 1928–9, the fourth front. In attempting to situate this work in Weimar we are not attempting either crude causal explanations, or even to make the more modest claim that Barth was 'influenced' by this or that current tendency. Rather, following Barth's own advice, we note that 'a whole mass of connections' is visible which serve to highlight, not just Barth's participation in his time, but his determined effort to resist intellectual hegemony.

In a lecture on the spiritual presuppositions for the rebuilding of Europe, at the end of the Second World War, Barth sketched out a fascinating analysis of Weimar as he had understood it. It was a period, he said, of deep and passionate questioning in the realms of politics, society, and ethics but at the same time a period in which the human spirit was completely undisciplined; a time of fatalism, of a passion for astrology, and of flight from responsibility; a time when the inhuman objectivity of capital dominated not only politics but the arts and the Church as well; a time of lack of solidarity in which every individual sought their salvation in their own private life, house, or allotment; a time of sharp conflicts and especially of denials; and finally a time of complete absence of sobriety with regard to ideas and principles, of the vast intoxication of heaven stormers and world rulers which led finally to nihilism and death.[27] Clearly there are ways in which Barth himself fits into this picture—in the vehemence of some of his denials for example. On the other hand I believe that an examination of his Weimar theology shows it to be characterized precisely by that *Nüchternheit* which he later urged on his German friends. To the brilliant mixture of cynicism, despair, and new life which was Weimar culture Barth addressed a message of sobriety and hope.

---

[27] 'Die geistigen Voraussetzungen für den Neuaufbau in der Nachkriegszeit' in *Theologische Fragen und Antworten*, 414–32.

THEOLOGY, CULTURE, AND
CULTURE PROTESTANTISM

At the beginning of 1923 Harnack, who had been shocked by Barth's Romans commentaries, and still more by his Aarau lecture on *Biblical Insights*, published a challenge to the 'despisers of scientific theology' in *Christliche Welt*, a journal which existed to reconcile religion and culture.[28] It consisted of fifteen questions which set out the objections to the new theology on the part of the 'scientific theology' which Harnack represented. The debate which followed about what constituted a rigorous theology was in fact a confrontation between two cultural worlds, for the world of the Prussian Academy, of which Harnack was for long president, was the acme of the old German high culture. Harnack was unaware that a cultural earthquake had taken place, that all the new institutes, groups, and movements represented a ferment which was transforming the culture of which he was the doyen.

For Harnack, Barth was an enthusiast, a gnostic, or a new Marcion, founding theology on claims to revelation which could not be reputably substantiated. Barth ignored the need for a critical appropriation of the Christian tradition. Granted that Christ stood at the centre of the gospel, how was it possible to know about him other than through critical-historical study? What other theology could there be but a theology with a 'blood relationship' to science? In his reply Barth fired a broadside against the whole movement of culture Protestantism. Harnack represented the old order, for which Beethoven and Goethe's *Faust* were part of the canon, absolutely untutored and unshaken by the war. Barth, like many of his contemporaries, was striving for a quite new approach to culture. We could say that the dispute was between the new and the old objectivity (*Sachlichkeit*).

For Barth, real statements about God are made only where one is aware of being placed under judgement instead of believing oneself to be on a pinnacle of culture and religion. Those who valorize critical historical study forget that we no longer know 'Christ according to the flesh'. As far as the relation to science was concerned Barth believed that 'If theology were to regain the courage to face up to concrete objectivity [*Sachlichkeit*], the courage to bear witness to the Word of revelation, of judgement and of God's love, the outcome might well be that "science in general" would have to seek "strong ties and a blood relationship" with theology instead of the other way around.'[29] Barth rejected the cultural hegemony of the *opinio communis*. Why should that be a yardstick for theological work?

An angry reply from Harnack led to a still more bruising reply from

---

[28] *Revelation and Theology*, 3.   [29] Ibid., 35.

Barth, after which Harnack signed off with a prophecy that Barth would become an 'object' and not a subject of theology like all 'who express their Christianity as prophets or witnesses'.[30] The dispute about objectivity turned on the question of 'science'. Barth seemed to transform the lecture desk into a pulpit. 'On the basis of the whole course of Church-history I predict that this undertaking will not lead to edification but to dissolution.'[31] His account of scientific objectivity is reminiscent of Weber's, elaborated at the same time. The scientific theologian 'whose aim it is to inspire and to edify brings a foreign flame to his altar . . . revelation is not a scientific concept; science can neither draw together under one generic concept nor explain in terms of "revelation" the God-consciousness of the paradoxical preaching of founders of religion and prophets'.[32] Barth, he felt, was trying to grasp the Word of revelation as something so objective that human mediation could be eliminated from its operation. This was a clear misunderstanding, but one which revealed that Harnack could not begin to comprehend the new view. Barth was perfectly clear on the human mediation of all revelation whatsoever, indeed that was part of his point. The testimony of revelation '*must* be described as a piece of unpleasantly dark human intellectual and cultural history'.[33] This only makes clear that faith is God's creation, and not something we arrive at by way of our historical critical reconstruction. Barth for his part denied that the action of God, whether in the Sermon on the Mount, the parables or the passion, ever became directly historically comprehensible. God was certainly not to be identified with the high points of culture but precisely in the No spoken to it. 'God is known as *God*, as the source and the goal of the *thoughts* of God which man, in the darkness of his culture and his decadence, is in the habit of forming'. This does not mean that culture is insignificant. Far from becoming insignificant it really becomes 'full of significance and promise, really serious and possible precisely through being moved out of the twilight of supposed fulfilment into the light of real *hope*'.[34]

Culture, Barth is telling us in this exchange, has above all to be understood eschatologically. A shift to a more Christological approach to culture is to be found in an address he gave three years later to the Continental Association of Home Missions in Amsterdam on 'Church and Culture'. Barth's work on dogmatics had in the meantime led him to adopt the principle of the *Extra Calvinisticum*, the doctrine that 'the Word became incarnate and yet remained on high'. This allowed Barth to see that 'creation could be viewed from the perspective of Christology as well as from eschatology, not merely in terms of redemption but of reconciliation. It was now possible to

[30] Ibid., 52.   [31] Ibid., 36   [32] Ibid., 53.
[33] Ibid., 48.   [34] Ibid., 50.

understand Christ not merely as the changing and renewing but as the supportive ground of all being.'[35] Here he called for 'prophetic objectivity' rather than 'methodological objectivity' in the assessment of culture. We can, as most people do, approach culture as a purely human affair understanding it either anthropologically or as the *Kultur* which Harnack represented, 'the final goal and totality of norms by which human activity should be guided'. With respect to this activity the Church could only speak negatively and polemically. From the point of view of the Church's presuppositions this culture was 'an impossible fantasy and an idol' because the Word of God ought to determine human activity and not other norms.[36] Christian preaching has, therefore, met every culture with ultimate, sharp scepticism. However, culture is not, in fact, apart from God, but has to be understood in the light of creation, reconciliation, and redemption. In view of the *regnum naturae* we have to say that God's image is not destroyed by the Fall. Because God speaks to us in Christ humanity is promise. 'Man is capable of partaking of this promise . . . The term culture connotes exactly that promise to man: fulfilment, unity, wholeness within his sphere as a creature, as man, exactly as God in his sphere is fullness, wholeness, Lord over nature and spirit, Creator of heaven *and* earth.'[37] The fact that the world is redeemed means that whilst we cannot sanctify cultural achievements, as Schleiermacher wanted to do, 'there is even less place for a basic blindness to the possibility that culture may be revelatory, that it can be filled with the promise'. The kingdom of God cannot be identified with any human cultural achievement but the Church will be 'alert for the signs which, perhaps in many cultural achievements, announce that the kingdom approaches'.[38] From the point of view of reconciliation culture is the law in reference to which the sinner, sanctified by God, has to practise her faith and obedience. Finally, in view of redemption, the Church confronts society, 'Not with an undervaluation of cultural achievement, but with the highest possible evaluation of the goal for which it sees all cultural activity striving.' It approaches art, science, business and politics, technique and education as a serious game, putting all human effort and achievement in the framework of the comfort and warning of eternity. The Word of God always speaks in a particular way to a particular time and Barth judges that the eschatological perspective is what is crucial for Weimar. 'What the Church of our time needs most of all to relearn in relation to the problem of culture is, in my

---

[35] Marquardt, *Theologie*, 262, who draws attention to the significance of Barth's adoption of the *Extra Calvinisticum*, which is very prominent in the *Christliche Dogmatik*, 257–64. Later it allowed Barth, as he said, to go back to natural theology via Christology. 'Ein Gespräch in der Brüdergemeinde' in *Civitas Praesens*, Königsfeld, 1961, nr 13.

[36] Barth, 'Church and Culture' in *Theology and Church*, 338.

[37] Ibid., 343.   [38] Ibid., 344.

judgement . . . the eschatological form of the Word of God . . . What has
been left out is the insight that all Christendom and its relation to culture
depends entirely on hope.'[39]

Not identification, then, which is what Harnack believed in, but critical
affirmation. When the Church witnesses in the light of redemption it is
bound to be subversive, and to risk unpopularity, but only thus can it fulfil
its duty to society which knows, 'better than it will admit to itself that
without this comfort and warning cultural achievement is ultimately impossible'.[40] Such critical affirmation also characterized Barth's political witness
within Weimar.

THE GOD WHO COMMANDS: THEOLOGY IN THE
SERVICE OF RESPONSIBLE POLITICS

Retreat to an Ivory Tower?

In the opinion of most historians Weimar was marked by a *trahison des clercs*,
in that most intellectuals either withdrew from politics or were openly
hostile to the Republic.[41] Klaus Scholder brings both of these accusations
against Barth. On the one hand he claims that after Barth took up his post in
academia, 'the world of political ideas and decisions no longer formed any
basic element of his theological thought'. His political involvement 'plainly
retreated'.[42] At the same time, whilst dialectical theology developed a sharp
ideology critique, 'For the Weimar period, this criticism was ambivalent, at
least in its political effects. It hit the attempts to establish and to preserve the
Republic on the basis of feelings of Christian responsibility just as hard as
the designs of the opponents of the Republic.'[43]

In a piece of self-reproach at the end of World War II, Barth himself
agreed that during his years in Germany, partly as a result of concentration
on his theological task, and partly as the result of 'a certain shyness of a
Swiss getting involved in German affairs' he failed to warn against tendencies both in the Church and in secular life, which to him were perfectly clear,
'not only implicitly but explicitly, not just privately but also publicly'.[44] But

---

[39] Ibid., 353–4.   [40] Ibid., 349.   [41] Craig, *Germany 1866–1945*, 480.

[42] Scholder, *The Churches 1918–1934*, 45.

[43] Ibid., 51; cf. 49, 122. Marquardt maintains that Barth came to Weimar from a position 'on
the extreme left' and that his Yes to the existing order came out of 'the most radical revolutionary position'. 'There was nothing positive about it in itself, it was a through and through
critical Yes.' *Marquardt, Theologie*, 166. I would put the emphasis elsewhere: critical but a real
affirmation.

[44] 'To the German Theologians Held Prisoner of War', letter of 8 July 1945, in *Karl Barth
zum Kirchenkampf, Beteiligung—Mahnung—Zuspruch, Theologische Existenz Heute* (New Series),
Munich, Kaiser, 1956, 92.

to what extent was Barth aware of what was going on, and to what extent is this hindsight?[45]

The old voice of Barth's years in Safenwil re-emerged at the end of 1929 in his article '*Quousque tandem*', in which he tore into church complacency. By then alarm bells were beginning to ring for all sorts of people all over Germany. We have to remember, however, that in the elections of May 1928 the German nationalists were reduced from 103 seats to 78, and the Nazis from 14 to 12, whilst the Social Democrats increased their representation from 131 to 152. For someone of Barth's political persuasion this was a good result. Scholder points out that Hitler plays no part in Barth's letters to Thurneysen between 1920 and 1930, but there is nothing in the least surprising about this. When *Mein Kampf* appeared in 1925 it caused no great stir.[46] Germany was full of splinter groups on both the left and the right, and both right wing coups of the early 1920s had failed. In 1928 it was a perfectly fair assumption that the democratic republic, the rapprochement between left and right represented by Stresemann, would continue to creak along.

On the other hand it is certainly surprising to find Barth speaking to a Youth Conference in October 1927 on 'Theology and the Modern Person' without making any mention of nationalism or anti-Semitism, but basically outlining the main thrust of his theology.[47] It is not that at this stage people were unaware of anti-Semitism as a problem. Otto Baumgarten had put it on the theological agenda in 1926, and Barth, along with other leading theologians including Rade and Tillich, was to provide a commendation of Eduard Lamparter's book on the same theme in 1928.[48] It is certainly implausible that the Barth of the previous decade would have dealt with this topic in this way. That he did so could have something to do with the desire of the *emigré* to identify with the host country. Here it was, in the midst of a wonderful autumn in the Thuringian woods, that Barth wrote to Thurneysen about how much at home he felt in Germany, and how he showed these people that 'he could drink beer with the best of them'.[49]

Barth later spoke of his time in the 1920s as 'ten years taken out of politics',[50] and this is doubtless true as measured by his union involvement in the previous decade, and the involvement in the church struggle at the begin-

---

[45] McCormack raises the same question, though he puts Barth's response two years later than I do. McCormack, *Barth's Theology*, 414.

[46] Cf. A. Bullock, *Hitler: A Study in Tyranny*, Harmondsworth, Penguin, 1990. As a political best seller 'it was a failure, which few, even among the party members, had the patience to read'. In 1925 it sold 9,473 copies, 6,913 in 1926 and 3,015 in 1928. These sales doubled in 1929, and shot up to 50,000 in 1930 and 1931. *Hitler*, 122, 133.

[47] *Vorträge 1925–1930*, 160–82.

[48] Scholder, *The Churches 1918–1934*, 116.   [49] B–Th II, 536.

[50] In a letter to Hans Asmussen, 14 January 1932, cited by McCormack, *Barth's Theology*, 414.

ning of the 1930s, but on the other hand Barth was not politically asleep either, as the Youth Conference lecture might suggest. On the contrary, as I now hope to show, Barth, far from being a lukewarm *Vernunftrepublikaner*, was squarely behind the republic throughout the 1920s, and doubtless felt that common sense and widespread support for the Social Democrats would prevail over the turbid nonsense of German nationalism.[51] When things changed, with the death of Stresemann at the beginning of October 1929, and the world wide economic crash, which brought Germany down with it, Barth was one of the first back in action. 'Quousque tandem' was written two months after Stresemann's death, and Barth joined the SPD, as earlier he had joined the Swiss Democratic Party, in May 1931. That he underestimated the danger posed by the Nazis is a failing shared by almost everyone on the left. In his own way, and *as a theologian*, he had thrown his weight behind the fledgling democracy.

The Lectures on Calvin

Barth's comment to Thurneysen, as he took up the study of Calvin, has become well known: 'Calvin is a waterfall, a primitive forest, something demonic, coming down direct from the Himalayas, absolutely Chinese, wonderful, mythological. I lack the organs, the suction caps, to take in this phenomenon not to mention presenting it rightly. What I take in is only a thin stream, and what I give out still thinner. I could cheerfully sit down and spend the rest of my life with Calvin.'[52]

Barth first seriously came across Calvin as a young student in his father's lectures in Bern, where Calvin's theology emerged, in what Barth regarded as an exemplary way, in the course of the account of his life.[53] At the end of his studies he had arrived in Geneva just as Calvin's 400th birthday was being celebrated, and preached in the very room in which Calvin had lectured, and this led him to study the 1559 *Institutes* carefully.[54] He was, then, taking up an old study and enthusiasm. Throughout his life Barth spoke of Calvin as providing perfect study material for young theologians, and we get a sense of why this is in these warm and vivid lectures, in which the 'shadow' which lies over Calvin, the 'tragedy' which accompanies him, is always in view alongside his greatness. After a careful 'setting in life', in which Barth

---

[51]   This is how he understood his position in an article on the Weimar period in 1961. See Busch, *Barth*, 189.

[52]   B–Th II, 80.

[53]   *Die Theologie Calvins*, ed. A. Reinstädtler and H. Scholl, Zürich, Theologischer Verlag, 1993, 174; ET, *The Theology of John Calvin*, tr. G. W. Bromiley, Grand Rapids, Eerdmans, 1995, 131.

[54]   See *Theologie Calvins*, p. vii; ET, p. xiii.

explored the relationship of the Reformation to the Middle Ages, and then Calvin's relations with Luther and Zwingli, he looked at his early years, the first edition of the *Institutes*, and his attitude to authority, law, and government, before taking up his early conflicts up to 1541.

What is especially remarkable about the lectures, given the letter to Thurneysen, is the emphasis in them on Calvin's practical political concerns. Barth stresses, as he does in all his historical lectures, that Calvin is our contemporary, and that he speaks to the present.[55] He begins with a word of Cicero that Calvin himself liked to quote: 'History is the teacher of life.' We have to remind ourselves, then, that this is 1922, a wild and chaotic time in Germany, a full eighteen months before the situation settles down. The pathos of the Reformation world, Barth remarks, is something we know again in our post-war present.[56] Barth had been told on his appointment that he was not to bring his politics into his teaching, but without any doubt we find Barth's own views on the situation in his account of Calvin.

Were Calvin alive today, Barth tells us, he would be both a great reader and contributor to newspapers—and present day politicians would have experienced something from him! He was no head in the clouds idealist, but 'the most practical amongst the practical men', an 'aristocratic republican'.[57] He was a representative of the new *Sachlichkeit* which Max Weber had already urged in 1918 as the only road to authenticity and moral sense.[58] 'Sobriety and objectivity are perhaps the best words to describe Calvin's attitude with regard to world politics . . . his tendency to keep a distance between heaven and earth gave him an inner freedom to act more certainly and determinedly on earth. He dealt with political matters not as an Enthusiast, not driven by 'religious feeling', but on his reading simply in obedience.[59] We have to regard him as one of the fathers of modern democracy.[60] Unlike Zwingli he was never utopian, but attuned to what was practically possible. Action, for him, was always 'a measured, well considered deed'.[61] His study of law stood by him, and law was in his view always the very foundation of the state, though this did not make him a legitimist.[62] Barth allows himself a pyrotechnic aside at Wernle's reading of Calvin as someone who affirmed the absolute power of government ('What on earth has this to do with the "Christian freedom" under which Calvin understands Romans 13!'[63]). Contrary to popular opinion Calvin did not believe in theocracy. His connecting of eschatology and ethics, of the absolute difference between God and human beings, disallowed any such possibility.[64] He therefore

[55] Ibid., 5, 7, 11; ET, 4, 6, 11.
[56] Ibid., 25; ET, 21.
[57] Ibid., 274; ET, 203.
[58] Gay, *Weimar Culture*, 126.
[59] *Theologie Calvins*, 541; ET, 400.
[60] Ibid., 305; ET, 225.
[61] Ibid., 149; ET, 111.
[62] Ibid., 290; ET, 214.
[63] Ibid., 299; ET, 220.
[64] Ibid., 171, 277; ET, 127, 205.

wanted no Christian state, no Christian socialism, or civil or criminal law. Of course, the demand of Christian obedience applied in the political sphere. Calvin expressly confirmed the state, but only as a parable, 'not directly but indirectly, not in its giveness, but in its correspondence as a temporal image of the eternal righteousness of God, in its correspondence to this its sense and origin'.[65] In Switzerland, Barth tells his students, Ragaz has claimed Calvin for the left, and revolution, and Wernle for the right, and reaction. 'The last word of Calvin's *Institutes* is neither one nor the other but Christ, the freedom of Christian people and the celestial homeland, from which proceeds Practice [*übung*]—serious, pertinent, passionate practice (but not more than practice), which is the right description for what human beings have to do.'[66]

Barth sees many analogies between the sixteenth century situation and his own. Zwingli is clearly Ragaz, the Anabaptists the starry eyed idealists. His students are the *Vernunftrepublikaner*. Modernity, he told his students, is frightened to shoot the arrow of longing too far. It is more weary and resigned than the Reformation age. With a scepticism which is partly more questioning and partly more dogmatic it halts before the doors of the upper world.[67] Barth's sympathies in the lectures are to a larger extent with Luther. There are two moments to the Reformation. The first is the discovery of the *ganz Anders*, the living, judging and forgiving God; but the second, perhaps the central theme of the lectures, is the discovery of the necessary connection between theology and ethics, which Luther knew of, but which Calvin worked out in detail.[68] This necessary move, the responsible and passionate addressing of political questions, is, I believe, what Barth is urging on his students to whom he has made clear that the past lives again, speaks, and works in the present.[69]

Explorations in Ethics

'Christianity is not ethics, nor does it *have* any special ethic . . . Christianity is knowledge of God and just for that reason knowing about the *commandments* being bound to them, and that means . . . keeping them.'[70] Christianity is not ethics, but Barth outlined in these years one of the most original ethical manifestos in church history. His work on Romans had already established that ethics was fundamentally about grace, and that the method of separating dogmatics and ethics he had learned from his teachers was

---

[65] Ibid., 299; ET, 221.   [66] Ibid., 307; ET, 226.
[67] Ibid., 87; ET, 65.   [68] Ibid., 98, 161–2; ET, 74, 120.
[69] *Theologie Calvins*, 11; ET, 8.
[70] Barth, *The Epistle to the Philippians*, tr. J. Leitch, London, SCM, 1962, 125.

impossible. This insight was developed in a lecture to pastors in Wiesbaden in September 1922 on 'The Problem of Ethics in the Present'. 'This lecture is giving me hell!' wrote Barth to George Merz. 'For ten days I've been trying to see what to say and how to say it—not academically-theologically (to the devil with that way of doing it!), not pious-biblicist and not in the hysterical post-war period style but *also* not down from the damned hellenistic heights, as both my brothers like to do.'[71] He begins, in a way which is vital for his theological method, by characterizing the ethical question as the fundamental ontological question: 'The ethical question is the question about being . . . There is no sense in posing the question about the Good as a logical question as if the question of truth were not the question as to what counts as our ultimate foundation . . . above all nothing can come of posing the ethical question as spectators . . . as if the necessity did not arise from understanding ourselves as those who live and act.'[72] Here again, as in *Romans*, theory arises out of praxis.[73]

Barth then turns to the facts of the present situation, which each of his hearers read in their newspapers: French colonial troops on the Rhine, the Russian revolution, inflation, the collapse of a whole vision of state, economics, and technology underwritten by religion, morality, and cultural progress.[74] The question of what to do in this situation, the ethical question, is the question 'regarding the truth about truth'.[75] Indeed, here the ethical problem is *the* theological problem.[76] We cannot possibly answer this question through some kind of logical or theoretical ethical investigation. Rather, we analyse the idea of *activity*, which is the most all embracing category of human being. *Life* is the object of theological ethics.[77] The ethical responses of Ritschl and Troeltsch are no longer viable—they have collapsed with the previous order—but neither can there be any cheap resort to dialectic.[78] The question has to be answered teleologically, but not in Kant's sense: 'Without at least a modicum of millenarianism we can no more have ethics than we could have ethics without an idea of moral personality.'[79] Why? Because it is only *hope* which gives shape and sense to ethics. Christian ethics affirms a goal to history, and just for

---

[71] B–Th II, 97. Barth's style to Merz is very different from anything he ever wrote to Thurneysen. His concern *not* to speak '*hysterisch-nachkriegzeitlich*' seems to me to call seriously in question R. H. Roberts's suggestion that what Barth did was precisely to capture that mood. See pp. 116–17 below.

[72] *Das Wort Gottes*, 125; ET, 137.   [73] So Marquardt, *Theologie*, 279.

[74] *Das Wort Gottes*, 130; ET, 144.   [75] Ibid., 125; ET, 137.

[76] So Plonz, on whom I draw for my account of this lecture. *Herrenlosen Gewalten*, 199. Cf. KD I/2, 884–6, CD 787–90 for the same sentiments.

[77] Plonz, *Herrenlosen Gewalten*, 175 ff.

[78] *Das Wort Gottes*, 135; ET, 151.

[79] Ibid., 140; ET, 158.

that reason cannot be limited to the individual. With a sharp look at the *Vernunftrepublikaner* Barth refers his hearers (positively this time) to Ragaz: 'Is it really a sign of ethical maturity to be so ostentatiously unenthusiastic about the social state and world peace, not to believe in these things from the depths of one's heart?'[80] 'What the enthusiasts, ideal- ists, communists, anarchists and (despite all true Lutheran teaching), note well, also the Christian hope sets out as a reality here on earth, is a task, not a daydream, a goal, not the end of ethical struggle.' This task and goal is:

Freedom in love and love in freedom as the pure and direct motive of social action, a society based on justice as its immediate object, the overcoming of patronage, or rather of exploitation and oppression, the overcoming of class conflict and national frontiers, of war, force and power, a culture of the Spirit in place of one based on things, humanity in place of objectivity, fraternity in place of each against all.[81]

For Barth this is not a utopian dream but the serious goal of human social and political endeavour in the light of the gospel. Of course, really in the light of the *gospel* of the forgiveness of sins, through which we are freed from cheap quietism for real struggle. Everything hangs on God's grace, which cannot be commanded but through which resurrection is a fact in history.[82]

In the same year Barth wrote a response to an attack on religious social- ism by Paul Althaus, in which Barth appeared as 'one of the most moderate religious socialists'. Those critics who believe that Barth withdrew from politics in the Weimar years can certainly not find any evidence here. Barth cheerfully confessed to his religious socialism. Naturally democracy, social- ism, communism, and anarchism do not represent the practical application of Christianity in the world but Barth claims the right 'of referring for a few years, inconsistently and indirectly, for instructional purposes, to these possibilities', just as Lutherans have appealed to the Prussian state.[83] The

---

[80] Ibid., 140; ET, 159.

[81] Ibid., 141; ET, 160. It is not easy to see how, in the light of this lecture, Scholder can con- clude that morality and conscience were *merely* walls against God and 'Thus any kind of polit- ical theology was already nipped in the bud.' Scholder, *The Churches 1918–1934*, 105. The point was precisely to oppose one kind of political theology and make way for another kind. The dialectic of love and freedom here is the anticipation of his later doctrine of God as Marquardt points out. *Theologie*, 236–9.

[82] Marquardt comments: 'This is a completely socialist programme for struggle, defined backwards through the old concept of chiliasm and forwards through the dogmatic concept of God.' *Theologie*, 238.

[83] 'Grundfragen der Chrislichen Sozialethik' in *Anfänge*, i, 155–6; ET, 49.

key difference between Barth and Althaus lay in the seriousness with v
they took the biblical critique. Althaus asked whether love was really t_____
able as the 'only structure of the world'. Barth answered: 'Yes: The love of
God which is "thought" in the Sermon on the Mount is either an illusion
or it is the only "structure of the world".'[84] To believe means to affirm
that the love of God is the only structure of the world despite the fact
that we find anything but love in the world. For Barth the righteousness
of God is the scales on which 'the pressing, burdensome, highly actual questions in all politics' are weighed. It is rat poison for all the ideologies
with which human beings seek to escape the truth, the supreme form of
ideology critique.[85]

These reflections on ethics were finally worked out in great depth in the
lectures Barth gave in Münster in 1928/9, a time of imminent danger. By
now Barth had fully realized the implications of the fact that ethics was part
of dogmatics. '*Good* means *sanctified by God* . . . To remember not only the
ethical character of dogmatics in general but also the express answer to the
ethical question that is given in the doctrine of sanctification is to ensure
that ethics is not possible as an independent discipline alongside dogmatics.'[86] At the same time, 'every revolt in dogmatics rests on a revolt in
ethics'.[87] The Word of God is both the origin and answer of the question of
human existence but 'the theme of the Word of God is simply human existence, life, or conduct'.[88] He sketched out a trinitarian ethics in which the
command of God the Creator was explored under the headings of life,
calling, order, and faith; of God the Reconciler as law, authority, humility,
and love; and of God the Redeemer as promise, conscience, gratitude, and
hope. Nigel Biggar has illustrated the way in which these ethics are far more
conservative than those Barth developed later, especially in their concern for
order.[89] In them Barth says a sharp and decisive 'No' to anarchy.[90] In my view
this is to be understood as Barth's quite deliberate attempt to respond to
his context. These lectures, in the Weimar Republic, give us a political ethic
which supports neither reaction nor revolution but responsible, critical participation in the democratic process. Consider, for example, the section on
education, which Barth deals with under 'Authority'. Education cannot be
self education, but training, and training means 'painful opposition'. None
of us go willingly to school. At the same time true pedagogy is always characterized by humanity, by the serious engagement of an I and a Thou which
respects the protest of the child. The goal of education is to fit a person for

---

[84] Ibid., 158–9; ET, 51–2.   [85] Ibid., 160, 164; ET, 53, 57.
[86] *Ethik* I, 25; ET, 16.   [87] *Ethik* II, 152; ET, 341.   [88] *Ethik* I, 26; ET, 17.
[89] N. Biggar, *The Hastening that Waits: Karl Barth's Ethics*, Oxford, Clarendon, 1993, 52–62.
[90] *Ethik* II, 335; ET, 447.

their position in the world. 'To be fit is to be able to do what is required, with a stress upon the word *required*. For the sinner, to have a calling cannot mean living one's own life, developing one's own talents and interests, engaging in one's pursuits . . . It means being claimed for, and required to be at, a particular place in human society and history with one's own particular abilities . . . All the real education that comes to us consists of being directed by people, in God's service, to this place and to these limits . . . to a goal, not that we set, but that is set for us.'[91] That Barth had an eye on the many experiments in education undertaken at the time (Rudolf Steiner set up his school in Basle in 1913) is beyond question.

Under the heading of 'order' Barth considers the 'external order of our life by which we are disciplined and human life is possible as life together'.[92] Order demands equality, which he prefers to the terms justice and equity. 'Equality in the state means the repression of the struggle of all against all, of the oppression of the weak by the strong, through the instrumentality of the law as this is upheld by force. Leadership in the state means the existence of the office of a watchman to preserve the law by the just use of force.'[93] At this stage, clearly, the *Führerprinzip* had not yet clearly emerged. Once it had, Barth could no longer speak like this. He likewise became much more reticent about the concept of 'order', which was co-opted by the German Christians to validate nationalism, so that it is tacit rather than explicit in the ethics he wrote twenty years later.[94]

The state Barth considered under the heading neither of law nor order but of 'humility'. It fulfils its aim and purpose 'by making all responsible for each and each for all through the establishment and maintaining of public law and the control of public education'.[95] It is neither the city of Satan nor the kingdom of God. Concretely we are commanded to confirm the state, 'to affirm and desire it as a sign of obligatory service to the neighbour and to be a sincere and constant citizen of it'.[96] This may well take the form of membership of a party which seeks to improve or alter the state, and in extreme circumstances to overthrow it by revolution. All states share in human corruption, but the task of a state which lives under the divine patience and forgiveness is to protect labour and make it possible, to prevent cartelization, if necessary by nationalization, to protect social structures

---

[91] Ibid., 208; ET, 373–4.

[92] *Ethik* I, 96; ET, 58. Biggar remarks, 'order here does not refer to the coercive order of the State, but rather to the natural order or law by which life is properly communal'. *Hastening*, 53.

[93] *Ethik* I, 414; ET, 244. It is also worth noting that Barth's sexual ethics were clearly at odds with the ethos of the liberal side of Weimar, with which Barth would otherwise identify.

[94] Cf. Barth, *A Letter to Great Britain from Switzerland*, London, Sheldon, 1941, 17.

[95] *Ethik* II, 331; ET, 445.   [96] Ibid., 334; ET, 446.

such as marriage and family, the possibilities of free education and re-- and the free activity of the Church.

The message that students took away from Barth's packed lecture halls was quite unequivocal: of course Weimar is not the kingdom, for that is true of no state, but our task is to engage in all the duties of society in order to forge something more human, more open, and more just. What we have here is a good example of the new objectivity, neither cynical or resigned nor an endorsement of the status quo, but an attempt to work realistically for change.

Eschatology

We have already seen that Barth chose to view Weimar culture within a fundamentally eschatological, which is to say hopeful, framework. Just as there is no ethics without *ein Quentchen Chiliasmus* so there is no eschatology without ethics. The problem with Althaus, Barth said in 1922, the reason that he does not know how the gospel critiques society, is that 'he knows so little how to begin with the *eschatology* of the New Testament'. 'At the basis of the removal of eschatology from ethics there lies the intention of making the former harmless and of removing the latter from the threatening shadow of the former.'[97] In the Münster lectures Barth understands conscience as an eschatological concept which commands us to march out into the future 'to fight, to build, to work, to organise, to fashion things'.[98] The connection between ethics and eschatology was spelled out in his short commentary on 1 Corinthians which was published in 1924.[99]

Barth found in the licence, the confusion and the enthusiasm of Corinth a vivid analogy for Weimar society. This kind of situation has 'something bordering on the end of history about it', it teeters on the edge of the abyss.[100] Do we not stand partly right in the midst of a similar situation?, he asks. How are we to respond to it? Through hysteria, or intuition, or suicide, or a step back into the order of bourgeois religious moderation? No. What is needed is 'a word of redemption . . . in the midst of this human world so full of the Spirit and so full of God, and for that reason so apparently unredeemed'.[101] In chapter 13 (the so called 'agape hymn') we have to realize that we are already in the realm of eschatology, seen from the human stand-

---

[97] Barth, 'Grundfragen', in *Anfänge*, i, 154, 163; ET, 47, 56.
[98] *Ethik* II, 404; ET, 490.
[99] Barth lectured on eschatology at Göttingen, but these lectures still await publication.
[100] Barth, *Die Auferstehung der Toten*, Munich, Chr Kaiser, 1926, 38; ET, *The Resurrection of the Dead*, tr. H. J. Stenning, London, Hodder & Stoughton, 1933, 75.
[101] *Auferstehung*, 39; ET, 75.

point. The theme of chapter 13 is a corporate way, unavailable to the individual, which passes between judgement and promise. Now the problem in Corinth was that religious enthusiasts believed that the kingdom had come already: like Roman Catholics on the right and liberal Protestants on the left.[102] Such a belief leads to two complementary errors. In the first place it overlooks the seriousness of God's struggle against all the powers of death, in which the Christian is caught up. It leads to a 'pious godlessness' in which our enjoyment of religious activity in itself becomes the meaning of Christianity. It misses the point that no complacent Christian satisfaction with the present state of things is possible because the kingdom of God is coming, 'in vollem Gang', under way amongst us, in conflict with all sorts of hostile autonomous powers.[103] Precisely this means that Christianity cannot be a comfortable celebration of religious emotion. 'Because *God* in Christ rules and wills to rule, Christianity is a serious opportunity; *that* is the meaning of faith.'[104] To have faith means to participate in the struggle against the powers of death.[105]

The other error, however, is to throw over the ideas of unity and order, and these have to be insisted on, precisely in the light of the coming kingdom.[106] To have faith is to live in hope in the resurrection of the body, to be set 'right in the middle of the struggle in which the resurrection is truth'. Indeed, the resurrection can be understood only from the standpoint of this struggle.[107] As we have already seen, Barth allowed no ethics without eschatology. Correspondingly, there is no eschatology without ethics. Christians are set in society to proclaim 'the menace and the promise of the Kingdom of God'.[108] In his lecture on 'The Holy Spirit and the Christian Life' in 1929 Barth noted that conscience is an eschatological concept. Given us by the Spirit it compels us to speak and act, no doubt in unexpected ways, but always in hope.[109]

Klaus Scholder speaks of 'the basic mood of desperation' encountered throughout Weimar, after 1928 to the point of hopelessness.[110] It was the eschatological cast of Barth's whole theology which challenged this mood throughout, and the promise of the renewal of all things, the affirmation of all created reality, which grounded the political imperative. In no way was it an expression of a mood which expected nothing of the present, and everything of the future.[111]

---

[102] Cf. the remarks in *Christliche Dogmatik*, 460.
[103] *Auferstehung*, 100; ET, 177.
[104] Ibid., 101; ET, 179.   [105] Ibid., 105; ET, 185.
[106] Ibid., 107; ET, 189.   [107] Ibid., 121–2; ET, 212–13.
[108] *Philippians*, 48.   [109] *Vorträge 1925–1930*, 516 ff.
[110] Scholder, *The Churches 1918–1934*, 7.
[111] So ibid., 49.

THE GOD WHO CANNOT BE COLONIZED:
THE SEARCH FOR A NEW OBJECTIVITY

When Barth turned to the preparation for his lectures on dogmatics in 1923 he found himself drawn to two handbooks of the old Protestant orthodoxy, and adopted formulae, such as the doctrine of the An- and Enhypostasia, which convinced some critics for ever that his programme was a 'return to orthodoxy'. In some quarters Barth's theology is still characterized as 'neo-orthodox'.[112] Dieter Schellong demonstrated many years ago that Barth's agenda is 'modern' through and through, that he is a 'theologian of modenity'. He takes up and seeks to 'overcome' the question of the individual, above all in his treatment of human freedom, he understands the Church as a vanguard movement in relation to the social movements of his time, and his theology is a profound expression of the activist side of modernity: history, act, and change are the fundamental categories of his theology.[113] His adoption of the ancient Christological categories is part of this, and not an exception to it. In his Münster dogmatics Barth remarks that 'The total failure of objectivity [*grosse Unsachlichkeit*] of modern theology cannot be better illustrated than by its horror of this part of the old Christology.'[114] *Unsachlichkeit* meant both a missing of the true theme, *die Sache*, and its replacement by subjectivity. *Sachlichkeit*, on the other hand, meant 'the most exact adaptation of knowing and of knowledge to the peculiarity of its object'.[115] Just as artists like Max Beckmann were seeking for a new realism, profoundly hostile to all sentimentality, so Barth sought to develop the insights of both Romans commentaries by developing a new theological realism, a 'realism determined by the object'. In this respect the theology Barth worked out in Göttingen and Münster was part of the quest for *neue Sachlichkeit*, which, even in the wider fields of literature and art, was never just a question of resignation and pragmatism.[116] To the contrary, the search for a deeper and truer objectivity was not for a moment a purely academic exercise but represented the appropriate theological response to the recognition that the gospel 'touches culture in the deepest and most final way', as he had said in 1921. Responding to the fears of his friend Georg Merz that 'a questionable scholastic autumn' had followed the prophetic spring Barth

---

[112] Paul Knitter may be taken as representative of a whole way of characterizing, or caricaturing Barth. *No Other Name?*, London, SCM, 1985, 80 ff.

[113] D. Schellong: 'Karl Barth als Theologe der Neuzeit' in *Karl Barth und die Neuzeit, Theologische Existenz Hente* (New Series), Munich, Kaiser, 1973, 35–102.

[114] *Christliche Dogmatik*, 353.

[115] Barth, *Unterricht in der christlichen Religion*, i, 10; ET, 8.

[116] As McCormack appears to read it. *Barth's Theology*, 330. In 1945 Barth observed that the objectivity we need is an objectivity which is affirmative of human life. *Theologische Fragen*, 422. Precisely this objectivity is what he found in the ancient Christological doctrines.

,ed: 'Both before and after my commentary on Romans I have gone my
,, and again gone my way, *on the earth*. That means for me concretely . . .
that I have no choice but to take up Christian Dogmatics.'[117] Dogmatics,
in other words, Barth understood to be part of his concrete 'prophetic'
concern.

Barth developed an entire dogmatic in Göttingen which was never published in his lifetime, two volumes of which have so far appeared in the
Gesamtausgabe. We see Barth as teacher here in a way which we do not in the
more polished and heavily revised texts of the later *Dogmatics*. We also see
the clear lines of Barth's later theology emerging. In a book of this kind it is
not possible to provide a detailed commentary on the lectures as a whole.
Rather, I will try to show how they, along with the lectures on Schleiermacher, and other important lectures on theology and church, represent a
struggle for new and responsible realism.

The Failure of Liberal Theology

Barth has some claim to be considered the greatest exponent of Schleiermacher in the twentieth century: exponent, not advocate. He notes in the
introduction to his 1923 lectures that he cannot deal with Schleiermacher
as he dealt with Calvin and Zwingli, 'genetically', because 'love' is the
necessary presupposition for objectivity in such setting in life.[118] Since this is
not his situation with Schleiermacher he proceeds thematically. These early
lectures are devastatingly critical. 'For me the results of this study are fairly
shattering. . . . I was prepared for something bad. But I was not prepared to
find that the *distortion* of Protestant theology . . . was as deep, extensive and
palpable as it has shown itself to be.'[119] In the great lecture on Schleiermacher which began the series on nineteenth century Protestant theology, first
offered at Münster in 1926, he offers a more balanced and open ended critique. The result, however, is the same, namely that what we have in this theology is 'a song of triumph to man, celebrating both his union with God and
his own cultural activity, and necessarily coming to grief in so doing'.[120] The
problem with his Christology is that Christ remains one of a series, a
symbol, a supreme achievement, a revelation in which nevertheless 'we have
a share all the time'.[121] What we have is not an absoluteness of Christ but a

---

[117] *Christliche Dogmatik*, 8. The italics are Barth's. I take *'auf die Erde'* to be an allusion to
Ecclesiastes, which had been Barth's 'text' at Tambach, but I understand it to mean not simply
that both prophets and theologians have to have 'both feet on the ground' (so McCormack) but
that they have a responsibility to the world in which they live.

[118] Barth, *Die Theologie Schleiermachers*, ed. D. Ritschl, Zürich, Theologischer Verlag, 1978, 8;
ET, p. xvii.

[119] Ibid., 461; ET, 259.   [120] Ibid., 410; ET, 230.   [121] Ibid., 190; ET, 103.

supreme relativity. That Schleiermacher makes a symbiosis of what can only be an eschatological synthesis points to a 'heresy of gigantic proportions' which calls for a 'theological revolution'.[122] The remarks in the letters to Thurneysen are stronger still. 'The stuff is really brittle wherever you touch it, a tremendous swindle, which makes one want to shout in anger. But then, the insight that the way taken by this highly intelligent and undoubtedly pious man simply won't go makes the situation clear. But then the question—well, what?—is all the more alarming. It's not enough just to refer to the Reformation.'[123]

In the Göttingen lectures Barth again and again lambasts sentimentality. The way liberal theology ascribes God consciousness to human beings, experiences of transcendence, unavoidable feelings, he told his students, involves 'boundless sentimentality and exaggeration'.[124] Protestant fideism is 'an ugly brew of emotion, experience [*Erlebnis und Erfahrung*] and feeling'.[125] Barth turned against this as savagely as Beckmann, Dix, and Remarque in their own spheres.

As soon as the tide began to turn against Schleiermacher Barth felt the need to right the boat, and the lecture in the series on the nineteenth century is far more appreciative, anticipating the *Nachwort* of forty years later. From these lectures, however, I wish to highlight his treatment of two other thinkers, namely Hegel and Feuerbach.

Hegel is, for Barth, the acme, indeed the true Messiah of modernity.[126] He is this, first, in his self confidence, as 'the man who absolutely and undeviatingly believes in himself', because he identifies his thinking and the things which are thought.[127] This is 'Titanism to the highest degree', but at the same time humility because it is confidence in God. Secondly, it is in rationality that the true nature and dignity of human being is found. With obvious significance for his own theology (probably what he meant by the 'bit of Hegeling' he enjoyed), for Hegel the key to everything is that reason, truth, concept, idea, mind, God, are understood as event. 'Essentially reason and all its synonyms are life, movement, process. God is God only in his

---

[122] Ibid., 192, 462; ET, 104, 259. On the positive side it is important to note that Barth is one of the few Schleiermacher commentators who emphasize his political concern, and more precisely his concern for social equality. Here the nineteenth century should have followed him, but failed to do so. *Theologie Schleiermachers*, 76 f.; ET, 38–9.

[123] B–Th II, 223; ET (*Revolutionary Theology in the Making*), 169. Cf. 207 ff.; ET, 158, where the Christmas eve dialogue is dismissed as 'a "Patmos" of the purest water!'

[124] *Unterricht* i, 99; ET, 82. This is obviously an extension of his view in R2 that theology involves a struggle against kitsch.

[125] *Unterricht* i, 210; ET, 171.

[126] Barth, *Protestant Theology in the Nineteenth Century*, tr. B. Cozens and J. Bowden, London, SCM, 1972, 386.

[127] Ibid., 391.

divine action, revelation . . . as an absolute act, as *actus purus*.'[128] His dialectical method was fashioned as 'a key to open every lock, a lever to set every wheel working at once, an observation tower from which not only all the lands of the earth but the third and seventh heavens too can be surveyed at a glance'.[129] Finally, Hegel brought the conflict between reason and revelation to a conclusion, but at the cost of a deadly abstraction: 'Hegel's living God . . . is actually living man. In so far as this living man is only after all thinking man, and this abstractly thinking man might be a man who is merely thought, and not a real man at all, it is possible that this living God . . . is a merely thinking and merely thought God, before whom real man would stand as before an idol, or as before nothing.'[130] What Hegel offered could only deceive the real concrete human being, and it was the realization of this deception that led to the collapse of the Hegelian faith which was expressed, above all, in 1914. Barth took over the concept of event, but in the service of an understanding of the God who takes form in the most concrete way, in the interests of changing world history.[131]

Just as Hegel reveals the face of modernity which Barth set out to critique so Feuerbach reveals where liberal Protestantism is heading—namely to the deification of humanity, the insight that 'theology long ago became anthropology'. In itself this was a trivial insight, but there are three reasons why Feuerbach is important. First, he throws light not only on liberal Protestantism but on Lutheran Christology and sacramental teaching. Luther insists that we find God in the *man* Jesus, that in the eucharist the communicant partakes of the nature of the risen Christ. 'All of the emphasis points plainly to the possibility of a reversal of above and below, of heaven and earth, of God and man, a possibility of forgetting the eschatological boundary.'[132] To meet Feuerbach's attack we have to know that the human relation with God is in principle irreversible.

Secondly, Feuerbach has an advantage in his determined 'anti-spiritualism'. He was opposed to all abstractions which run out into ideology. And thirdly, his affinity with the ideology of the socialist movement. In his concern with overthrowing those hypostases on which people feel dependent his teaching was an important part of the struggle for emancipation. 'Of the right and necessity of this struggle not only the bourgeoisie glorifying itself with idealistic philosophy but also the Christian Church knew nothing at all.'[133] The 'God' who was rejected by most working people was an ideological fiction of bourgeois idealism, and Feuerbach knew this. 'If only the Church had been compelled before Marx to show in word and

[128] Ibid., 399.   [129] Ibid., 406.   [130] Ibid., 419.
[131] So Schellong, 'Barth als Theologe', 80–6.
[132] 'Ludwig Feuerbach' in *Theology and Church*, 230.   [133] Ibid., 233.

action, and had been able to show, that it is just the knowledge of God which automatically and inevitably includes within itself liberation from all hypostases and idols, which of itself can achieve liberation!'[134] Here, then, was Barth's own understanding of theology and church. Of course Feuerbach would not do, because in the first place he had far too optimistic an understanding of human being, ignorant of evil and death, and because all programmes of self redemption end up with new ideologies and idols. He points up, however, that all theology worthy of the name is both ideology critique and for that very reason, a means of liberation.

Ad fontes

'O this swamp of many hundreds of years in which we are stuck!', Barth exclaimed to Thurneysen, as he struggled to prepare his lectures in Göttingen. 'It is so fearfully hard just to keep *thinking* the opposite always, to say nothing of *speaking* it, or of *formulating* it and setting in *context*.'[135] From the liberal 'swamp' Barth looked for help to 'the old war cry the Reformers understood better and more profoundly than the humanists who first raised it: *Ad fontes!*'.[136] He recommended to his students the works of Bonaventura, Melancthon, Zwingli, and Calvin, but also two nineteenth century handbooks of Reformed and Lutheran dogmatics edited by Heinrich Heppe. 'After much racking of my brains and astonishment I have finally to acknowledge that Orthodoxy is right on almost all points and to hear myself saying things in lectures which neither as a student nor as a Safenwil pastor would I ever have dreamed could really be so.'[137] Discussing options with Brunner he toyed with the Loci method of Melancthon, the Sentence commentaries of the early Middle Ages, the biblical theology of Beck, prophetic theology like Calvin, or Confessional theology. He realized, in an insight that we find again and again in the *Church Dogmatics*, that if one moved too fast in the direction of biblical and Reformed theology the result would be nothing but 'a new mixture of Enlightenment and Pietism'.[138] The way to avoid that was to learn from the Reformers as teachers of the *Church*, which was possible through the vast careful arguments of the seventeenth century. Confronted with a suspicious and somewhat militant Lutheranism in Göttingen, Barth found in the Reformed tradition in particular a number of advantages such as a priority given to God rather than human experience, emphasis on God's freedom, and an equal emphasis on both religious and

---

[134] Ibid., 234.   [135] B–Th II, 252; ET, 183.
[136] *Unterricht* i, 51; ET, 41.   [137] B–Th II, 328; ET, 221.
[138] Barth, 'Zum Geleit' in H. Heppe, *Die Dogmatik der evangelisch-reformierten Kirche*, ed. E. Bizer, Neukirchen, 1935, p. iii. Cited in McCormack, *Barth's Theology*, 335.

ethical elements.[139] At the same time the Göttingen lectures reveal how attentively Barth read Aquinas from the beginning, as well as his nineteenth century predecessors. He mentions Martensen, Lipsius, and Wichelhaus with particular respect.[140]

His respect for tradition notoriously led him even into angelology, not without some initial embarrassment. At the same time he felt free to critique the tradition: constructing a Reformed dogmatics did not involve merely repeating it.[141] Bultmann charged Barth with having failed to enter into debate with modern philosophy, and having naively adopted the patristic and scholastic ontology. 'What you say . . . is beyond your terminology, and a lack of clarity and sobriety is frequently the result.'[142] Barth replied that he had 'come to abhor profoundly' the spectacle of theology constantly trying above all to adjust to the philosophy of its age, 'thereby neglecting its own theme.'[143] He felt it quite possible to use patristic or orthodox formulations without subscribing to the underlying ontology and, as we saw in the last chapter, owned a cheerful 'gypsylike procedure' in relation to all philosophical systems.

Barth's confessionalism did not mean a repristination of the older Christian or Reformed dogmatics, any more than biblicism meant a reproduction of the thoughts of Scripture. Dogmatics listens and learns from the tradition but 'As regards content, it is a free and not a captive science.'[144] Our task is to witness to God's revelation in our situation in the same way that the Reformers did in theirs.[145] It is also formed by rigorous engagement with the present: 'At each moment, in each historical situation, the church has a word to speak . . . Dogmatics must not ignore the present, the moment . . . Naturally, what it has to relate to is not just the political, intellectual, or economic situation but the word which is hidden beneath this surface—the word which the church speaks, or ought to speak.'[146] What is at issue, in dogmatics as in preaching, is 'the Word of God which must be addressed to people today'.

The New Objectivity

What we find, in the Göttingen lectures, and in the letters to Thurneysen, is Barth's struggle to recover a truly rigorous, objective science of theology. His immersion in the orthodox teaching of the seventeenth century, as well

---

[139] McCormack comments that the final result was a combination of Loci and sentence approaches, with Heppe's textbook replacing Lombard's *Sentences*. *Barth's Theology*, 349.
[140] *Unterricht* ii, 101; ET, 390.   [141] Ibid., 186; ET, 456.
[142] B–B, 38.   [143] B–B, 41.   [144] *Unterricht* i, 356; ET, 294.
[145] 'The Doctrinal Task of the Reformed Churches' in *Das Wort Gottes*, 212.
[146] *Unterricht* i, 357; ET, 295.

as in Aquinas and a great mass of other dogmatic teaching, was indispensable in this, but what emerged was something absolutely new. It has the same kind of relation to the past as, say, Chagall's 1938 *Crucifixion* has to the countless Crucifixions of the thirteenth to the sixteenth centuries. The theme is the same. Some of the details are the same. But the perspective, the working, the imaginative construction is radically modern.

Barth's breakthrough to a new theological position in Safenwil was three-cornered: it involved him as a *preacher* trying to make sense of *Scripture* within the context of his social and political *situation*. The Barth–Thurneysen correspondence reveals how they struggled and agonized over preaching, a struggle reflected on in many of Barth's early lectures.[147] It also provided the foundational insight for his dogmatic work. 'Main viewpoints', he wrote in a sketch of his lectures to Thurneysen and friends: 'Dogmatics is consideration of the Word of God as revelation, Holy Scripture, *and Christian preaching*. Thus the primary object is not biblical theology, not church doctrine, not faith, not religious consciousness, but Christian preaching that is actually preached, which on the one hand is to be recognised *as* the Word of God by reference to Scripture and revelation and on the other is to be defined critically *by* the Word of God. Thus the concept of dogmatics: exposition of the *principles* of Christian preaching based on revelation and Scripture.'[148]

In the preface to the second commentary on Romans Barth spoke of the need to get at 'the Word in the words'. The point of dogmatics, he told his Göttingen students, is to investigate 'the meaning or concealed reality within the very ambiguous phenomenon of Christian speech'.[149] The point of this critical investigation is to get free of the swamp of pious feeling. Following Schleiermacher at this point Barth defines preaching very widely, as Christian speech about God, 'from pulpits and in the streets, oral and written'.[150] It is specifically speech about God. Barth recognized that God may speak to us through nature or art or history but we take from the Reformed tradition the truth that preaching is 'God's Word in the present for the future'.[151]

How can this claim be made? Is it not inevitably based on 'my experience as the subject'? What allows it to be said of preaching that 'God has spoken'? The attempt to answer these questions led Barth through the canon, the questions of authority and freedom in the Church, to the doctrines of the Trinity and the incarnation. Using ancient formulae here he actually elaborated Dogmatic Prolegomena in a way that had never been done before. The attempted put down 'neo-orthodox' completely missed

---

[147] E.g. 25.5.1915; 1.1.1916; 11.11.1918; 2.12.21; 9.2.23.
[148] B–Th II, 251; ET, 182.   [149] *Unterricht* i, 30; ET, 182.
[150] Ibid., 34; ET, 28.   [151] Ibid., 44; ET, 35.

the wood for the trees. It saw an affirmation of the canon, or the ancient doctrines of the *an-* and *enhypostasis*, and read an obscurantist retreat back beyond the Enlightenment. In fact Barth took up these ideas in the course of a rigorous attempt to wrestle with the question of hegemony. Are we left on our own? Can we do nothing but give voice to our experience? If so, what help is there for us? Simple assertion that we are not on our own is clearly inadequate. Barth's response, developed in ever greater depth in the three *Dogmatics* of Göttingen, Münster, and Bonn, begins with the self evidence of Scripture. 'Revelation gives rise to scripture and itself speaks in it. This is what makes scripture God's Word without ceasing to be historically no more than the words of the prophets and apostles, sharing the relativity, the ambiguity, and the distance that are proper to everything historical.'[152] Objectivity becomes possible because God in revelation 'becomes a necessary object'. At the same time revelation never becomes something we can appropriate and make our own, as happens in the idea of religious experience. All theology, Barth frankly admits, is a 'begging of the question par excellence'. 'We always have as the theme of this science an axiom, a final and non derivable thing that is grounded in itself and is original in the absolute sense.'[153] This 'axiom' is God's revelation: 'There is nothing more objective than this'. 'To talk about revelation means strictly and exclusively to talk on the basis of revelation. The ontic and noetic basis is one and the same on this matter.'[154]

Reflection on the meaning of the 'Deus dixit' led directly to the central doctrines of Trinity and incarnation. 'In regard to the incarnation,' he wrote to Thurneysen, 'it is best to proceed cautiously so as not to run one's head into the "Jesus Christ" pit of the Lutherans . . . *Essential* Trinity [*Wesentrinität*], not just the economic Trinity. The doctrine of the Trinity above everything! If I could get my hands on the right key there everything would be just fine . . . *Zwischen den Zeiten* would at last become interesting when this battleship shows itself on the horizon!'[155] A month later: 'I am just now in the midst of the mysteries of the Trinity . . . ever again pondering over the runes the ancients have left for us: *essentia, persona, notiones* . . . Don't think . . . that that is old rubbish; all, all of it, seen in the light, seems to have its own good sense. I understand the Trinity as the problem of the inalienable subjectivity of God in his revelation.'[156]

[152] Ibid., 68; ET, 57.   [153] *Unterricht* i, 97; ET, 81.
[154] Ibid., 133; ET, 109.   [155] B–Th II, 245; ET, 176.
[156] B–Th II, 253 ff; ET, 185. This formula appears in *Unterricht* i, 120, ET, 98. Barth tells how he wrestled so concretely with these problems that he dreamed of this 'unheard of subjectivity' *sehr plastisch*. Marquardt remarks: 'This is the experience in which the concept of objectivity was expounded, which has much less to do with theory of knowledge than with its practice.' *Theologie*, 324.

Taking up these doctrines was Barth's way of exploring ho
became 'objective' for us. His placing of the Trinity at the head of do
reflection was, like the identification of preaching as the starting poi
goal of dogmatics, fundamentally new. Barth's insistence on the 'inalienable
subjectivity' of God was directed against either the divinizing of human
beings—as in the Jesus centred piety of Lutheranism—or the humanizing of
God, the true direction of liberal Protestantism, revealed in Feuerbach.
Taking a 'radically unsentimental' view of church history, open to all the
unpleasant and even downright wicked processes out of which the dogma
developed, we still are forced to see that the doctrine of the Trinity is the
Church's way of insisting that in revelation we are dealing with God in
Godself. We are forced to acknowledge the deity of the Son the moment we
acknowledge that through God alone can God be known. But then why a
Trinity? Why not a binity? Because 'God would not be God if the relation to
us were not intrinsic to God from the very first.'[157] The Spirit is the way that
we talk of this intrinsic relation. The doctrine helps to safeguard objectivity
by shifting the focus radically away from the Christian religious self
consciousness.

Asserting that the Son is 'wholly God' forces us in turn to ask how we
make sense of the incarnation of the Son. Barth was especially concerned
to insist, against liberal Protestantism, that we cannot make Jesus 'directly
and nondialectically . . . into an entity that is God'.[158] That, too, finally compromises the truth and objectivity of revelation. The divine incognito has to
be total, for a direct revelation would not be a revelation of the hidden God.
This means, amongst other things, that talk of our having a 'turning point
in world history' in Christ misses the point. 'Where would be the concealment? Where the need for faith in it, and for faith alone?'[159] To guarantee the
indirectness but truth of the revelation in Christ as an act of God Barth
believes we have to go back to the fifth century ideas of the *an-* and *enhypostasis*, the idea that the human person Jesus is wholly formed and constituted by the Word. There are more modern ways of trying to say the same
thing but 'to put it mildly, they rest upon a much less profound and serious
knowledge of the matter'.[160]

The significance of the virgin birth, Barth maintains, in what was to
become a familiar assertion, is the fundamental blow struck at patriarchy.
The sequence which must be broken, restored, and renewed, in economics,
politics, art, and science, is male history. It is crucial therefore that Christ as
male 'cannot participate in the typically male position of a presiding father,
lord and ruler. If he did it would mean a prolonging and continuing of the

---

[157] *Unterricht* i, 157; ET, 128.   [158] Ibid., 147; ET, 120.
[159] Ibid., 182; ET, 148.   [160] Ibid., 206; ET, 167.

old history.'[161] The virgin birth means that the male is 'ejected' from his role as creator.

To be scientific, for Barth, we have seen, means allowing our thinking to be determined by the object. For theology this means 'thinking after' and 'thinking with' Scripture.[162] 'Free thinking with the help of authorities, that's the way we have to go about it.'[163] Authority and freedom—submission to the tradition of the Church, independent contemporary investigation—these were the two arcs drawn by the compass of theological investigation. 'Objectivity' is to be had at the point of intersection. Catholicism has emphasized the first, and liberal Protestantism the second, to the exclusion of the other. The two need regaining together. What is *not* involved is the doctrine of verbal inspiration, an exhibit from 'one of the darkest corners of the orthodox chamber of horrors'.[164]

CHRISTIAN DOGMATICS IN OUTLINE

Barth moved to Münster in October 1925. Münster was very Catholic, and Barth was forced to take Roman Catholicism seriously as a dialogue partner still more seriously than he had in Göttingen, where he had already noted that in many ways it was much closer to the truth than liberal Protestantism. On arrival he completed the lectures he had prepared on eschatology, and then lectured on 'Nineteenth Century Protestant Theology'. His seminars were on Calvin and Anselm. Anselm duly figured more prominently in the Münster *Dogmatics* than he had done in Göttingen, and the method of 'thinking after', which is set out as a methodological principle in the Anselm book, is clearly adumbrated.

When he came to lecture again on dogmatics he found himself once again forced to rewrite everything so that, as he had said about Romans, 'no stone was left upon another'. Bruce McCormack has argued that the main lines of Barth's theological work are anticipated in the Göttingen *Dogmatics*, and that there were not major changes of substance in the two *Dogmatics* which followed.[165] Whilst we can agree with this what we find each time is a massive deepening of the foundations. The early sketches are manifestly by the same artist, manifestly on the same lines, but the detail in the two later works is incomparably richer. Here I shall briefly outline in what ways this 'famous false start', as Barth later called it, differed both from the Göttingen material and the *Church Dogmatics*.

---

[161]   Ibid., 201; ET, 165.   [162]   Ibid., 315; ET, 257.   [163]   Ibid., 317; ET, 260.

[164]   *Unterricht* i, 286; ET, 235. For Catholicism see the lecture: 'Roman Catholicism as a Question to the Protestant Churches' in *Theology and Church*, 307–34.

[165]   McCormack, *Barth's Theology*, 375.

In comparison with the Göttingen material thirteen paragraphs have been expanded to twenty-five, each one with three or four sub-paragraphs. Every section is treated in much greater detail but the greatest expansion is in the account of the doctrine of the Trinity. In the earlier material lectures on the 'Deus dixit' were followed by those on 'man and his question', in which Barth explored the way in which the Word answered the contradiction in which human beings found themselves. Both of these sections disappear in favour of a massive exposition of 'The reality of the Word of God'.

Barth once again began with preaching, understood very broadly, and with echoes of Schleiermacher, as 'Christian speech'—'from the simple words with which a mother teaches her children to the Sunday sermon of the studious pastor, from the religious expressions of the Christian individual to the solemn Summa or Institutio of recognised Church teachers'.[166] It demanded, he emphasizes, 'existential openness, readiness and devotion [*Hingabe*]'.[167] He develops this theme in what he describes as 'phenomenological' fashion.[168] Preaching is always marked by a response to command (it is *auftragsgemässe*), by responsibility, and by the way it calls forth faith and trust.[169]

When, in the fifth paragraph, he turned to the question of 'The Word of God and the Human Being as Preacher' he announced a certain change of course. Hitherto, he says, we have proceeded phenomenologically. Now we must proceed more existentially. The person confronted by the Word is no unconcerned observer. What has been said hitherto relates to a concrete situation, an action in which we are existentially involved. 'Where human beings are really concerned, there the subjective is the objective.'[170] Preaching is the means used by God but also, from our side, a venture, a form of daring. Here the preacher places the hearer before an inescapable 'Thou', which cannot be colonized.

As if I have digested all the world's wisdom, I dare to set in brackets immeasurable nature in all its dimensions and viewpoints, the Sphinx of past and future history, the wonder and the terror of human culture, the puzzle of the individual, sexual and social need, the never ending crisis of abstract thought, guilt and destiny, sickness and death, and deal with it from outside by interpreting it through words such as Creation, sin, redemption, assurance, the kingdom of God, eternity.[171]

It was paragraphs 5 and 6 of the *Christian Dogmatics* with which Barth was most unhappy in retrospect. They are omitted entirely from the *Church Dogmatics* and Barth includes a lengthy account of why this has to be the case. One reviewer had cited the turn from phenomeological to existential

---

[166] *Christliche Dogmatik*, 34. [167] Ibid., 35, 37.
[168] Ibid., 70. [169] Ibid., 33–6.
[170] Ibid., 71. [171] Ibid., 73–4.

thinking and said: 'On this foundation he proposes to build his dogmatics.' Barth was aghast. Neither the lectures on 'Man and his Question' in Göttingen nor these paragraphs on human beings as preachers and hearers of the word of God were in the least designed to predicate dogmatics on an existential analysis, but Barth had to concede that he had given room for such a conclusion. He caught himself advancing an anthropology as the basis for statements about God's Word: 'I was paying homage to false gods, even if only after the manner of the *libellatici* of the Decian persecution.'[172] To begin with the concrete situation is to make the Word a predicate of human being. Such a move he regarded as impossible in the light of human sin: 'There is a way from Christology to anthropology, but there is no way from anthropology to Christology.'[173] At the same time Barth's concern in these paragraphs in the *Christliche Dogmatik*, to emphasize that the Word of God really addresses human beings in their entire life situation, and is no 'purely religious' phenomenon, remained. Furthermore Barth continues his insistence, over against liberal theology, that God meets us as a sovereign Lord, whom we have to obey, and whom we cannot subordinate to our principles, no matter how lofty. It is the doctrine of the Trinity which establishes once and for all that God can only be Lord in our thinking: 'We cannot master God. We cannot come behind God. We cannot grasp God, but only be grasped by God. That is only secured when God is placed over against human beings . . . as *Du*, as the Subject who cannot be colonized [*unauflösliches Subjekt*].'[174]

Again in the *Christliche Dogmatik* it is the fact that God and human beings are incomparable which necessitates dialectic. Reason and religion stand on one side, and faith and revelation on the other. These 'incomparables' cannot be set on the same level but can only be related to one another in a 'strongly dialectical' fashion. Revelation can be understood in analogy, but in no sense in terms of continuity.[175] The incarnation is the model for such understanding, where the unity of divine and human also has to be understood 'strongly dialectically' as unity in difference.[176]

In these *Dogmatics* he uses the concept of *Urgeschichte* which he had used in *Romans*, and in the lecture on 'Unresolved Questions for Today's Theology' in 1920. The meaning here is somewhat different. Barth wants to emphasize that whilst revelation is history it is also more than history. That God speaks with us is the historicity of revelation. 'That it is God in person who speaks with us is its . . . special "more than historicity".'[177] *Urgeschichte* 'has no historical continuity. It is history, but realised directly as the Word of God to the nearest and the furthest times'.[178]

---

[172] KD I/1, 133; CD, 127.   [173] KD I/1, 135; CD, 131.
[174] *Christliche Dogmatik*, 232.   [175] Ibid., 181.   [176] Ibid., 301.
[177] Ibid., 312.   [178] Ibid., 319.

Barth eliminated this usage in his Bonn Prolegomena, once again because he thought it sent a confusing message. 'We may not first of all speak of history in order subsequently or by epithet to speak with force and emphasis about revelation. When the latter happens, we betray the fact that we have gone our own way in interpreting, valuing, absolutising.'[179]

It was only in the interval between this book and the *Church Dogmatics* that Barth finally attained to complete clarity on the need to put reality before possibility—a fundamental strategy of his mature thought. Here, for example, Barth spoke of both the objective and subjective possibility of revelation, only then establishing their reality. In the section on the subjective *possibility* of revelation Barth dealt with the possibility and reality of grace, its conditions, and with baptism as the ground of our knowledge of grace. Karl Heim duly found in this section the question of faith and the answer to 'man in despair about himself'. Once again this was quite against Barth's intentions, but Heim forced Barth to realize that possibility remains in the air so long as it is not a possibility already realized in revelation. Grounded awareness that God's revelation meets human beings 'has first to be regarded simply in its reality, and only then, and on that basis, in its possibility'.[180]

What we can already see emerging in the Münster *Dogmatics* is also the change from an individual, Protestant perspective to a much more church centred one. The second paragraph of the chapter on Holy Scripture was called 'Freedom of Conscience'. We hear God in Scripture, Barth tells us, 'subjectively determined through the concrete freedom of conscience, i.e. in the independent, responsible deed of the individual'.[181] We 'appropriate' Scripture through a threefold process of thinking after, thinking with, and *selberdenken*. This last happens when 'the Word of others becomes my word, when I not only say it is said to me, but that I really say it'.[182] In the *Church Dogmatics* the priority of conscience has gone. The turn away from the individual is foreshadowed in the third form of the dogmatic norm, *Kirchlichkeit*. Dogmatics must be biblical, confessional and 'churchly'. 'Church relatedness' is Barth's name for the responsibility of dogmatics to the present. This is exactly *not* connivance with the *Zeitgeist*, because the Word of God is always engaged in a struggle with the *Zeitgeist*. Dogmatics is no private work, or game, no romantic retreat to the fourth or sixteenth centuries. In dogmatics we do not think practically and parenetically in the same way as the preacher but like the preacher the theologian has to bear all the burdens of her contemporaries. 'Dogmatic thinking and speaking must be full of

---

[179] KD I/2, 64; CD, 58.   [180] KD I/2, 225, CD, 206.
[181] *Christliche Dogmatik*, 506.   [182] Ibid., 513.

homely reality, full of indirect relation to the church militant, with relation
to what should be spoken from pulpits right now. Every dogmatic sentence
must be an arrow which, from no matter how great a distance, is directed to
real life.'[183] This was as important a criterion in Weimar as it was ten years
later, when *Church Dogmatics* I/2 appeared.

THEOLOGY AS A DIALECTICAL SCIENCE

That God truly speaks to us, and does so in Scripture and preaching, gives
Barth both the structure of his Prolegomena, and his account of the task of
dogmatics. In preaching, the relation between God and human beings
takes the form of speech, and it is such speech which forms both the material and the purpose of dogmatics. Dogmatics exists to measure Christian
speech about God against the standard of the scriptural revelation, a
task which involves, as we have seen, a continuous conversation with 'the
living past'.[184]

The need to develop a sharp critique of existing theological trends had
made Barth's Romans commentaries, and especially the second, highly
dialectical. When the new edition of *Suchet Gott* was due out in 1928 Barth
wrote to Thurneysen that he was wondering whether it was a good idea to
show people 'absolutely clearly that the "Dialectic" wasn't cooked up in a
brew of concepts but in a furious attack on the ethics and sensibility of the
older generation'.[185] This attack was intensified all along the line when he
turned to systematic work. Furthermore, he found dialectic at the heart of
the theology to which he turned for guidance. Lecturing on Calvin's 1536
Institutes he notes at every point of his theology a dialectical hinge, in which
every statement is illuminated through a counter statement. This gives us a
highly dynamic theology, always in movement, the force of which is always
that we have to take the vertical and horizontal, the divine and the human
together, to learn to understand God from the human side and human
beings from God's side. For this very reason we always have here a humble
theology which cannot form a system because God, the object of theological reflection, can alone provide system or synthesis.[186]

Barth spelled out what he meant by dialectic in a lecture on 'The Word of
God as the Task of Theology', given at the same time as the Calvin course.
All those who have to speak of God lie under a great embarrassment: we
have to speak of God, but because we are human we cannot do so. What
then? 'We must recognise both, our obligation and our inability, and thereby

---

[183]   Ibid., 566.
[184]   For dogmatics as continuous conversation, see *Unterricht* i, 25; ET, 20.
[185]   B–Th II, 589.   [186]   *Theologie Calvins*, 224; ET, 169.

give God the glory.'[187] As a way of carrying out the obligation Barth recognized three broad routes, dogmatic, critical, and dialectical. The problem with the first is that we are tempted to confuse the dogmatic formulation with the reality itself; the problem with the second is that it can end up with the radical negations of mysticism. We are left, then, with dialectic, 'not only because it is the Pauline–Reformed route, but on account of its objective superiority'.[188] At its heart is the Nicene paradox that the one who is truly God becomes truly human. This God requires dialectic to be brought to speech. The Yes has to be interpreted through the No, and vice versa, without becoming fixated on either. To the exasperated 'plainsman' who wants a straightforward answer the 'hillsman' replies 'I've done what I could to make plain that neither my affirmation nor denial pretend to be the truth of God, but only a witness to the God who stands between all affirmations and denials.'[189] The true answer can only be a question, itself raised by God, because God is the living truth which is both question and answer. This possibility that God might speak is not part of the dialectical way but rather occurs where dialectic breaks off.[190]

In the Göttingen lectures Barth developed these insights to speak of dogmatic thinking as necessarily dialectical thinking, though with a sharp warning not to take dialectic in itself too seriously. 'Do not use it too often,' Barth told his students. 'Learn to be relaxed when you come across it, for it is absolutely unavoidable.'[191] Dialectic is rooted in the distinction between God and human beings: 'Before God human thoughts *become* dialectical.'[192] At this stage Barth links dialectic strongly to the human situation, marked by 'disorder, disruption, curse'. To think dialectically is to acknowledge that we are in contradiction, sinful and fallen. Life itself constitutes a true dialectic: 'Pilgrim man stands between Scylla and Charybdis, between two truths that make each other, and man as a third thing between them, impossible.'[193]

Barth's theology was, from the start, dialectical, but he never had a dialectical method in the sense that, say, Hegel had. Rather, dialectic is partly a mark of the brokenness of all human thought before God but much more the mark of any authentic response to the living God who is always in movement, and whom we can only follow. To this extent I have to disagree both with von Balthasar's account of a 'dialectical period', which is followed by a 'turn to analogy', and with his attempt to root Barth's dialectic within the structure of dialectical thinking in general.[194] Barth's dialectic followed from

---

[187] *Das Wort Gottes*, 158; ET, 186.   [188] Ibid., 170; ET, 206.

[189] Ibid., 173; ET, 209.   [190] Ibid., 174; ET, 211.

[191] *Unterricht* i, 373; ET, 305.   [192] Ibid., 376; ET, 311.   [193] Ibid., 83; ET, 76–7.

[194] von Balthasar, *Theology of Barth*, 73 ff. Cf. McCormack: 'Barth's dogmatic method presupposes an initial dialectical movement of negation in which God's judgement is invited to fall

his subject matter and was never surrendered, though it is true that analogy came to play a much larger part in his theology than it did in the 1920s. There may be analogies between other forms of dialectic and that of Barth, but its function as contradiction and pointer is deeply implicit in the subject matter. It emerges *out of* the pointing finger of John the Baptist, as Barth liked to say, rather than this being an illustration of it.[195] Von Balthasar is on much surer ground when he comments that the absolute actuality of God in revelation, and the alienation of human beings from God through sin, 'radically distinguish Christian revelation from every philosophy about God'. We have to add, also from every dialectical 'scheme'.[196]

Methodologically the 'following' of God's movement involves us in a *petitio principii*. 'To the question—how do you know the Word of God? I answer—I knew it before I know it in that God spoke the Word to me.'[197] The reality of God's self communication is both our presupposition and our conclusion, thus making a starting point in human subjectivity impossible.

Barth's fullest statement of theological method in these years is the complex of lectures which were published as 'Fate and Idea in Theology'.[198] The lectures explore the debt of theology to both realism and idealism. By 'fate' (*Schicksal*) Barth means the idea that God is simply given us, perhaps in our God consciousness or in a world from which we can infer God's identity. By 'idea' he has in mind the critical contribution of idealism. Theology is indebted to both. To realism to the extent that we have to say that God can become an object of knowledge for us, and to idealism because this stresses God's non-objectivity, and reminds us that our thinking and speaking are inadequate. For theology at any rate the relation to a philosophy which respects its limits will not be one of neutrality but a 'deeply instructive working relationship'.[199] What is illegitimate is either for philosophy to attempt to arrogate the place of theology, in which case there has to be 'war to the knife', or for theology to transform itself into philosophy. In either case what is missed is the freedom of God in revelation. The event in which

on all previous efforts (including our own).' *Barth's Theology*, 345. When McCormack says that 'dialectical method would never simply disappear' (346) I agree with the central contention that Barth's theology always remained dialectical but find the term 'dialectical method' misleading.

[195] Barth kept a print of Grünewald's Crucifixion above his desk throughout his life. The artist gave John the Baptist an elongated index finger, with which he pointed to the crucified Christ, which was, for Barth, a fundamental image of the Church, to which he often referred.

[196] von Balthasar, *Theology of Barth*, 81.

[197] *Christliche Dogmatik*, 143.

[198] Barth, 'Schicksal und Idee in der Theologie' in *Theologische Fragen*, 54–92. McCormack demonstrates the extent to which these lectures represent a response to Prywara's formulation of the *analogia entis*. McCormack, *Barth's Theology*, 388–9.

[199] *Theologische Fragen*, 85.

God comes to us is 'strictly momentary'. Theology has to think dialectically because the contradiction in all human existence 'has been placed into the world of thought and existence by God's Word as something it and only it resolves'.[200] The art of theology cannot therefore be synthesis as it legitimately is for philosophy. At the same time, dialectical *method* is not the answer for theology either, because that too can be an attempt to capture God in a theory. Rather it has to realize that it is always justified by faith, that it must begin with the doctrine of election.

THE PRACTICAL SIGNIFICANCE OF THEOLOGY: THE CHURCH IN WORLD OCCURRENCE

The Word which is life and death for all human beings, and not just for Christians, is nevertheless heard in the Church. The renewal of the Church was the point of the whole theological movement, Barth wrote to Thurneysen:

Of course we don't want a *new* church, but the *church* as opposed to sects or our own personal prophecy. Our protest against the church, to the extent that it was any good, was precisely intended to be churchly (*kirchlich*), far more churchly than people from Benz to Grob thought they had to hold against us. It led us first to the Bible and then and in consequence to dogma, and at least to the insight that the proceedings regarding the understanding of the sacraments are not yet closed. It has made church ministry important once more, in principle, first simply as a duty for ourselves, but then in connection with my task here, and as part of any theology worthy of the name.[201]

That the Church has a crucial role to play in world occurrence follows from the fact that the Word is heard there, and its nature and task was the subject of many of Barth's lectures during this period, making it natural for him finally to write a 'Church' (as opposed to 'Christian') dogmatics.

The Church Militant

In his Calvin lectures Barth gave the doctrine of the Church particular attention. He found the key to an understanding of church in the tension between visible and invisible, human and divine. With Zwingli, and against Luther, Calvin laid all the emphasis on the *relation* of God and human beings, and therefore on the sanctified Church, but with Luther against Zwingli also on the 'What?', on the *substance* of this relationship, and therefore on the Church as a believing reality.[202] Of course the doctrine of the

---

[200] Ibid.   [201] B–Th, 318–19.   [202] *Theologie Calvins*, 238.

Church is bound up with that of predestination. We cannot say that predestination is the centre point of this theology, but it is essential to keep it, unlike present day sentimental forms of Swiss and American Reformed theology, because it is a hedge against the moralizing of the gospel.[203] The free election of grace as the constitutive principle of the Church is the dynamite which blows sky high the peace, security, and continuity which we prize as the most essential aspect of church life. Predestination is an eschatological doctrine. Precisely because the Church has its roots in heaven it will take shape on earth, cost what it may, 'in the visibility of the empire of Charles V' (for which we must certainly also read: the Weimar Republic, T. G.).[204] But who are the elect? 'Humility, objectivity [*Sachlichkeit*], prayer is the way one learns whether or not one is elect.' It is not an object of fear but of affirmation, making the point that the Church is truly *God's* Church.[205] Despite all reservations at heart Calvin sought a visible Church, engaged with its contemporary situation, its purpose to honour God in the world, with the advantages, and without the disadvantages, of a sect, a combatant Church, not imprisoned in itself but with a real fighting capacity (*Schlagkraft*).[206]

The insistence on a combatant Church can also be found in the lecture Barth gave to a meeting of the Reformed Alliance in Cardiff in 1925. The Church has to have something to say which concerns people's concrete lives. 'Precisely in its ethical stand, the Church declares unmistakeably to those outside what it is and what it has.' It has to act whilst the issue is still 'hot' and not come thirty years too late.[207]

The church must have the courage to speak today (I mention only one specific problem) upon the fascist, racialist *nationalism* which since the war is appearing in similar forms in all countries. Does the church say yes or no to this nationalism? Does the church, deliberately and in principle, say Yes to war or has it . . . a final, principled No to set on the lampstand? A No which is unqualified and fully audible, not a pacifist's No, but a specifically Christian No against the war?[208]

We have already seen how, in the following year, in the 'Church and Culture' lecture Barth had insisted that eschatological hope, a word of both comfort and criticism, was the proper framework for understanding the culture of the time. Had the Church known this, he concluded, it would have spoken differently both in 1914–18, and at the meeting of the Faith and Order Conference in Stockholm in 1925.

[203] *Theologie Calvins*, 239.   [204] Ibid., 240–1.
[205] Ibid., 242.   [206] Ibid., 249–50.
[207] *Vorträge 1922–5*, 641. On this cf. *Theologie Schleiermachers*, 77; ET, 39.
[208] Ibid., 640; *Theology and Church*, 133.

A Universal, *not* Völkisch, *Movement*

In Germany Barth encountered an identification of church and nation, or rather '*Volk*', which he had never known in Switzerland.[209] The *völkisch* movement gained strength throughout the 1920s, and had many theological representatives. Barth's letters to Thurneysen contain many observations on this theme, especially in the form of fiery exchanges with his Göttingen colleague Hirsch, who represented, at his worst, 'a Prussian betrayal of Christianity . . . a theological paraphrase of Ludendorff's war memoirs'.[210] It is therefore natural that in his Göttingen lectures we find the sharp dismissal of any national church: 'I need hardly say that this office of the church as watchman and leader, which it should discharge every historical moment as an organ of the truth which is truth here and now today . . . should naturally be absolutely free from all national, social, and cultural ties, and is an authority only in such freedom.'[211] In Münster his encounter with the Catholic Church impressed him because, with all its errors, it maintained its hold on the truth of the Church far better than Protestant modernism, not least in its universal nature. When Barth added in an aside that we had to be grateful that Bismarck's name was not added to the list of Protestant saints he found that this remark raised 'a small tempest of indignation, as if I had attacked the sanctuary with a "These are thy gods, O Israel!" '.[212]

In fact *völkisch* ideas were by no means dominant in the Church.[213] What was dominant, at least in official circles, was a feeling of satisfaction at the success of the Church throughout the 1920s which could offer no resistance to these trends and which continued to believe in 'the German soul'. Just before Christmas 1929 an article appeared in the *Kirchliches Jahrbuch* which claimed that in the previous decade 'The divine "nevertheless" has triumphed' over atheists and scornful intellectuals. 'It has been shown that religious thoughts are far more deeply rooted in the German people's soul [*Volkseele*] than had appeared.' The empirical 'church' has held its own. 'The church leadership of the last decade was masterly.'[214] Barth was stung to fury, and wrote a scathing response, published in *Zwischen den Zeiten*, which Thurneysen hailed as 'at last a word spoken to the situation'.[215] 'It is a scandal which cries to high heaven that the German evangelical church constantly talks like this . . . where we have this kind of language, there is Catiline, there is actually the most dangerous conspiracy against the evangelical

[209] B–Th II, 109.   [210] Ibid., 163.
[211] *Unterricht* i, 298; ET, 244.
[212] *Vorträge 1925–1930*, 341; *Theologie Calvins*, 331.
[213] Scholder, *The Churches 1918–1934*, 120.
[214] *Vorträge 1925–1930*, 527.   [215] B–Th II, 696.

church.' In peddling this self satisified opium the church is betrayed. It is only distinguished from all the other groups which muster around flags and banners by the fact that it is more unbroken, cherub faced and unrestrained than they are. It dares to talk like this in the middle of an acute housing shortage and huge unemployment! The Church exists not to praise itself, not to win youth or the workers, or to keep one eye on the German soul, but to preach the gospel fearlessly. When this Church says 'Jesus Christ' all that is heard is its own self satisfaction and security, and the real needs of real people are ignored.[216]

The General Superintendent of the Prussian church, Otto Dibelius, who was partly in view in this article, responded vigorously and heated controversy now ensued. Scholder believes that two views of the Church were at issue here: that of the church leaders, keen to set standards for public life, on the one hand, and that of Barth, aimed exclusively at the individual on the other.[217] He quotes in support a passage from *Die Christliche Dogmatik* in which Barth notes that God addresses human beings in the centre of their humanity, in their naked humanness, and therefore as individuals. Barth writes: 'Anyone who wants to avoid a German theology, a youth theology or a theology of the proletariat, in other words a polytheism, will have to be very hard hearted here.'[218] He goes on to quote Galatians 3.28. Scholder misses the entire point of this passage, which is not in the least intended to prevent the 'realization of the proclamation' but to insist that the Church cannot be the possession of competing groups, but is truly universal. In his dogmatic work throughout the 1920s Barth was laying the foundations for the struggle against fascism which was to follow.

BARTH: CRITIQUE AND CONSTRUCTION IN WEIMAR

Richard Roberts, reading Weimar purely as a period of unparalleled crisis, argues that Barth created, in response to this, 'an eschatological discourse, a rhetoric of the dialectics of God and negation, which answered immediate contemporary needs with extraordinary efficiency'.[219] When the times changed, however, he was left behind and became a prisoner to this rhetoric. The reading proposed here is very different, partly because the understanding of the Weimar period is so different. Of course, the period to the end of 1923 was one of great crisis, but from the start there were those who were hopeful. In response to this Barth argued first, against the cynics and

[216] B–Th II, 531–4.
[217] Scholder, *The Churches 1918–1934*, 124.   [218] *Christliche Dogmatik*, 92.
[219] R. H. Roberts, 'Barth and the Eschatology of Weimar' in *A Theology on its Way?: Essays on Karl Barth*, Edinburgh, T. & T. Clark, 1991, 175.

the pessimists, the highbrow *Vernuftrepublikaner*, that there is no theology without ethics, and that this entailed patient humdrum work for the building up of the common good. Secondly, against the ideologues, and in particular those in the Church, people like Hirsch, whose *Deutschlands Schicksal* he read before even arriving in Göttingen, he developed the insight gained in Safenwil, that theology involves an attack on idols, namely, ideology critique. But ideology critique is quite ineffective if there is not something better to put in its place: hence ten years spent largely on architectural sketches and foundations, digging to substantiate the insights already won through to. 'The concern of the Word of God is daily life.' For Barth there could not be a divide between practical and dogmatic theology because there is nothing more practical, more vital for every human concern, than God's Word. For this reason, on both fronts, the theology of this period is political theology.

But are Roberts and von Balthasar right in characterizing Barth's theology in this period as 'dialectical theology'? 'Dialectical theology', wrote von Balthasar, 'is expressly designed for a journeying People of God who are merely on their way to God but not there: a *theologia viatorum*.'[220] This is well said, though the 'merely' expresses the opposition of an entire theology—and a pre-Vatican II theology at that. To call a theology dialectical, I have tried to argue, is simply to draw attention to the necessary brokenness of all human language in talking about God, in attempting to follow a journeying God. In this sense analogy cannot replace dialectics. As Barth put it in the *Christliche Dogmatik*, God can speak an undialectical Word: 'We, however, are human beings. That is the simple and decisive ground for the exclusive possibility of dialectical theology.'[221] But Barth from the start kept a cool distance from any notion of a school of dialectical theology, and most certainly never committed himself to any dialectical principle. What he was trying to do in these years, by way of critique and construction, was to find a proper theological response to hegemony. Like his contemporaries he was searching for a *neue Sachlichkeit*, a new sense of reality. In his exchange with Harnack Barth ackowledged that he wished to replace a determinative object for the determinative method of liberal theology.[222] The struggle to see what lay at the heart of liberal theology, which led Barth through the Schleiermacher lectures, and the lectures on 'Protestant Theology in the Nineteenth Century', was an effort at diagnosis, to understand what it was which led a theology to become captive to its culture. Part of the diagnosis was that it was fatal to become captive to philosophical categories. This led Barth to be deeply suspicious of Brunner and Gogarten's enthusiasm for

[220] von Balthasar, *Theology of Barth*, 79.   [221] *Christliche Dogmatik*, 583.
[222] *Revelation and Theology: An Analysis of the Barth–Harnack Correspondence of 1923*, ed. H. M. Rumscheidt, London, Cambridge University Press, 1972, 41.

␣ner's I–Thou categories and of Bultmann's enthusiasm for Heidegger. By February 1930 Barth had had enough. He saw the theology of Bultmann, Brunner, and Gogarten forming a pattern: 'From my standpoint all of you, though your concern differs from mine in different ways, represent a large scale return to the flesh pots of Egypt . . . all of you—in a new way different from that of the nineteenth century—are trying to understand faith as a human possibility . . . and therefore you are once again surrendering theology to philosophy.'[223] Not to do that was one of Barth's most pressing concerns, for he was sure that it ended up in submission to a new form of hegemony. 'Where people play around with a natural theology and are so eager to pursue theology within the framework of a preunderstanding that has not been attained theologically, the inevitable result is that they end up in rigidities and reactionary corners which are no better than the liberalism of others . . . where this happens, I would rather be in hell with the religious socialists than land up in the heaven in which it will be one's lot to be condemned to a "state of life" for all eternity, to have to gaze at a "Thou" that is foreordained by creation.' We can see that the stage is already set for the theological confrontation with fascism which was to dominate the coming decade.

[223] B–B, 49.

4

The Struggle against Fascism

March 1930—December 1941

> It was on the truth that God is one that the 'Third Reich' of Adolf
> Hitler made shipwreck . . . Beside God there are only His creatures or
> false gods, and beside faith in Him there are religions only as religions
> of superstition, error and finally irreligion.
>
> Karl Barth, 1939

HITLER'S SEIZURE OF POWER AND THE POSITION
OF THE CHURCHES

Barth moved to Bonn in March 1930, already deeply concerned about
both political and theological developments. The last months of 1929 saw
growing unemployment in Germany, and gains in local elections for
both Communist and National Socialist candidates. The centre government
formed at the end of March 1930 was committed to radical fiscal reform.
When this was rejected by the Reichstag new elections were called for September in which the National Socialist vote rose from the 809,000 of two
years previously to nearly 6.5 million. With 6 million unemployed there was
widespread and serious poverty which Hitler played on with promises of
restoring work, bread, and order. In the following year street violence, in
which Hitler's *Sturmabteilung* (the SA) took a leading part, directed first
against socialists and Communists, and then against Jews, was almost inces-
sant. Barth took this opportunity to join the main opposition party, the
Social Democrats. The SA were briefly banned in 1932 but their relegaliza-
tion prior to July elections of that year led to 120 deaths in five weeks. The
collapse of all interim governments led to Hitler's being made chancellor in
January 1933. The Reichstag was burned down on 27 February, almost certainly by the SA and SS, but it was blamed on Communists. During that
night 4,000 Communists were arrested and interned and a state of emergency declared. March elections still did not give the National Socialists an
overall majority but an Enabling Act was passed with the aid of the Catholic
Centre Party and the Bavarian People's Party, and Hitler became dictator on

the 23rd of that month. Four million people had voted Communist but their deputies either were arrested or fled. The SPD was banned in June and by the next month the National Socialist party was the only political party in Germany.

Commenting on the situation in the SPD the historian of the German resistance, Peter Hoffmann, remarks that after January 1933 'everything was confused, politically obscure and undefined; no one knew what to do'.[1] This confusion puts the church resistance in a relatively good light. Here the source of weakness was that both Roman Catholic and Protestant churches were affected by *völkisch* ideas which drew popular support from the perceived injustice of the Versailles treaty. This was especially a problem for the Protestant churches whose origin was bound up with the emergence of German identity. Martin Luther was not just a Reformer but also a national hero, and as such was co-opted by the right. The idea of a church which would give expression specifically to the German soul was already current by the end of the 1920s and found solid academic support from the likes of Althaus and Hirsch. Matters were stirred up by the call of Barth's ally Gunther Dehn to a Chair in Halle in 1931. Three years previously he had criticized Germany's role in the First World War. This provoked vigorous nationalist attacks at the time which were now renewed and included attacks in the Press by Hirsch and others. Reluctant at first to intervene Barth finally published a response in February 1932 in the *Frankfurter Zeitung*, in an article entitled 'Why Not Attack along the Whole Line?'. He read the opposition to Dehn as a veiled attack on dialectical theology. Hirsch responded, as Gogarten was later to do, by alleging that Barth's theology was purely speculative and lacked roots in the historic structures essential to human existence, a failure he traced to Barth's republican Swiss roots.[2]

The first step in the emergence of the Confessing Church was taken in the northern city of Altona. A Nazi rally prior to the elections of July 1932 provoked conflict with the Communists which left 17 dead and many wounded. The local church arranged emergency church services which protested these events and set up a commission under the chairmanship of the Lutheran Hans Asmussen to think about the next step. Its report, in January 1933, significantly anticipates the Barmen declaration. As Scholder notes, 'The long road from the Tambach lecture . . . the road from dispute in the church and about the church to the confession of the church, the road of Karl Barth's theology, here issued in a new perception of itself by the church.'[3]

---

[1] P. Hoffmann, *The History of the German Resistance*, tr. R. Barry, Massachusetts, MIT Press, 1979, 6.

[2] It meant, he said, that Barth could not respond to German realities as someone would who was a German through and through (*von der Wurzel bis zum Wipfel*).

[3] Scholder, *The Churches 1914–1934*, 185.

Likewise in 1932 the German Christians made their first public appearance, founding their own newspaper in October, *Evangelium im Dritten Reich*. Taken together the Catholic and Protestant churches were an enormously important force in German life and Hitler knew he had to reckon with them. His ultimate aim, as Scholder has shown, was their destruction, but meanwhile he moved carefully.[4] He concluded a concordat with the Catholic Church in September 1933, but the Protestant churches, with no centralized authority, were more of a problem. In April 1933 Hitler proposed the formation of an Evangelical Reich Church, and appointed the naval chaplain Ludwig Müller to coordinate affairs. The appointment and then the fall of Bodelschwingh as Reich bishop provoked Barth's pamphlet *Theologische Existenz Heute!*, in June 1933, which sold 12,000 copies in the first month and 37,000 copies before it was confiscated a year later. The next month the temperature was raised by church elections. Hitler himself intervened, declaring on a nationwide radio broadcast both that the state demanded the support from the churches which it needed 'for its existence' and that the National Socialist state guaranteed the 'inner freedom of the religious life'.[5] The result was a huge victory for the German Christians. One of the people who clearly understood the significance of this was Martin Niemöller, who at once demanded 'a modern confession' to counter this movement. In September he was instrumental in founding the Pastors Emergency League in response to the Prussian Church's adoption of the 'Aryan Paragraph', according to which neither non-Aryans nor those married to non-Aryans could be employed for service in the Church.

Despite German Christian success in the elections, the extent of the support that church opposition to Hitler enjoyed was evident when Barth travelled to Berlin to speak at the Reformation festival on 30 October, on 'The Reformation as Decision'. Though the lecture was not advertised the hall (in the Academy of Singing!) was packed. Barth spoke of the Reformation as the decision to recognize the rule of God as absolute. At any given time there are other possibilities besides faith—morality, reason, humanity, culture. Today it was *Volkstum* and the state. All of these involve the same disloyalty to the Reformation decision, which had now reached its most consummate form. Strengthened by the Reformation teaching those who have not succumbed to the movement have to offer resistance. At this word, 'resistance', tremendous applause broke out for several minutes. Resuming, Barth appealed to an old Swiss story of resistance to the Austrian army, when one of the Swiss had cried out: 'Smite their spears, for they are

---

[4] For Hitler's view of Christianity see Scholder, *Requiem for Hitler*, 180.
[5] Scholder, vol. 1, 446.

hollow!'. And Barth continued: 'They *are* hollow!'. This story became a watchword for the Confessing Church.

In December a free Reformed Synod was called, which actually met at the beginning of January 1934. Barth's lecture at this event was a precursor of the decisions taken at Barmen in May. Affirmation of the sole sufficiency of revelation and the rejection of natural theology stood at the heart of the address:

> The church has its origin and its existence solely from revelation, from the authority, the consolation and the guidance of the Word of God, which the Eternal Father has uttered once and for all in Jesus Christ, the Eternal Son, in the power of the eternal Spirit, when the time was fulfilled. This is a rejection of the view that apart from the revelation of the Triune God the church may and must base itself upon and find recourse to divine revelation in nature and history.[6]

Barmen itself was a key moment in the church struggle, and yet theological differences, especially over the relation of church and state, continued to dog the Confessing Church. From the start the Lutherans had difficulties with it on account of their doctrine of church and state. A synod in Dahlem in October clarified the significance of Barmen for church law but to Barth's dismay these decisions were overturned in November, partly on account of Bishop Marahrens, who regarded Barth as the principal threat to the Church in Germany and who believed that the Nazi world view was binding on every Evangelical Christian. Quite apart from the church struggle Barth was also affected by the Nazi seizure of power as a Party member and academic. Membership of the SPD was prohibited in 1933 and though Barth refused to take advice and resign from it, it quickly became a dead letter.[7] Non-Aryans were removed from university posts in 1933. In that year Tillich published his *The Socialist Decision*, and then emigrated to the United States, along with virtually all of the scientists of the Max Planck institutes. Leading literary and artistic figures such as Thomas and Heinrich Mann, Käthe Kollwitz and Ricarda Huch resigned their membership of the Prussian Academy of Arts. Huge book burnings of the works of Marx, Heine, Freud, Remarque, Kästner, Tucholsky, and others took place in 1934. This forms the background of Barth's own dismissal, part of a purge in which 45 per cent of academic posts changed hands by 1938.

---

[6] Cited in Scholder, *The Churches 1914–1934*, 581.

[7] Barth's exchange with Tillich on this question is most instructive. Barth joined the Party, he said, because it was the party (1) of the working class, (2) of democracy, (3) of antimilitarism, (4) of a conscious but judicious affirmation of the German people. Precisely because he could not 'confess' socialism as a world view he felt obliged to remain a member, as an exercise of his God given freedom to adopt purely political decsions. It is the question of freedom which is crucial. Text in Hunsinger, *Barth and Radical Politics*, 116–17.

Barth's dismissal was connected with the Hitler oath. When Hindenburg died in August 1934 Hitler became both chancellor and president and required an oath of allegiance from all state officials, who included university teachers. Barth agreed to give the oath only when qualified by the phrase, 'within my responsibilities as an Evangelical Christian'. The expression of this reservation was sufficient cause for dismissal. Appeals lasted until June 1935, but a negative outcome then resulted in his move to Basle.

In hindsight the move to war in the next four years seems inevitable, but this was notoriously not the case for many contemporaries, whose war weariness Hitler was able to exploit as he moved steadily towards his first goal of acquiring more *lebensraum* for Germany. In 1938 Austria was annexed and the Munich treaty surrendered the Sudetenland to Hitler. The destruction of Jewish synagogues and property, the *Krystallnacht*, took place on 9 November of that year. In March 1939 what remained of Czechoslovakia was occupied. The attack on Poland in September prompted the Second World War.

Back in Basle Barth had greater freedom to intervene politically and did so with increasing frequency and vehemence. He published yearly updates on the German church struggle in the Swiss press. From 1938 onwards appeared what became a celebrated series of letters, first to the evangelical theologian Hromadka in Prague, and then to French and Dutch pastors, and to the Church in Britain, in which Barth insisted on the need to resist Hitler. This was taken seriously enough in Germany for all his work to be banned there in October 1938. In 1941 the Reich authorities protested in a diplomatic note about Barth's anti-German stance. This was also far from welcome to the Swiss government, which until well into the war carefully sat on the fence and sought to preserve its position in the event of a final German victory. A number of these open letters, and some of his lectures, were censored, and Barth was also publicly rebuked by Basle university.

Throughout this period it is fair to say that the struggle with Fascism, recognized as a struggle for humanity, was uppermost in the minds of most people in Europe, and Barth was no exception. Six volumes of the *Dogmatics* were either completed or under way from 1931 to the end of the war, but this did not mean that Barth had his head down and was indifferent to what was going on in the wider world. It was not just his more overtly political lectures and publications, let alone his service in the Swiss frontier guard during the war (of which he was certainly proud) which constituted Barth's practical contribution to the struggle. He considered dogmatics the most practical, and therefore political, of all activities.[8] It was not, he wrote in

---

[8] KD i / 1, 77; CD, 76.

hat he suddenly began to write explicitly political material, but ῀..ange in the political situation gave his familiar insistence on the first commandment and on the critical significance of Scripture a new cast.[9] It is essential to understand this correctly. Noting the responsibility of church proclamation in *Church Dogmatics* I/1 (written in 1931) he writes,

Church proclamation ... cannot let itself be questioned as to whether it is in harmony with the distinctive features and interests of a race, people, nation or state. It cannot let itself be questioned as to its agreement with the demands of this or that scientific or aesthetic culture. It cannot let itself be questioned as to whether it is contributing what is needed to maintain or perhaps even to overthrow this or that form of society or economy. A proclamation which accepts responsibilities along these or similar lines spells treachery to the Church and to Christ himself. It only gets its due if sooner or later its mouth is stopped by some refined or brutal ungodliness.[10]

The first sentence here is clearly directed against German political theology. The third seems to represent a disavowal of any political responsibility on the part of theology, an impression some believe to be confirmed by the angry language of the farewell from *Zwischen den Zeiten* written two years later. Barth observed there that just as some traced his departure from the 'dialectical theology' group to his Reformed origins so others saw his politics behind all his church political decisions:

I warn you. Of course I have my own thoughts on these matters. But if I were really to be interpreted from that standpoint then I could damage the German religious socialists as badly as I did in 1919, as Ragaz bears witness; then my theological and church affinity with Marxism and Liberalism and so forth during these notorious fourteen years must somehow or other become visible; then at this time, and in this year 1933, those of my audience now politically victorious, and committed in quite an opposite direction to myself, will have to demonstrate this evil causal connection and conduct themselves accordingly. One can demonstrate this connection from my books, essays and sermons, if one can, or enquire in Göttingen, Münster and Bonn what I have and have not done, but only then pursue, if possible, this talk about my political background. Until this is done I consider it conduct unworthy of gentlemen.[11]

The shrill tone warns us that there is more than theological argument going on here. Just five years later he wrote in *The Christian Century*: 'The abstract, transcendent God, who does not take care of the real man . . . the abstract, eschatological waiting, without significance for the present, and the just as

---

[9] Barth, *How I Changed my Mind*, Edinburgh, St Andrew Press, 1969, 46.

[10] KD I/1, 73; CD, 72.

[11] Reprinted in K. Kupisch (ed.), *Der Götze Wackelt*, Spennr, Waltrop, 1963, 68–9; cf the comments in Jüngel, *Barth*, 40–1.

abstract church, occupied only with this transcendent God, and separated from state and society by an abyss—all that existed, *not* in *my* head, but only in the heads of many of my readers.'[12] Unsurprisingly we find in much of Barth's writing during his last two years in Germany an attempt to guard his position. Barth wanted to stay in Bonn and was well aware that outright opposition to the regime would spell his immediate departure. At the same time he is completely in earnest in denying that his theology is at the disposal of any political movement—even the anti-Fascist movement. This is not to say that theology does not have political consequences. It does, but precisely as *theology*. This is what any exposition of Barth's theology in these years has to make clear.[13]

DOGMATICS AS SCIENCE AND STRUGGLE

We saw in the last chapter how Barth worked out his break with *Kultur-Protestantismus* in terms of an attempt at a new theological objectivity, through a doctrine of the Word of God, and a restatement of the doctrines of the Trinity and the incarnation. In the course of Barth's reworking, 'Christian' dogmatics became 'Church' dogmatics. Barth adduces as reasons for doing this his dislike of 'lighthearted use of the great word "Christian"' which he had protested about in the 1929 lecture on 'The Holy Spirit and the Christian Life'.[14] Materially, however, he wished to show that dogmatics 'is not a free science. It is bound to the sphere of the Church, where alone it is possible and meaningful'.[15] This represented a final move away from the liberal Protestantism which was preoccupied above all with the individual.

In the semester immediately prior to his reworking of the Prolegomena Barth studied Anselm again, and wrote his famous 'treatise on method' in the summer of 1930. Barth later liked to direct people to it as a 'key' to reading the dogmatics, and this is where we shall begin.

[12] Reprint of the 1938 article in Barth, *How I Changed my Mind*, 48.

[13] George Hunsinger puts this well: 'It is not salvation which is to be accounted for in terms of social action, but social action which is to be accounted for in terms of salvation. Salvation is conceptually prior to and independent of social action, and social action is conceptually subsequent to and dependent on salvation.' *How to Read Karl Barth*, Oxford, Oxford University Press, 1991, 142.

[14] 'Der heilige Geist und das christliche Leben', in H. Barth and K. Barth, *Zur Lehre vom heiligen Geist*, Munich, Kaiser, 1930, 39–105; ET *The Holy Ghost and the Christian Life*, tr. R. Birch-Hoyle, London, Frederick Muller, 1938, 92–3. Barth criticized the use of the word as an adjective applied to art, world views, parties, newspapers, and societies, etc.

[15] KD I/1, p. vii; CD, p. xiii.

Anselm

For some critics the dialectics which remained a feature of Barth's mature theology were a sign of capitulation to irrationality. Barth finds adherents, noted Paul Schempp in 1928, 'because his theology corresponds more to the contemporary spiritual situation than do other theologies, because the *sacrificium intellectus* satisfies those who have little to sacrifice here, because the paradoxicality seems to be profound'.[16] The accusation was that Barth's theology was but part of the exaltation of irrationality which was the other side of the 'community of reason' in Weimar.[17] But, as we have seen, Barth's insistence on dialectic and the theological *petitio principii* was precisely his attempt to be rigorous, to escape from that swamp of the identification of theology with religious psychology which his senior colleague at Göttingen, Wobbermin, had got stuck in, and to overcome the idealism which characterized liberal theology.[18] Barth had struggled to set out a new theological method from 1923 onwards. To make matters absolutely clear he decided to lay it out *more geometrico* in his study of Anselm in 1931.

As with Calvin, Barth had studied Anselm intensively as a student, and he ran a seminar on him in 1926, and then again in 1930, stimulated especially by a lecture of his Münster friend Heinrich Scholz. The two originally planned a double publication, but only Barth's appeared. In a brilliant *tour de force*, against the grain of all previous readings, Barth argued that, so far from Anselm providing a foundation for natural theology through the ontological argument, his *Proslogion* presupposed the objective givenness of God which then called for obedient but rational exploration. Anselm is not seeking to 'prove' at all, but simply to understand, and he sets out to do this through the Credo of the Church, which includes Scripture. Only such a positive (as opposed to speculative) theology is possible. 'Anselm is distinguished from the "liberal" theologians of his time in that his *intelligere* is really intended to be no more than a deepened form of *legere*. But—and this distinguishes him just as definitely from the "positivists", the traditionalists of his day—it does involve a deepened *legere*, an *intus legere*, a reflecting upon.'[19] This was the decisive methodological move of the book. It represented Barth's account of what 'faith seeking understanding' meant.

---

[16] Cited in Scholder, *The Churches 1914–1934*, 49.

[17] See Gay, *Weimar Culture*, 66.

[18] *Christliche Dogmatik*, 398.

[19] *Anselm: Fides Quaerens Intellectum. Anselm's Proof of the Existence of God in the Context of his Theological Scheme*, tr. I. Robertson, London, SCM, 1961, 41.

That theological method involves thinking through (*nachdenken*) what has already been given us in revelation had been implied as early as the Preface of the second *Romans* and thoroughly adumbrated in Göttingen and Münster.[20] Here he makes it a manifesto. Barth distinguishes noetic, ontic, and ultimate levels of rationality. The noetic level refers to our capacity to order experience, but this depends for its rationality on the ontic level—in this case, the rationality of Scripture, the creeds and Confessions. In turn, however, this ontic rationality is derived from the source of all rationality, God.[21] Theology is a rational enterprise because it is reflection on God's self-communication, attested in human words in Scripture and preaching. It is the attempt to understand this self-communication, to penetrate from the outer text to the inner text of Scripture. Theology begins where biblical quotation stops.[22] It is the attempt to think through what is given us in Scripture until its essential rationality becomes manifest, and it is this process of reflection which prevents theology from being a merely positive science.[23] The heart of Barth's dogmatic method is thus taking seriously the fact that God is known through God alone, and that therefore reality precedes possibility.

This account might confirm suspicions that Barth's theology is after all purely an affair of the Academy. Sabine Plonz has shown, however, that even this most abstract of Barth's productions has a practical turn. The Anselmian 'proof' integrates the questions of knowledge and existence in that all reality is grounded in God. The argument is directed against metaphysical speculation, against a God who might or might not be. In place of such a being is the God who is objectively given over against us. But this insistence on God's objectivity makes it impossible, for faith seeking understanding, not to recognize the concrete objective action of the Creator. She discerns an analogy between Barth's reading of the argument and the first commandment in the Hebrew Bible. In both, confession of the Name, action, the exclusion of other gods and the demand for obedience are bound together. The question then is not—How can God be known?, but—To what extent do we know God?[24] The answer to that question is only given in praxis. Marquardt draws attention to the analogy between the concerns of Barth's theological method and Marx's second thesis on Feuerbach: 'The question whether objective truth can be attributed to human thinking is not a question of theory but is a practical question. Man must prove the truth,

---

[20] McCormack's conclusion is therefore just: we have in *Anselm* 'at most a *relatively* more faithful unfolding' of the method Barth was already employing. McCormack, *Barth's Theology*, 441.

[21] *Anselm*, 44–5.   [22] Ibid., 31.   [23] Ibid., 41.

[24] Plonz, *Herrenlosen Gewalten*, 252–3; 344.

i.e. the reality and power, the this-worldliness of his thinking in practice. The dispute over the reality or non reality of thinking which isolates itself from practice is a purely scholastic question.'[25] Plonz comments, 'Barth's reflections in his Anselm book point to a "proof of truth" on the basis of the objective (*in intellectu et in re*) knowability of God. The concept of knowledge itself can . . . only be understood as a process of active participation in the movement of the kingdom of God, that is, as a unity of theory and praxis.'[26] This unity is the starting point of his dogmatic prolegomena.

Dogma and Hegemony

The doctrine of the Word of God, Barth's dogmatic prolegomena, takes the form of a massive reflection on revelation—on the Triune God who is Lord of the whole process of revelation, on Scripture, and on proclamation. This huge exposition is topped and tailed by an account of the task and nature of dogmatics in which Barth strenuously wards off all forms of hegemonic discourse.

It is in this sense that we are to understand the combative remarks of the opening paragraphs of 1/1, where Barth insists that dogmatics only accepts the law of non-contradiction in a severely limited sense, and that theology has nothing whatever to learn about method in the school of the secular sciences.[27] If theology accepts the designation of 'science' it does so as a protest against a concept of science which is 'admittedly pagan' and which manifests a 'quasi religious certainty'.[28] The task of theological science is the self examination of the Church, the attempt to see whether the language of the Church is faithful to Christ. Unlike every other science it presupposes faith, and it is thus an activity which happens only within the Church: dogmatics is *church* dogmatics. We recognize, of course, that God can speak through an unlimited variety of means—through Russian communism, a dead dog, or a flute concerto, but the Church's task is exposition of the Word of God, whose threefold form is the incarnate Word, Scripture and proclamation.[29]

The aim of dogmatics, then, is to unfold and present the content of this Word—but not in terms of a system, which would negate the obedience in

---

[25] K. Marx and F. Engels, *Collected Works*, v, Moscow, Progress, 1975, 6; Marquardt, *Theologie*, 277.

[26] Plonz, *Herrenlosen Gewalten*, 346.

[27] KD 1/1, 6; CD, 8.   [28] KD 1/1, 10; CD, 11.

[29] Barth claims that it is Tillich's failure to distinguish these questions which makes his teaching 'ultimately irrelevant' as a contribution to the task of theology KD 1/1, 55; CD, 55.

which it has to prove its freedom. 'Essentially dogmatic methc
openness to receive new truth, and only in this.'[30] This obviously ru.
to safeguard theology from every form of hegemony but the reason for th.
openness is the living nature of the subject of theology. The object of theology 'stands outside and above all possible viewpoints from which human
beings can attempt to survey and master it'.[31] Barth returned to the image
of the empty space which he had used in *Romans*. There is an empty space
at the hub of the wheel of Christian doctrine which is reserved for the
present speaking of God's Word here and now. 'In the last resort we may say
that dogmatic method consists simply in this: that the work and activity of
God in His Word are honoured and feared and loved (literally) above all
things.'[32]

Proclamation must speak to the present—*reality* (*Wirklichkeit*) is one of its
marks. It is responsible. But not only can it not be questioned as to whether
it is in harmony with the distinctive features and interests of a race or state,
but it cannot seek to contribute to the establishment or overthrow of this or
that society or economy. 'Just because of its real responsibility Church
proclamation must be unconditionally free in every other area.'[33] Of course,
we have to recognize that the fulfilment of its intention to be the Word of
God may very well result in the overthrow of a particular regime but Barth's
point is that this cannot be the central theme of proclamation. Its one
concern is to be faithful.

The key to the Church's ability to resist hegemony is the existence of
Scripture. Against both the appeal to the religious self consciousness of neo-
Protestantism, and the teaching office of the Catholic Church it is in Scripture that we have a pronouncement which is not the Church's dialogue with
itself, but an address to the Church. As a canonical text Scripture has the
character of a free power. 'After any exegesis propounded in it . . . [the
Church] has to realise afresh the distinction between text and commentary
and to let the text speak again without let or hindrance.'[34] The Bible is 'the
absolute authority set up over against Church proclamation'. This is not,
however, simply in view of the nature of Scripture as text, nor with its
use by the community but in virtue of God's act through it. 'The Bible is
God's Word as God causes it to be his Word.'[35] Dogma, by contrast, is the
agreement of church proclamation with the revelation attested in Scripture
and as such a limiting or eschatological concept, something we aim at but
never achieve this side of the kingdom.[36]

We cannot defend the position of Scripture as a witness to revelation with

---

[30] KD 1/2, 962, 970; CD, 860, 867.   [31] KD 1/2, 969; CD, 866.
[32] KD 1/2, 990; CD, 867.   [33] KD 1/1, 73; CD, 72.   [34] KD 1/1, 109; CD, 107.
[35] KD 1/1, 112; CD, 109. Webster, *Barth's Ethics*, 31–2, makes this point very clearly, and I
draw on his discussion here.   [36] KD 1/1, 283–4; CD, 268–9.

rational arguments, or arguments not derived from Scripture. 'When the Bible has spoken as a witness to divine revelation, and when it has been recognised and acknowledged as such, we are forced into this position; we have our work cut out to do what we have to do in this position . . . we are neither able to find reasons nor justifications for our attitude.'[37] Scripture has 'self attesting credibility' (*sich selbst bezeugenden Glaubwürdigkeit*).[38]

Because theology is the science of faith it takes place under the authority of the Word and in the freedom of the Word. What this means is apparent especially in Barth's treatment of church confession. He has Barmen in mind as a paradigmatic account of what is involved in such confession. The task of confession is the same as that of dogmatics, namely to expound Scripture in the speech of its own age. It is a challenge, question, and attack on the world around, which is threatened not chiefly by brutal godlessness but by the situation in which state and society, school and university, all seem to be saying the same thing.[39] Thus at the time of writing, Barth notes (1937), the debate about authority in the Church is threatened by the return to authority of the fascist state. It would be fatally easy to understand one in terms of the other. Equally fatal, however, would be to understand freedom in the Church in terms of the liberal protest against such authoritarianism. Barth insists that whilst we must expect parallelisms between church history and world history 'we cannot and must not interpret either by the other.'[40] Yes, of course the Church must speak a word to its own age. The proclamation dogmatics exists to critique relates to the whole fabric of human life, and involves a concrete attitude to state and society.[41] However, the very possibility of the Church speaking a liberating word depends on the recognition that authority and freedom in the Church are both of and under the Word, and thus not at the service of any ideology.

THE IDOLS OF DEATH AND THE GOD OF LIFE

The Declaration of Barmen, which Barth wrote through the night 'whilst the Lutherans slept', is 'the most important ecclesiastical expression of Barth's christological concentration' and 'can truly be read as the basic text of Barth's theology'.[42] It is certainly the vital commentary on the first two volumes of the *Dogmatics*, the essential clue to what Barth means there by 'the Word'. The second article reads:

[37] KD 1/1, 510; CD, 461.   [38] KD 1/2, 599; CD, 539.
[39] KD 1/2, 721; CD, 644.   [40] KD 1/2, 744; CD, 664.
[41] KD 1/2, 860; CD, 770.   [42] Jüngel, *Barth*, 43.

Jesus Christ became for us wisdom from God and righteousness, and sanctifica...
and redemption (1 Cor. 1.30)

As Jesus Christ is God's declaration of forgiveness of all our sins so in the same
way and with the same seriousness he is God's mighty claim upon our whole life.
Through him we obtain joyful deliverance from the godless bondage of this world
for the free and grateful service of his creatures.

We reject the false doctrine that there are spheres of our life in which we belong
not to Jesus Christ but to other masters, realms where we do not need to be justified
and sanctified by him.[43]

When Barth says 'Word' he means Jesus Christ, and this is a Word which
claims our whole life, not an academic creation. It has profound political
consequences, obscured, perhaps, by Barth's need to take account of the
Lutheran insistence on the separation of church and state. Given the
German Christians' fervid political theology, Barth could not simply oppose
it with another of a different hue, but rather follows the traditional Calvinist
emphasis on Christ's supremacy over every aspect of life without
exception. It is the rendering of Christology into politics. Anglo-Saxon
commentators, in particular, have often been preoccupied by Barth's attack
on natural theology. In reading the early volumes, in both their affirmations
and negations, we have to bear the theology of Barmen in mind.

The Denial of Natural Theology

From the start National Socialism had a pronouncedly religious, or idolatrous, rhetoric. Goebbels spoke of Hitler in the language of the Christian
tradition. 'Only one man in Germany', he said in 1928, 'is capable, by means
of fate-given perception and the power of the word, of creating political
works for the future. Many are called, but few are chosen. We are all convinced, so that our conviction can never be shaken, that he is the mouthpiece and the pathbreaker of the future. Therefore, we believe in him.
Beyond his human form, we can see in this man the active grace of destiny,
and we cling to his thought with all our hopes and bind ourselves to that creative power that drives him and all of us forward.'[44] In his inaugural address
as Rector of the University of Freiburg in 1933 Martin Heidegger hailed
Hitler as a leader called by destiny, sanctioned by all the primal forces of the
German soul that made the Leader and the led one flesh.[45] Hitler himself, as
Barth noted, frequently invoked 'providence'. 'Providence', said Hitler in
November 1939, 'has spoken its last word to me and brought me success.'[46]

---

[43] A. Burgsmüller and R. Weth (eds), *Die Barmer Theologische Erklärung*, Neukirchener
Verlag, 1983, 37.

[44] Cited in Craig, *Germany 1866–1945*, 545.

[45] Cited in Craig, *Germany 1866–1945*, 643.

[46] Cited in ibid., 673.

This religious strain was emphasized by Alfred Rosenberg, the editor of the Nazi paper the *Völkischer Beobachter*, who published a lurid account of the new religion in 1930, *The Myth of the Twentieth Century*, in which he called for 'a new faith, the myth of blood', and claimed that Aryan blood was the new sacrament of the German people.

Along with this blasphemous use of language the political theology of Hirsch and those like him became more strident. In response to Barth's article in the *Frankfurter Zeitung*, Hirsch asked whether Barth wished to deny that 'integration into *Volk* and state is so interwoven with my existence as a human being that I could deny it only by being disobedient to the one who has placed me in it, and could fail to make it the fundamental point of that understanding of *Volk*, state and war which is my task as a theologian only by lapsing into non-existential, i.e. theologically insignificant chatter.'[47] 'Not one people in the world', he wrote in 1933, in the leading National Socialist newspaper, 'has a statesman who takes Christianity so seriously. When Adolf Hitler ended his great speech on 1 May with a prayer, the whole world felt the wonderful sincerity of it.'[48]

It is against this background—the shading of explicitly pagan ideas such as Rosenberg's into Christian theologies which affirmed the primacy of nation and *Volk*—that we are to understand the mounting vehemence and intransigence of Barth's attack on natural theology through the 1930s. He had learned not to approve of natural theology from Herrmann, and the theology of revelation he was developing from Göttingen on logically had no place for natural theology, but there are few references to it, and those quite ironic, in the Göttingen and Münster dogmatics. Barth had long identified the theological movement which began with Schleiermacher as the cause of what he regarded as the devastation of the Protestant Church. What now happened was that Barth came to believe that Protestant liberalism and existentialism were equally forms of that natural theology whose classical form in the *analogia entis* was so stoutly defended by the Jesuit Pryzwara. All gave pride of place to human experience, all made it their starting point. But this was no more than Hirsch was doing with his theology of blood and soil. The demand to recognize the political events of 1933 as a source of special new revelation Barth regarded as a paradigm of the procedure of natural theology.[49] Making human experience the starting point was the shared weak point which could allow such a development. In his lecture in March 1933, on 'The First Commandment as a Theological Axiom', Barth declared that the fight against natural theology was 'unavoidable in view of the first commandment' and represented the fight for 'right

[47] Scholder, *The Churches 1918–1934*, 177.
[48] Ibid., 334.   [49] KD II/1, 194; CD, 173.

obedience in theology'.[50] At Barmen just over a year later the response to the German Christians took the form of an absolute denial of theological starting points other than in revelation. Article 1 of the declaration ran:

'I am the Way and the Truth and the Life; no one comes to the Father but through me'... Jesus Christ, as he is witnessed to us in Holy Scripture, is the one Word of God whom we must trust and obey in life and in death. We reject the false doctrine that the Church can and must recognise as a source of its preaching, alongside the one Word of God, other events and powers, forms and truths than God's revelation.

In this context opposition to natural theology took on a confessional significance. Only this can explain the vehemence of Barth's arguments.[51] In Barth's 1933 lecture on the First Commandment he had complained that the present 'complete darkening of the theological situation' had been brought about by 'the staggering statements of Bultmann, Brunner and Gogarten'.[52] Brunner responded in a pamphlet on 'Nature and Grace' the following year, in which he tried to show that natural theology was both biblically required and thoroughly grounded in Reformation teaching. Barth took it on holiday with him to Rome and wrote his most famous and impassioned piece of polemic in fascist Italy, overlooking St Peter's, in October 1934.

The struggle for the truth in the Church, he argues, now has an urgency it has lacked for centuries. It is not possible to say 'no' to Hirsch without doing the same to Brunner, 'because at the decisive point he takes part in the false movement of thought which today threatens the church'.[53] Just as he had found it necessary to attack Ragaz and those who stood for revolutionary change in *Romans*, because they stood so much closer to the truth, so now he reckoned Brunner a more dangerous opponent than Hirsch, for the very same reason. Barth considered that 'the most undesirable figures' of evangelical Germany were those who stood midway between the German Christians and the Confessing Church.[54] The

---

[50] *Zwischen den Zeiten* 11 (1933), 313; ET in *The Way of Theology in Karl Barth*, ed. M. Rumscheidt, Allison Park, Pa., Pickwick, 1986, 77.

[51] So Marquardt: 'Barth's total negation of natural theology was a polemical action from a not yet fully developed theological position and a means of political encounter with Nazism. In politically quieter times both before and afterwards Barth could not only affirm this theology but take it up. The extra Calvinisticum made this possible.' Marquardt, *Theologie*, 263. On rather different grounds so also Stephen Webb: 'Barth confronts the unlimited power of fascism with the jealous power of God, playing off one exclusive rhetoric against another; this explains, in part... his condemnation of natural theology.' Webb, *Refiguring Theology*, 168. H. Diem disagrees, arguing that Barth never totally rejected natural theology and did not deny it on political grounds. 'Karl Barth as Socialist' in Hunsinger, *Barth and Radical Politics*, 135.

[52] *Zwischen den Zeiten* 11 (1933), 313; *The Way of Theology*, 77.

[53] Barth, *Nein! Antwort an Emil Brunner*, Munich, Kaiser, 1934, 4.

[54] Barth, *Nein! Antwort an Emil Brunner*, Munich, Kaiser, 1934, 40.

implications of Brunner's arguments were made clear by the praise they had won from German Christian sympathizers such as Karl Fezer, Otto Weber and Paul Althaus. The fact that Brunner had showered Barth with love and praise in his pamphlet made the need to emphasize differences all the more urgent. By natural theology here Barth meant 'every (positive or negative) ostensibly theological formulation of a system which claims to set out a divine revelation whose object is fundamentally different from the revelation in Christ and whose method is not that of the exegesis of holy Scripture'.[55] We are compelled to reject such abstract systems by the 'hermeneutical rule, forced upon the exegete by the creed (e.g. by the clause *natus ex virgine*) and by revelation'.[56] What especially provoked Barth's wrath was the way that Brunner 'with astonishing self understanding and logical consistency' summoned Calvin to his aid, 'leaving out the very important brackets within which Calvin always speaks of the natural knowledge of God'.[57] As opposed to all natural theology is the fact that it is the Holy Spirit who creates a 'point of contact ' in human beings, an event which can only be acknowledged as miracle.

Barth's final reckoning with natural theology is to be found in more than a hundred pages of *Church Dogmatics* II/1, which was completed in summer 1939. The *analogia entis*, and in particular the chapter on revelation in the Vatican I document on faith (the 'Vaticanum'), is the centre of his attack. Barth considers the scriptural arguments, as well as the arguments from pedagogy and mission, in favour of natural theology. In effect he has three related arguments against it. In the first place he considers that natural theology represents the human struggle against grace, the desire to be self sufficient and autonomous. From this desire for mastery follows the fact that we cannot in fact have natural and revealed theology together as the Vaticanum imagines. 'A natural theology which does not strive to be the only master is not a natural theology.'[58] This desire, however, leads inevitably to idolatry. 'Quite apart from grace and miracle, has not man always had what is in relation to the being of the world the very "natural" capacity to persuade himself and others of a higher divine being? All idols spring from this capacity.'[59] This tendency was only too visible in National Socialism.

Secondly, he identifies natural theology as a supremely middle class enterprise. It represents the *Verbürgerlichung* of the gospel. It is the Christian as bourgeois who speaks in natural theology— 'and which Christian does not wish to speak as a bourgeois?'. Precisely as bourgeois theology it can boast of its achievements and pedagogic success. As such its success repre-

[55] Ibid., 11–12.   [56] Ibid., 13.
[57] Ibid., 45.   [58] KD II/1, 195; CD, 173.   [59] KD II/1, 92; CD, 84.

sents the domestication of the gospel.[60] Barth does not deny the reality of natural theology. What he denies is that it can serve as a source for Christian preaching. 'When the Church proclaims God's revelation, it does not speak on the basis of a view of reality of the world and of man, however deep and believing; it does not give an exegesis of these events and powers, forms and truths, but bound to its commission, and made free by the promise received with it, it reads and explains the Word which is called Jesus Christ and therefore the book which bears witness to him.'[61] The way to deal with it is to deny it any kind of tragic seriousness. 'The illusion that we can disillusion ourselves is the greatest of all illusions. And a theology which thinks it can persuade man against natural theology and forbid it to him is still definitely natural theology.'[62] We have to be so taken up with our proper theme, the Word of God, that natural theology drops away as superfluous.

Thirdly, Barth argues that natural theology puts in place of the objective liberating biblical God the illusory abstraction of speculative being. As in the Romans commentary, Barth regards abstraction as the original sin in theology for it represents a failure of engagement with theology's real object.

The Word of God

As opposed to natural theology Barth wants to insist that 'the Word of God' is the proper source and theme of theology. We have seen how, in Göttingen, Barth effectively constructed a new type of theology which began with the task of the critical measuring of Christian preaching. His doctrine of the Word is elaborated from there. When Barth speaks of revelation he means first and foremost Jesus Christ. The concept 'Word' is merely a 'preliminary and veiling' one, purely representative, an ideogram for the name Jesus Christ. We do not learn who Jesus is from the concept 'Word' but the other way about.[63] 'The equation of God's Word and God's Son makes any doctrinaire understanding of the Word of God impossible.'[64] If Barth's theology is a theology of the Word this is only because Christ, the Word, is its starting and finishing point. Christology 'describes as it were an inner circle surrounded by a host of other concentric circles in each of which it is repeated, and in which its truth and recognition must be maintained and expounded'.[65] It is Christ who is the 'objective reality of revelation'.

[60] KD II/1, 157–8; CD, 141–2. The English translation obscures the sharpness of Barth's political critique.

[61] KD II/1, 290; CD, 178.   [62] KD II/1, 190; CD, 169.   [63] KD II/2, 103; CD, 96.

[64] KD I/1, 142; CD, 137.   [65] KD I/2, 147; CD, 133.

Jesus was the life which was light, the revelation of God, the saying, or address, or communication in which God discloses Himself to us. But as this revelation He was not something other outside and alongside God. He was God himself within the revelation . . . He was revelation in its complete and absolute form. It was to show this that the Evangelist—no matter where he derived the concept . . . made use of the term Logos. 'Word' [*das Wort*] or 'saying' [*der Spruch*] is the simple but genuine form in which person communicates with person. It is by the Word that God communicates with man. Because it is God's Word it is not called 'a' word but 'the' Word, the Word of all words.[66]

Because Scripture and preaching witness to Christ, Barth speaks of a 'threefold form' of the Word of God, though Scripture and preaching have to 'become' the Word of God, whereas with Christ we have to do not with becoming but with being. There is a becoming involved here but it is an event within the Trinity, the election of God by God. Still, in the circle of theological knowledge, we only know this through Scripture. What is meant by calling Scripture 'the Word of God'?

The question Barth had wrestled with since 1915 was: How is the Church to avoid the kind of cultural imprisonment which had disabled it in the First World War? What is it that prevents the Church simply talking to itself? He found the answer in Scripture. 'Apart from the undeniable vitality of the Church itself there stands confronting it a concrete authority with its own vitality, an authority whose pronouncement is not the Church's dialogue with itself but an address to the Church, and which can have *vis-à-vis* the Church the position of a free power and therefore of a criterion.'[67] This authority is Scripture. It is partly the written character of Scripture that accounts for this, but what distinguishes it from all other written texts is its self evidential power. 'It is the Canon because it imposed itself upon the Church as such and continually does so.'[68] If we thought we could say why this is so, we should be 'acting as if we had in our hands a measure by which we could measure the Bible and on this basis assign it its distinctive position. Our ultimate and decisive wisdom would then be once again the wisdom of a self dialogue about the Bible'.[69] All that we can say is that the Word of God becomes knowable by making itself known. We cannot go a single step beyond this.[70] To the obvious objection that Scripture is open to radically divergent readings Barth opposes free exegesis and a free Bible.[71] The lordship of God is expressed in the fact that we cannot compel Scripture to be revelatory. Barth famously appeals to the image of the pool of Bethesda: only when the angel stirs the waters is there revelation.[72]

Like Scripture, preaching can 'become' God's Word. The Word of

---

[66] KD II/2, 104; CD, 97.   [67] KD I/1, 108; CD, 106.   [68] KD I/1, 109; CD, 107.
[69] KD I/1, 109; CD, 107.   [70] KD I/1, 260; CD, 246.   [71] KD I/1, 108; CD, 106.
[72] KD I/1, 114; CD, 111.

God preached means human talk about God 'on the basis of God's own direction, which fundamentally transcends all human causation, which cannot, then, be put on a human basis, but which simply takes place, and has to be acknowledged, as a fact'.[73] It is 'proclaimed' to the extent that it presents and places itself 'as an object over against us' and is never our possession.

The 'becoming' of Scripture and preaching is the meaning of the important Barthian category of 'event'. To say 'God reveals Godself' is 'a statement about the occurrence of an event [*Ereignis*]'.[74] A theological 'event' is the meeting of the Word of God with human beings, which is independent of any causal nexus (*bloßes Geschehen*).[75] Not intrinsically, but in virtue of the divine decision, the Bible and proclamation are God's Word. The supreme theological event, however, is the incarnation, and Barth recants the idea of revelation which he had advanced in the second Romans commentary which 'merely bounded time and determined it from without'. Then, he notes, such a conception had a certain antiseptic task but 'John 1.14 does not have justice done to it.'[76] Prolegomena, for Barth, are not the outlining of the conditions for speaking of God prior to doing dogmatics, but are themselves dogmatics. He accordingly sketches an entire Christology, maintaining the Chalcedonian pattern he had opted for at Göttingen. This pattern—truly divine and truly human without division, separation or confusion—was to become one of the most important motifs of his theology and is used, for example, to illustrate the way in which Scripture is 'wholly the word of man and wholly the Word of God'.[77]

In speaking of the sovereignty of God we speak of the sovereignty of the *Word*. As in the previous decade Barth continued to oppose the anti-intellectualism and irrationalism which was prepared to meet God almost anywhere but in an appeal to reason. 'Whatever "the holy" of Rudolf Otto may be, it certainly cannot be understood as the Word of God, for it is the numinous, and the numinous is the irrational, and the irrational can no longer be differentiated from an absolutised natural force. But everything depends on this differentiation if we are to understand the concept of the Word of God.'[78] The Word of God is spiritual, personal, and purposive. The personal character of the Word presents 'an absolute barrier against reducing its wording to a human system or using its wording to establish and construct a human system'.[79]

That God remains free in the event of revelation is expressed by the

---

[73] KD I/1, 92; CD, 90. [74] KD I/2, 50; CD, 45.
[75] KD I/1, 162; CD, 156. [76] KD I/2, 56; CD, 50.
[77] KD I/2, 555–6; CD, 501. For Chalcedon as a structural pattern in Barth see Hunsinger, *How to Read Barth*, 85 f.
[78] KD I/1, 140; CD, 135. [79] KD I/1, 143; CD, 139.

y familiar dialectic of veiling and unveiling. 'Revelation in the Bible is the self unveiling, imparted to men, of the God who by nature ot be unveiled to men.'[80] The God who can be colonized is at the end of the day just the largest member of the universe, perhaps the end of the series but not utterly distinct from it. The dialectic of time and eternity of the second Romans is now replaced by the veiling and unveiling of the incarnation. That God remains 'veiled' means that although God takes form the result is not a third thing between God and the creature—in which case God would be manipulable.[81] When we say 'revelation' it is Jesus Christ that we mean. 'God wills to veil himself by becoming a man, in order by breaking out of the veiling to unveil himself as a man. He wills to be silent and yet also to speak.'[82] 'To say revelation is to say "The Word became flesh".'[83] Even here we have to recognize that 'Jesus Christ is also in fact the Rabbi of Nazareth who is hard to know historically and whose work, when he is known, might seem a little commonplace compared to more than one of the other founders of religions and even compared to some of the later representatives of his own religion . . . The veil is thick.'[84] As we saw, in constructing his Göttingen lectures, Barth sought to avoid 'the Jesus Christ pit' of the Lutherans. The 'historical Jesus' was in his view 'purposely discovered, or invented, in order to indicate an approach to Jesus Christ which circumvents his divinity, the approach to a revelation which is generally understandable and possible in the form of human judgement and experience'.[85] It was the attempt to understand Christ as the Word, and as the heart of what we mean by revelation which is what Barth had in mind in claiming to derive his theology exclusively from revelation. Precisely because the Word is Christ it is also the case that no system is possible, and that we cannot reduce revelation to 'a fixed sum of revealed propositions'.[86]

Barth's understanding of revelation is bound up at every level with the affirmation of God's lordship. 'Godhead in the Bible means freedom, ontic and noetic autonomy . . . The self-sufficiency or immediacy so characteristic of the biblical revelation is the very thing that characterises it as God's revelation on the one side and as the revelation of lordship on the other.'[87] The first two volumes of the *Dogmatics* are the minute examination of this claim. 'Lordship' is, of course, a political category and the heart of this affirmation is that if we are genuinely to speak of revelation it must be in terms of the disclosure of the God who cannot be colonized, and wheeled in to the service of this or that race, nation, or political party. From the beginning, as is clear from the correspondence with Harnack, revelation meant the critique of idols, or as we might also say, ideology critique. This is not to say that the doctrines of revelation or of the being and attributes of God were elaborated in the interests of ideology critique—quite the reverse. Neither would it be true to say that the significance of Barth's doctrine of revelation could be reduced to the implications of God's lordship. If we can risk any generalization about Barth's theology it is that simplistic or reductionist readings are sure to be wrong. However, revelation is both an act of God's lordship and the establishment of this lordship, and as such it involves a head to head struggle with the lordless powers.

God is lord of the event of revelation in the sense that we can only speak of it in terms of a miracle of the Holy Spirit. The statement 'God reveals himself' must be 'a statement of utter thankfulness, a statement of pure amazement, in which is repeated the amazement of the disciples at meeting the risen One'.[88] The freedom of human beings for God is created by the Spirit—it was precisely the failure of neo-Protestantism that it believed human beings had a natural knowledge of God independent of miracle.[89] Knowledge of God, in fact is always *acknowledgement*—faith, response— and consists decisively in the recognition that we have a master in Christ. Barth prefers the term Master to *Führer*, teacher, or Lord, and this choice, in 1938, the time of writing, is without doubt deliberate. 'To stand unavoidably under any other master is a sign of sickness. But to stand under this Master is not only the normal thing, it is the only possible thing.'[90] To have our master in Christ means to have someone over against us from whom we cannot withdraw, to whom we are always responsible and subject in all our obedience and disobedience, and to be subject to a very definite formation and direction.[91] To fail to see this is to open the door to idols, including, Barth adds, in case the message is not clear, 'those with which we have to do today'.[92]

James Barr, writing as one for whom the Barthian theology long ago 'collapsed in ruins', has for many years attacked Barth's preoccupation with revelation.[93] He argues that the concept of revelation occupies no great role in Scripture, and therefore that it has no business operating as a 'controlling concept' for a theology which gives the place to Scripture which Barth's does, and also that its use is a response to post-Enlightenment priorities such as concern as to whether God exists or not, and if so, how knowledge of God relates to scientific knowledge.[94]

These objections seem to me to miss the reason for the priority of

[88] KD I/2, 65; CD, 65.   [89] KD I/2, 223–4, 228; CD, 204, 209.
[90] KD I/2, 295; CD, 270.   [91] KD I/2, 295; CD, 270 ff.   [92] KD I/2, 275; CD, 252.
[93] J. Barr, *Old and New in Interpretation*, London, SCM, 1966, 12.
[94] Ibid., 89–96; *The Bible in the Modern World*, London, SCM, 1973, 18 ff.

revelation in Barth's theology, which is bound up with the struggle against hegemony. That God cannot be colonized is the implication of Barth's language about the objectivity of revelation.[95] 'The Word of God as directed to us is a Word which we do not say to ourselves and which we could not in any circumstances say to ourselves. The Word of God always tells us something fresh that we had never heard before from anyone. The rock of a Thou which never becomes an I is thrown in our path here.'[96] It is the dialectic of authority and freedom which is intended to prevent the obvious objection that what we end up calling the Word of God is simply our own invention.

The Knowability of God

In the Preface to the first volume of the *Dogmatics* Barth made plain that he intended to reject all forms of philosophical existentialism. This would mean, he felt, a resumption of the line from Schleiermacher to Herrmann and 'in any conceivable continuation along this line I can only see the plain destruction of Protestant theology and the Protestant church'. It approximated too closely to the doctrine of the *analogia entis* which 'I regard . . . as the invention of Antichrist.'[97] This is not irony: Barth writes in anger. What lies behind such intemperate language about what many might regard as a theological technicality? At the end of the decade Barth returned to the question of analogy, and set out his objections in detail. In the first place he felt that a distinction between revealed and natural knowledge of God implied a division in God as well. The God whom we can know apart from revelation seems to be a construct of human thinking. More fundamentally, the dogma of Vatican I which sets out the account of the analogy of being has not a single word 'to suggest that the God referred to is engaged in a work and activity with man which is for man a matter of life and death'.[98] We have to begin, in our knowledge of God, with the God who condemns to death and leads from death to life. It also fails to respect the truth that God is not a member of any universe, and this failure inevitably ends in idolatry.

[95] Joseph Bettis spells this out in his fine article on 'Barth's Rejection of Natural Theology and the Hermeneutical Problem', *SJT* 22 (1969). That God is the One who loves in freedom is a prescriptive not a descriptive definition. All things we can know are objectifications, a phenomenon constructed by the active functions of perception and cognition. What we objectify we make in our own image and exercise some control over, but 'God breaks through this to confront us as he is in himself.' The distinction between natural and revealed theology implies that there are anthropological statements that have no direct theological ramifications, and vice versa, but 'Theology is not a two step dance in which one first discusses the structures of human existence and then the dynamics of divine love. The only vocation for theology is the understanding of human existence.'
[96] KD I/1, 146; CD, 141.   [97] KD I/1, p. viii; CD, p. xiii.   [98] KD II/1, 88; CD, 81.

'The really wicked and damnable thing in the Roman Catholic doctrine is that it . . . obviously derives from an attempt to unite Yahweh and Baal, the triune God of Holy Scripture with the concept of being of Aristotelian and Stoic philosophy.'[99]

Barth recognized that analogy was unavoidable but in place of the analogy of being wished to put the analogy of faith. When revelation 'commandeers' language a genuine correspondence and agreement is set up between our language and God. God takes what properly and originally belongs to God. 'We use our words improperly and pictorially . . . when we apply them within the confines of what is appropriate to us as creatures. When we apply them to God they are not alienated from their original object and therefore from their truth, but, on the contrary, restored to it.'[100] Thus Barth felt that the words 'father' and 'son', for example, applied properly to God, and only secondarily to ourselves, and the same could be said of 'patience', 'love', and even 'arm' and 'mouth'. In revelation 'God controls his property, elevating our words to their proper use.'[101]

Concern about whether or not God can be known had been a major preoccupation since the Enlightenment, but, Barth maintained, we simply cannot worry about this. In his Word God becomes an object for us, a possibility which rests on the fact that God is first and foremost an object to Godself, just as the knowability of God is grounded in God's knowability to Godself. God's objectivity to Godself Barth speaks of as God's primary objectivity. God's secondary objectivity is that which God has for us in revelation, in which God gives Godself to be known by us. We stand indirectly before God, but directly before another object which is used by God as God's clothing, temple, or sign. Knowledge of God in faith is always at bottom knowledge of God in God's works. The acknowledgement of the fact that revelation has taken place is what we mean by faith. Once again we have the dialectic of veiling and unveiling. 'When God sets up his lordship it means the self humiliation and self alienation of God, when he reveals himself his hiddenness is confirmed.'[102] The humanity of Christ is the basic sacrament. In his self-giving to us God is known 'in a cognition which progresses from one present to another, which constantly begins afresh in every present, in a series of single acts of knowledge'.[103] We know God in faith. This is the total positive relationship of the person to the God who gives Godself to be known in the Word. Knowledge of God is always a matter of grace. 'Grace is the majesty, the freedom, the undeservedness, the unexpectedness, the newness, the trespass [*Eigenmacht*], in which the relationship to God and therefore the possibility of knowing him is opened up to man by

---

[99] KD II/1, 92; CD, 84. [100] KD II/1, 259; CD, 229.
[101] KD II/2, 260; CD, 230. [102] KD II/1, 60; CD, 55. [103] KD II/1, 67; CD, 61.

God himself.'[104] There is a readiness of man for knowledge of God but it is effected by grace. The problem with natural theology is that it elevates this readiness into an independent factor. Natural theology is 'the unavoidable theological expression of the fact that in the reality and possibility of man as such an openness for the grace of God and therefore for the knowability of God in his revelation is not at all evident.'[105] Instead of an object of faith the gospel becomes an object of the experience of faith. The only remedy for this is to focus our attention on Christ. 'If we look past Jesus Christ, if we speak of anyone else but him, if our praise of man is not at once praise of Jesus Christ, the romance and the illusions begin again.'[106] Through Christ we are included in the knowledge which God has of Godself. We cannot get away from the hiddenness of God, but come back to Christ infinitely often.[107] Our knowledge always consists in approximations, but we must not for that reason doubt its truth.[108] We always remain 'on the way'.

Barth's account of the knowability of God, of the readiness of God and of human beings, is a sort of theological castling move: it guards the freedom of God from any hostile human takeover. It is not sceptical: authentic knowledge of God is certainly possible. What is denied is the possibility of any knowledge on the grounds of innate human capacity. The political force of this doctrine in the 1930s is obvious. Of course, it does not represent a simple reaction to these events, as it is the outworking of insights Barth had grasped in Göttingen, but it seems most probable that these events influence the polarized statement of alternatives.

Religion and Unbelief

The paragraph on religion in *Church Dogmatics* I/2 is both the continuation of the polemic Barth had developed in *Romans* but also a complement to the attack on natural theology. In the *Christliche Dogmatik* this section had been devoted to a detailed rebuttal of Schleiermacher, but here the net was cast far more widely. Barth places it after the exposition of the objective reality and subjective possibility of revelation, in both dimensions God's gift. In contrast religion, like natural theology, is part of the human attempt to do without grace. 'Sin is always unbelief. And unbelief is always man's faith in himself. And this faith invariably consists in the fact that man makes the mystery of his responsibility his own mystery, instead of accepting it as the mystery of God. It is this faith which is religion.'[109] That Christianity exists alongside a sea of more or less adequate parallels and analogies is part of the divine hiddenness.[110]

[104] KD II/1, 80; CD, 74.   [105] KD II/1, 150; CD, 135.
[106] KD II/1, 167; CD, 149.   [107] KD II/1, 283; CD, 250.
[108] KD II/1, 227; CD, 202.   [109] KD I/2, 343; CD, 314.
[110] KD I/2, 307; CD, 282.

As with *Romans*, Barth's critique of religion is not timeless and
but closely related to events at the time of writing. If knowledge oı ᴜ_
not acknowledgement of a gift then it becomes a contravention of the first
commandment through the production of idols.[111] It is religion which characteristically provides ultimate legitimation for all kinds of human projects,
as it did for nationalism in the war. Concretely we see that human religion
leaves us defenceless against the German Christians.[112] 'The religion of
man is always conditioned absolutely by the way in which the starry
heaven above and the moral law within have spoken to the individual. It
is, therefore, conditioned by nature and climate, by blood and soil, by the
economic, cultural, political, in short, the historical circumstances in which
he lives.'[113]

Of course religion is under attack from all sorts of atheist philosophers
but, drawing especially on Fritz Mauthner's great history of atheism, Barth
contends that this does not pose a truly radical challenge. Mauthner concludes his work with an appeal to mysticism as a form of atheism. Barth
agrees with the analysis but considers that both mysticism and atheism are
merely parasitic on religion as that against which they need to protest.[114]
The nameless, formless, and unrealized oneness to which mysticism deliv-
ers us is a bizarre parody of the Speech, Act, and Mystery of the Word of
God which critique our social reality.[115] That atheism very easily ends in religion is clear to Barth from National Socialism. In 1936 Otto Petras had valorized the existence of the lonely hero, typified in the heroes of the First
World War, who are stripped of all illusions and fears and 'march just for the
sake of marching'.[116] This was the very type glorified in the Stormtrooper.
Such a creed can be simply lived out, in which case it remains a private affair,
or it can be publicly proclaimed. 'But if that is the case it cannot dispense
with some sort of basic, declarative ideology and mythology . . . and the
result of this critical turning against religion is simply the founding of a new
religion—and perhaps even the confirmation of an old.' The significance of
this in 1937, when Barth was writing, is quite unmistakeable. Against such
revived paganism, and as our necessary defence against idols, stands the
Word of God, revelation.

As with natural theology, the affinity of religion with the capitalist
process is part of the subtext of the critique. The religious man is 'like a rich
man, who in the need to grow richer (which cannot, of course, be an
absolute need) puts part of his fortune into an undertaking that promises a
profit'.[117] Religion has a certain non-necessity and weakness which means
that we can 'withdraw our capital from an undertaking which no longer

---

[111] KD 1/2, 355; CD, 324.   [112] KD 1/2, 318; CD, 292.
[113] KD 1/2, 345; CD, 316.   [114] KD 1/2, 353; CD, 323.
[115] KD 1/2, 354; CD, 324. Plonz, *Herrenlosen Gewalten*, 275.
[116] KD 1/2, 353; CD, 322.   [117] KD 1/2, 344; CD, 315.

appears to be profitable'.[118] There is, then, an analogy between the religious
circle and that of capital accumulation which indicates the fundamental
questionableness of both.[119]

The God of Life

In the *Church Dogmatics* Barth repeated his exposition of the doctrine of the
Trinity as part of his exposition of God in revelation, taking care to emphasize that it could not be understood as a grammatical or rationalistic
exposition of the phrase *'Deus dixit'*.[120] With two exceptions in the early
scholastic period the tradition had been to begin with the being and attributes of God and then come to the Trinity. Barth reverses this model and puts
the doctrine of the Trinity at the head of the entire dogmatics. 'The doctrine
of the Trinity is what basically distinguishes the Christian concept of God as
Christian . . . in contrast to all other possible doctrines of God or concepts
of revelation.'[121] Why? Because in it we learn who God is. We have to begin
with the 'Who' before we turn to the 'What' of God's being and attributes.
The doctrine of the Trinity is an 'explanatory confirmation' of the name
Yahweh-Kyrios, which embraces both Old and New Testaments.[122]
The root of the doctrine of the Trinity , says Barth, is that God reveals
Godself as Lord. This is not to say, as critics of the *Christliche Dogmatik* had
objected, that the doctrine of the Trinity emerges from the analysis of the
concept of lordship. On the contrary, it is revelation which allows us to
understand lordship. Godhead in the Bible means 'freedom, ontic and noetic
autonomy'.

> The self sufficiency or immediacy so characteristic of the biblical revelation is the
> very thing that characterises it as God's revelation on the one side and as the revela-
> tion of lordship on the other. But all this becomes fully characteristic only when we
> note that what we have here is not an abstract revelation of lordship, but a concrete
> revelation of the Lord, not Godhead . . . but God Himself who in this freedom
> speaks as an I and addresses by a Thou.[123]

The concept 'personality' Barth referred to 'the one unique essence
of God', and preferred 'modes of being' (*Seinsweise*) for the three persons.
God meets us 'as an I existing in and for itself with its own thought and
will . . . thrice God as Father, Son and Spirit'.[124] Emphasizing each individual 'person' ran the risk of tritheism in Barth's view. To talk of modes of
being emphasized the fact that the 'persons' are to be understood 'in terms

---

[118] KD I/2, 347; CD, 317.   [119] So Plonz, *Herrenlosen Gewalten*, 275.
[120] KD I/1, 312; CD, 296.   [121] KD I/1, 317; CD, 301.   [122] KD I/1, 368; CD, 348.
[123] KD I/1, 323; CD, 307.   [124] KD I/1, 379; CD, 359.

of their distinctive relations and indeed their genetic relations to one another'.[125]

Barth turned to the exposition of the being and attributes of God six years later, in 1937/8, when the dominant fact in Europe was the Nazi regime, arbitrary, violent, justifying the 'will to power', underwritten by propaganda and the big lie. The exposition of the true God, who is power and truth in God's self, necessarily contradicts this deeply idolatrous regime at every point. At the very start of his account Barth emphasizes that the existence of God changes all things: 'in great things and in small, in whole and in part, in the totality of their existence as human beings, they should and must live with the fact that not only sheds new light on, *but materially changes*, all things and everything in all things—the fact that God is'.[126] As Marquardt points out this reads like an allusion to Marx's eleventh thesis on Feuerbach, that the point is to change rather than to interpret. In any event Barth speaks of God not in primarily ontological categories but in 'salvation history-eschatological ones' and the field of concern is 'the whole of human existence'.[127]

We have to bear this qualification of the statement that 'God is' in mind in further exposition of Barth's account. God's being is in *act*: 'with regard to the being of God, the word "event" or "act" is *final*, and cannot be surpassed or compromised' (the italics are Barth's).[128] In his exposition of the Trinity Barth sought to signal this fact by replacing *Dreieinheit* with *Dreieinigkeit*, which emphasizes that the unity of God is always a becoming.[129] This fundamental move of Barth's doctrine of God represents in the first instance his attempt to understand what is involved in saying that God is the God of *life*, the living God who not only creates but constantly engages with all reality. The gods and idols 'have no life', and it is Barth's decisive objection to natural theology, restated as a counterpoint in the course of the exposition of the doctrine of God, that it involves a lifeless deity. Barth notes polemically that we have to refuse to be tied to the superstitions of a spirit nature system, which confuses theology with metaphysics. It was the determination of the orthodox doctrine of God by the philosophy of late antiquity which paved the way for the Enlightenment, with its God who is either nothing but first cause, or who cannot be known save as the logical implication of moral behaviour.[130] Barth finds the negative way of Neoplatonism 'disastrous', an exemplification of Feuerbach's thesis.[131] As opposed to this is the being of the God who loves in freedom, and who does

---

[125] KD I/1, 383; CD, 363.
[126] KD II/1, 289; CD, 258. Marquardt makes this passage the heart of his exposition of Barth's doctrine of God and I have adopted his emphasis here. Marquardt, *Theologie*, 240.
[127] Marquardt, *Theologie*, 240–1.   [128] KD II/1, 295–6; CD, 263.
[129] KD I/1, 389; CD, 369.   [130] KD II/1, 298; CD, 266.   [131] KD II/1, 341; CD, 303.

so in and through an engagement with creation and history. Barth's 'actualism', his spelling out of God's existence as the living God, is at the same time his account of the God who is not just engaged, but the meaning and ground of all engagement. In other words, in his doctrine of God Barth offers us the deepest possible rationale for political or liberation theology because the God who loves in freedom can and does ground all life-giving action.

To speak of God's being in act is to speak of God's being as personal. This is not to invoke an analogy from our life. 'The definition of a person—that is, a knowing, willing, acting I—can have the meaning only of a confession of the person of God declared in his revelation, of the One who loves and who as such (loving in his own way) is *the* person . . . Man is not a person, but he becomes one on the basis that he is loved by God and can love God in return.'[132] Unlike the God of Schleiermacher, this God can show mercy. 'The personal God has a heart. He can feel, and be affected. He is not impassible.'[133] As triune God is relationship in Godself—God's innermost being is self communication.[134] 'His innermost self is his self communication, and loving the world, He gives it a share in his completeness.'[135] God's love is free—which is to say, determined and moved by itself. The exposition of freedom takes the place of the 'Wholly Other' of Barth's earlier period. It enables him to make clearer that, whilst God can in no way be manipulated, God must be understood as existing in the profoundest relationship to creation. 'God Himself is the Son who is the basic truth of that which is other than God . . . because this is so, the creation and preservation of the world, and relationship and fellowship with it, realized as they are in perfect freedom, without compulsion or necessity, do not signify an alien or contradictory expression of God's being, but a natural, *the* natural expression of it *ad extra*.'[136]

In a provocative and detailed study of Barth's doctrine of time, Richard Roberts has alleged that in Barth's theology 'The reality of the divine denies, subverts and supersedes the reality of the mundane.'[137] As we shall see shortly, Barth embraces worldly time with divine time. The effect of this, Roberts believes, is that 'a vast and "unnatural" theological growth chokes

---

[132] KD II/1, 319; CD, 284.   [133] KD II/1, 416; CD, 370.
[134] KD II/1, 311; CD, 277.   [135] KD II/1, 311; CD, 277.
[136] KD II/1, 356–7; CD, 317. G. S. Hendry objects that Barth equivocates between five senses of freedom: as gratuity, choice, self determination, initiative, and energy, and that this equivocation leads him to the borders, if not across the borders, of a Hegelian emanationism. *SJT* 31 (1978), 229–44. I think Barth is much more aware of what he is up to than Hendry allows. Barth's emphasis is on self determination (3), but this is the self determination of the gracious God (1), who elects in love (2), and who acts in creation and history (4 and 5).
[137] R. H. Roberts, 'Barth's Doctrine of Time' in S. Sykes (ed.), *Karl Barth: Studies of his Theological Methods*, Oxford, Clarendon, 1979, 139.

and smothers the natural order and its reality, for grace consumes nature in a putative, but merely apparent recreation.'[138] Were this true the claim that Barth's theology might function in and through its main doctrines as a political theology would obviously fall to the ground. But far from leading to an alienation of the natural order the Christological grounding of Barth's theology is in fact the most detailed and profound reworking of Aquinas's famous assertion that grace does not destroy but perfects nature. Because Christ is 'the basic truth of that which is other than God', including time, it is precisely not alienated but redeemed. What it *cannot* have is a purely autonomous reality, for that would be a reality without God. As it is, all reality, including political reality, finds its ultimate truth in Christ. It is for that reason that even abstruse debates about analogy and the knowability of God have not simply critical, but also positive political significance.

We can see the effect of this in Barth's reworking of the doctrine of the attributes of God, which become in his exposition the perfections of God. The moral and metaphysical attributes become the perfections of the divine freedom and of the divine loving. The exposition has both critical and constructive significance. Critically we find the exposition of God's power turned decisively against the arbitrary and unjust power of the Third Reich. 'Power in itself is evil. It is nothing less than freedom from restraint and suppression; revolt and domination.'[139] Failure to ground our understanding of power on the Word, which is to say on the event of Christ, leads to 'the irruption of a Third Reich of madness'.[140] Of course God's power is that which preserves the stars, moves the sea, and directs the lightning but absolutely decisively it is the Crucified who is the power of God, and from the cross that we learn what it means to say that the power of God is the love of God.[141] Again, over against a 'vast waste of falsehood' is the knowledge of God which sets itself limits. The limit is non-being, death, and hell. We may fall into these, but in doing so we do not fall out of the realm of God's grace and judgement. 'This is the comfort and the warning contained in the truth of the divine omniscience.'[142] Most remarkable of all, by way of political critique, is the way that Barth could, in 1938 or 1939, in the passage used as an epigraph for this chapter, speak of the downfall of the Third Reich as stemming from its idolatrous challenging of the first commandment—its denial of the unity of God.[143] So profound was his conviction that God *constitutes* our reality, and cannot therefore be ultimately contradicted.

More important than the critical turn of the doctrine is the significance of

---

[138] Ibid., 124.
[139] KD II/1, 589; CD, 524.
[140] KD II/1, 604; CD, 537.
[141] KD II/1, 684, 675; CD, 607, 598.
[142] KD II/1, 623; CD, 554.
[143] KD II/1, 500; CD, 444.

the positive exposition, which culminates with an account of the beauty and joy of God's being. It is relationship with God which makes us truly persons, through which we learn to love and through which we become free. It is the richness of God's being which grounds the richness of our life. God is our future, but the future is no dull abstraction, but characterized by grace and holiness, mercy and righteousness, patience and wisdom, by the celebration of God's beauty. Because God is the living God this bears on our life here and now. Where a natural theology or religion could endorse all sorts of principles, some good and some demonic, the God who loves in freedom calls forth a response of righteousness, mercy, and love. Human beings live in correspondence to the God who is not just righteousness in God's self, but who actively seeks the creation of that which corresponds to the divine righteousness in creation. 'A political attitude', says Barth, follows from the righteousness of God, 'decisively determined by the fact that human beings are made responsible to all those who confront them as poor and wretched, that they are summoned on their part to espouse the cause of justice, and to espouse it for those who suffer injustice.' Why?

Because in them it is manifested to him what he himself is in the sight of God; because the living gracious action of God towards him consists in the fact that God Himself in his own righteousness procures right for him . . . The man who lives by the faith that this is true stands under a political responsibility. He knows that the right, that every real claim which one man has against another or others, enjoys the protection of the God of grace . . . He cannot avoid the question of human rights. He can only will and affirm a state which is based on justice. By any other attitude he rejects the divine justification.[144]

Moreover, God always takes his stand unconditionally and passionately on this side and on this side alone: against the lofty and on behalf of the lowly, and to correspond to God is to take the same stand. Because God is the 'all in all' God concerns the 'totality' of human existence. God not only illuminates but also transforms reality. As Marquardt comments, 'that is Marx's eleventh thesis on Feuerbach applied to the concept of God'.[145]

As already noted, Barth profoundly reworked the concept of eternity. Traditionally this rested on an opposition of eternity and time which Barth regraded as a 'Babylonian captivity'. He liked Boethius's definition of eternity as 'total, simultaneous and complete possession of unlimited life', but felt that this had hitherto not been properly exploited. This he now set out to do. Barth prefers to speak of eternity as 'God's time'. It is not that there is no past and future in God but 'In God there is no opposition or competition or conflict, but peace between origin, movement and goal, between present,

---

[144] KD II/1, 434–5; CD, 387.
[145] F. Marquardt in Hunsinger, *Barth and Radical Politics*, 68.

past and future.'[146] God is pre-temporal (*vorzeitlich*), supra- or co-temporal (*überzeitlich*, i.e. accompanying our time), and post-temporal (*nachzeitlich*). God thus has a 'positive relationship' or 'readiness' for time. Understanding God's time like this enables Barth both to affirm the reality of God's engagement with history and at the same time to reject that immanentist eschatology which the German Christians appealed to. It has been necessary, Barth notes in the course of this exposition, to speak much more positively and clearly about church and state than has been possible for a very long while. Why should this follow from an account of the eternity of God? Precisely because 'The life of man in time and his various responsibilities must be brought into the light of God's supra temporality in a manner quite different from that previously practised.' When God's eternity is understood as the unity of redeemed time then we are free to understand the present, with which God engages, in the light of God's *nachzeitlichkeit*. Political action is grounded in the hope which follows from the fact that God is our future, and it is this which makes the privatization of faith found in neo-Protestantism impossible.[147]

By the same token we must understand the marvellous richness of the life of God as the goal of our political process. We are not confined to protest. The *Frui Dei*, human celebration of the divine joy, beauty, and humour, is the goal of human history.[148] The whole point of creation is that God should have a reflection in which he reflects himself, and in which the image of God as the Creator is revealed. 'The glory of God in its glorification by the creature must assume the form of correspondence, or it does not take place at all . . . In this sense . . . the glorifying of God consists simply in the life-obedience of the creature which knows God.'[149] This existence in correspondence is in praise, thanksgiving, gratitude, freedom, righteousness, and love. The doctrine of God thus plays an analogous role in the *Dogmatics* to Marx's famous vision of liberated labour in *Capital*. And as a last salvo against natural theology Barth remarks that it is questionable because it is 'so profoundly tedious and so utterly unmusical'.[150]

CHOSEN PEOPLE

The Context of the Doctrine of Election

Church Dogmatics II/2 was written between autumn 1939 and winter 1941—the darkest days of the war when, in the eyes of many contemporaries, Nazi

---

[146] KD II/1, 690; CD, 612.   [147] KD II/1, 714, 719; CD, 634, 638.
[148] KD II/1, 736, 745; CD, 653, 661.   [149] KD II/1, 760; CD, 674.
[150] KD II/1, 751; CD, 666.

victory seemed inevitable. Just at this time Barth turned to the doctrine of election which, uniquely in the history of Christian exposition, he decided to include in the doctrine of God. Barth was a Reformed Christian who had at first expected to be able to follow Calvin. In fact, alerted by a lecture of Pierre Maury at the Calvin conference in 1936, and also by the work of his brother Peter, who had in the meantime become a noted Calvin scholar, Barth reshaped it from the ground up. In traditional Calvinism election had been expounded as the doctrine of the twofold predestination which embraced all people—a few being predestined to salvation and the others predestined to damnation. This was the view which most of the participants at the Calvin conference continued to defend. Also in the background were a number of secular or pseudo-religious discourses about election— Zionism, and its demonic gentile shadow, the doctrine of the master race, which carried with it a likewise demonized account of the election of the individual in the Führer principle. Election meant the election of Israel, and Barth's exposition of this doctrine could not be without awareness of the savage persecution of Jewry which had been in force since 1933 and was steadily getting worse. Barth responded to all of these movements and events in the course of his exposition.

The leader concept Barth understood as a secular imitation of the concept of the election of Jesus Christ. It is the utter reversal and caricature of that election. In it we have the apotheosis of Western individualism. The leader is the individual 'besides whom there are finally no individuals . . . All freedom and all responsibility, all authority and power . . . belong to him . . . Emerging from the ranks of the many and elevated over them as the other who alone may be an individual, the leader is an absolute usurper in relation to other individuals.'[151] Christ is the reverse of this because what he has, he has for others.

Parallel with this are two secular imitations of the election of the community, the one in the idolatrous exaltation of the nation state, the other in the idea that the proletariat is the true agent of history, according to Soviet communism. From this side too the individual is annulled. It reveals the impotence and inner uncertainty inherent in the idea of individualism.[152] Although in his concern with nationalism Barth is thinking mainly of fascism he also considers that Zionism is 'the prototype of all bad nationalisms'.[153]

Both here and in his lectures at this time Barth insists in the strongest terms on the impossibility of anti-Semitism. 'A Church that becomes antisemitic or even only a-semitic sooner or later suffers the loss of its faith by losing the object of it.'[154] The Jewish question, Barth insists, simply

[151] KD II/2, 342; CD, 311.   [152] KD II/2, 342–3; CD, 312.
[153] KD II/2, 309; CD, 280.   [154] KD II/2, 257; CD, 234.

cannot be relegated to the realm of eschatology. In relation to Israel 'the responsibility of the Church, which itself lives by God's mercy, is already a wholly present reality'—and he adds 'he that has ears to hear let him hear'.[155]

The doctrine of election entails, finally, on the part of each individual, 'an invasion of the dark kingdom of lies', a retreat from its godless glorification. Election, in other words, in 1940/1 especially, entails resistance to fascism.[156]

Election as Good News

Max Weber, to whose famous thesis about Protestantism and the rise of capitalism Barth often refers, had highlighted the role played in the development of capitalism by the Calvinist need to establish for oneself that one was actually one of the elect. Always in the background was the dark prospect of damnation. In Barth's recasting of the doctrine it becomes, on the contrary, 'the sum of good news', the gospel in *nuce*.[157] It is this in the first instance as the election of the God who loves in freedom. Election, says Barth, is analytic to love. Love is never general and abstract but always particular—love of this particular beloved.[158] Election characterizes the love of God as absolutely free, not determined by the worth of the object. It presents us with an ultimate beyond which we cannot enquire—the love of God is the mystery of God which knows no 'wherefore' because 'our ears have heard the Therefore which is the truly satisfying and convincing answer to every question'.[159] This electing love says 'nevertheless' to the creature. In the Tambach lecture Barth had said that we stood deeper in the No than the Yes. Now, by contrast, with the world at war, he insisted that though the Yes could not be heard unless the No was also heard nevertheless 'the first and last word is Yes and not No'.[160] God's freedom amounts to the divine refusal to despair. In his righteousness God avenges sin, but he does so by forgiving it.[161]

God's being is in act, and election is therefore a living act. Once again abstraction emerges as the hallmark of any doctrine which ignores revelation and which consequently plays into the hands of the forces which dehumanize us. The concept of 'decree' favoured by the older Calvinists 'reminds us inevitably of a military or political ordinance, a law, a statute, a rule which lays down in black and white . . . the will of a regnant power'.[162] Election, however, is an act of the divine life in the Spirit, which occurs

---

[155] KD II/2, 335; CD, 305.
[157] KD II/2, 11, 13; CD, 12, 14.
[159] KD II/2, 22; CD, 22.
[161] KD II/2, 30, 35; CD, 29, 34.

[156] KD II/2, 461; CD, 417.
[158] KD II/2, 26; CD, 26.
[160] KD II/2, 12, 13; CD, 13.
[162] KD II/2, 198–9; CD, 181.

in the midst of time, the movement between the electing God and
the elected human being.[163] This activist and concrete understanding of
election depends entirely on identifying it with Jesus Christ. 'Who and what
Jesus Christ is, is something which can only be told, not a system which can
be considered and described.'[164] Failure to make this step was what rendered
the teaching of, for example, the Synod of Dort, 'decadent and profoundly
incredible'.[165] There is a failure in orthodox Calvinism to see that the 'Word'
to which they appeal is Christ. At this point, according to Barth, they felt
impelled to look behind Christ to the *decretum absolutum*, God's absolute will
apart from Christ.[166] Whether such an absolute decree produces horror
or peace it is thoroughly anti-Christian, 'an idea which belongs to natural
theology'.[167]

Jesus Christ, then, the Word made flesh and therefore both electing and
elected, is the heart of Barth's account of election. God's will to become
creature for the good of the creature is the original meaning of election. In
the old dispute between those who maintained that the incarnation was a
response to the Fall (infralapsarians) and those who believed that God's
determination to become human was an eternal resolve (supralapsarians)
Barth came down on the side of the latter. To understand election as the
sum of all good news we must see that Jesus is both the beginning of all
God's ways and works, that his election is specifically to suffering in our
place, and that we must see our own election in that of the man Jesus.[168]
Because when we speak of election we speak of Christ we see that the
content of the No of rejection is the justification of the sinner in him. 'Predestination is the non rejection of man. It is so because it is the rejection of
the Son of God.'[169] More, God's free electing in Christ in turn frees us and
awakens our individuality and autonomy.[170]

The Dialectics of Election

Barth himself does not speak of the dialectics of election. I use the phrase
to speak of the way both community and individual, and more importantly
election and rejection, belong together and cannot be separated out from
each other.

Again breaking with tradition Barth places the election of the community before that of the individual, as he had done as early as the lectures in
Göttingen. But the community is in the first instance Israel, and here we
come to the unavoidable significance of what Barth was saying at this time.

---

[163] KD II/2, 203–4; CD, 185–6.   [164] KD II/2, 206; CD, 188.
[165] KD II/2, 366; CD, 333.   [166] KD II/2, 163–5; CD, 151–3.
[167] KD II/2, 172; CD, 158.   [168] KD II/2, 129; CD, 120.
[169] KD II/2, 182; CD, 167.   [170] KD II/2, 195, 121; CD, 179, 121.

He later reproached himself that at Barmen he had not included an article on the Jews. How does the doctrine of election fare?

Barth proceeds largely through an analysis of Romans 9–11. On the one hand we find the strongest statements affirming Israel's eternal election, in the face of the basic lie of anti-Semitism, that because it was the Jews who crucified Christ they were rejected and destined for shame and punishment. Barth will have none of this. By virtue of their election it is impossible to exterminate Israel, it is impossible to be anti-Semitic, we have to recognize that the Church always needs Israel.[171] In election the Church and Israel belong together.[172] Israel is the people to whom Jesus Christ belongs, a fact that neither Israel nor Church can overlook.[173] On the other hand Israel rejects its election—it is an obdurate people. It represents the 'passing man', the 'form of death'. 'Over against the witness of the Church it must now be a typical expression and incorporation of the human need consequent on sin, of man's limitation and pain, of his transiency and the death to which he is subject . . . It must now live among the nations as the pattern of a historical life which has absolutely no future . . . in this way it punishes itself.'[174] Passages like these make very painful reading in the light of the behaviour of the empirical Church, with its concordats and its shameful silence or even overt anti-Semitism, about which Barth was only too well aware, on the one hand, and the literal death which was the fate of most of Europe's Jewry on the other, which Barth could not know about, but which was bad enough even in terms of what he did know. These passages raise a question which we have to put to all of Barth's theology, namely whether to give absolute priority to exegesis, over against empirical observation, does not reintroduce that abstraction which Barth sees so clearly to be the fatal flaw of the theology he opposes, and especially 'natural' theology.

At the same time it is important to recognize what I am calling the dialectic here. When he turns to the election of the individual he notes that the difference between the godless and others is not a matter of absolute antitheses.[175] Apart from anything else the exegesis of Romans 11 makes quite clear that to believe that the Church's position *vis-à-vis* Israel is final represents unbelief. 'God has not ceased to dispose but is free to dispose again . . . this is the supreme warning and consoling truth in relation to every contemporary situation.'[176] But anyway 'to be rejected of God is the threat whose fulfilment would be the inevitable lot of every single human life.'[177] The sins of the rejected are the sins of the elect also: 'Apart from Jesus Christ they have no advantage over the rejected whose existence the godless

---

[171] KD II/2, 249, 257, 307; CD, 226, 234, 279.   [172] KD II/2, 222; CD, 199.
[173] KD II/2, 259–60; CD, 235–6.   [174] KD II/2, 289; CD, 263.
[175] KD II/2, 373; CD, 339   [176] KD II/2, 324; CD, 294.
[177] KD II/2, 381; CD, 346.

undertake to manifest and repeat and reproduce with their false witness.'[178]
Those who are 'cut off' are not utterly rejected but 'do in their own way
remain in a positive relation to the covenant of God'.[179] The paradigm of this
fact is Judas, who in 'handing over' Jesus, as many of the medieval carols recognized, actually made redemption possible, a truth which Barth spells out
in one of the most powerful pieces of exegesis in the *Dogmatics*. It is Judas
who accompanies Jesus in death. Like all the rejected he insists on passing
judgement on himself, and with him go all the negative figures who came
to bad ends—Pharaoh, Saul, and Ahitophel and all their kind. But all the
'rejected' remain a witness to the elect in that they depend on the grace of
God and that grace is there for the rejected also.[180] Decisively, 'the rejected
man exists in the person of Jesus Christ only in such a way that he is assumed
into His being as the elect and beloved of God . . . With Jesus Christ the
rejected can only *have been* rejected. He cannot *be* rejected any more.'[181]
Pressed as to whether this did not commit him to universalism Barth always
insisted that it did not. 'The Church will not . . . preach an *apokatastasis*, nor
will it preach a powerless grace of Jesus Christ or a wickedness of men
which is too powerful for it. But without any weakening of the contrast, and
also without any arbitrary dualism, it will preach the overwhelming power
of grace and the weakness of human wickedness in face of it.'[182]

GOD'S COMMAND

Ethics as Part of Dogmatics

The recognition that dogmatics and ethics belong together is to be found in
the first *Romans*, but it is not until the *Church Dogmatics* that the full implications of this recognition are worked out.[183] In 1/2 Barth advances two
reasons for the necessary integration of ethics with dogmatics. Negatively,
were we to have an independent ethics it would subject theology to anthropology, as all ethics presuppose a view of the human. Positively, the Word of
God necessarily claims people, and the spelling out of that claim is ethics.[184]
These arguments are much more fully developed in 11/2. There Barth denies
that Christian ethics are one party in a contest with all sorts of other ethical
views: 'It is not one disputant in debate with others. It is the final word of the
original chairman.'[185] It listens to other ethics to receive material for its
deliberations, and to that extent is comprehensive, but it is fundamentally

---

[178] KD 11/2, 382; CD, 347.   [179] KD 11/2, 392; CD, 356.
[180] KD 11/2, 506; CD, 456.   [181] KD 11/2, 502; CD, 453.
[182] KD 11/2, 529; CD, 477.   [183] Cf. R1, 392.
[184] KD 1/2, 876, 887–8; CD, 783, 793.   [185] KD 11/2, 575; CD, 519.

critical. To act rightly or to realize the good is to hear God's command and to be obedient to it. The grace and forgiveness with which God meets us is at the same time a claim on us. 'The Gospel itself has the form and fashion of the Law. The one Word of God is both Gospel *and* Law.' The gospel claims—and enables—human freedom. It is the grace of God which is the answer to the ethical problem, and thus the obedience called for is not heteronomous but joyous and freely willed.

Christian ethics is the theory of the praxis of obedience. It is not sufficient to talk of a command of God, for that may be denied. 'What "there is" is not as such the command of God. But the core of the matter is that God gives his command, that he gives himself to be our Commander. God's command, God himself, gives himself to be known. And as he does so, he is heard. Man is made responsible.'[186] Human action follows and is determined by the action of God. Moreover there is no divine claim in itself but only concrete divine claims which meet us afresh in every different situation.

The danger of such a command ethic can be that it seems to warrant an ethical occasionalism, and to be entirely arbitrary. Barth often gave grounds for such assumptions. After his 1934 lecture on 'The Christian as Witness' he was asked how he would give a psychological account of what he had just said. He referred to the Oxford Group movement habit of keeping a spiritual journal. If you say: it is essential to do that, the reply is—on the contrary you can be quite negligent in this respect. If on the other hand keeping such a journal is prohibited then Barth would insist on it.[187] Similarly in relation to the war with Germany Barth insisted that in this case armed struggle was commanded, though in other circumstances this could be rank disobedience. 'The Church cannot identify the command of God with any "ism", with pacifism as little as with militarism.'[188] Where, then, do we find any ethical continuity? The answer is in the rigorous attempt to be faithful to Scripture.

The Church is most faithful to its tradition . . . when linked but not tied by its past, it today searches the Scriptures and orientates its life by them as though this had to happen today for the first time . . . the principle of necessary repetition and renewal, and not a law of stability, is the law of the spiritual growth and continuity of our life.[189]

The living God becomes our commander in and through the witness we have in Scripture. Christian ethics therefore does not rest on our hearing 'the

---

[186] KD II/2, 609; CD, 548.
[187] *God in Action*, Edinburgh, T. & T. Clark, 1937, 119, 120.
[188] *Eine Schweizer Stimme 1938–1945*, Zürich, Theologischer Verlag, 1945, 63.
[189] KD II/2, 720; CD, 647.

voice of conscience'. The command is not revealed *by* conscience but *to* it. All that conscience does is to warn us against every perversion of the command into the dictates of our own self will.[190] As regards pacifism and war, therefore, 'The Church can and must preach peace, but she must be open in every new situation to learn from God's Word exactly what is to be understood by peace.'[191]

The Being of the Church as Political Responsibility

The Word of God summons us: it makes us responsible. It calls forth a 'continuous answer' from us which has an essential political dimension. *Romans* makes clear that Christians should participate in the work of the state. 'Because Christians recognise the order of God in the order of the sword, compulsion and fear, they themselves can be neither anti-political nor a-political . . . They will then understand . . . that their reasonable service, consistently with the will and work of God himself, must take the form of the service of God in politics.'[192] This essential political work, however, also consists in the Church truly being the Church. 'Everything depends upon whether Christians are really the host that is awakened and astir in the midst of many sleepers.'[193] Barth has especially in mind the corruption of the understanding of the Church we find amongst the German Christians. Thus Paul Althaus had insisted in 1933 that the only true Church was a *Volkskirche*: 'that means, in the first place: serving the *Volk* as *Volk*, as a totality of life; then, serving it according to its nature, which again involves two things: a true German proclamation of the gospel and the entrance of the church into the organic life forms and living customs of the *Volk*'.[194] By contrast what Barth meant was spelt out over these years above all in three lectures: 'The need of the Evangelical Church', in 1931; and two 1938 lectures, 'The Church and the Political Problem of our Day', and *Rechtfertigung und Recht*, translated as 'Church and State' but concerned, as the German (lit. 'justification and justice') implies, with the Christological basis for politics.

The 1931 lecture takes up the theme of *Quousque tandem*. No one could at this stage predict how bad things would become within two years, but as noted earlier, Barth had heard alarm bells ringing. Delivered to an audience of 1,400 people in Berlin University the lecture was frequently interrupted by applause indicating, as with the later lecture on the Reformation as decision, how many people heard from Barth a key and critical word addressed to the time. Barth distinguished between a true and a false need. The first,

---

[190] KD II/2, 745; CD, 668.   [191] *Eine Schweizer Stimme*, 63.
[192] KD II/2, 807; CD, 722.   [193] KD II/2, 808; CD, 723/4.
[194] Cited in Scholder, *The Churches 1914–1934*, 209.

genuinely evangelical need, is that the Church is constituted by the marginality or excludedness (*Draussenseins*) of the crucified Christ. What this means is that the Church is both a Church of sinners, of excluded ones, but also a Church under the cross. Concretely, the Church cannot seek validity, influence, or spiritual or material power for itself. The Church is not the kingdom of God or the present realization of reconciliation or the sacrifice of Christ. All the Church does is witness to God's deed and God's promise. The true Church is always a Church in need, a Church at every point with empty hands.[195] The second, false, need however takes the form of both a flight *from* visibility, in which the necessary institutional form of the Church is denied, and a flight *into* visibility, and it is here that Barth finds the real contemporary problem. The one is the problem of a false idealism, exemplified by Tillich, the other of a false realism, where Barth's opponent was above all General Superintendent Dibelius. Barth saw in the Church which was concerned with its own position in society the preaching of a middle class ideology, and particularly attacked the hyphen between Church and nation, German and evangelical. The German people need an evangelical church, not a *German* evangelical church, they need a church which is truly able to witness because truly independent of all the powers of the day, whether of left or right.[196]

As we have seen, the political responsibility of the Church was a key aspect of the church struggle. The deteriorating situation in Germany, and the annexation of Austria in March 1938, led Barth to clarify his thought on the Church's political task. In these years Barth moves from a primarily critical to a primarily constructive approach to the state. Reformed teaching on the relation to the state, he realized, was quite inadequate, and he sought to spell out its Christological basis, to demonstrate an integral connection between justification and human political justice. The state, Barth insists, in accordance with Reformed teaching, is ordained by God, and even in its demonic forms fulfils God's will. In the New Testament the state is spoken of in the language of the angelic 'powers', but these are subject to Christ. Therefore, 'when the New Testament speaks of the State we are, fundamentally, in the Christological sphere'.[197] It is not inevitable that the state will play the role of the Beast from the abyss because it is created in Christ, through him and for him. All authority is ultimately Christ's, and this applies to state authority also. Whilst both church and state have their basis in Christ they have different functions. The state exists to establish a secure and peaceful existence for all people. The Church exists to preach justification, and the service it owes to the state is to preach the gospel and celebrate the

---

[195] 'Die Not der Evangelischen Kirche' in *Der Götze Wackelt*, 33–40.
[196] Ibid., 56, 57.   [197] 'Rechtfertigung und Recht' in *Eine Schweizer Stimme*, 30.

sacraments. The roles are distinct, and it is fatal either for the Church to seek
to become the state, for example in some kind of theocracy, or for the state
to seek to become a church, and to demand from its citizens not merely
obedience but love. But the command to discern the spirits applies to political spirits as to all others and a state which threatens the freedom of preaching has to be resisted for the state's own sake, to restore it to the function to
which it is called. In Zwingli's phrase it may be necessry to 'overthrow with
God' unjust states.

In establishing a just state Barth recognizes that the New Testament
speaks only of subjects and not of citizens. 'For us the fulfilment of political
duty means rather responsible choice or authority, responsible decision
about the validity of law, responsible care for their maintenance, in a word
political action, which may and must also mean political struggle.'[198] Barth
can find this in the New Testament by taking Romans 13 together with the
command to intercede for rulers in 1 Timothy 2. 'Can serious prayer, in the
long run, continue without the corresponding work? Can we ask God for
something which we are not at the same moment determined and prepared
to bring about, so far as it lies within the bounds of our possibility?'[199] Fundamentally Barth considered that the New Testament justified a democratic
understanding of the state, and when the Church fulfils its function he
believes that it is possible to have a true order of human affairs in which
justice, wisdom, and peace, equity, and care for human welfare can be established, not as a kingdom of God on earth but an image (*Abbild*) of the eternal
kingdom.[200]

Barth's most outspoken account of the Church's political responsibility,
the lecture on 'The Church and the Political Question of our Day' was delivered in December of the same year, a few weeks after the destruction of
Jewish homes and synagogues, the *Krystallnacht*. He developed his theme in
eight stages. The Church is a people (*Volk*) who witness to Christ's priestly,
prophetic, and kingly ministry. That they are a people speaks of the connection, indeed unity, with the people of Israel. Because the Lord to whom
all power is given is the theme of their preaching the Church cannot retreat
to a concern only for the inner life. It is impossible to hear Christ without
hearing the sighing of the creature, and especially of the oppressed. Second,
true witness to Christ demands concrete decisions in relation to the world

---

[198] Ibid., 53.   [199] Ibid.

[200] Ibid., 56. R. Williams argues that Barth goes beyond *Rechtfertigung* in the pages on the
state in KD II/2 'The shift from the 1938 lecture is in the idea that the state not only preserves
social peace for the sake of preaching of the gospel, but safeguards the possibility of active and
creative reconciliation within ordered bounds.' 'Barth, War and the State' in N. Biggar (ed.),
Reckoning with Barth, London and Oxford, Mowbray, 1988, 182. Of course the fundamentally
Christocentric approach to the state already informs the earlier lecture.

in which we live. Confession cannot be a matter simply of thinking and discussing. The decisive political question of the day Barth judges to be National Socialism. It is this because it is not simply a political experiment but makes idolatrous claims for itself, presenting a demonic inversion of both kingdom and messiah.[201] This makes any Christian affirmation of National Socialism impossible—an assertion which brought an angry denial from Hirsch, and the accusation that he was 'the bitter enemy of the German people'.

The fundamental theological ground for opposition to National Social- ism is that it is in principle anti-Semitic: 'Whoever is in principle an enemy of the Jews is . . . in principle an enemy of Jesus Christ. Anti-semitism is sin against the Holy Spirit. Anti-semitism is rejection of the grace of God.'[202] In face of this any faith decision has to be a political decision to resist it. The Church has to pray for its suppression and elimination as in former days it prayed for the overcoming of Islam. In face of it silence is impossible and only speaking out will do.

Barth's passionate opposition to anti-Semitism brought him once again into conflict with Brunner, who disputed that it was possible to say that salvation *comes* (as opposed to 'came') from the Jews. Since 1938 Barth had treated this affirmation as an *articulus stantis et cadentis ecclesiae* and was once again completely unable to compromise with his Zürich colleague here.[203]

For Barth, doing theology was crucial to the Church's task as watchman: a church without theology is a pagan church. Barth was convinced that it was neo-Protestantism which at least prepared the ground for National Socialism, in that it led the Church to lose its true theme. Over against God's will revealed is the world of our wishes, calling to us with voices of blood, or conscience, or genius, or destiny. 'Let us not deceive ourselves: these voices are always the echo of our own voice.'[204] It is obedience to the Word of God which enables us to resist this hegemony. Because the Church is con- stituted by the Word it is engaged in a struggle against idols. Just because those in the Church are hearers of the Word they are most keenly aware of their profanity. In the Church nothing human is foreign, but the Church's solidarity with the world is deepest where it is distinguished most sharply from the world. 'In the Church the boundaries of the human are watched and guarded—no idols are worshipped there, and no ideologies cultivated.'[205] If we think about the job of the pastor—of course human

---

[201] 'Die Kirche und die politische Frage von Heute' in *Theologische Fragen*, 85.
[202] Ibid., 90.
[203] See Busch, *Barth*, 313.
[204] 'Gottes Wille und unsere Wünsche' in *Theologische Fragen*, 151.
[205] 'Offenbarung, Kirche, Theologie' in *Theologische Fragen*, 169.

sympathy and political understanding are taken for granted but the key thing is preaching the Word of God. As those who are called our task is to tell others what we have heard: that Christ is salvation, the Lord, the Word become flesh.[206]

War against Hitler as Obedience to God's Command

The letters to Christians all over Europe between 1938 and 1942 may be regarded as examples of Barth's ethical stand in action. We find in them, first, a sovereign confidence in God's overruling of all events. Even in the darkest days of the war Barth never doubted that Hitler would ultimately be defeated. In December 1939 he wrote to a French pastor that it might well be that the war would take a turn for the worse with 'signs and wonders of Antichrist'. Only if Christians were prepared to submit themselves to the judgement of God could they resist Hitler 'joyfully and confidently'.[207] Some took Barth's warning—only too dreadfully fulfilled—as encouraging defeatism. Barth's response, in October 1940, was that resignation in the face of defeat was impossible. There were those who were preaching humility before God's judgement. This, said Barth, we have heard before—in 1933 in Germany. Hitler was able to produce paralysis in people but this power of his has nothing to do with our proper humility before God. On the contrary, that humility reminds us that the word 'total' applies only to God, and so there can be no talk of 'total defeat'. Since only God's omnipotent grace is total we have to retain our inward joy and courage in the face of what for the moment represents the victory of the big battalions.[208]

Resistance to Hitler as obedience to God's command was enjoined in the strongest language possible. Every Czech soldier who resists Hitler fights for the whole of Europe but also for the Church of Jesus Christ, he wrote to Hromadka in September 1938.[209] This war, he wrote to the Christians in Britain in July 1941, is not only a just war, but commanded us by God.[210] 'Christians who do not realize that they must take part unreservedly in this war must have slept over their Bible as well as their newspaper.'[211] The command of God is that justice be done on earth, the purpose for which the state is established. The Church cannot remain neutral in the face of flagrant injustice.[212]

This insistence goes alongside an absolute refusal to demonize the Germans, or even Hitler, a refusal to preach a crusade. On the one hand he is clear about the evils of National Socialism, and about what, in German history, enables its political success.

---

[206] 'Der Dienst am Wort Gottes' in *Theologische Fragen*, 206.
[207] *Schweizer Stimme*, 115.   [208] Ibid., 153, 154.
[209] *Schweizer Stimme*, 58.   [210] Ibid., 181.
[211] Ibid., 189.   [212] Ibid., 111.

The German people suffer from the heritage of a paganism that is mystical and that is in consequence unrestrained, unwise and illusory. And it suffers, too, from the heritage of the greatest Christian of Germany, from Martin Luther's error on the relation between Law and Gospel, between the temporal and spiritual order and power. This error has established, confirmed and idealized the natural paganism of the German people, instead of limiting and restraining it.[213]

Fascism is an *Ungeist*—an anti-Spirit, part of the revolution of nihilism, a spirit of conscious lies, intentional injustice and fundamental contempt and violation of human values.[214] Without doubt we encounter in it the principalities and powers. The enterprise of Hitler is a spirit of mischief given freedom in the world for a while to put our faith in the resurrection and our obedience to the test.[215]

At the same time, every people has just such an inheritance from paganism. The Allied cause is not the *causa Dei*, and we cannot take up the crusade. 'The one who died on the cross died also for Hitler, and for all the confused people who, willingly or unwillingly, stand under his banner.'[216] Barth insists over and over again in these letters that the whole of Europe is responsible for National Socialism, because of the mistakes made at Versailles in 1919. Contrary to his former colleague Hirsch's allegations, he was never a bitter foe of the German people. At Christmas 1940 he broadcast a message to German Christians on the BBC: 'We do not forget you. We don't know everything, but we know a good deal about what makes it difficult for you to be joyful this year—about your sorrow and care . . . about the terrible things you and our Jewish brothers and sisters are going through in Germany . . . you must know that we pray for you. Pray also for us!' He concludes with a verse from a joyful carol.

Whilst bearing in mind the 'poor Germans' he was scathing about his own government's failings. Against defeatism in Switzerland he insisted that the country was worth fighting for but that did not mean it was past reproach. The Swiss political covenant of 1815 was introduced 'in the name of Almighty God'. In view of that fact Barth asked why so little was being done for the unemployed and the poor to secure food and other necessaries, why the largest political party, the Social Democrats, were excluded from the wartime government, why freedom of speech was so vigorously censored, why refugees were being turned away, and why Switzerland was trading so vigorously with the Reich government. Christians at least had to understand what was entailed in referring to Almighty God in the Constitution, in having the cross on the national flag. What was required of Swiss Christians was solidarity and courage in all undertakings of the country against its enemies, but also simply that they be the Church, witnessing to

---

[213] Ibid., 113.   [214] Ibid., 133.
[215] Ibid., 185, 186.   [216] Ibid., 111.

God's grace and forgiveness in every village and thus acting as salt and light in the wider community.[217]

This talk was given at huge rallies, and the critique of Swiss trade caused uproar. Barth had taken the precaution of having 16,000 copies secretly printed, and these had all been distributed before the censor banned it a fortnight after its delivery. When accused by the government of confusing theology with politics Barth denied that they could be separated, but also rejected the implication that his theology was nothing but a disguise for political arguments.[218] These critics, like many later friends and enemies of Barth's, had failed to understand the way in which, for him, theology, as part of the Church's task, was necessarily *both* political *and* critical of all politics.

THEOLOGY AS POLITICS

In her profound examination of feminist theology since the 1960s Angela West remarks that idolatry always offers a solution to the problem of the last judgement, making a division between those for whom God's mercy is reserved and those made to bear the weight of human sin and thus receive the judgement of God. It is the theology of the final solution. The twentieth century Church, she notes, has embraced this theology, preserving a superstructure of religious idealism, but resting on a foundation of racism, sexism, and class privilege. What has to be preached instead is Christ the mercy of God and the judgement of God.[219] It is my contention that Barth understood this and that this was the heart of his struggle against idolatry.

The decade under review was, in terms of world events, the most momentous of Barth's life, the one where he played a part, albeit a small one, on the world stage. Barth himself understood this part as remaining true to his theological vocation. He spelled this out in his interview for *The Christian Century* in 1938. What has been at stake in the Church struggle, he asks. 'Simply this, to hold fast to and in a completely new way to understand and practice the truth that God stands above all gods, and that the church in the *Volk* and society has under all circumstances, and over against the State, her own task, proclamation, and order, determined for her in the Holy Scriptures.' The church theological conflict contained within itself the political conflict. Europe has not understood the danger posed by National Socialism because 'it does not understand the First Commandment . . .

---

[217] 'Im Namen Gottes des Allmächtigen' in *Eine Schweizer Stimme*, 201 ff.
[218] Busch, *Barth*, 310.
[219] A. West, *Deadly Innocence*, London, Mowbray, 1995, 210.

Because it does not see that this transgression, because it is sin against God, drags the corruption of the nations in its wake'.[220]

From the start Barth felt that opposition to National Socialism meant opposition to natural theology. Barth says over and over again that natural theology and neo-Protestanism are at least powerless against the German Christian ideology, if they do not actually lead there. There is a revealing exchange in the Barth–Bultmann correspondence. At a meeting in November 1934 Barth told Bultmann, to his dismay, that he had expected to see him amongst the ranks of the German Christians. In reply to a shocked letter Barth wrote:

Do not be upset any more that I was in fact filled with distrust to the extent that I had expected to see you turn up among the D.C. It has been proved by the facts that I made a mistake in this case and therefore that something may have been wrong in my basic suspicions as well. You must grant me not only the general truth that it was possible to suspect anyone of anything in this crazy year but also the particular truth that you did not make it easy for me to see clearly in advance that you would not do what Heidegger has done with drums and trumpets and also Gogarten, whom I had to regard as the normative theologian in your eyes. According to my observations it was a fact that all those who worked positively with a natural theology or the like *could* become D.C. and that most of them incidentally or definitively *did* so. One may validly infer reality from possibility. It was plain in your case that I was wrong about the reality. But you will need to explain to me how far the possibility did *not* reside in *your* fundamental theology.[221]

The point about Heidegger is well taken, but of course Barth never allowed himself to consider that he had made a mistake in his basic presuppositions. Throughout this period he continues to speak of natural theology as the mother of all evils.

In 1937/8 Barth was invited to give the Gifford Lectures in Aberdeen, which are expressly for the consideration of natural theology. He did so largely by ignoring it, and commenting on the Scots Confession of 1560 instead. The denial that a Reformation theologian could have anything to do with natural theology was in fact quite new, like many of what appeared to be Barth's 'traditional' positions. In the series given just over fifty years later James Barr has examined Barth's attitude to natural theology. He argues that natural theology was not a necessary part of German Christian theology, and that it could even be used to inspire resistance to fascism. He argues, as Brunner did, that Scripture, Barth's ultimate criterion, does in fact contain a good deal of 'natural theology'. In his view the immediate consequence of Barth's opposition to natural theology was that preoccupation with the issue distracted attention from the urgent business

---

[220] *How I Changed my Mind*, 46, 47.   [221] B–B, 76.

of opposition to fascism, whilst the long term consequence was a serious skewing of biblical studies, making a dogmatic system prior to critical exegesis.[222]

At this point I shall take up only the first of these charges. To the extent that 'theology of the Word' empowered Barmen, and later South African Kairos theology in the struggle against apartheid, it has shown itself an effective political instrument. There may be more to the charge that natural theology is prone to co-option by the status quo than Barr allows. Barth's hostility to natural theology develops as part of his original discovery that it is in 'the strange new world of the Bible' that there is a critical principle to free us from supine endorsement of the reigning culture. In a sense he uses the term 'natural theology' for any position which does so endorse the status quo. But here we have to bear in mind the very important observation of Klaus Scholder, which is in line with Barr's suggestions. Speaking of those who protested at the Aryan laws in 1933 he writes:

> The minority in both churches which did not keep silent but rather spoke up, had no common criterion other than uneasy consciences. Having an uneasy conscience was obviously independent of age, confession, estate or political alignment. It bound together the old Bavarian nobleman with the young socialist pastor in the Rhineland, the liberal professor of theology in Hessen with the Berlin Dominican Father, the Protestant German Nationalist with the Catholic Centre Party member. These uneasy consciences remained, and remain, underivable, personally as well as socially.[223]

It was thus independent of any subscription or otherwise to natural theology. The question is, if Barth is wrong here, if natural theology did not carry with it all the implications which he so often implied, does this not in turn place a significant question mark against Barth's theological enterprise?

We may put this another way. If resistance to idols is a matter of conscience more or less evenly distributed amongst all forms of religious and political belief, as Scholder implies, does Scripture have the unique critical role Barth assigns it? These questions cannot be lightly dismissed. What can be said with confidence is that Barth's understanding of the Word of God in Christ enabled the articulation of a clear opposition to fascism, and that more recently it has done the same *vis-à-vis* apartheid.[224] If it is true, as James Barr argues, that natural theology can empower political opposition it has to be granted that what is 'natural' at any given time is only too likely to be an expression of the status quo, which is what Barth is getting at in speaking

---

[222] J. Barr, *Biblical Faith and Natural Theology*, Oxford, Clarendon, 1993, esp. chs. 1 and 6. His series of lectures were delivered in 1991.

[223] Scholder, *The Churches 1914–1934*, 279.

[224] See Villa Vicencio, *On Reading Barth*.

of natural theology as the domestication or 'middle class-ification' of the gospel.

In any event, whilst the critique of natural theology looms large, the work of fresh creation in the doctrine of God and the doctrine of election looms larger still, and at the end of the day it is these doctrines which are Barth's creative political resources, constituting as they do an ontology of freedom which goes beyond liberal ideas of the autonomous agent. Here there are profound resources for those of us whose being is defined by the laws of the market, an election which is not consumption, in which consumer choice is a parody of true choosing in the same way that the *Führerprinzip* was a parody of the election of Jesus Christ. And it is here above all that Barth shows us what it is for theology to be political.

5

Nevertheless!

January 1942–Spring 1951

1756–1791! This was the time when God was under attack for the Lisbon earthquake, and theologians and other well meaning folk were hard put to it to defend Him. In face of the problem of theodicy, Mozart had the peace of God which far transcends all the critical or speculative reason that praises or reproves.

Karl Barth, 1949

In June 1941 Hitler ordered the invasion of Russia, and massive gains were made before the end of the year, in the course of which the Russians sustained more than 4.5 million casualties. The 'final solution' began at the same time, leading to the death of 6 million Jews, and millions of gypsies and others by 1945. In December came Pearl Harbour, and Hitler announced that Germany was at war with the United States. For a further six months things seemed to go Germany's way. Rommel captured Tobruk and advanced to within 60 miles of Alexandria by July. The U-Boat war was in full swing and 4.5 million tonnes of shipping were sunk in the first six months of 1942. The tide turned in the autumn. In October Rommel's army was routed, and surrendered the following May. In November the German Sixth Army was encircled at Stalingrad, and capitulated in February. New anti-submarine devices led to the sinking of a sixth of the U-boat fleet in May 1943. The same month saw the start of round the clock bombing of German cities. France was liberated in August 1944. The gas ovens continued in operation until the Allies entered the camps in the spring of 1945, as did the punitive Gestapo machine with regard to German 'traitors' like Bonhoeffer. Hitler finally committed suicide in his bunker in Berlin on 1 May 1945. Germany surrendered on 8 May.

Barth's frequent interventions on the need for resistance to fascism, and his words of encouragement to Christians in Holland and Norway, stopped by the end of 1942, when it was already clear to him that an Allied victory was inevitable. 'It is no accident', he noted in his post-war collection of writings, *Eine Schweizer Stimme*, 'that this volume contains no statement of mine from the end of 1942 to the middle of 1944. On 22 January 1943 Tripoli fell;

on 31 January Stalingrad followed. On 6 June 1944 the invasion of France followed. It was the time of the decisive turn in the war, and, until other issues obtruded, I was only too glad to keep quiet.'[1] The date of his next public statement on contemporary issues is 23 July 1944, when he lectured on 'The Promise and Responsibility of the Christian Community in Present Circumstances', addressing what he saw as the special temptations of the post-war period. At this time he joined the 'Movement for a Free Germany', in which he and Charlotte von Kirschbaum served alongside Communists and others. He began to insist on the need to befriend the Germans, and took the earliest opportunity to return to Germany himself, lecturing twice in Freiburg in July 1945, and in September visiting Frankfurt, Marburg, and Bonn.

Germany was in chaos. Every fifth inhabitant of the Western zone of Germany, occupied by France, Britain, and the United States, was a refugee. Between 1945 and 1952 about 2 million refugees left the Soviet zone to come to the West. Political parties were restarted in Germany in 1945 but Barth's old party, the SPD, which was far too intransigently socialist for the occupying powers, quickly lost ground to the newly formed Christian Democratic Union, under the leadership of Adenauer. During the winter of 1945/6 the Communist Party gained absolute control of East Germany, under Walter Ulbricht. Tensions between the two blocs gradually escalated. Churchill made his 'iron curtain' speech on 5 March 1946. During 1947 the three Western blocs were gradually brought more and more into alignment, and in June 1948 a currency reform was carried out for the whole of the Western sector, which was opposed by Stalin. As a protest he imposed the blockade of Berlin, which lasted until May of the following year. This level of antagonism prompted the formation of Nato, whose treaty was signed in April 1949.

Outside Germany, economic recovery in Europe was rapid after the temporary setback of 1947, when disastrous weather caused acute food shortages. The years which immediately followed saw the large scale mechanization of European agriculture. From the end of 1947 Marshall Aid sought to restart the market economy of Western Europe, and in the next three years the output of goods and services across Europe rose by 25 per cent, so that by the end of 1950 it was 35 per cent above pre-war levels. During the 1950s Germany in particular witnessed an extraordinary growth in its gross domestic product, the 'German economic miracle'.

Barth taught the summer semester of 1946 in Bonn and, in a wide ranging tour, met Ulbricht and the leaders of the German Communist Party in the Russian sector of Berlin, and criticized the Allied military occu-

---

[1] *Eine Schweizer Stimme*, 306.

pation for doing insufficient to nurture democracy. The semester in Bonn was repeated the following year, and his open lectures on theology published as *Dogmatics in Outline*, but Barth felt it was notably less successful. He refused the invitation for a third year, and the invitation to become Rector of Bonn University. He was disappointed with the course of the German Protestant Church, preoccupied as it was with questions about the Stuttgart Confession of guilt, denazification, the grievous divisions left by the church struggle, and on top of that the demythologizing controversy, and with reorganization. He next returned in 1951 for a seminar in which he urged church opposition to reactionary tendencies in Germany.

During the years between 1942 and the spring of 1951 Barth wrote the four volumes of his doctrine of creation, a huge volume of work, but if all of his occasional pieces on political and social themes from this period were put together they would also make a very substantial book. It is important to understand this, as these writings constitute the decisive commentary on the doctrine of creation which, as the church struggle of the 1930s had shown, often had very conservative political implications. This could not be the case for Barth, whose interventions were directed first towards reconstruction in Europe, and especially in Germany, and then towards the urging of sanity in the 'Cold War'.

In the introductory chapter I noted that Barth's later work did not fall neatly into blocks of historical time in the way his earlier work did. His many addresses on the Church from this period, and especially on church and state, anticipate the teaching which was to follow not only on the Church but on justification and sanctification and are essential in understanding the concrete and practical orientation of that teaching.[2] Conversely, his treatment of war in the ethics of creation needs to be supplemented, as he himself recognized, by the intervention on nuclear weapons which he made in 1958. In 1950 Barth was still thinking primarily of the Second World War; very shortly thereafter he realized that this was inadequate to the new situation introduced by nuclear weapons. The problem of the Cold War was on the agenda from 1946 to the end of Barth's writing career, and is reflected more obviously in the doctrine of reconciliation than in the doctrine of creation. However, it is also the case that the two decades of economic growth which began after the war shaped the cultural climate decisively only as the 1950s advanced, whereas the war and reconstruction still dominated public attention throughout the period in which the doctrine of creation was written.

---

[2] B. Klappert has shown how Barth's lecture on 'The Christian Community and the Civil Community' anticipates his teaching on justification (paras. 15–16), on freedom (17–21) and liberation(22–6) in KD IV/1 to IV/3, in 'Die Rechts-, Freiheits und Befreiungsgeschichte Gottes mit dem Menschen', *EvT* 49 (1989), 474–6.

PARABLES OF THE KINGDOM

'What is Europe now?' asked Winston Churchill in 1947. 'A rubble heap, a charnel house, a breeding ground of pestilence and hate.'[3] Before the First World War, Barth told a student audience in Budapest in 1948, 'the walls of old Europe were still standing; its light, though already somewhat clouded over, was still shining'.

Today it shines no more. Western civilisation is out of joint. Instead of leading us to still further heights, the progress of the centuries has suddenly brought us to the depths of two world wars which have left a sea of ruin behind them and destroyed millions upon millions of lives, though no one can say what they all really died for. . . . there is no doubt that in recent years the whole conception of a Christian civilisation in the West has been pitilessly exposed as an illusion.[4]

Barth's first concern in this situation was to analyse the causes of this 'sea of ruin' and to set out what he understood as the Church's contribution to its remedy.[5] In this situation the Church must witness to the kingdom, to the fact that God rules. Jesus is the kingdom and 'where two or three are gathered together something of the wind of the kingdom of God, of certainty and hope, will breathe through contemporary events'.[6] Secondly it has to witness to the fact that a just and free state is a divinely willed necessity: 'True politics is, according to the clear Word of the Apostle Paul (Romans 13.4), also the service of God.'[7] Thirdly, it is responsible for preaching the forgiveness of sins. It was on the basis of this necessity that Barth urged friendship to the Germans. 'What the Germans need today', he urged at the beginning of 1945, 'are true friends—not the friends of Job . . . whose one fault was that they wanted to be teachers, and not friends.' Preaching was useless. What the Germans need to experience is the reality of forgiveness, that the gospel comes before the law. 'With the moral and social law at the front of our minds we can only be teachers, and so against them. With the gospel at the front of our minds, and in our hearts we can and must be their friends, unreservedly for them.'[8]

The second point, the need for a true and honest politics, was expounded in Berlin and other German cities in the celebrated lecture on the Christian community and the civil community in 1946. The Christian community,

---

[3] Cited in W. Laqueur, *Europe in Our Time: A History 1945–1992*, Harmondsworth, Penguin, 1992, 105.

[4] 'The Christian Community in the Midst of Political Change' in *Against the Stream: Shorter Post War Writings*, London, SCM, 1954, 56–7.

[5] I have outlined Barth's analysis in Chapter 3.

[6] 'Verheissung und Verantwortung der christlichen Gemeinde im heutigen Zeitgeschehen' in *Theologische Fragen*, 326.

[7] Ibid., 327.   [8] 'Die Deutschen und wir' in ibid., 351–4.

Barth argued, had 'ultimate and supremely political significance' in that it witnessed to the original and final pattern the state represented, namely the kingdom of God.[9] He regarded the Church as the inner circle, and the state as the outer circle of Christ's kingdom. Though the state certainly cannot be equated with the kingdom of God it exists 'as an allegory, as a correspondence, and an analogue to the Kingdom of God' in virtue of the fact that the kingdom is its ultimate goal.[10] There is an 'analogical but extremely concrete relationship' between the Christian gospel and certain political decisions and modes of behaviour. Though Barth maintained that no political model amounted to *the* Christian concept of the state he did allow a certain priority to democratic socialism—a priority spelled out in his later doctrine of the Church. 'The essence of Christian politics is not a system . . . but a constant direction, a continuous line of discoveries on both sides of the boundary which separates the political from the spiritual spheres, a correlation between explication and application.'[11] This constant line was a commitment to the poor, to the weak, and to social justice.[12] To the indignation of many German hearers he insisted on tracing the catastrophe of National Socialism back to Bismarck, with his exaltation of *potentia*, power that masters and breaks the law, over *potestas*, power which follows and serves the law.[13]

The category of *Gleichnis* (parable) and of *Entsprechung* (correspondence) are vital terms in Barth's theology, as Helmut Gollwitzer noted. 'The concepts of "parable" and "correspondence" display a central significance in Barth's theology. It is indicative of academic theology's idealist way of thinking that it is not these concepts but their correlate from the theory of knowledge—the concept of analogy—which has held the centre of attention in the discussion and interpretation of Barth. In reality the entire direction of Barth's thought leads to praxis: to faith as the praxis-determining element, not to faith as the enabling of dogmatic utterances.'[14] It also indicates the continued separation of ethics and dogmatics in European theology. The concept of parable goes beyond the eschatological proviso and shows that the kingdom of God is not an individual and symbolic reality but presses us towards the realization of a 'brotherly human society filled with salvation in communion with God'.[15]

[9] 'The Christian Community and the Civil Community', in *Against the Stream*, 20–1.

[10] Ibid., 32. Gregor Smith translated *Gleichnis* as 'allegory'.

[11] Ibid., 42. For commitment to democracy, though not what is called democracy in the West, see p. 44.

[12] Ibid., 36.

[13] Ibid., 40; *Theologische Fragen*, 359, 405.

[14] H. Gollwitzer, 'The Kingdom of God and Socialism' in Hunsinger, *Barth and Radical Politics*, 97.

[15] Ibid., 99.

The years immediately after the war, during which the Cold War emerged, were a time of appeal to noble principles on both sides, and Barth opposed himself to them more than ever, even those of progress and development. 'Since God himself became human, human beings are the measure of all things . . . even the most wretched person . . . must be resolutely defended against the autocracy of every mere "cause". Human beings do not have to serve causes; causes have to serve human beings.'[16] The breath of principles and postulates and world views, he insisted, was not the breath of life.[17] The Church had to be the place where 'false ideas were seen through and rendered innocuous'.[18] As opposed to principles Barth urged a new humanism, which he believed was implied by the gospel. Already in 1949 he was talking about the 'humanism of God'.[19] It was, of course, supremely the gospel of Christ he believed Europe needed, but he also looked forward to a period in which 'the music of Mozart and the poetry of Goethe will be received with ever more sensitive ears and open hearts'.[20] The 'spiritual presuppositions' for the healing of Europe were in his view a newly serious approach to the *human* spirit (and not just the divine), a sense of responsibility instead of withdrawal, a human (and not heaven storming) objectivity, social solidarity instead of competition, affirmation in place of denial, and sobriety.[21]

By 1948 Hungary, like the rest of the Eastern bloc, was under communist rule, and Barth sparked off a long running debate and opposition by publishing the account of his journey.[22] He praised the Hungarian church for its refusal either of simple opposition or of collaboration. Although he warned them privately later that he thought they were going too far in the direction of collaboration with communism, his refusal to condemn communism in the same terms as he had condemned fascism earned him opprobrium at home, and an attack from Emil Brunner. Brunner observed that from the start he had opposed all 'totalitarianisms'. Was Barth urging 'passive unconcern' again, as he had in 1933? 'Dear Emil Brunner,' Barth replied, 'You do not seem to understand.' Barth pointed out, not only here but in many publications of this period, that the decisive difference was that Nazism had been profoundly seductive. People had flocked

---

[16] 'The Christian Community and the Civil Community' in *Against the Stream*, 35.

[17] 'Die Christlichen Kirchen und die Heutige Wirchlichkeit'(1946) in *Der Götze Wackelt*, 105. An especially strong rejection of principles and world views as powerless to stop the war is found in Barth's address on Remembrance Day 1954, in ibid., 171–2.

[18] Ibid., 103.

[19] 'The Christian Message and the New Humanism' in *Against the Stream*, 184.

[20] 'The Christian Community in the Midst of Political Change' in *Against the Stream*, 60.

[21] 'Die geistigen Voraussetzungen für den Neuaufbau in der Nachkriegszeit' in *Theologische Fragen*, 414–32.

[22] In *Against the Stream*, 53–105.

to it, and theologians and philosophers eulogized its aims. With the exception of a few Western intellectuals, however, he saw no one entranced by 'communism'. What was the point of repeating as a theologian what every newspaper was saying in every column?[23] Barth urged, instead, a 'third way' between communism and capitalism which anticipated the 'non-aligned' politics of Nehru, Nyerere and other Third World leaders, which was profoundly critical of capitalism; socialist, but not committed to Stalinism.[24] The Church, he said, had to walk between East and West, and stand all the more emphatically for those things which might be overlooked or forgotten in the West. 'It can only stand for Europe: not for a Europe controlled by the West or the East, but for a free Europe going its own way, a third way. A free Church is perhaps the last chance for such a free Europe today.'[25]

Throughout these years which, as the record of his interventions show were exceptionally busy, Barth worked steadily at the *Church Dogmatics*. He began the doctrine of creation in 1942 and completed it by the end of the next year. The volume on anthropology took much longer, mainly as a result of the guest semesters in Bonn—it was finished early on in 1948. The volume on providence was completed by the summer of the next year. The ethics of creation were completed in a further two years, by the spring of 1951, with Barth writing a steady 8 pages a day. Of course the exposition of creation was what Barth intended in his overall plan for his dogmatics, and to that extent they represent the intent to do theology 'as if nothing had happened', but in the light of his other lectures we must also understand them as his response to the terrible events of the time. Talk of the divine 'nevertheless' runs back to his work on Romans—the sober facing of evil and wickedness whilst at the same time affirming the sovereignty of grace. The famous intervention on Mozart in the course of the doctrine of providence is probably the high point of this *dennoch*—for if God was under attack from the Lisbon earthquake how much more from the Holocaust and Hiroshima!

During his years in Germany Barth had given his great lectures on eighteenth and nineteenth century philosophy and theology, only published in 1947. These were not repeated, but the volumes on creation saw a very intensive debate with a whole variety of philosophers—above all with Descartes, Leibniz, Schopenhauer, Marx, Nietzsche, Heidegger, Sartre, and Barth's Basle colleague Jaspers, which form some of the most

---

[23] 'Theologische Existenz "heute"' in *Against the Stream*, 113–18. Also *Der Götze Wackelt*, 122, 151.

[24] 'Fürchtet euch nicht!' in *Der Götze Wackelt*, 150–7. Also, 'The Church between East and West' in *Against the Stream*, 127–46; and 422–3 in *Theologische Fragen*.

[25] 'The Church between East and West' in *Against the Stream*, 145.

interesting material in the *Dogmatics* and continue the profound engagement with 'secular' thinkers of the earlier lectures.

GOD'S YES

Grace and Reality

Joy over the Abyss

The Church's mission is not to take the world to task, he told the Hungarian churches on his visit in 1948. 'It would be the servant of quite a different Master if it were to set itself up as the accuser of its brethren. Its mission is not to say "No", but to say "Yes"; a strong "yes" to the God who, because there are "godless" men, has not thought and does not think of becoming a "manless" God—and a strong "Yes" to man, for whom, with no exception, Jesus Christ died and rose again.'[26] This 'strong affirmation' is the dominant note of these years. 'The spirit we now need', he said three years earlier, 'is a constructive, not a destructive, an affirmative not a denying spirit.' We have to learn that human beings are set in the Garden to build it up and watch over it.[27] Like the divine 'nevertheless' this affirmation has the deepest roots in Barth's theology but it is characteristic that it becomes dominant just at this time. The emphasis on ideology critique, whilst by no means abandoned, is now in the background. The affirmation rests on an 'ontology of grace' which we have already glimpsed in his reworking of the doctrine of God, but which is massively worked out in the remaining volumes of the *Dogmatics*.[28] Hans Urs von Balthasar's account of 'the centrality of analogy' in Barth's thought is above all true of the doctrine of creation.[29] The analogy of faith is used to explicate an understanding, springing from the incarnation, of all reality—of time, of the body, of the sexual, and of the political—as a product of divine affirmation.

Doctrine of creation, like any other theological locus, is a product of faith seeking understanding. Our views on creation do not rest on reasoning back

---

[26] 'The Christian Community in the Midst of Political Change' in *Against the Stream*, 73.

[27] 'Die geistigen Voraussetzungen für den Neuaufbau in der Nachkriegszeit' in *Theologische Fragen*, 426.

[28] The phrase 'ontology of grace' is used by W. Härle, *Sein und Gnade: Die Ontologie in Karl Barths Kirchlicher Dogmatik*, Theologische Bibliothek Töpelmann, Berlin, de Gruyter, 1975. I agree with Härle's account but I cannot follow his objection, which is that it fails to allow for the contingent character of sin and reconciliation and abstracts from real experience. Here the old debate about grace and human freedom is restated and Barth effectively gives the old answer.

[29] Balthasar, *Theology of Barth*, 114–67. Of course these were the volumes which appeared as von Balthasar was writing.

to a first cause nor on the elaboration of world views. The Christian doctrine of creation cannot base itself on, become, guarantee, or come to terms with a world view because these rest on thinking which is not based on revelation. Theology expects 'an increasing elucidation and precision of its own attitude to its own theme' from engagement with world views but it pursues its own particular task of a 'faithful and exact reproduction' of the self witness of the Creator in revelation.[30] For this reason, though Barth had expected to have to begin with exploration of all sorts of contemporary science, he seems quickly to have come to the view that exegesis was in fact the central task of a theology of creation. Whilst the bulk of III/1 is an exegesis of Genesis 1 and 2 this is based on an understanding that the whole Bible speaks 'figuratively and prophetically' of Christ.[31] We know the Creator only through the Redeemer. Only from this standpoint can we truly affirm that creation is grace but from this standpoint this is what we have to do. Creation as we know it in Christ is not Yes and No but Yes—Yes to Godself, and Yes to that which is willed and created by God. Creation is good because it is the product of the divine joy, honour, and affirmation. It is the goodness of God which takes shape in it, and God's good pleasure is both the foundation and end of creation, and is therefore its ontological ground.[32]

Revelation not only permits but commands us to laugh and weep, to be glad and sorrowful. Barth never understates the dark side of creation. On the other hand he turns decisively against every type of Manichaean dualism, the substance especially of his debate with Schopenhauer. Schopenhauer makes clear to us that the creation from which God is excluded can only be evil. 'His pessimism cannot be refuted once his presuppositions are granted.'[33] At the root of such a pessimism is doubt about the reality of the world, which, philosophers often suggest, is pure appearance. 'All the wretchedness of human life is bound up with the fact that sound common sense and the *natura docet* have no power at all firmly to plant our feet on the ground of the confidence that the created world is real.'[34] This is not just Barth enjoying a rhetorical flourish, but represents his reading of the origins of contemporary (1940s!) nihilism in the early seventeenth century. Descartes already saw the necessity of belief in God to ground the certainty of our own existence, but his account of the ontological proof does not work, and he had to fall back on common sense. It is doubt of reality which underlies nihilism, a doubt which can never be quite suppressed and which it is better not to deny. To affirm that we exist with any degree of security we have to be told that we do

[30] KD III/1, 394; CD, 344.   [31] KD III/1, 24; CD, 23.
[32] KD III/1, 378–9; CD, 330–1.   [33] KD III/1, 389; CD, 340.
[34] KD III/1, 414; CD, 362.

so.[35] Reversing the movement of European thought from Locke onwards, Barth finds real security in revelation rather than in sense data. In revelation God vouches for God's own divine existence, and therefore by implication for the existence of the knower and of the being which is distinct from God. The ontological order demonstrates itself in the noetic.[36]

The world whose reality is made known to us in revelation is good because it corresponds with the God who is good. Creation is good because God both actualizes it and justifies it. Its rightness, goodness, worth, and perfection spring from its correspondence to the work of God's own Son as resolved from eternity and fulfilled in time.[37] We have to love and praise the created order because, as is clear in Christ, it is so well pleasing to God. Creation therefore calls forth joy—a note sounded intensively throughout the account of creation. That we should seek joy is not merely a concession or permission but a command.[38] What is especially forbidden us is the 'sadly ironic smile'—perhaps not very distant from Camus's heroes—which conceals 'an evil superiority, a wholly inadmissible resistance to the divine revelation, which so illumines the created world that it demands our brightest and not an obstinately clouded Yes'.[39]

To the surprise of many of Barth's readers this emphasis on the goodness of creation led him to a very positive appreciation of Leibniz. What helped him to this, he said, was an intensive listening to Mozart, especially the flute concertos, the horn concertos and the *Magic Flute*. 'If one rightly hears that music then you truly understand that period.'[40] Barth found himself compelled to affirm Leibniz's famous claim that we live in the best of all possible worlds. 'It is notable that in the whole history of ideas there is hardly a single verdict which verbally corresponds so closely to the Christian verdict as that of 18th century optimism.' Leibniz and his followers certainly proclaim glad tidings. Their problem is that they turn evil, sin, and death into a margin of the positive side of creation. They lack not a knowledge of these things but 'a compulsion to face this other aspect of life without running

---

[35] Macken maintains that the consequence of Barth's ontology of grace is that 'nature is never said to possess any real substance. It is never said to be more than a shadow, an insubstantial outer shell, an empty theatre, a foil for grace'. Macken, *Autonomy*, 157. But Barth's views here make plain that he was concerned to establish the very opposite. Grace establishes reality, it does not deny it.

[36] KD iii/1, 400; CD, 349.

[37] KD iii/1, 423; CD, 370.

[38] Macken speaks of 'an ungenerous and anxious depreciation of God's gifts to us in creation out of anxiety that we might claim them for ourselves', *Autonomy*, 170—a bizarre response to the command to rejoice in the created order, which finds concrete expression, for instance, in relationships and work.

[39] KD iii/1, 424; CD, 371.

[40] *Der Götze Wackelt*, 112. Barth did not follow it up by noting that we truly understand our own period through Shostakovitch, Britten, and Schoenberg.

away'.[41] Because this is the case there is a certain forced and moralistic character to their joy also. Their fundamental presupposition was human self confidence, and as such they shared in the absolutism of the day, and they also remain ivory tower thinkers for whom everything is a panopticum. 'These optimists are incorrigible spectators and . . . as such they successfully evade and resist . . . the necessity for decision and action.'[42] Barth did not feel able to urge a 'Christian optimism' but rather 'joy over the abyss', which he also at one moment characterized as 'Christian realism'.[43] That Christian joy is grounded in the events of Good Friday and Easter means that it has a freedom of judgement in face of shattering disturbances which is lacking to Enlightenment optimism.

Barth's description of Mozart best describes his stance with respect to optimism and pessimism. Mozart, he notes, was neither an optimist nor a pessimist. 'What he translated into music was real life in all its discord. But in defiance of that, and on the sure foundation of God's good creation, and because of that, he moves always from left to right, never the reverse.[44]

The Scope of Demythologizing

Rudolf Bultmann, who had, in the general view, occupied a common platform with Barth in the 1920s, had published his famous essay on 'The New Testament and Mythology' in 1941. It is senseless and impossible, he declared, to ask 'modern man' to embrace the mythical view of the world as if this was identical with the gospel. On the contrary, it is 'simply the cosmology of a pre-scientific age'.[45] In a famous sentence Bultmann observed that it was impossible to use electric light and the wireless and avail oneself of modern medicine and at the same time to believe in the New Testament world of demons and spirits. Barth commented: 'Who can read this without a shudder?'—presumably because these wonderful discoveries made possible Auschwitz and the transport system which fed the camps, and the experiments carried out there. He went on to ask whether the modern world view were really as final as all that, or modern thought as uniform as the Marburg Kantians believed.[46]

Discussion of Bultmann's thesis began in Germany even during the war; and no sooner had the war ended than an intense church controversy broke

[41] KD III/1, 467; CD, 406.   [42] KD III/1, 473; CD, 411.

[43] The phrase 'joy over the abyss' occurs in 'Brechen und Bauen' in *Der Götze Wackelt*, 112; 'Christian realism' is urged in 'Wie können die Deutschen gesund werden', an article which appeared in the *Manchester Evening News* in April 1945, in *Theologische Fragen*, 381.

[44] Barth, *Wolfgang Amadeus Mozart*, tr. C. Pott, Grand Rapids, Eerdmans, 1986, 33–4.

[45] R. Bultmann, 'The New Testament and Mythology' in *Kerygma and Myth*, tr. R. Fuller, London, SPCK, 1960, 3.

[46] KD III/2, 536; CD, 447.

out over this essay, and there were calls for Bultmann to be declared hereti-
cal, calls which Barth strenuously resisted. To some extent Barth had his
own sympathies with 'demythologization'. When he visited Bultmann in
Marburg in 1946 he found people there talking of confronting demons. He
retorted that they had better just admit that they had been political fools.[47]
However, his more fully considered answer is to be found not just in the
essay 'Rudolf Bultmann: An Attempt to Understand Him', published in
Kerygma and Myth, but in large tracts of the *Dogmatics* where Bultmann is in
the background and not least in the 150 pages on the angels which form part
of the doctrine of providence.

Barth dealt with 'good and evil angels' in his Göttingen lectures, at least
initially with some embarrassment. 'The old Adam', he told his students,
would rather not take a position on the subject but, in following the old
primer of dogmatics Barth felt obliged to do so.[48] He devoted four lectures
to the topic setting out Catholic, Lutheran and Reformed views and anticipating his later teaching on the lordless powers.[49] There is no mention of
these lectures in the correspondence with Bultmann, but we know that the
Marburg students kept a keen eye on Barth's doings, and it is unlikely that
Bultmann did not know of them. We may suspect, then, that Bultmann's
dismissive views on good and evil angels must have had Barth in mind. In
expounding such views Bultmann was seeking a response to a 'shallow
enlightenment' by uncovering the existential dimension of the ancient
myths. Barth, on the other hand, considers the tract on angels to form a
model part of what it means for theology to be 'faith seeking understanding'. The angels have to be taken seriously because of the role they play in
Scripture, and cannot simply be written off as remnants of an obsolete
world view.

The tract on angels, then, originated in Barth's wrestling with the
dogmatic tradition, in particular in allowing himself to be tutored by
Burmann's 1678 *Theological Synopsis*. However, following Barth's advice
and looking for the 'mass of connections' which may always be found
amongst contemporaries, I believe some light is thrown on this mature
exposition, written in 1949, when we recall that Adorno and Horkheimer's
Dialectic of Enlightenment had appeared (in America) in 1944. The Enlightenment, they alleged, aimed at liberating men from fear; its programme
was 'the disenchantment of the world; the dissolution of myths and the
substitution of knowledge for fancy'. The result, however, was 'disaster
triumphant'.[50] What constitutes the dialectic of Enlightenment is the fact
that the genuine impulse to freedom in fact produces conformity, disen-

---

[47] Busch, *Barth*, 328.   [48] *Unterricht* II, 310.   [49] Ibid., 319.
[50] T. Adorno and M. Horkheimer, *Dialectic of Enlightenment*, London, Verso, 1973, 3.

chantment, and terror. Enlightenment issues in the 'rationality' of the holocaust.

It is the doctrine of creation which is, above all, Barth's own dialectic of Enlightenment. On the one hand freedom is the key note of Barth's ethics and, speaking in Hungary in 1948, he quoted with approval Kant's famous description of Enlightenment as having the courage to use one's own intelligence.[51] On the other hand no tradition emphasized human corruption more strongly than that which Barth represented. Accordingly he insists that both glory and corruption are true descriptions of the human condition, but only true when taken together. The tract on the angels is part of this dialectic, his refusal of the levelling down of the Enlightenment process according to which only the human counts and, in Adorno and Horkheimer's words, 'whatever does not conform to the rule of computation and utility is suspect'.[52] Barth in effect argues that freedom does not have to be won at the cost of disenchantment. In his own way Barth affirms what a survivor of the camps was to call, many years later, 'the uses of enchantment'. Bettelheim was referring to fairy stories and their role in preparing us for reality. Barth does not question the existence of angels— they are not fictions, in his view. But they are part of the reality of enchantment, which exists despite the camps.

The tone of the *Church Dogmatics* is nowhere better weighed than here. There is a certain austerity about the treatment, a refusal of any sentimentality, a judicious but ultimately very decided weighing of the tradition of Dionysius and Aquinas, but a weighing not devoid of charity and humour. What he calls 'the angelology of the weary shrug of the shoulders', for which the existence of angels cannot be ruled out, but for which they have no significance for saving faith, receives much severer treatment.

What, then, is the significance of angels? Barth insists that we have to take the language of 'heaven' seriously, that it too is part of creation. Heaven is, according to Barth, the 'Whence, the starting point, the gate from which [God] sallies with all the demonstrations and revelations and words and works of His action on earth'.[53] Barth considers that the existence of God's special 'place' is essential for there to be genuine dialogue and intercourse between God and human beings. It is another created place which confronts our own, but otherwise unknown and inconceivable, and therefore a mystery. It has its own 'inhabitants', and these are the angels.

In the tradition, alongside huge volumes of speculation on the heavenly hierarchies which he discounted entirely, the angels were spoken of as having a primarily liturgical existence, and as mediators between God and

[51] *Against the Stream*, 60.   [52] Adorno and Horkheimer, *Dialectic*, 6.
[53] KD iii/3, 504; CD, 433.

the world. Barth reworks these two traditions. Like all creatures, angels are witnesses to God but this does not mean that we should look to experience their reality. 'He would...be a lying spirit, a demon, if he were to tarry, directing attention and love and honour and even perhaps adoration to himself, causing even momentary preoccupation with himself and enticing man to enter into dealings and fellowship with himself instead of through him into dealings and fellowship with God.'[54] They do not mediate between God and human beings but they constitute the 'atmosphere' in which there can be a creaturely witness. Their presence gives the cosmic character to the relationship between God and the creature, 'the concrete form of the divine mystery perceptible on earth'.[55] It is this aspect I refer to as the use of enchantment. Their work is above all that of pure—absolutely genuine and authentic—witness. All witness to God lives by the angelic witness. 'In their so utterly selfless and undemanding and purely subservient passing, in their eloquently quiet pointing to God which is always a pointing away from themselves, heaven comes to earth.'[56]

The 'atmosphere' of the angels is discerned above all in music. An old antagonist, Eric Peterson, had insisted that there was only vocal music in heaven. Barth, with Mozart in his ears, disagreed. 'Surely the playing of musical instruments is a more or less conscious, skilful and intelligent human attempt to articulate before God the sound of a cosmos which is otherwise dumb. Surely the perfect musician is the one who, particularly stirred by the angels, is best able to hear not merely the voice of his own heart but what all creation is trying to say, and can then in great humility and with great objectivity cause it to be heard by God and other men. Hence the harps in the hands of these angels.'[57] Curiously neither this perception, nor his passion for Mozart, ever enabled him to overcome his Calvinist suspicion of church music! To believe that the angels are present where music is made does not legitimate church organs! On the contrary, it locates the ministry of angels in the 'secular' world, though Barth was prepared to allow that for the angels divine service might take the form of both worship and a concert! At this point we can note that if there is a natural theology in Barth, it is certainly in his writings on music in that he allows Mozart, at least, and those who listen to him, to hear the 'peace which passes understanding' mediated quite independently of the Word. It is typically part of his austerity that he never allowed himself to develop this, as he very easily could have done, but that he remained rigorously focused on the Word in Christ.[58] At the same

[54] KD III/3, 563; CD, 481.   [55] KD III/3, 580; CD, 495.
[56] KD III/3, 568; CD, 485.   [57] KD III/3, 552; CD, 472.
[58] This austerity is marked also in his treatment of *eros*, which he obviously had a very profound experience of, but which he did not allow to cloud his judgement of the relations of *agape* and *eros*.

time the joy which is the hallmark of his writing on Mozart is the mark of
his theology as well, and forms part of the impenetrable barrier to any
moralism we find in his work.

Nothingness

How was it possible to be so affirmative of Leibniz, to agree with 'the best
of all possible worlds', in the midst of the war, and in the light of what the
end of the war disclosed? This is a question which has insistently to be put
to Barth and which will not lightly go away. We noted, however, that unlike
Leibniz Barth did not minimize the reality of evil. He discusses it, famously,
in what many critics have considered to be the creation of a new mythology.
According to Barth, God's Yes has a recoil. There is a 'necessary rejection'
of everything which by God's own nature God cannot be.[59] The darkness
of untruth is that which God rejects—the relation of darkness and light has
to be understood on the analogy of the elect and the rejected.[60] After the
most vehement insistence on the absolute rule of God over all creaturely
occurrence Barth then asserts that after all there is an 'entire sinister system
of elements' which is not preserved, accompanied nor ruled by God. It is
comprehended by providence, but in a peculiar way. This is *Das Nichtige*—
nothingness. Barth insists that nothingness is neither the positive work of
God nor the simple product of the creature. It must be neither underesti
mated nor overestimated. 'We have here an extraordinarily clear demonstration of the necessary brokenness of all theological thought and
utterance, the clearest evidence that theological systems are impossible.'[61]
Objectivity means taking with equal seriousness God's holiness and
omnipotence, the joy and seriousness which accompanies this as every
other piece of theological work, and the need to rate Nothingness as low as
possible in relation to God and as highly as possible in relation to ourselves.

Nothingness is not to be confused with the normal facts of suffering and
death, the 'shadowside' of creation. The contrasts these facts lead to remain
part of the goodness of creation, and it is Mozart's supreme gift to have
heard this. In his music we hear the harmony of creation in which the
shadow is not darkness, nor sadness despair.[62] The danger is in confusing
this shadowside with nothingness, in which case it is finally validated and
exculpated—the danger exemplified by eighteenth century optimism. The
failure of that movement was to recognize that it was nothingness which
brought Christ to the cross, that there is an assault on God in the assault on
the creature.

---

[59] KD III/1, 378; CD, 330.   [60] KD III/1, 133, 136; CD, 120, 123.
[61] KD III/3, 332; CD, 293.   [62] KD III/3, 338; CD, 298.

Although nothingness is not simply the work of the creature, nevertheless the concrete form of nothingness is human sin, the attempt of human beings to be their own master, their lust for what is not their own, the falsehood, hatred, and pride in which they are enmeshed in relation to the neighbour. A concrete illustration is the war. 'That we have in this war an enemy who today is called "Hitler", and then sadly "Germany",' Barth wrote to an American enquirer in 1942, 'signifies only that the sickness from which we all suffer has broken out there . . . so much nihilism has accumulated in all possible forms throughout the world that finally it had to come to an explosion in the anarchy and tyranny of Hitler's Germany.'[63] Nothingness is also, however, the evil and death we suffer under in connection with sin. In order to come to grips with the theme Barth has long debates with Leibniz (again), Schleiermacher, but also with his contemporaries Heidegger and Sartre. Barth considers that in both we have to do with a theogony—in the one case that of the human creature as deity, in the other that of 'nothing'. They witness to the encounter with nothingness which all modern people have had the opportunity of encountering, but they still do so in the confidence that they can choose the ground from which nothingness is to be seen. Neither author really describes the sickness unto death which is involved with true nothingness.[64]

What then is true nothingness? It has a third form of reality which is neither divine nor creaturely. Its ontic ground is God's defining 'No'. God is the Lord both on the left hand and the right, and it is as God is Lord on the left hand that God is the basis of nothingness. 'It "is" problematically because it is only on the left hand of God, under his No, the object of his jealousy, wrath and judgement . . . Yet because it is on the left hand of God, it really "is" in this paradoxical manner.'[65]

Not only what God wills but what God does not will has potency. The character of nothingness derives from this ontic ground. It is that which God did not create, chaos, the world God did not choose or will. 'As that which God has denied it has the tendency and power to negate the creature of God. It has the attractive force of a whirlpool . . . in whose eddyings the creature in itself and as such can only sink and perish.'[66] Evil, then, is essentially what is alien and adverse to grace. As such nothingness is primarily the problem of God rather than of the creature. Because it is not created by

---

[63] 'Brief an einen amerikanischen Kirchenmann' (1942) in *Theologische Fragen*, 279.

[64] Barth was especially shocked by Sartre's *Huit Clos* which tells us that 'the true humanist, the one whose life is most fulfilled, is the person who is capable of the greatest boredom'. It closes with the word *Continuons!* Barth commented: 'Let us not even begin like this, let alone "continue", or if we have already made a start in this direction, let us turn back as quickly as possible!' 'The Christian Community in the Midst of Political Change' in *Against the Stream*, 59.

[65] KD III/3, 405; CD, 351.   [66] KD III/3, 87; CD, 77.

God, and God has no covenant with it, it has no perpetuity. Barth maintains that it was defeated on the cross so that it is now past. 'It is no longer to be feared. It can no longer "nihilate".'[67] Of course Barth concedes that our consciousness of reality does not bear this out but in faith we can only regard it as destroyed and therefore seek to make a new beginning in remembrance of the one who has destroyed it. To the extent that it still has a semblance of validity it does so under God's permission. 'God still permits his kingdom not to be seen by us, and to that extent he still permits us to be a prey to nothingness . . . He thus permits nothingness to retain its semblance of significance and still to manifest its already fragmentary existence. In this already innocuous form . . . it is an instrument of his will and sanction. He thinks it good that we should exist "as if" He had not yet mastered it for us— and at this point we may rightly say "as if".'[68]

Lecturing in Berlin in 1946, Barth noted that human beings were always on the verge of opening the sluices through which 'chaos and nothingness' would break in and bring human time to an end'.[69] Obviously he is thinking of nuclear weapons, used less than a year before the lecture, but of course the Holocaust also exemplifies what nothingness is and how it works. Barth speaks of the Holocaust most fully in his 1944 lecture on 'The Promise and Responsibility of the Christian Church'. He reads it through Isaiah 53 and the crucified Christ whom we see 'as in a glass darkly' in the 'innumerable Jews who were shot or buried alive, suffocated in overcrowded cattle wagons or murdered with poison gas'.

What kind of revelatory sign, what kind of writing on the wall [*Buchstabe*], what kind of Word, what kind of exceptional proof of God is this! Is it possible that a Christian community cannot see towards what or whom this points? That a Christian cannot sink to the knee: You have borne all sins! Lord have mercy on us! Not the Jew, but in silhouette the tortured and crucified Jew whose rejection in all its total incomprehensibility is once more visible, of whose lonely death we are once more reminded. In the destiny of his bodily [*leiblichen*] brothers and sisters the way in which God gave his only Son for us is once more set forth. What should we now say concerning the Jews when it has pleased God in the midst of our time to erect this sign on this people?[70]

Like Orthodox Judaism, Barth does not shrink from the affirmation that God is to be found even in the Holocaust. The three temptations he thought the Christian community was faced with in 1944 were complacency, denial of God, and the worship of false gods, and the second obviously followed from the Holocaust. Barth, however, reads it as what follows from

---

[67] KD iii/3, 419–20; CD, 363.   [68] KD iii/3, 424; CD, 367.

[69] 'The Christian Community and the Civil Community' in *Against the Stream*, 20.

[70] 'Verheissung und Verantwortung der christlichen Gemeinde im heutigen Zeitgeschehen' in *Theologische Fragen*, 319.

commitment to nothingness. Germany has behaved with such shocking terror in the prosecution of the war, he says, because it has opposed the divine election. It seized the one thing which binds together God and humanity, and wished to cancel the reconciliation which had been acccomplished. In doing that Germany lost all foundation whatsoever (*Man wird damit bodenlos*). The power and reality of nothingness emerges from believing that we ourselves are gods, and turning resolutely against the true God. Any attack on the Jews, Barth believes, will always have that consequence.[71]

It is frequently objected to Barth that his teaching on nothingness smacks of mythology. Is there really biblical ground for thinking that God's 'No' has the power to bring things into existence, and if so is not evil intrinsic to cration? If a 'No' necessarily accompanies God's 'Yes' then nothingness necessarily exists, and to the extent that the 'No' is eternal does it not exist eternally?[72] Are we to trace the Holocaust and the whole record of human destructiveness to this necessary root in God? To the 'ontology of grace' (not Barth's phrase) is opposed the 'ontology of chaos' (*Ontik des Nichtigen*, Barth's phrase) against which the divine *conservatio* protects us.[73] Berkouwer protests: 'We do not find [in Scripture] a dimension of chaos which according to its nature is related to creation as a rejected and non willed reality . . . It bears the hallmarks of speculative thinking wherein the human choice of one possibility, involving the rejection of other possibilities, is transferred to God and is turned into an independent conception from which all kinds of conclusions are drawn.'[74] The problem of theodicy which Barth seeks to circumvent returns with a vengeance for we seem to have not just the divine *permission* of evil, but its creation. Again, we are told both that sin is the concrete form of nothingness, and that it is Pelagianism, and an underestimation of evil, to trace nothingness to sin. Which of these two options is Barth really recommending to us?

Barth has warned us that the brokenness of theological thought appears here more than anywhere. Responding to Berkouwer's criticisms some years later he insisted that evil always has to be characterized as that which God did not will: 'It will always be obscure, unfathomable and baffling that

---

[71] 'Verheissung und Verantwortung der christlichen Gemeinde im heutigen Zeitgeschehen' in *Theologische Fragen*, 320. Barth also deals with the Holocaust in the 1954 Remembrance Day Sermon, *Der Götze Wackelt*, 168. The omission of the theme from the *Dogmatics* makes these documents all the more crucial hermeneutical keys to that work.

[72] Here I have more sympathy with the view of Härle and Macken that an ontology of grace tends to treat sin and reconciliation as ontologically necessary rather than contingent. Macken, *Autonomy*, 173. On the other hand, it is not primarily a matter of Barth's ontology, but more a result of his refusal of any ultimate dualism, and any theology has to come to terms with this issue. See KD iv/1, 453; CD, 408. Barth's insistence that sin is contingent is contained in his concept of 'impossible possibility'.

[73] KD iii/3, 407; CD, 353.

[74] Berkouwer, *Triumph of Grace*, 246.

something which is merely opposed to the will of God can have reality. We do not understand how this can be. But it is of a piece with the nature of evil that if we could explain how it may have reality it would not be evil.' His self understanding, then, is that he is not trying to provide an 'answer' to the problem of evil, but to spell out its unintelligibility.[75]

The Healing of Time

> . . . to us poor men
> Is given no place to rest.
> Harried by pain,
> We grope and fall
> Blindly from hour to hour.
> Like water dashed
> From cliff to cliff,
> In lifelong insecurity.

These words of Hölderlin's, quoted by Barth in the volume on anthropology which he wrote as the war was ending, must have summed up human experience for hundreds of thousands of inhabitants of *Mitteleuropa* in these years, awash as it was with refugees, returning prisoners, and occupation troops. How to come to terms with the past, to find a way in the present, and to steer some kind of course for the future in the dark days of a Cold War which threatened to plunge the world once again back into chaos? These are the questions Barth addressed in his reflections on Jesus as Lord of time. Of course, they have a relevance which transcends their period, but they have an added seriousness and pertinence against this background.

Experience of the loss of time—of the impossibility of changing the past, and therefore of doing anything constructive with the present and the future—is a major marker, perhaps the crucial marker, of the meaning of human sin. Barth speaks of the 'monstrosity of general human being in time'—a monstrosity witnessed to only too well by Barth's existentialist contemporaries, who responded to the fractured and hopeless mood of the time. Death, Barth agrees with them, marks a judgement on human beings. Although it is good that we have our allotted span, as it gives direction and urgency to our lives, death is always resisted by life as an assault of nothingness. But the No of the New Testament is underlain by a much greater Yes. 'The No uttered by preachers of the Law, including Heidegger and Sartre, is always too human a No.'[76] The No of the New Testament, by contrast, is that of judgement and mercy.

Barth often gave powerful expression to the transience of life and to the inevitability of death—nowhere more so than in this part of the *Dogmatics*.

[75] KD iv/3, 202; CD, 177.   [76] KD iii/2, 736; CD, 605.

If the late twentieth century has seen a flight from death and its treatment as *the* major social *pudendum*, then this owes nothing to Barth's work. To this mood Barth responded with the gospel—good news. According to his understanding of revelation, the redemption accomplished in Christ includes decisively the healing of time. Healing requires antiseptic, and the gospel exposes the way in which our time is condemned to disintegration and extinction. The primary significance of the revelation in Christ, however, is not critical but a message of hope. In the resurrection Jesus is revealed as the Lord of time, as the one who is and was and is to come. That he lives at the right hand of God means that he is always present but this presence does not mean that the historical Jesus disappears. 'On the contrary, his presence stimulates interest in the past and in the tradition of Jesus, revealing the unfathomable but clear depths of his prior life on earth.'[77] That he entered time shows that it is not the abyss of non-being, but that we really have time to live and to enjoy. We learn in the incarnation that God also has time—according to Barth it is this which allows God to be our God. But it also means that the reality of time is rooted in God. Time is the presence and gift of God, not Chronos the devourer. Time is therefore as a form of human existence 'always in itself and as such a silent but persistent song of praise to God'. To have time 'is to be allowed to exist as and with light under and by the divine Yes; it is not to be overtaken by God's No; it is to be preserved and sheltered before him'.[78] The hidden meaning of time is the covenant with human beings as materialized in God taking time in the incarnation. Because this has occurred, all other times show traces of God's eternal time. 'In all its hiddenness it is the rustling of the Holy Spirit by which, however deaf to it we may be, we are surrounded in virtue of the fact that we are in the movement of time.'[79] If there is an analogy to the role of prevenient grace in Barth's theology then it is surely in the role time plays, especially in his anthropology.

God redeems every aspect of our being in time. It is the fact that the living God is present which makes our present real, weighty, and important because God's presence redeems and rescues our weakness and stupidity. 'Though we are sinners who have forfeited our time, and indeed ourselves, we are not lost, but as we were created so we are sustained and delivered.'[80] Likewise, it is God's reality which rescues us from a romantic historicism in which the past is falsified. Again, we have to understand these words in the context of a Europe, and especially of a Germany, desperately trying to come to terms with what had happened in the previous twelve years or, according to Barth, the previous century—for Barth caused great offence by tracing the roots of Germany's catastrophe back to Bismarck. Without

---

[77] KD III/2, 562; CD, 468.   [78] KD III/1, 140; CD, 126.
[79] KD III/2, 634; CD, 526.   [80] KD III/2, 643; CD, 532.

God 'the fact that the past is irrecoverably behind us, and that even the present hour and our future days rush irresistibly into the past, would be the leak in virtue of which we could understand our whole being in time as one which is condemned to perish'.[81] In the knowledge of God it is possible to have the courage to face up to reality and not to seek refuge in escapism. Resignation is incompatible with the fact that life is created by God. At the same time there has to be movement beyond facing up to the past. 'We need to forget. And we are enabled to do so. If it were otherwise we should be in a terrible plight.'[82] Again, knowing time as the gift of the living God rescues us from the extremes of optimism and pessimism and frees us for sober, hopeful, and cheerful engagement with our task—'unreflectiveness' (*Unbedenklichkeit*) Barth calls it. In conclusion, then, 'neither ontological godlessness nor ontological inhumanity' can be predicated of human beings.[83] This was why, in a lecture given all over Switzerland in January and February 1945, recalling an incident in which defeated German troops had been reviled and spat on by Swiss women, Barth was able to insist on the gospel promise of forgiveness. The Swiss, he said, had to show the Germans that they understood the question, 'Who is my neighbour?' The call to the weary and heavy laden is addressed to unsympathetic Hitler youth, brutal SS soldiers, evil members of the Gestapo, sad compromisers and collaborators. Even if the Swiss, puffed up with their democratic freedoms and ideals, reject them, Christ addresses them: 'Come to me. I am for you! I am your friend!'[84]

Much of the literature which emerged from the war wrestles with futility and transience, the chaotic and meaningless stop to life which was reality for so many in Europe for nearly six years—one thinks of Böll's *The Train was On Time* for example. Richard Roberts finds in Barth's Christological grounding of time a desperate attempt to retract and save some reality when 'all but a single thread connecting his theological system to the world of the commonplace has been severed'.[85] On substantially the same reading of Barth—that there is no dimension of reality not immediately derivable from his primal sources (i.e. God revealed in Christ)—Ingolf Dalferth comes to very different conclusions. Our world of common experience is, he says, an 'enhypostatic reality' for Barth, 'which exists only in so far as it is incorporated into the concrete reality of God's saving self realisation in Christ'.[86] This does not *deny* the secularity of the world but reinterprets it theologically in the light of Christ. Far from alienating us, this seems to me

---

[81] KD III/2, 649; CD, 537.   [82] KD III/2, 652; CD, 540.
[83] KD III/2, 670; CD, 553.   [84] *Eine Schweizer Stimme*, 354.
[85] Roberts, 'Barth's Doctrine of Time', 139.
[86] I. Dalferth, 'Karl Barth's Eschatological Realism' in S. Sykes (ed.), *Karl Barth: Centenary Essays*, Cambridge, Cambridge University Press, 1989, 29.

an invitation to experience all reality as potentially hopeful and open ended—the source of Barth's notorious tendency towards universalism, of what Marquardt calls the 'revolutionary humanity' of his thought.[87] In the anthropology, which was written as the war was in progress, we find a tremendous affirmation of 'human beings in their time', which, as Fergus Kerr has argued, emphasizes limitation as gift.[88]

THE HISTORY OF CREATION

Creation as History

In the spring of 1940, a few months before he took his life, Walter Benjamin drew up his 'Theses on the Philosophy of History'. Observing that medieval theologians had regarded the inability to recover the past as the root of *acedia* he went on: 'The nature of this sadness stands out more clearly if one asks with whom the adherents of historicism actually empathize. The answer is inevitable: with the victor. And all the rulers are the heirs of those who conquered before them.'[89] In seeking grounds of hope for the victims of history he noted that it was impossible to do without the notion of a present which is not a transition, but in which time stands still and has come to a stop. He recognized that such a time was bound up with the coming of the Messiah who comes 'not only as the redeemer, but as the subduer of Antichrist'.[90]

Barth's profound theology of history reads almost like a commentary on these theses, with the risen Christ in the place of Klee's *Angelus Novus*, not blown by the storm of progress into the future but binding together past, present, and future, redeeming because subduing Antichrist. Barth learned the historical method Benjamin condemns as historicism from Herrmann, as did Bultmann, and like Benjamin he rejected it in the name of a messianic reading of history.

In the Christian tradition there has been a deep rooted division between nature and grace, creation and redemption, which has led to the doctrine of creation being treated as a branch of philosophical theology. 'Creation' deals with nature and questions about the environment; 'redemption' with history. Barth sought to overcome this division by radically conceiving of creation in every dimension—heavenly as well as earthly—as history. This is true even of the order of nature where, though we have to talk of 'deep "his-

---

[87] Marquardt, *Theologie*, 309.

[88] F. Kerr, *Immortal Longings: Versions of Transcending Humanity*, London, SPCK, 1997, ch. 2.

[89] W. Benjamin, *Illuminations*, tr. H. Zohn, London, Fontana, 1992, 248.

[90] Ibid., 247.

torical" twilight', there is not 'absolute obscurity'. 'Even here there is always a certain relationship and similarity with other creaturely and to that extent visible history.' And though it transcends all the bounds of normal historiography, the very act of creation is 'pre-historical history'.[91] The foundation of this wholistic reading is his understanding of God's being as historical. God's being is not non historical but 'historical even in its eternity'.[92] The creation of a God whose eternity was opposed to time might itself be indifferent or hostile to time but as it is, 'The aim of creation is history. This follows decisively from the fact that God the Creator is the triune God who acts and who reveals Himself in history.'[93] The God witnessed to by Scripture is not present everywhere and nowhere but is known in specific acts. God is not non historical because as the Triune God 'He is in his inner life the basic type and ground of history. And he is not non temporal because his eternity is not merely the negation of time, but an inner readiness to create time, because it is supreme and absolute time, and therefore the source of our time, relative time.'[94] It follows that 'believing' signifies a relationship to the specific historical act and attitudes of God. The *acedia* of the medieval monks would not have been possible with this doctrine of God.

We learn of our radical historicality, that we are historical through and through, from the event of Christ. It is the existence of Jesus which shows us what is meant by history. 'What happens in this existence, i.e., that the Creator shows his concern for his creation by himself becoming a creature, is the fulness and sum of what we mean by talking about history.'[95] Here, Barth remarks, looking backwards towards *Romans*, the concept of *Urgeschichte* might be allowable. Opposed to the idea of history is that of a state (*Zustand*). The key markers of a 'state' are limitation of possibilities and being self enclosed (*Geschlossenheit*). History is not bound up with movement, first and foremost, but with the possibility of change *in response to factors transcending itself*. History begins when a movement from without breaks through its imprisonedness, or enclosedness.[96] In this case a being

---

[91] KD III/1, 85–7; CD, 79–80. In IV/3 Barth gives only a very guarded assent to the idea that creation (i.e. the natural world) has its own history. 'This theatre is not itself a history. It is not immovable, rigid or lifeless. Yet it is basically the same at all stages in the history. It cannot, then, be described in the form of the narration of a history and histories.' But he then goes on to say that it is of course an event, or series of events, that 'histories are found in it too' but that 'even when seen and understood as history, it is a sequence and repetition of the same or very similar events'. KD IV/3, 54–5; CD, 136–7. The point is to distinguish the drama of salvation history, which includes all human history, from the regularities and continuities of the creaturely world. As continuous creation, however, it is still the scene of God's ongoing work.

[92] KD III/1, 70; CD, 66.   [93] KD III/1, 63; CD, 59.
[94] KD III/1, 73; CD, 68.   [95] KD III/2, 188; CD, 157.
[96] KD III/2, 189; CD, 158.

(*Wesen*) does not have a history but exists in a history. This is how human beings exist. In virtue of the incarnation we can say that human being is what it is as creature in a dynamic movement of the Creator to itself and the creature to the creator. 'It does not "have" a history from which it can itself be distinguished as a substratum. But it "is" in this history, i.e., it is, as it takes place that the Creator is creature and the creature Creator.'[97]

Not only is the incarnation thus the ground of our understanding of our being as history, but Jesus himself is 'wholly and utterly who he is' in the continuity of the evangelical history. The only non historical element to do with him is his name, but this, in its meaning 'Yahweh saves', itself tells a story.[98] This applies also to the events of the resurrection, which Bultmann rejected in the name of historicism. In opposition to him, Barth insists that the Church is founded on a specific memory and not by a timeless and non-historical truth. It is not that faith created the history but 'the fact of faith was created in this history'.[99] The Easter history is the clue to all history. It was the Easter history which opened the eyes of the disciples to the nature of this man and his history, to the previously concealed character of this history as salvation history, and therefore to the fact that what had happened had done so once and once for all. The 'once' of this event of the resurrection differed absolutely from that of every other 'once'.[100] What Barth is saying is that the axis of history is resurrection—precisely what ensures that Benjamin's nightmare, that even the dead will not be safe if the enemy wins, can only ever be a nightmare, and not reality.

Not only the earthly creation but the angels as well are involved in history. The presence of angels means that even in that which seems to belong only to the nexus of creaturely occurrence, human beings are summoned to see the intervention of God, 'and therefore an element of the salvation history or universal history directed by him, and within this context an element in his own life history as controlled by God'.[101] Amongst the German Christians some theologians had made much of the idea of national angels. Whilst not ruling out the possibility of such beings Barth maintains that, 'always in the context of the covenant as the guiding thread of the whole' the angels are, rather, witnesses to God's mystery in the course of political history.[102]

It is the Christological reading of history which informs Barth's exegesis of the Genesis stories, which become a witness to the history of the relations between God and humankind. In a typically paradoxical insight Barth calls the first creation narrative, of the Priestly writer, 'the more prophetic of the two accounts'. This begins with the formless void, the creation of

[97] KD III/2, 190; CD, 159. [98] KD III/2, 67; CD, 58.
[99] KD III/2, 538; CD, 449. [100] KD III/2, 545; CD, 454.
[101] KD III/3, 580; CD, 496–7. [102] KD III/3, 606–7; CD, 517–8.

light, and then the earth and non human world, and is understood as making creation the external basis of the covenant. The more sacramental Yahwist account, which begins with the creation of the male and ends with the creation of woman, makes the covenant the internal basis of creation. For the first account the story of the covenant of grace requires a stage. This is not to make human beings the centre of creation, but God's *dealings* with human beings. In the second account we are dealing with 'a history of creation from inside'.[103] It begins with the start of the history of the covenant between God and human beings, and the creation of man and woman prefigures all the history which follows.

History thus begins with creation, and creation has an historical character and is an event fulfilling time. Barth makes clear that there is 'no *metabasis eis allo genos* between creation and what follows it. Nor does creation itself break off or cease when the history of the covenant begins and continues.'[104] It follows that theology is not concerned with the 'history of salvation' as the history of Israel and church, as a kind of red thread which runs through all other history. Rather, the history of salvation encloses all other history, and all other history to some extent belongs to it. Conversely, the fact that Scripture begins with creation makes plain that faith is concerned with all reality and not just with a special sphere of it.

Following Regin Prenter, Berkouwer objected to this that running creation and redemption together in this way

leaves the impression that everything has already been done, all the decisions have been taken, so that one can hardly say that the *historical fall* and the *historical reconciliation* are at issue, but only the *revelation* of redemption in history, the *revelation* of the definitive Yes of God's grace. There is no question of a 'stepwise', one after another, of creation and redemption.[105]

So does Barth *affirm* history, or does he *reduce* it to the playing out of a script already decided? The sense that Barth's tendency to supralapsarianism empties history of its real significance is widely shared. It is here that the need to read the *Dogmatics* alongside the political writings of the immediate post-war years is so important, to take seriously Marquardt's methodological principle that Barth's theological method is his biography. Barth's response to Berkouwer is most illuminating. He appeals to Blumhardt, whose 'story and influence' have not yet penetrated Berkouwer's Calvinist environment. What Barth is trying to do is to take with absolute seriousness the fact that 'Jesus is Victor'.[106] This does not empty history of its significance: neither Blumhardt, the social democrat, nor Barth, vigorously engaging with communists and anti-communists at this time, could

[103] KD III/1, 263; CD, 232.   [104] KD III/1, 64; CD, 60.
[105] Berkouwer, *Triumph of Grace*, 250.   [106] KD IV/3, 200; CD, 175.

possibly think that. What it does is to draw Christians into a struggle which they believe will be victorious: it is a question of faith. Blumhardt did not believe he could control Jesus: 'He did something which is very different, and which is the only thing possible in relation to this person. He called upon him for two years. He did so with absolute confidence. But he still called upon him.'[107] Thus history is not negated. History is a history of struggle. But it is history seen in the light of faith in Christ's victory: 'In relation to the name of Jesus I see no alternative to my understanding.'[108]

To claim that creation is history challenges historicism as much as, if not more than, Barth's insistence on the historical nature of the resurrection. In order to make the claim he developed a concept of 'saga' (*Die Sage*) to distinguish the sense in which he was claiming it was historical from historicism on the one side and myth on the other. The history of creation is obviously not susceptible to the usual canons of historical investigation. Barth calls it 'non historical history'. All history has this character in terms of its immediacy to God, something which cannot be verified by the canons of academic historiography. The history of creation, however, has only this element. 'Saga' refers to 'a pre-historical reality of history which is enacted once and for all within the confines of time and space'.[109] It rests on 'divination'—a vision of the historical emergence which precedes historical events and which can be guessed from the history we know. 'Where divinatory and poetical saga is not allowed to speak, no true picture of history, i.e., no picture of true history, can ever emerge.'[110] To regard this history as untrustworthy or worthless Barth regards as 'a ridiculous and middle class habit of the modern Western mind which is supremely phantastic in its chronic lack of imaginative phantasy, and hopes to rid itself of its complexes through suppression.'[111] If the immediacy of history to God is lost then we are left with 'an ocean of tedious inconsequence and therefore demoniac chaos'.

Barth distinguishes this kind of history from myth, which is concerned with 'the essential principles of the general realities and relationships of the natural and spiritual cosmos'.[112] It has a timeless, non-historical, abstract sense. The biblical material, however, does not simply use narrative, as myth does, but it is set in a narrative frame, even if material like Proverbs and Psalms is not itself narrative. No philosophical system accompanies it, which can express abstractly what it says concretely. Myth is really concerned with a view or solution of the enigma of the world and as such human beings find themselves fully at home with it, whereas in the biblical creation stories humans find themselves confronted by their Maker.

---

[107] KD IV/3, 201; CD, 176. [108] KD IV/3, 202; CD, 176. [109] KD III/1, 88; CD, 81.
[110] KD III/1, 90; CD, 83. [111] KD III/1, 87; CD, 81. [112] KD III/1, 91; CD, 84.

Von Balthasar argues that for Barth, 'formally all of creation is one vast symbol for grace'.[113] Creation is not grace but there is an analogous relation between the two. Creation is, says Barth, 'a unique sign of the Covenant, a true sacrament; not Jesus Christ as the goal, but Jesus Christ as the beginning (the beginning just because He is the goal) of creation'.[114] In this way, von Balthasar remarks, Barth gives us a justification for Alexandrian theology, which thought in such symbolic terms. '*Everything* in the Bible, and above all its great moments of articulation, are images and signs and expressions for the great salvific events that take place between God and the human race'.[115] This insight, that creation is affirmation, benefit, and that this is grounded in Christology, is important, but von Balthasar understates, in my view, the relation of creation to history and therefore obscures the way in which it is already caught up in the dynamism of redemption.

In the years since Barth's doctrine of creation was completed attention has been focused ever more on the demands of the non-human creation, increasingly at risk from human rapacity, and it has been felt that Barth's insistence that creation is but a stage for the covenant fails to do justice to the non-human creation. It has to be granted that Barth would be unlikely to write as he did had he done so under the shadow of the damage to the environment which began to emerge in the late 1960s.[116] His doctrine of creation is decisively determined by the same preoccupations as Walter Benjamin. It is a doctrine for the refugee, for those who mourn the dead, for those who have to find hope in history. At the same time we have to remember that according to him it is not anthropocentric, but the account of the relation of God and human beings, and thus speaks to human beings whose freedom, as we shall see, can only be mentioned in the same breath as responsibility.

The Lord of History

If creation is history then the doctrine of providence is an account of what it means to say that God is the Lord of history. In the history of the creature 'we need not expect turns and events which have nothing to do with His lordship and are not in some sense acts of His lordship. This Lord is never absent, passive, non-responsible or impotent, but always present, active,

---

[113] Balthasar, *Theology of Barth*, 124.
[114] KD III/1, 262–3; CD 232.   [115] Balthasar, *Theology of Barth*, 124.
[116] Gollwitzer surmised that in KD V Barth would have gone back to the first *Romans* and 'presented the hope for God's kingdom as a cosmic fulfilment, as a reconciliation of man and nature, and as social in magnitude—as a new community amongst human beings'. 'The Kingdom of God and Socialism' in Hunsinger, *Barth and Radical Politics*, 95.

responsible and omnipotent.'[117] Like the doctrine of creation it is Christologically grounded, and thus represents belief in the rule of the Father of
whom Christ spoke, something the Reformers missed. The goal of providence is the fulfilment of the covenant, and presupposes that this history is
exalted above all other history. The goodness and perfection of creation consists in the fact that God has made it serviceable for the rule of grace.

Barth follows the outline of the old Reformed dogmatics in speaking of
God preserving, accompanying, and ruling world process. He begins by
laying enormous emphasis on the total remit of God's rule. As God accompanies world process his will is 'unconditionally and irresistibly fulfilled'.
God's operation is 'as sovereign as Calvinist teaching describes it. In the
strictest sense it is predestinating.'[118] The operation of God's Word, which
is the operation of providence, is 'unconditioned and irresistible'.[119] We
cannot make of God a being who is much in much, but must insist that God
is all in all. God foreknows and forewills all things. That God is the Lord
means that his activity determines our activity even to its most intimate
depths and origins. God rules over us as God foreordained before us. The
creature is God's instrument. Creaturely occurrence provides us with a
mirror or reflection of God's working. It is a theatre for the work of God. 'If
we are clear in our minds that what concerns us is the knowledge and the
will and work of the Father of Jesus Christ, this proposition is not a dangerous one.'[120]

The mode of God's operation is the speaking of God's Word to all creatures, the moving of all creatures by the force and wisdom and goodness
which are the Holy Spirit, the Spirit of God's Word.[121] At the same time
Barth insists that prayer plays a part in God's rule. 'If ever there was a
miserable anthropomorphism, it is the hallucination of a divine immutabil-
ity which rules out the possibility that God can let Himself be conditioned
in this or that way by His creature. God is certainly immutable. But He is
immutable as the living God and in the mercy in which He espouses the
cause of the creature. In distinction from the immovability of a supreme
idol, His majesty, the glory of His omnipotence and sovereignty, consists
in the fact that He can give to the requests of this creature a place in His
will.'[122]

Barth writes after Auschwitz. We need only consider one tiny part of our
history, he admits, to ask whether such affirmations of God's rule are not
empty words. 'We start back from what we say, for it obviously goes far
beyond what we can see and know from our experience and conviction, and

---

[117] KD III/3, 13; CD, 13.   [118] KD III/3, 132, 148; CD, 117, 131.
[119] KD III/3, 163; CD, 144.   [120] KD III/3, 137; CD, 121.
[121] KD III/3, 161; CD, 142.   [122] KD III/4, 119–20; CD, 109.

what we can see and know and say responsibly falls far short of what is said with this confession.'[123] If theology begins with experience, or conceptions of cosmic process like the eighteenth century doctrine of progress, then it would be impossible to make such a confession. We do so simply because we are required to do so by the Word of God. 'If it is a confession of this faith, it is *eo ipso* a solid confession, because *eo ipso* one which has reference to this objective content and derives from the revelation of this objective content.'[124] It is in the doctrine of providence above all that we have to affirm the 'Nevertheless'. 'It can only be a Nevertheless [*Dennoch*]. What man sees is simply the multiplicity and confusion of the lines of creaturely occurrence, which in itself and as such. . . cannot be identified with the doing of the will of God.'[125] Only by beginning with faith can we hang on to the Nevertheless, believing that the story of Christ helps to understand the true meaning of world history and world process.

Of course our knowledge of providence, though based on an infallible Word, is fallible knowledge. 'Not everything which the serious believer seriously listening to the Word of God regards as such is in fact a divine disposing and directing in history, a hint and sign of providence. He might have misunderstood what God has really said to him.'[126] We have such misunderstandings in Eusebius of Caesarea's identification of Constantine with a second Moses or J. A. Bengel's belief that 1836 was the date for the revelation of the beast from the abyss. Such failures, and in particular mistakes in biblical prophecy, Barth believes, teach us not that the doctrine is false but that human beings must not rest on their own achievements. We must always be willing to withdraw with respect to detailed insights and to receive new and better instruction.

Apart from the counterintuitive nature of the assertion of God's providence there is also the ancient question of how God's foreknowledge and forewilling of all events is consistent with human freedom. Barth's answer, too, is the ancient one, namely that grace does not destroy nature but renews and transforms it.[127] The operation of the creature, Barth affirms, is free and autonomous. God gives it space for its own work, its own being in action, 'its own autonomous activity'.[128] The foreordaining activity of the

---

[123] KD III/3, 14; CD, 15.   [124] KD III/3, 16; CD, 16.

[125] KD III/3, 51; CD, 44.   [126] KD III/3, 28; CD, 25.

[127] KD II/1, 572; CD, 509: 'How can grace meet [human beings] as grace if it simply decks itself out as nature, if nature as such is grace? Grace is the secret behind nature, the hidden meaning of nature. When grace is revealed, nature does not cease to exist . . . Nature itself becomes the theatre of grace, and grace is manifested as lordship over nature.' Cf. KD II/1, 463; CD, 411, where Barth spells out his difference from Aquinas, a difference based on the fact both that grace is Jesus Christ, and that there is no natural potential in human beings which is taken up and perfected. Grace is always a miracle. See Hunsinger, *How to Read Barth*, 146, 193.

[128] KD III/3, 103; CD, 91.

creature is not constraining or humiliating, which would only be the case were God's omnipotence a supreme cause and no more.[129] The uncondi- tioned and irresistible lordship of God means not only that the freedom of creaturely activity is not jeopardized nor suppressed, but rather that it is confirmed in all its particularity and variety.[130] It not only leaves the creature free but makes it free. The secret of making such affirmations is escaping the God of our projections, the father figure of Freudian imagination. This fear of God is 'At root. . . the only relevant form of human sin.'[131]

The objection that Barth minimizes human freedom, or even disallows it altogether, fails to understand that Barth is speaking of the reality of *grace*. Berkouwer asks: 'Is it possible to give too much attention to grace?. . . In terms of Roman Catholic conceptions it is possible and necessary to counter Barth's theology with the objection that it fails to do justice to human freedom of the will and to human co-operation in salvation. . . Reformed theology faces a wholly different situation here.'[132] He has understood Barth's central contention that human freedom is freedom for God, and does not include the possibility of following two directions, so that 'sin can never be explained in terms of man's freedom'.[133] As von Balthasar puts it, Barth has a noticeably Augustinian concept of freedom.

In this view, freedom is primarily a life lived in the intimacy of God's freedom. This freedom, in other words, cannot be defined negatively, as merely a neutral stance towards God, as if freedom were merely presented with a 'menu' of options from which the *liberum arbitrium* would make its selection. On the contrary, when freedom is authentic, it is a form of living within that mysterious realm where self- determination and obedience, independence and discipleship, mutually act upon and clarify each other. And this domain is that of the Trinity, which grace has opened up for us.[134]

In the exercise of the divine freedom God makes the activity of the creature part of God's own activity. In this respect Barth does not shrink from talking of God cooperating with the creature. In the course of this, God maintains

---

[129] KD III/3, 147–8; CD, 130.
[130] KD III/3, 166; CD, 146.   [131] KD III/3, 167; CD, 147.
[132] Berkouwer, *Triumph of Grace*, 349–50.   [133] Ibid., 216.
[134] Balthasar, *Theology of Barth*, 129. He goes on, 'This concept of freedom . . . is the ulti- mate foundation of Barth's anthropology.' Nigel Biggar joins Macken and others in believing that Barth's implicit universalism makes Barth's doctrine of freedom a failure. Human beings are determined to choose freely what is right, and this yields a notion of freedom more appar- ent than real. Biggar, *Hastening*, 5. But for this very reason Barth is most careful to avoid com- mitting himself to a principled universalist position. So J. Bettis, 'Is Barth a Universalist?', *SJT* 20 (1967), 423–36. The answer to the question is, of course, 'no'! 'The problem is not that uni- versalism ties God to all men, but that it ties God to men at all. The goodness of God's love lies in the fact that God gives it freely and not out of necessity.' Precisely because God is gracious, freedom cannot be compelled. What Barth allows himself is hope for all creatures, which is a very different thing.

the creature by means of the creature. It is not that the creature cooperates with God. 'By the grace of God the events of nature and history are authorised and qualified to cooperate with him.'[135] They do so above all on the individual level. God harmonizes and controls the creatures with one another but this does not make the individual merely a cog in the machine. Barth regarded this insistence as of the 'greatest practical importance'. 'At the end of the thread which begins here there lies in the ethical sphere . . . political or economic totalitarianism . . . the forces at work in this conception of the divine rule are the motives and logic and law of an immanent hierarchy of power and value. The articulated whole is greater and more important than the sum of its component parts.'[136] Barth considered this an impossible account of the divine ruling because God's kingdom is a kingdom of righteousness. That God deals with each individual in direct and immediate encounter is what distinguishes divine rule from the hierarchy of a universal collective whole. God loves and rules all beings 'in their interdependence, their mutual association. But on this account he does not love and rule them any the less but to the highest degree possible in their particularity and singularity'.[137]

Medieval theology theorized the coexistence of divine and human freedom, which can be understood in terms of Barth's fundamental Chalcedonian pattern, in terms of 'double agency', so that an event can be truly human, but it is still proper to see God acting in and through it. As Barth recognizes, this possibility is supremely realized in prayer.[138]

As instances of God's rule Barth singles out the history of holy Scripture, of the Church, the limitation of human life and—of the Jews. Since the dispersion after AD 70 the Jews have had neither a common language, nor culture, nor even ethnicity. They are a people who are not a people, with no true history—and yet they survive. Their survival, Barth believes, can only be understood against the background of the Old Testament covenant. They constitute 'the declared mystery of God, the mystery of his faithfulness and grace, of the constancy of his will and decree'.[139] Because the Jews are 'the apple of God's eye', they can be 'despised and hated and oppressed and persecuted and even assimilated, but they cannot really be touched;

---

[135] KD III/3, 124; CD, 110.

[136] KD III/3, 196; CD, 173.   [137] KD III/3, 197; CD, 173.

[138] KD III/3, 321–4; CD, 284–5. See Hunsinger, *How to Read Barth*, ch. 7.

[139] KD III/3, 247; CD, 218. In an article written for the American political quarterly *Foreign Affairs* in 1942 Barth wrote that, 'The existence of the Jews is actually the exponent and the sign, independent of all spiritual counter movements or objective metaphysical facts, that the Christian root of Western culture is alive.' The Jew is the factual witness to revelation, and where revelation is understood there always has to be struggle against National Socialism. *Eine Schweizer Stimme*, 256.

they cannot be exterminated; they cannot be destroyed. They are the only people that necessarily continues to exist, with the same certainty as that God is God.'[140] This continued existence of the Jew is the trace of divine world governance in all creaturely occurrence. Properly understood the Jews are both the elect people and the people who are constantly untrue to their election.

It costs something to be the chosen people, and the Jews are paying the price. Everything has to fall away that makes a man great and glorious in himself, all the pride of his own religion and culture and language and race. Living only by the grace of God, he is not allowed anything of his own by which to justify or adorn himself, or to vindicate himself and make his way in world history as a whole. All that he can do is simply be there. He cannot be overlooked, or banished, or destroyed—for the grace of God holds and upholds him—but he is not allowed the glory which counts in world history generally. He is everywhere the minority. He is everywhere the guest and stranger.[141]

Barth finds the reason for anti-Semitism in the idea that the Jew is mirror of us all, the one who resists and opposes God, who wants to elect God rather than to be elected by God. 'Our annoyance is not really with the Jew himself. It is with the Jew only because and to the extent that the Jew is a mirror in which we immediately recognise ourselves, in which all nations recognise themselves as they are before the judgement seat of God.'[142] Anti-Semitism also draws on the irritation others feel at the marks of their election, that they continue to exist without any of the usual securities, and that they persist when other peoples assimilate or disappear into history. We learn through them that we are not elect, or rather that we are elect only through them.

The shadow which hangs over all theological work is undoubtedly darker in Barth's treatment of Israel than anywhere else in the *Dogmatics*. On the one hand there are the affirmations: the covenant promises to Israel are unbreakable. Israel will exist to the end of time as a sister to the Church. There should be witness, but no Jewish missions. On the other hand Israel is the mirror of the damned, not of the elect. Dieter Kraft notes that Barth strove to combat anti-Semitism in his theology from 1933 onwards but 'his theological philo-semitism is dominated by an objective dialectic to such an extent that it is hardly distinguishable from the cynicism of anti-Semitism'. The logic of Barth's argument that anti-Semitism is a manifestation of the universal opposition to God, that the Jew is the mirror of us all, is bad news indeed, for if that is the case, can we not expect the Holocaust to

[140] KD III/3, 247; CD, 218.   [141] KD III/3, 248; CD, 220.
[142] KD III/3, 251; CD, 222.

happen again?[143] Others have pointed out the many theologians who have developed Barth's theology in the direction of dialogue with Israel, whilst the Jewish theologian Michael Wyschogrod remarks that Barth's deep devotion to the biblical Word ties him to the Jewish dimension of the Christian faith. Whilst the Bible might be part of the problem, it is also part of the solution.[144]

Though Barth does not mention Auschwitz in the *Dogmatics*, he does discuss and affirm the State of Israel. To that extent it may be said that Jewish existence was out of the shadow. Still, that Barth chooses to understand Jewish existence in this way, with only very indirect allusions to the attempt to exterminate them, may be felt to be extraordinary. It is their survival, however, which is for him a key mark of God's rule in history, a survival against all odds which calls into question once more the massive confidence of Barth's account of providence. And it is here that we have to return to nothingness, that whole element in world occurrence not preserved, accompanied, and ruled by God, to which the Holocaust of course belongs, which means that 'the whole doctrine of God's providence has to be investigated afresh'.[145] We have seen how Barth refuses all dualism in this regard and insists that it is embraced by providence nevertheless, but the effect of this strategy is to relativize the positively triumphant affirmations of God's rule, and to turn the whole into one great 'Nevertheless'.

Ending Time

Christians live not just in the memory and presence of Christ but also in expectation of his coming. Without this eschatological dimension hope would simply mean confidence in the power of the gospel to cleanse and sanctify society, the idea of a progressive immanent development of the new life opened up by the resurrection. The New Testament does not support this utopian view. Instead, it sets a term to time and looks

---

[143] D. Kraft, 'Israel in der Theologie Karl Barths',*Communio Viatorum*, 27/1–2 (1984), 59–72.

[144] M. Wyschogrod reviewing K. Sonderegger's *That Jesus Christ was Born a Jew: Karl Barth's Doctrine of Israel, Modern Theology* 9/3 (July 1993), 307. In addition to Sonderegger the classic treatment of Barth on Israel is F. W. Marquardt, *Die entdeckung des Judentums für die christliche Theologie: Israel in Denken Karl Barths*, Munich, Kaiser, 1967. Also B. Klappert, *Israel und die Kirche*, Munich, Kaiser, 1979; M. Wyschogrod, 'Why Was and Is the Theology of Karl Barth of Interest to a Jewish theologian?' in H. W. Rumscheidt (ed.), *Footnotes to a Theology The Karl Barth Colloquium 1972*, Canadian Corporation for the Publication of Academic Studies in Religion, 1974; Dieter Kraft and H. Jansen have pointed out the way in which Barth's work has generated philo-Semitic Christian theologies such as those of Marquardt. Kraft, 'Israel'; H. Jansen, 'Anti Semitism in the Amiable Guise of Theologica; Philo-Semitism in KB's Theology before and after Auschwitz', in F. H. Littell et al. (eds), *The Holocaust: Remembering for the Future*, London, Sage, 1996, i, 72–9.

[145] KD iii/3, 326; CD, 288.

forward to a wholly new order. Barth energetically disputed the thesis of the delay of the parousia and suggested that those who insisted on it caused 'a great and maliciously ignored source of unsettlement' to more usefully employed angels as well as to humans and animals![146] A resolution of the Congregation of the Sacred Office in 1944 to the effect that belief in a visible second coming could not be taught as a certainty provoked Barth's wrath. The lively expectation of Christ's coming was, in his view, what kept the Church humble, and prevented it from elevating itself to a position alongside Christ. Wherever the Church has an exaggerated estimate of itself we have a de-eschatologized Christianity, a Christianity without a gospel of hope.[147]

Here and now both the jubilee year and the sabbath are types of redeemed time. Both show that time is destined for festivity, liberation, and restitution. That the sabbath is the completion of creation shows that human time begins with a day of rest and not of work, with freedom and not with obligation, the gospel and not the law. Not the creation of human beings but the divine rest is the completion of creation. 'There is no avoiding an eschatological explanation of this rest. God does not only look upon the present of his creation nor does he only look back to that which he did in creating it. God knows its future, and he knows more, and more gladdening things, about the future of the work which is finished before him, than is to be seen in the present state of things themselves.'[148] This eschatological connection is reinforced when, in the New Testament, the day of resurrection is celebrated as the holy day. The resurrection of Christ is the prelude to his return in judgement, and this is what is remembered on the sabbath, when, with the Reformers, we look forward to the eternal sabbath of the last day.

HUMAN BEING

Christology and Anthropology

Amongst Barth's contemporaries the war, and the course of the twentieth century in general, not unnaturally led to pessimistic views of what it meant to be human. 'Man is a useless passion,' concluded Sartre in 1943. Barth engaged in extensive polemics with nineteenth and twentieth century proponents of these views, above all Fichte, Nietzsche, Jaspers, and Sartre, as well as with Darwinianism. The latter he regarded as especially pernicious. 'Today we are reaping the evil fruits of the seeds partly although not exclu-

---

[146] KD III/2, 613; CD, 509.   [147] KD III/2, 614; CD, 510–11.
[148] KD III/1, 255; CD, 222.

sively sown by this world view. To try to deny man his humanity, and to understand him as the expression of a universal dynamic, was to do something which could only avenge itself, and has done so, and will probably do so further.'[149] Supposed champions of freedom and human spiritual superiority like Fichte, however, offer nothing better because his absolute idealism leaves human being without an 'other', and without a limit. 'The god in whom Fichtean man believes is himself, his own mind, the spirit of the protesting voice in which he puts his confidence and in the power of which he knows himself to be free.'[150] In existentialism, as exemplified by Jaspers, on the other hand, human being is understood in its historicity and relatedness. The problem is that the negative situation, which Jaspers called 'frontier situations', simply does not have the power to teach which the existentialists ascribe to it. 'According to the present trend, we may suppose that even on the morning after the day of Judgement . . . every cabaret, every night club . . . every nest of political fanatics, every pagan discussion group, indeed, every Christian tea party and Church Synod would resume business to the best of its ability, and with a new sense of opportunity, completely unmoved, quite uninstructed, and in no serious sense different from what it was before.'[151]

In outlining his anthropology, then, this is what Barth was opposing. Like every other aspect of his doctrine of creation Barth's anthropology is a vindication of the creature.[152] And like every other aspect it is grounded in Christology. His doctrine of the human is predicated on a series of analogies between Christ and all other humans: we cannot *read off* human nature from Christ but, because in Christ God became human, we have to learn from the analogies. Between the man Jesus and ourselves stands the mystery of our sin and his identity with God, so that there cannot be direct knowledge of human nature from that of the human being Jesus. Jesus derives his being definitively from the movement of God in the Holy Spirit in a way which cannot be said of us. Nevertheless, his being as human has ontological implications for all other human beings for they are creatures 'whom this man is like for all his unlikeness, and in whose sphere and fellowship and history this one man also existed in likeness with them.'[153] The

---

[149] KD III/2, 98; CD, 84.   [150] KD III/2, 127; CD, 108.   [151] KD III/2, 135; CD, 115.

[152] I cannot share Macken's view that Barth treats human beings as 'a mere epiphenomenon of divine grace and the divine will'. Macken, *Autonomy*, 157. What is the force of the word 'mere' here? Or of 'epiphenomenon'? It follows from belief in God as a Creator that, if that being is benign, creation is a matter of grace. But grace has its name because it affirms freedom. I agree with Webster that the notion of freedom as spiritual neutrality seems to be presupposed here. Webster, *Barth's Ethics*, 227.

[153] KD III/2, 158; CD, 133. It has implications for other creatures as well because 'it is also true in some mysterious way of all creatures, since man is in biological, physical and ontological solidarity with all creatures'. Von Balthasar, *Theology of Barth*, 127. The difference between human beings and animals, for Barth, rests on election, and therefore on the exercise of a task.

light of Christ is truly part of what we are. For this reason Scripture does not address us on the basis of our rationality, responsibility, human dignity, or intrinsic humanity but simply in virtue of the fact that 'in the person of this One we are confronted by the divine Other'.[154] To be human is to be with God, which concretely means listening to the Word of God. The word 'real' with respect to human beings is equivalent to 'summoned'. To the question, Who am I? we have to answer, 'Summoned by the Word'.[155] God in God's Word is the fundamental presupposition of human being. 'Godlessness is not, therefore, a possibility, but an ontological impossibility for man.'[156] To call sin an impossibility is not to deny its existence but to recognize it as a radical attack on the foundation of what it means to be human.

The analogy between the human being Jesus and all other humans is spelled out in four dimensions: his being for God, his being for his neighbour, his unity of soul and body, and his lordship of time. That God takes flesh in Christ teaches us that relationship to God is a key aspect of human identity. To exist for God means to exist for the divine deliverance and therefore for God's glory, freedom, and love. But, to draw on the ancient Christology of the two natures, if Christ's divinity means that he exists for God, then his humanity means that he exists for his neighbour. 'In the light of the man Jesus, man is the cosmic being which exists absolutely for its fellows'.[157] There is in Christ no secret recess in which he is alone with God, untouched by the fate of his neighbour. Barth claims that 'His relationship to his neighbours and sympathy with them are original and proper to him and therefore belong to his innermost being.'[158] In taking our place Jesus allows himself to be fully claimed by our lowliness and misery, and this is the glory of his humanity which reflects the inner being and essence of God. The love of Jesus for his neighbour is an analogy of the love in the Triune God and it is in virtue of this that we have in Jesus the image of God.

Jesus is also the truly human in being a unity of soul and body. We find in the New Testament no hint that there is any 'war of the flesh against the spirit' in Jesus. His body is in his soul and vice versa. Soul and body exist in an ordered unity of super- and sub-ordination. 'The soul and body of Jesus

---

[154] KD iii/2, 159; CD, 134.   [155] KD iii/2, 180; CD, 150.

[156] KD iii/2, 162; CD, 136. In iv/3 Barth defends the term 'ontological impossibilty', which Berkouwer had criticized. 'What it means is that the nature of evil as the negation negated by God disqualifies its being, and therefore its undeniable existence, as impossible, meaningless, illegitimate, valueless, and without foundation.' KD iv/3, 203; CD, 178.

[157] KD iii/2; 248, CD, 208.

[158] Barth supports this statement by exegesis of the word *splagchnizesthai*. James Barr comments: 'The insistence on the untranslatability of the word is a consequence of insisting on reading into it an impossible sense.' *The Semantics of Biblical Language*, Oxford, Oxford University Press, 1961, 57. For comments on Barr's criticism of Barth, see below, Ch. 7.

are mutually related to one another as are God and man in his person, and himself and his community.'[159] Finally, Jesus lives as the one who redeems time and who overcomes therefore the despair of the past and the slippage of the present. In all of these ways to be human is to exist in correspondence with him.

Being in Relation

Christ may be the image of God, but when it comes to humanity in general it is relationship which constitutes the image. The relationship of I and Thou is the 'basic form of humanity'. 'I am' means 'I am in encounter'. At the root of all human being is encounter with the being of a Thou. The humanity of human being 'is this total determination as being in encounter with the being of the Thou, as being with the fellow man, as fellow humanity'.[160] The encounter is a history. 'I am as thou art' brings together two histories. There is no 'pure subject' apart from encounter. The hallmarks of this history of encounter are looking the other in the eye, mutual speech and hearing, the rendering of mutual assistance, and the fact that all of this is done with gladness. True encounter cannot be a matter of existing for the other or seeking only to enrich oneself through the other. There cannot then be any true encounter between tyrant and slave. Encounter can only be genuine in the atmosphere of freedom. 'Companions are free. So are associates. So are comrades. So are fellows. So are helpmates. Only what takes place between such as these is humanity.'[161] Human essence is, then, mutual determination in freedom.

The opponent against whom Barth pitches himself here is Nietzsche. He is the prophet of humanity without the neighbour. It was because he understood the significance of fellow humanity in Christianity that he attacked it so ferociously. Nietzsche is the man of 'azure isolation', 6,000 feet above time and man, the superman, beyond good and evil. But Christianity places before the superman 'the Crucified, Jesus, as the Neighbour, and in the person of Jesus a whole host of others who are wholly and utterly ignoble and despised in the eyes of the world . . . a whole ocean of human meanness and painfulness'.[162] In an age when bourgeois Christianity was the norm Nietzsche saw that 1 Corinthians 1 was at the heart of the gospel and attacked it, and sought to replace it with the strong, lonely individual, but what we learn from him is precisely what humanity is not rather than what it is.

---

[159] KD iii/2, 413; CD, 343.
[160] KD iii/2, 295; CD, 247. An abbreviated account of this teaching is found in the 1949 lecture, 'The Christian Message and the New Humanism' in *Against the Stream*, 183–91.
[161] KD iii/2, 325; CD, 271.   [162] KD iii/2, 287; CD, 241.

Amongst the special forms of encounter Barth investigates are the relations of parents and children, and 'near and distant neighbours'—his discussion of the question of nationality. In the case of the latter Barth insists that there is no specific command and obedience as there is in our more fundamental relationships. Of course there are common histories and cultures which constitute the place in which we hear the command of God, and limits are essential to our formation. But frontiers, cultures, and languages are all fluid and removable. None of these boundaries are original or final. The *völkisch* theologies of the 1920s and 1930s, for which neo-Protestantism cannot be blamed, failed to see this, obliterating the distinction between creation and providence, the divine command and the divine disposing. Once again it is Israel which has to be recognized as a people on a different level from all others. The Jews are the universal horizon of all peoples. 'The individual within the nations and the nations themselves, can no longer be on the way to themselves or to one another. Or rather, they can be on the way to one another only as they are engaged in looking and breaking out to the one people of God.'[163]

The fundamental form of relationship to which Barth devotes a great deal of space in three of the volumes on creation is that of man and woman. In understanding this, as well as his teaching on *agape* and *eros*, there is no doubt that a vital part of the context is his long standing relationship with Charlotte von Kirschbaum. His friend Georg Merz introduced them in 1924 and in 1928 she formally became his assistant. In fact she was more than this. She lived in the same house, spent most of the holidays in which the *Dogmatics* were written with him, and was finally buried in the same grave with Barth and his wife Nelly.[164] In the foreword to the volume on providence he thanked her, using the words the Genesis writer applies to man and wife: 'I know what it really means to have a helper.'[165] Commenting on the accusation that she had been colonized by Barth, and that he had effectively made use of her to his own ends, Georges Casalis, a long time friend of both Barth and von Kirschbaum wrote:

She would probably have laughed ironically if someone had suggested to her that she had become a sacrifice to Machismo . . . For her he was the meaning and centre point of her existence. She was totally wrapped up in her love of him, in her total attachment to him she had given of herself to the uttermost and was burned out.

---

[163] KD III/4, 362; CD, 320.
[164] The relationship between Barth and von Kirschbaum urgently raises the need of a proper critical biography of Barth whose personal options, as Gollwitzer noted, 'were exceptionally free from bourgeois motivations'. 'The Kingdom of God and Socialism' in Hunsinger, *Barth and Radical Politics*, 106. The matter is not one of prurient interest but of understanding the freedom, integrity, as well as brokenness, of his own discipleship.
[165] KD III/3, p. vii; CD, p. xiii.

She sank into spiritual night the moment he stopped writing . . . we are deeply involved in the struggle for justice and freedom. But in the midst of all that there is also, and there will always be, the wonder of love, and one cannot wish more than to love and be loved. This was the deepest secret of this remarkable and in many respects courageous woman.[166]

Barth and his wife could have gone for divorce but Casalis believed that the option all three took to live together might have been the truly evangelical course. Somehow or other, he recalled, amidst all the fracturedness and conflict of the relationship there were moments of mutual friendship, of relaxation, and somehow each of the three remained loyal to the other two.[167] Indeed, the impression one gains from the relationship of friends like Casalis, the Thurneysens, and above all Barth's children to *all three* testifies not only to great generosity but to great integrity no matter how 'abnormal' the situation. This relationship has to be understood in the background as the commentary to everything Barth writes on man and woman.

In his account of the relations of men and women marriage stands at the centre, though he is careful to make clear that marriage is not the be all and end all of such relations. Marriage is a unique, unrepeatable encounter and life partnership between a particular man and woman. It is the context for the celebration of the sexual, which is part of the command to freedom just the same as every other aspect of human activity. The call to freedom means that our sexuality has to form part of our total humanity as male or female.

The presupposition of Barth's dealing with sexuality is his view of human being as a body–soul unity informed by Spirit. To have Spirit means that we are grounded, constituted, and maintained by God as the soul of our bodies. Spirit is not something we possess but God's operation in relation to the creature and therefore the principle of the human relation to God. That we have Spirit is what makes our being as soul and body possible. Failure to take Spirit into account is what leads us to either a monistic materialism or a monistic spiritualism, both equally as false as the other. As the principle of the soul, Spirit is the principle of the whole person. Soul and body are inextricable—the soul is not the immortal essence in a mortal shell, but they exist in an order. The soul rules and the body serves. That we cannot have a soul without a body means that 'every trivialisation of the body, every removal of the body from the soul, and every abstraction between the two immediately jeopardises the soul'.[168] Body is openness of the soul whilst the soul is our self consciousness taking place in the body.[169]

---

[166] The letter is part of the appendix to R. Köbler, *Schattenarbeit*, Cologne, Pahl-Rugenstein, 1987, 131.

[167] Ibid., 130.   [168] KD III/2, 448; CD, 373.   [169] KD III/2, 481; CD, 401.

In sexual relationships, then, we seek the spirit impelled soul of the body of the other. Sexuality is not to be separated off from any of the other areas of our life. It is properly fulfilled in marriage. 'Marriage is "chaste", honourable, and truly sexual when it is encompassed by the fellowship of the spirit and of love, but also of work and of the whole of life with all its joys and sorrows, and when this total life experience justifies at the right time and place this particular relationship. . . If it does not take place in this context, it is neither chaste, right nor salutary. . . coitus without coexistence is demonic.'[170] Properly speaking *eros* is the decision for mutual understanding, self giving and desire. Desire is legitimate when controlled by the joy of being the other's, the confidence of being well placed with them, the willingness to make common cause with them.[171] Marriage is a supreme divine vocation, a task which involves labour at the work of art of the couple's common being, a total and all embracing fellowship for life. It involves the affirmation and generous liberation of the other in which the two always remain fundamentally a mystery to each other. Although it may be expected that each partner has friends of the opposite sex it is an exclusive partnership, monogamy. 'How can the order of life partnership be fulfilled if there are two firsts and two seconds? In every dimension a third party, whether male or female, can only *eo ipso* disturb and destroy full life-partnership.'[172] Neither a fickle eroticism nor polygamy are possible in the man–woman relation. Although there can be no true marriage without love it is not love but God's calling and gift which is the true basis of the marriage. Barth allowed for the possibility of divorce but believed that it was extraordinarily difficult to know that a particular relationship had come into being and been lived out contrary to the divine will and command. No marriage whatsoever stands completely outside of the shadow, just as all people are at fault in relation to the prohibition of adultery as formulated by Jesus. Absolute purity is not required of us, but we must be led to repentance and to a position of remoteness from transgression and vigilance against it. In words which it is difficult not to see as autobiographical he concludes,

There is also loyalty even in the midst of disloyalty and constancy amid open inconstancy. And, let it not be forgotten, there is genuine, strong and whole hearted love even in relationships which cannot flower in regular marriage, but which in all their fragmentariness are not mere sin and shame, and do not wholly lack the character of marriage. Furthermore, in this sphere especially there is to be noted a certain zealously practised restraint against the desire or preference for strange fruit.[173]

---

[170] KD iii/4, 147; CD, 133.   [171] KD iii/4, 245; CD, 219.
[172] KD iii/4, 220; CD, 197.   [173] KD iii/4, 268; CD, 239.

Measured by God's command such relationships may all be a heap of ruins. They can be good only on the basis of God's forgiving grace and the remembrance that both judgement and mercy apply to all.

Barth's teaching on the relations of men and women has much wider implications than the doctrine of marriage. Already in his exposition of Genesis 1.26 Barth had advanced the original thesis that being in the image of God did not consist in rationality or the exercise of dominion, but in the relationship of man and woman. 'As the only real principle of differentiation and relationship, as the original form not only of human confrontation with God but also of all intercourse between human beings, it is the Human (*das Humane*) and therefore the true creaturely image of God.'[174] The exposition of the second creation saga leads to the same result, namely that only man and woman together constitute the human. In this account Barth regards the completion of man by the creation of woman as 'not only one secret but *the* secret, the heart of all the secrets of God the Creator'.

Barth died in 1968, as second wave feminism was just beginning to make itself felt. What has caused most offence in the intervening years is his emphatic assertion of an order, a super- and subordination in the relations between men and women. Christian exegesis had consistently spoken of a relation of such an order. Barth opposed gender stereotyping and recognized that different ages had very different ideas as to what was appropriate and salutary for the different sexes to do.[175] 'The question what specific activity woman will claim and make her own as woman ought certainly to be posed in each particular case as it arises, not in the light of traditional preconceptions . . . above all, woman herself ought not to allow the uncalled for illusions of man, and his attempts to dictate what is suitable for her and what is not, to deter her from continually and seriously putting this question to herself.'[176] Nevertheless, he believed that there was a distinction which had to be insisted on, and in his account of the life long relation of men and women he followed the older tradition. In the Yahwist saga woman is created from the rib of man. We learn from this, according to Barth, that man recognizes woman as part of himself, that he cannot

---

[174] KD III/1, 209; CD, 186. James Barr speaks of Barth's exegesis of Genesis 1.26 as 'ill judged and irresponsible'. Exegetically it is impossible and in fact derives from the need to deny a 'point of contact' to human beings. 'It makes an apparent contact on the one side with the exegesis of the older Church . . . and on the other it empties the image of all actual contact between humanity and deity, leaving only a relationship within humanity which has some analogy with a relationship with God . . . the interpretation is stimulating, interesting and ingenious, but totally incredible.' Barr, *Biblical Faith*, 163. Aside from the exegetical criticism it seems to me that the impact of personalist philosophies and theology, and his own experience of the man–woman relation, is likely to be more important than the need to 'overcome Brunner', which was not very urgent at this stage.

[175] KD III/4, 169–70; CD, 153–4.   [176] KD III/4, 172; CD, 155.

produce woman himself and therefore that he cannot rule her, that he only becomes fully human in relation to the woman, and that in the woman man recognizes a being 'with its own autonomous nature and structure'. In this way the saga points to the 'reality and multidimensional depth of the unmistakeable mystery of the existence of woman and the sex relationship'.[177]

That woman is taken from the rib of man indicates that the relation of man and woman is not one of reciprocity and equality. 'The supremacy of man is not a question of value, dignity or honour, but of order. It does not denote a higher humanity of man. Its acknowledgement is no shame to woman. On the contrary, it is an acknowledgement of her glory, which in a particular and decisive respect is greater even than that of man.'[178] So central is the relation of man and woman to Barth that it is the content of his exegesis of humanity as likeness and hope. In his account of the so called 'house tables' of Ephesians 5 Barth speaks of a reciprocal subordination in which each gives to the other that which is proper. 'This is the meaning of the house table . . . It has nothing really to do with patriarchalism, or with a hierarchy of domestic and civil values and powers. It does not give one control over the other, or put anyone under the dominion of the other . . . what it demands is mutual subordination in respect before the Lord.'[179] The subordination involved emphasizes 'mutual adaptation and co-ordination'. It is absurd to suppose that woman's relationship to God is mediated through her relationship to man.[180] Nevertheless, in marriage it is the man who represents Christ and the woman the community, just as in the Old Testament 'Man is primarily and properly Yahweh, and woman primarily and properly Israel.'[181] When the order is observed the strong but not tyrannical man who serves the order and does not make it serve himself is met with the mature woman. In regard to the precedence she sees the man assume 'she will feel no sense of inferiority nor impulse of jealousy. She will not consider herself to be attacked by this, but promoted and protected. She will see guarded by it just what she desires to see guarded. She has no need to assert herself by throwing out a challenge to man . . . She will not merely accept his concern for the order and for herself, but make it her joy and pride as woman to be worthy of this concern, i.e. to be a free human being alongside man and in fellowship with him.'[182] Not only does the strong and loving husband summon her to maturity but to 'self restriction'. It is not part of her maturity to see that the marriage is a fellowship in freedom, which is primarily the man's responsibility. She is called 'upwards' into fellowship with the man.

---

[177] KD III/1, 338–9; CD, 296–7. [178] KD III/1, 344–5; CD, 301–2.
[179] KD III/2, 378; CD, 313. [180] KD III/3, 196; CD, 173.
[181] KD III/2, 358; CD, 297. [182] KD III/4, 197; CD, 177.

In the letter previously mentioned, Casalis speaks of the way in which Charlotte von Kirschbaum opened the door for a feminist reading of Scripture, for the creative breakthrough of women into theology, and to a new understanding of the relations between men and women in politics, the community, and in love.[183] Barth himself was a determined advocate of votes for women in a Switzerland which was extremely reactionary in this regard.[184] In his account of the relations of women and men he is, unsurprisingly, at one with the views of von Kirschbaum herself in her booklet on 'The Real Woman', which appeared in 1949. In the same year Simone de Beauvoir had published one of the seminal works of twentieth century feminism, *The Second Sex*. Barth understood feminism as the attempt on the part of women to 'occupy the position and fulfil the function of men'. Barth was opposed to the idea of androgyny, as he believed the encounter of male and female to be the normative form of encounter with the other. In de Beauvoir he could not accept the emphasis placed on sexuality as a cultural construct. In his view she proclaims a new myth of the human individual who in the achievement of freedom overcomes his masculinity or her feminity, mastering it from a superior plane, so that sexuality can be ultimately dispensed with or at least controlled.[185] Against both androgyny and de Beauvoir's view he believed that human beings were called to rejoice in their gender and 'fruitfully use its potential'.[186] He disallowed any self contained and self sufficient male or female life, and disliked the cloister. His remarks on Goethe's betrayal of his 'finest love affair' and his capture by the 'secularised cloister' make this point with especial force. The Greek erotic world, to which Goethe belonged, 'was a man's world in which there is no real place for woman; and for this reason it was necessarily a world of the I without the Thou, and therefore a world of the I wandering without limit or object, a demonic and tyrannical world. . .the only safeguard against these disasters is Christology and a little knowledge of life. . .a placid and cheerful and sure knowledge of the duality of human existence, of the original form of the I and Thou in the continuity of human being as the being of male and female.'[187]

There is no possibility that Barth's teaching on the relation of men and women can be followed. Does it, then, call his whole theological method into question? A number of theologians, basically sympathetic to his approach, have argued that he can be understood *in meliorem partem*, and that following his own principles does not necessarily produce this result. Thus Paul Fiddes, for example, argues that rather than thinking in terms of

---

[183] Köbler, 131.
[184] See 'The Christian Community and the Civil Community' in *Against the Stream*, 38.
[185] KD III/4, 180; CD, 162.   [186] KD III/4, 165; CD, 149.
[187] KD III/2, 350; CD, 290.

super- and subordination a Barthian account of the man–woman relationship, indeed of all relationships, might well be guided by the idea of peri-
choresis. Noting that Barth refused gender stereotyping he concludes:
'Barth's theology of covenant. . .leaves us with a direction and a quest.' As
we give up the idea of what is specifically 'men's' and 'women's' work so 'we
may take the clue from the image of the Trinity that the difference will lie in
the mode of being of a person *within* the activity'.[188]

E. Frykberg, meanwhile, presses the logic of Barth's analogy of relations
and argues that Barth should have taken account not just of gender
but of age, as he does in his ethics. From that perspective it becomes
clear that the inner Trinitarian relations are more directly analogous to
male–female relations *within a generation* than to parent–child relations.
Barth was led to the problem of subordination because Christ was the analogue in his understanding of the relation of God to Godself, of humans to
each other, and of God to humanity. In understanding the relations of men
and women Barth ran the first and the last together. What he should have
seen, and what his logic leads him to see, is that it is the first analogy which
obtains between men and women: as the Son is distinct from the Father but
still God the adult male and female are different and distinct, but still equal.
We can accept his fundamental theological principles without his unaccept-
able conclusions.[189]

FREEDOM IN HOPE

Freedom was a major theme of Barth's theology from start to finish,
but it was especially to the fore as he addressed the last two volumes on
creation. The war against Hitler had been a struggle for freedom. In 1948 the
United Nations Charter outlined the four essential freedoms it believed
all people were entitled to. At exactly the same time, the rhetoric of the
struggle for freedom was being harnessed in the interests of the Cold
War. Meanwhile, Barth had not lost sight of the discussion of what constituted true human freedom with which he was familiar in the socialist
meetings in Safenwil: he saw very clearly how the 'almost unequivocally
demonic process' of capitalism dissipated society and led to widespread

---

[188] P. Fiddes, 'The Status of Woman in the Thought of Karl Barth' in J. M. Soskice (ed.),
After Eve, London, Collins, 1990, 138–53; here 153. He also argues that on Barth's logic women, as true receivers of the Word, ought to be initiators, inspirers, and leaders on the human
scene.

[189] E. Frykberg, 'The Child as Solution: The Problem of the Superordinate–Subordinate
Ordering of the Male–Female Relation in Barth's Theology', *SJT* 47 (1994), 327 ff. Her argument about the relation between peers might be extended to Barth's views on homosexuality,
which he rules out of court on the grounds of Romans 1.25–7. KD III/4, 184; CD, 166.

alienation.[190] This whole background informs his complex discussion of the ethics of creation, which is an ethics of freedom.[191]

Freedom and Responsibility

On 2 November 1945 Barth addressed a large gathering of politicians and others in Stuttgart in a talk published as 'A Word to the Germans'. He appealed to German common sense (*Nüchternheit*), which ought to consist in the recognition that there is a duty which goes beyond that of obedience, namely that of freedom. 'Freedom means responsibility, not running away from but taking responsibility oneself, responsibility of the spirit, of the heart, of thinking, of the conscience, of each individual and of the whole people . . . freedom is found where each individual makes themselves responsible for the leadership of the whole. It is there where the responsibility of each individual is for the benefit of the leadership, maintenance and shaping of the whole.'[192] Three years later, talking to a youth gathering in Hungary, he quoted with approval Kant's call to enlightenment—*Sapere aude!*—but he noted that Enlightenment freedom had degenerated into freedom for godlessness and inhumanity. Freedom, he said, meant freedom for God and the neighbour. 'Wherever it is something different from that it is not freedom for responsibility.'[193] Freedom and responsibility were what Barth saw to be the key words for post-war Europe, and they form the heart of his ethics of creation.

'Real humanity' finds expression in gratitude. In thanking God we confirm the divine separation of light from darkness. But thanksgiving takes the form of self commitment to God, or responsibility. 'The summons of the Word of God . . . aims at responsibility realised in action and event . . . What makes him real man is that he is engaged in active responsibility to God.'[194] Responsibility is active affirmation of the Word of God through which a person makes themselves the active response to God's Word; it is obedience to the Word and commitment to action; it is to invoke God as our Judge and to await God's verdict; but then finally it is freedom. Freedom is the decisive mark of what it means to be human, and it has to be seized and won in knowledge, obedience, and asking before God.[195]

---

[190] KD III/4, 609–10; CD, 531–2. There are stringent critiques of capitalism and of 'mass man' which anticipate Marcuse in 'The Church between East and West' and 'The Christian Community and the Civil Community' in *Against the Stream*, 36, 133, 140.

[191] Nigel Biggar points out that the concept of order, explicit in the Münster ethics, is predominant throughout this account, though incognito, so that the concept of created orders has 'a more fundamental role'. Biggar, *Hastening*, 58.

[192] 'Ein Wort an die Deutschen' (1945) in *Der Götze Wackelt*, 96.

[193] 'The Christian Community in the Midst of Political Change' in *Against the Stream*, 61.

[194] KD III/2, 209; CD, 175.   [195] KD III/2, pp 209–36; CD, 176–96.

The reality of human freedom rules out casuistry.[196] Casuistry makes the human being rather than God responsible for choosing between good and evil, it assumes that God's command is a universal rule, but above all it is a destruction of Christian freedom. Barth's ethics is from first to last an ethics of freedom. God's Word calls us to obedience, but casuistry destroys the freedom of this obedience. 'It openly interposes something other and alien between the command of God and the man who is called to obey him. It replaces the concrete and specific command of God's free grace and there-fore the authentic will of God which man must freely and voluntarily choose, affirm, approve and grasp, by the interpretation and application, invented by himself or others, of a universal moral truth fixed and pro-claimed with supreme arbitrariness.'[197]

From the beginning Barth was accused of ethical occasionalism, and recently Robin Lovin has argued that Barth's ethics provide us with no guid-ance for making 'public choices'. 'An ethical theory can only provide specific guidance if it includes some general propositions . . . For all its theological integrity, Barth's position is impossible for a public ethics.'[198] Given Barth's intervention on the public stage throughout his life, on matters ranging from trades union legislation to nuclear weapons, this points either to radical inconsistency in Barth, or to something which Lovin has missed. Barth clearly believed he had grounds for making 'public choices'. In brief this was a matter of attending what he liked to call 'the school of the apos-tles and prophets'.[199] We are *schooled* in our ethical decision making in the community of the Church. The need to disown the theology of his teach-ers, as later the need to combat the German Christians, and at this stage of his life to refuse to join in any anti-communist hysteria, taught Barth at the same time the need to swim against the stream, theologically, politically, and therefore ethically. 'General propositions' may be desperately unreliable for making public choices, as the Nuremburg trials demonstrated. It is in *this* sense that each individual, be they soldier, politician, accountant, or what-ever, needs to respond to the command of God's Word 'that reaches her

[196] For a sensitive and critical account of Barth's understanding of casuistry see Biggar, *Has-tening*, 12, 40–5.

[197] KD III/4, 12; CD, 13.

[198] R. Lovin, *Christian Faith and Public Choices: The Social Ethics of Barth, Brunner and Bonhoef-fer*, Philadelphia, Fortress, 1984, 42.

[199] One of the most concrete examples of his ethics in action is his underground letter to friends in Holland in 1942. They had posed a series of questions to him about how they should act during the Occupation. To the question whether Christians could belong to 'illegal' orga-nizations Barth responded: 'Not merely allowed, but commanded!' Should one lie in opposi-tion to the Robber State. Answer: The Word of truth is bound up with the struggle for freedom, and cannot be separated from that. This is not 'situation ethics' but an understanding of what it means to say 'God is truth in God's revelation'. 'An meine freunde in den Niederlanden', *The-ologische Fragen*, 247, 248.

through—and often in spite of—her social context'.[200] If we then object that even in the West Christians account for only a tiny minority of the population Barth cheerfully reminds us that the task of the Church is *witness* to the living God whose command has immediate contemporary relevance.

What takes the place of casuistry in Barth's ethics is, then, knowledge of the ongoing history between God and human beings as this is made known to us in Scripture. In his ethics of creation Barth develops the dimensions of human freedom in correspondence with the four aspects of anthropology outlined earlier, namely human being for God, for the neighbour, in the unity of soul and body, and in respect to time.

If freedom is the hallmark of humanity, then the hallmark of freedom is prayer and praise, which stem from knowledge of God as the basic act of human reason, a theme to which Barth constantly returns. The reality of God's providence, for example, is acknowledged in faith, obedience, and prayer. 'Christian prayer means thanksgiving and praise, then confession and intercession, and then again thanksgiving and praise.'[201] Prayer is the most intimate and effective form of Christian action, the true and proper work of the Christian. It is a genuine and actual share in the universal lordship of God, a gift of the free God which invites the exercise of our freedom.[202] Praise takes the concrete form of confession which, in its freedom from purpose, has more of the nature of a game or song than of work.[203]

The keeping of Sunday is a special form of the exercise of this freedom, given us to celebrate, rejoice, and be free to the glory of God. By making people free from themselves it makes them free for themselves, and makes them free for God, giving them space to hear and attest the Word of God. Because it is concerned with freedom for God its meaning is joy, the celebrating of a feast. 'The Church must not allow itself to become dull, nor its services dark and gloomy. It must be claimed by, and proclaim, the lordship of God in the kingdom of his dear Son rather than the lordship of the devil or capitalism or communism or human folly and wickedness in general.'[204] The freedom, release from care, and lack of a programme which characterize it must stream from it in the form of joy and openness for others in the course of the week.

All forms of prayer, confession, or worship are fundamentally the work of the community rather than of the individual. 'We' pray and the 'we' 'is ontological, not homiletical in character'.[205] It is always either I who pray as one of a fellowship, or we of whom I am one. 'We' are those summoned and

---

[200] Biggar, *Hastening*, 145.   [201] KD III/3, 287; CD, 252.
[202] KD III/3, 322; CD, 285.   [203] KD III/4, 84; CD, 77.
[204] KD III/4, 75; CD, 69.   [205] KD III/4, 114; CD, 104.

claimed by Jesus of Nazareth, intimately bound to all those who have not heard that summons. ' "We" are united and made brethren among ourselves in order that we may be responsible for the world around us, representing our Lord among them and them before our Lord.'[206]

Freedom for Life

Human beings exercise their freedom *vis-à-vis* God and their neighbour. Barth deals with many of the most contentious issues of ethics, including euthanasia, suicide, war, and work, under the heading of freedom for life, that freedom which is grounded on respect for life, and which is directed towards the preservation and the furthering of life. It is in this context that, to some extent, Barth addresses the concerns of the non-human world. He refused to dismiss Schweitzer's contention that 'ethics is infinitely extended responsibility to everything that lives' as 'sentimental'. 'Those who can only smile at this point are themselves subjects for tears.'[207] With regard to non-human life human beings have to think and act responsibly. They are not lords over the earth, but on the earth, and the exercise of freedom is one of care and stewardship. Barth allowed the possibility of killing animals for food but only as 'a deeply reverential act of repentance, gratitude and praise on the part of the forgiven sinner in face of the One who is the Creator and Lord of man and beast'.[208]

The emphasis on joy in the exposition of respect for life is entirely characteristic. The biblical commands go far beyond ethics in pulling us directly into joy. To be joyful means to look out for opportunities for gratitude, distinguished from empty pleasure by the fact that it is hope for a receiving, and not the covetous glance at a grasping. It is essentially social: we can have joy only as we give it to others, and we cannot have joy at the expense of others, nor at the expense of our conscience. There are material joys, and we should not avoid them, but the deep triviality in every person can easily rise to the surface. Truly speaking, we experience joy when the Holy Spirit comes and is present. Although we experience joy when we reach a goal or fulfil some task most joy is anticipatory, and to that extent has an eschatological character. To this extent the will for joy is the faith and hope which clings to God and to God's future.[209]

Barth's early socialist concerns reappear in this section of his ethics. Discussing health he points out that the principle *mens sana in corpore sano* is short sighted and brutal unless complemented by the understanding that it is only possible *in societate sana*. This has to mean that 'the general living

---

[206] KD III/4, 112–13; CD, 102.   [207] KD III/4, 397; CD, 349.
[208] KD III/4, 404; CD, 355.   [209] KD III/4, 426–39; CD, 374–82.

conditions of all, or at least as many as possible, are to be shaped in such a way that they make not just a negative but a positive preventative contribution to their health. . . The will for health of the individual must therefore take also the form of the will to improve, raise and perhaps radically transform the general living conditions of all men.'[210] He recognized the roots of war in the operations of capital: 'It is when interest-bearing capital rather than man is the object whose maintenance and increase are the meaning and goal of the political order that the mechanism is already set going which will send men to kill and be killed.'[211] War is basically a struggle for coal, potash, oil, and rubber, for markets and communications, for more stable frontiers and spheres of influence as bases for the deployment of power to acquire more power. In particular the world wide armaments industry demands that war should break out from time to time so that existing stocks be used up and demand for new ones generated. The real issue in war, then, is the economic power which possesses us.[212] As opposed to the doctrine that it was always necessary to prepare for the eventuality of war he maintained that peace was the real emergency to which all our energies should be devoted, and he believed that the idea that war was inevitable was 'satanic'. 'Neither rearmament nor disarmament can be a first concern, but the restoration of an order of life which is meaningful and just.'[213] Writing at the time of the Cold War he refused to endorse the ethic of the just war, and insisted that war could only be undertaken *in extremis*. Althaus had taught in 1931 that 'the law of conflict has a more elemental basis than the human will' and the question of German remilitarization was producing, Barth noted, 'similar pernicious nonsense'.[214] The Church needs to learn the lesson of Christian concern for fashioning true peace among nations and of Christian concern for peaceful measures and solutions among states to avert war; and it might then have the confidence to say that it did not accept the absolutism of the pacifist thesis, and that Christian support for war was not entirely beyond the bounds of possibility. The Church at any rate should exist within the state as 'a genuinely unreliable element upon whose cooperation it is impossible to count unconditionally, since it may at any time be found in opposition'.[215]

The existence of human beings, like the existence of God, is a being in act, the realization of freedom. We alter, shape, and effect something in relation to God, our neighbour, and the environment. This is the active life to which all are called. We are called to accomplish something, transcend ourselves, and do so as an act of freedom. Our activity corresponds to the divine activity and has to be understood fundamentally as service. In activity we

[210] KD III/4, 413; CD, 363.   [211] KD III/4, 525; CD, 459.
[212] KD III/4, 517; CD, 452.   [213] KD III/4, 525; CD, 459.
[214] KD III/4, 523; CD, 457.   [215] KD III/4, 538; CD, 469.

seize the unique opportunity given us. Barth does not follow either the medieval or Reformation theology of vocation, but believes that all people are recipients of the divine calling. The command to seize the time meets us with an urgency which can only be described as eschatological.

The basic form of the active life, according to Barth, was direct or indirect cooperation in the fulfilment of the task of the Christian community. He recognized that the Church would always be a tiny minority, but maintained this church activity was the most secular of all activities because it was that which 'truly binds the world together and which is the ultimate goal of all else that is done'.[216] The Church cannot be a national church but only the body which exists to serve people; it is not identical with a particular institution; it is constituted by the call of Christ; in it all are useless and all are used, all are clergy and all are laity. The life of the community must be human and natural in its Christianity. 'Its strictly Christian character can flourish only on the soil of a serious and cheerful secularity [*Profanität*]; yet, on the other hand, it can live a meaningful human and worldly life only as this has an unassuming but self-evident Christian impress.'[217] It does not constitute an end in itself but exists for 'the world', the great majority of non-Christians. It cannot be against the world, but only for it. Although it knows that the attempt to live without God is impossible its decisive task is not to meet people with criticism and negation and a plan for improvement, which is the way of Moral Rearmament. With regard to every person the decisive presupposition with which the Church has to approach them is that Christ has died for them and therefore 'The whole credibility of the Christian service of witness as a human act depends on whether the work of active human love precedes and follows it, accompanying and sustaining it as the commentary and illustration of an eloquent parable.'[218] The heart of the message with which the Church is entrusted is the divine 'Yes'. Christians cannot be nourished by opposition to the godlessness of others. In its prophetic witness the Church has to speak to the events of the day, for there is no timeless or supratemporal gospel. It will sometimes be surprisingly conservative and sometimes extremely revolutionary, but its word will always be one of grace and hope and not scolding and quarrelsome.

Membership of the Christian community forms the centre of the active life, but our daily work forms its circumference. Work is our active affirmation of our existence as human creatures, the affirmation of body and soul in their ordered unity. 'To live as man is to fashion nature through the spirit, but also to fulfil the spirit through nature. It is the subjectivisation of the object but also the objectivisation of the subject.'[219] Along with the

[216] KD III/4, 556; CD, 485. [217] KD III/4, 568; CD, 496.
[218] KD III/4, 577; CD, 504. [219] KD III/4, 595; CD, 519.

older Christian tradition Barth puts a question mark against work which is intrinsically useless or superfluous. The hallmarks of true work, on the other hand, are that it should be done to the best of one's ability, that it serves human existence, that it be done cooperatively and that it have an element of reflectivity. He opposed competition as the guiding principle in work, believing that it revealed man's isolation and hostility.[220] He found it highly questionable, in the Europe of Germany's 'economic miracle', whether the amassing of capital, directed to a purely illusory yet dynamic and almost unequivocally demonic process, could possibly be honest work or be a source of salvation for the nations.[221] In an implicit critique of the market economy he attacked the revolution of 'empty and inordinate desires' which he saw constituted 'the true social explosive'.[222] 'In these circumstances is it not almost inevitable that the Marxist tyranny should finally overwhelm us, with its new and very different injustices and calamities, to teach us *mores*, true ethics, in this respect?'[223] The gospel always involved a championing of the weak against the strong and for this reason the Christian community 'can and should espouse the cause of this or that branch of social progress or even socialism in the form most helpful at a specific time and place and in a specific situation'. As in the two Romans commentaries, however, he at once warns that the Church's decisive word 'cannot consist in the proclamation of social progress or socialism. It can consist only in the proclamation of the revolution of God against 'all ungodliness and unrighteousness of man (Romans 1.18), i.e., in the proclamation of his kingdom as it has already come and comes'.[224]

THE AFFIRMATION OF THE CREATURE

The 'greedy dialectic of time and eternity' which Barth had spoken of in *Romans*, and the 'infinite qualitative distinction' between God and human beings proved for many to be the definitive word on his theology. What they failed to see was that these emphases were not the sum of what was said in either commentary on Romans, and that the dogmatics he began to develop in Göttingen began to take up other more affirmative themes. Although the groundwork for these is laid in the first four volumes it is in the doctrine of creation that these above all become evident. Barth's four volumes on creation need to be put into the context of the dogmatic tradition if their full originality is to be appreciated. Creation was often the sphere in which theologians turned to philosophical theology and examined issues of

---

[220] KD III/4, 616; CD, 537.　　[221] KD III/4, 609–10; CD, 531–2.
[222] KD III/4, 617; CD, 538.　　[223] KD III/4, 611; CD, 532.
[224] KD III/4, 626; CD, 545.

causation, which underlined the gulf between creation and history.[225] Providence on the other hand was often, as by Aquinas and Calvin, for example, taken together with predestination. Anthropology was the place to dialogue with current or received views of the human. Barth breaks with this tradition at every point. Creation is understood through the covenant, and therefore as itself a history. Anthropology is expounded from the standpoint of Christology. Providence is understood as God's accompanying and ruling of the creature. Whilst Bruce McCormack is right that there is no final and radical turn from dialectic to analogy what is clear is that the analogy of faith, set out in detail in II/1, is vital to Barth's exposition of creation. The first three volumes, and above all III/2, are a fugue on the analogy which is made available to us in Christ. The effect of this is, not to undo, but to sublate and incorporate into a richer synthesis the earlier onesided emphases of *Romans*. In place of the infinite qualitative distinction is an ontology of grace, in which the fundamental theological decision of II/2, the doctrine of election, is spelled out in its implications for the creature. Creation, and the human creature above all, is the product of God's good pleasure. Sin and fall is neither the first word nor the last word. Indeed, to emphasize its entirely relative status Barth invents the idea of *das Nichtige*, the power of God's non-willing. After the fireworks of Barth's 'No' of 1934 we now read even of an autonomy and a cooperation of the creature with the Creator. This is not, as might be suspected, cussedness on Barth's part, but rather his following through of what must be said if all creation is elect in Christ. 'God saw all that God had made, and behold it was very good.' The four volumes of Barth's doctrine of creation are an affirmation of that sentence.

A barrage of questions accompany Barth's exposition. Is his scriptural exegesis, in James Barr's words, ill judged, irresponsible, and even downright ridiculous?[226] If so, what are the implications for a theology which claims to be based on exegesis, as Barth famously told his students on leaving Bonn? (Above all, he said, they should do exegesis, exegesis, and more exegesis.) In his concept of nothingness is he not guilty of the mythologizing of which he accuses his opponents, and to a far more shocking degree? Does his account of time and eternity mean that time is in fact swallowed up and devalued? Is his work not relentlessly Christomonist, involving a failure to honour the common sense of which he often speaks, a failure to recognize the precious insights of the human and natural sciences? These are genuine

[225] Aquinas, for example, discusses 'how things flow from their original source', and questions such as whether God can create something and what exactly is produced by creation (*Summa Theologiae* 1a 45), whilst Schleiermacher expounds the universality of the Spirit–nature system as this follows from the feeling of absolute dependence (*Christian Faith*, para. 46).
[226] Barr, *Biblical Faith*, 160. More on this in Chapter 7.

questions to which there are not yet agreed answers. What I have attempted to show in this chapter is what happens when we understand his account of creation not only within the framework of the tradition, which is of course essential, but as a response to the tragic years in which it was written, a period which would justify the darkest Calvinist condemnation of the creature. If ever there was a period when the prophet of doom could wag his finger it was this one. Barth refuses. When we think we know what to expect he puts himself alongside—Leibniz! Not uncritically, of course, but nevertheless in affirmation of his main emphases. He tells us that he wrote his doctrine of providence with Mozart in his ears, and it shows. No doctrine of creation, apart from that of Leibniz, has been more gloriously affirmative of the goodness of the creature and of the created order. The ethical correlate of this is an ethic of responsibility and freedom, of bodily joy on the one hand and the necessary political opposition to capitalism, as well as to all forms of political totalitarianism on the other. It is a blazing 'nevertheless' to the misery of the years of war and the Holocaust.

6

Jesus Means Freedom

Spring 1951–Summer 1961

What needs to take place today in the interests of peace is in the first place . . . a spiritual Reformation and thus a conversion of Christians and of the Christian churches themselves—a conversion to the truth of their own message. Among other things . . . a good deal of better theology is needed! And so . . . we come to the contribution which . . . I have to make to peace among the nations.

Karl Barth, January 1963

Barth's massive doctrine of reconciliation, the four volumes of *Church Dogmatics* IV/1 to IV/3, was written between 1951 and 1959. IV/4, and the unrevised fragments published as *The Christian Life*, were written between 1959 and 1961. This decade was the period of European industrial and economic recovery, and in particular of the German 'economic miracle'. Standards of living rose dramatically in all the central European countries, and Macmillan's 1959 slogan, 'You've never had it so good,' was true for most of the people of northern Europe. Eric Hobsbawm, in his review of world history from 1914 to 1991, refers to the decades between 1950 and 1970 as 'the golden years'.[1] The significance of this dimension of Barth's context for his developing theology cannot be overstated.

In this decade the LP record came into its own, a development Barth particularly appreciated. He quickly accumulated a large Mozart collection. Towards the end of the decade car and television ownership became general. These developments greatly hastened the arrival of that mass culture which Adorno and Horkheimer, whom Barth met in 1956, had already criticized as destructive of real democracy. The middle of the decade also saw the emergence of rock and roll and a pop music culture of hitherto unprecedented dimensions.

The lifting of restrictions on censorship, and the swift growth in 'permissiveness' following the advent of really effective contraception, were part of

---

[1] Eric Hobsbawm, *Age of Extremes*, London, Abacus, 1994, 257 ff.

a much broader cultural movement, in some ways picking up threads from the end of the previous century, which had been deferred by the two world wars. Part of this was the beginning of a massive decline in church attendance, a phenomenon quickly analysed in terms of secularization.[2] Barth hailed aspects of it, noting that the great Constantinian illusion was finally being shattered.[3]

The affluence of the West, and the speed of technological development, led to the emergence in both Europe and North America of the 'end of ideology' theory—or in other words to the victory of pragmatic welfare reformism, committed to a mix of free market and limited state regulation.[4] In point of fact this theory was itself highly ideological, part of the war of ideologies which characterized the whole period, which Barth responded to very pointedly.[5] The 'never had it so good' society quickly bred its own disillusionment which, in Walter Laqueur's view, left the literary intelligentsia 'the writers and poets, the theologians and philosophers, as the only ones to fulfil what they thought of as the real mission of the intellectual; to be an outsider, to undertake a comprehensive critique of society, radically to reject existing conditions, and to appeal to the conscience of mankind'.[6] Laqueur is thinking of the 'angry young men' of the 1950s, with whom Barth had little sympathy, but critique was by no means the dominant mode.[7] Bloch's three volumes of *The Principle of Hope*, for example, appeared in 1954, 1955, and 1959, alongside Barth's volumes on reconciliation.[8] Hope figured prominently in the work of both. Camus's *L'Homme révolté* had appeared in 1951, a passionate attack on all forms of nihilism, and a plea for a new humanism. The parallels and contrasts between Barth and Camus are particularly fascinating. Both were centrally concerned with human freedom. As Barth got down to the doctrine of reconciliation and his account of human pride Camus, looking back over European history since 1789, felt that 'The prodigious history evoked here is the history of European pride.'[9] In a diagnosis which closely mirrors Barth's, Camus notes that

---

[2] One of the earliest analyses was by F. Gogarten, *Verhängnis und Hoffnung der Neuzeit. Die Säkularisierung als theologisches Problem*, Stuttgart, Vorwerk, 1953. Gogarten understood it positively as liberation from a mythic world view. As far as I know Barth never responded to this overtly, though he took up the idea in IV/3 in the treatment of Christ as 'The Light of Life'. KD IV/3, 132–40; CD, 119–26. The best known account by a German sociologist was T. Luckmann, *Das Problem der Religion in der modernen Gesellschaft*, Freiburg, Rombach, 1963.

[3] KD IV/3, 1053; CD, 918.

[4] Daniel Bell published *The End of Ideology* in 1960, but was anticipated by an article of Edward Shils in 1958 and by Raymond Aron's *The Opium of the Intellectuals* in 1956.

[5] See the discussion in *Christian Life*, 224 f.

[6] W. Laqueur, *Europe in Our Time: A History 1945–1992*, Harmondsworth, Penguin, 1992, 270.

[7] For Barth's view of 'angry young men' see *Christliche Leben*, 180; ET, 111.

[8] These were published in 1953, 1955, and 1959.

[9] A. Camus, *The Rebel*, tr. A. Bower, Harmondsworth, Penguin, 1962, 16.

the old slogan that *homo homini lupus* becomes in the contemporary world *homo homini deus*. Twentieth century human beings have valorized freedom but 'the real passion of the twentieth century is servitude'.[10] Camus, like Barth, calls people to rebellion, but here the resemblances end. The only salvation the agnostic Camus can see is 'to learn to live and die, and in order to be a man, to refuse to be a god'.[11] For him grace and rebellion are incompatible. Human beings have to learn to live both without grace and without justice.[12] Barth, on the other hand, asserts an ontological ordering of grace, and therefore of justice, and believes that it is grace which leads us to rebel against the powers which keep us in servitude.[13]

Incomplete as it is, the doctrine of reconciliation and the material in *The Christian Life* constitute nearly 3,500 pages of text. This was a stupendous achievement, especially considering the fact that Barth celebrated his seventieth birthday in 1956, the year in which his well known essay *The Humanity Of God* appeared. In these volumes there is much less overt debate with contemporaries, and especially secular contemporaries, than in earlier volumes of the *Dogmatics*, though the habit of 'debate without allusions' continues.[14] There is no doubt that Barth concentrated his energies in order to do this writing, trying to get as much of his life project completed as he could. This should not deceive us into thinking that here we have 'pure' Barth, doing theology in antiseptic isolation from his surroundings— 'Jerome in his cell' as the Basle press sometimes referred to him. 'Everything concerning everyday life and world events and daily politics occupied him and aroused his criticism and lively interest,' wrote Carl Zuckmayer of Barth at the end of his life.[15] Politically this decade was dominated by three questions: the Cold War, nuclear weapons, and decolonization. Barth intervened publicly on the first two, and followed especially the Algerian war keenly.

A political thaw seemed to be promised after Stalin's death in 1953, but tension rose again with the invasion of Hungary in 1956. Barth had been in

[10] A. Camus, *The Rebel*, tr. A. Bower, Harmondsworth, Penguin, 1962, 200.

[11] Ibid., 269.

[12] J. Webster also explores the similarities between Barth and Camus. *Barth's Ethics*, 207–10.

[13] I agree with Marquardt that Barth is not interested in a systematic and abstract ontology, but feel that the 'category of praxis', which he takes to be fundamental is itself rooted in a view of reality as stemming from and grounded in Christ. Marquardt, *Theologie*, 276–92; 321–6.

[14] There is an extended debate in *The Christian Life*, for example, with Max Weber's thesis of *Entzauberung*, the disenchantment of the world through the bureaucratic rationalism of capitalism—a debate wholly obscured by the translation. Cf. *Christliche Leben*, 367f.; ET, 215f.

[15] K. Barth and C. Zuckmayer, *A Late Friendship*, Grand Rapids, Eerdmans, 1982, 71. Similarly, Barth wrote to South Asian Christians in his last open letter: 'I read the newspaper attentively every day in which I always learn something new about your constantly changing corner of the world.' *Offene Briefe 1945–68*, 552.

trouble in Switzerland for some time for being supposedly 'soft' on communism. A correspondence on the issue with a Swiss Federal Councillor in 1951 was published and produced 'storms of protest and dismay for months in almost all the Swiss newspapers and magazines'.[16] After the Hungarian invasion Reinhold Niebuhr attacked Barth for remaining silent, maintaining, 'we know the reason why'! Barth, however, regarded the invasion as communism's own self condemnation, which was not in need of further commentary from the West. More controversy followed in 1958 with his letter to an East German pastor, in which he suggested that East Germany might be 'God's favourite' rather than the West. For this he was severely criticized by both the Swiss and the West German press. Writing for *The Christian Century* in 1958 Barth noted that he had no inclination whatever toward Eastern communism but 'I regard anticommunism as a matter of principle an evil even greater than communism itself.' 'What kind of Western philosophy and political ethics—and unfortunately even theology—was it whose wisdom consisted of recasting the Eastern collective man into an angel of darkness and the Western "organization man" into an angel of light? And then with the help of such metaphysics and mythology . . . bestowing on the absurd "cold war" struggle its needed higher consecration?'[17] Barth's stand during these years was so unpopular that, on his retirement in March 1962, the pro Rector of Basle University saw fit to criticize him for it publicly in a farewell speech.

In his account of war in *Church Dogmatics* iii/4 Barth had not grappled in depth with the question of nuclear weapons, something for which he reproached himself later.[18] As time went on he took a more and more resolutely opposed view, though he had disappointed Ilya Ehrenburg in 1950 by refusing to sign the Stockholm peace accord (he thought it was too obviously a propaganda move). When the German Evangelical Church sought to draft a resolution on nuclear weapons in 1958 they asked Barth to do it for them. He drew up ten theses which in effect proposed that nuclear war was a confessional issue for the churches:

The prospect of a future war waged with the use of modern means of annihilation has created a new situation, in the face of which the Church cannot remain neutral . . . Even the preparation for such a war is in all circumstances a sin against God and neighbour, and no Church, no Christian can share in the guilt of this.[19]

---

[16] Busch, *Barth*, 384.

[17] *How I Changed my Mind*, 63–4.

[18] 'An Outing to the Bruderholz' in *Fragments Grave and Gay*, tr. E. Mosbacher, London, Fontana, 1971, 81–2.

[19] Text of the ten theses in Rowan Williams, 'Barth, War and the State', in N. Biggar (ed.), *Reckoning with Barth*, London and Oxford, Mowbray, 1988.

All the elements of *confusio hominum* meet in the case of atomic weapons, he wrote in IV/3, at about the same time: 'the good creation of God in the form of a newly discovered and glorious cosmic supply and a newly developed and no less glorious human capacity; man himself, who after a brief period of hesitation combines it with nothingness and places it at the service of the latter; and the recoil in which it becomes in all its glory an enemy threatening man with destruction'.[20] Barth did not, like E. P. Thompson later, set aside his academic work to devote his energies to peace campaigning. But his letter to the Japanese theologian Kagawa, quoted as an epigraph to this chapter, shows that he believed his theology continued to have a political dimension and relevance just as it had done in 1933.[21]

Apart from this political involvement Barth was also involved in three of the preparatory conferences for the Evanston Conference of the World Council of Churches and he followed developments in the Roman Catholic Church critically, but with warm interest. The doctoral dissertations of the Catholics von Balthasar, Hans Küng, Henri Bouillard and Jerome Hamer, which appeared in this decade, represented, in his view, 'the most penetrating analyses, and even the most interesting evaluations of the *Church Dogmatics* and of the rest of my work'.[22] Barth's interventions on Mariology, the Church and the sacraments constitute his response on the Catholic side.

Protestant Europe, at least in the German speaking areas, was still obsessed with Bultmann and his disciples and thus with existentialism and the 'word event'. Barth devoted the winter seminar of 1951/2 to Bultmann and published the 'results'—a string of questions—the same year, punning on Bultmann's preoccupation with 'understanding': 'Rudolf Bultmann: An Attempt to Understand Him'. He warns his readers in the Foreword to IV/1 that much of what follows must be understood in terms of a debate with Bultmann, and rumblings of that debate can be found right into *The Christian Life*. Barth disliked the later Bultmann school, whom he called 'flat tyre' theologians, but he never disliked Bultmann. He often compared him with Schleiermacher and it seems that the questions Bultmann put to him exercised him in the same kind of sustained way. At the same time, he suspected that Bultmann's theology led to reactionary politics, a suspicion which, whether justified or not, throws a great deal of light on Barth's own theology.[23] Barth saw very clearly that the all conquering capitalist society of his

---

[20] KD IV/3, 802; CD, 701.

[21] The letter is in Barth, *Letters 1961–1968*, tr. G. Bromiley, Edinburgh, T. & T. Clark, 1981, 88–91.

[22] Barth, *How I Changed my Mind*, 69.

[23] Barth felt the predominance of the Bultmann school had to be seen 'in close connection with what I have felt with increasing misgivings to be the reactionary character of politics,

day generated manifold forms of alienation and destruction. The powers of Leviathan, Mammon, and the ideologies, he said, tear apart the individual and society as well.[24] If one considered the overcoming of the orientation towards death in the resurrection of Christ to be a myth then one could also miss the liberation from the lordship of death he brings.[25]

Perhaps the most important theological publication of the decade (aside from the *Dogmatics!*) was not work by von Balthasar, Bultmann, or Tillich, but Bonhoeffer's prison correspondence, published as *Widerstand und Ergebung* (*Resistance and Resignation*) in 1951, which caught the theological imagination in a very profound way.[26] Writing from his Nazi prison cell Bonhoeffer explored the ideas of 'man come of age', of a 'religionless Christianity', of the need to speak to human beings in their strength rather than their weakness, and of the need to live *etsi Deus non daretur*. In the great letter of 30 April 1944 he writes:

How can Christ become the Lord of the religionless as well? . . . Barth, who is the only one to have started along this line of thought, did not carry it to completion, but arrived at a positivism of revelation, which in the last analysis is essentially a restoration. For the religionless working man . . . nothing decisive is gained here. The questions to be answered would surely be: What do a church, a community, a sermon, a liturgy, a Christian life mean in a religionless world?[27]

Barth used Bonhoeffer's *Cost of Discipleship* with gratitude, but he was very doubtful about the letters, and wondered whether a service had been done in publishing them. He said that he did not understand either the phrase 'world come of age', or 'non-religious interpretation', nor the 'positivism of revelation' of which Bonhoeffer accused him.[28] Nevertheless the frequency with which he mentions these themes, along with von Balthasar's allegation of a 'Christological constriction' and Regin Prenter's charge of 'christomonism', show that they gave Barth much to think about.[29] Bonhoeffer had, with astonishing sureness of touch, put his finger on many of the key questions of the age. The question about Christ—Who is Christ for us today?—voiced the unease about the traditional theological categories

---

the church and church politics in West Germany since the end of the war'. Letter to A. Hege, 3 April 1962, cited in Busch, *Barth*, 449.

[24] *Christliche Leben*, 398; ET, 233.

[25] So Sabine Plonz, to whose brilliant analysis of *The Christian Life* I am much indebted. *Herrenlosen Gewalten*, 324.

[26] His questions still continue to set the theological agenda. See, for example, Peter Selby's *Grace and Mortgage*, London, Darton, Longman & Todd, 1997.

[27] D. Bonhoeffer, *Letters and Papers from Prison*, 3rd edn, London, SCM, 1967, 280.

[28] Barth, *Fragments Grave and Gay*, 121–2.

[29] Webster notes that 'The late writings of Barth frequently show how alert he was to the difficulty . . . [of] Christological totalitarianism in which the reality of God in Jesus Christ simultaneously grounds and absorbs all other realities.' *Barth's Ethics*, 137.

which found garbled but tremendously popular expression in John Robinson's *Honest to God* in 1961. The question of 'man come of age' and 'religionless Christianity' foreshadowed the astonishing fall away from the churches in the Fifties and Sixties and the debate about the meaning of human freedom and autonomy. The questions about the Church picked up the debate about the proper shape of human community. I do not wish to suggest that Barth's doctrine of reconciliation is a point by point attempt to respond to Bonhoeffer's agenda but on the other hand it is certainly responding to the social and theological trends these give voice to. I shall use these questions to structure the exposition.

All doctrines, Barth noted, had an architectural quality.[30] The *Church Dogmatics* as a whole was intended as a four sided courtyard with the imposing portico of Volume 1 standing as the entrance to the whole. Each of the three parts actually erected have their own architectonics, but none more impressive than those of the doctrine of reconciliation.[31] The shape of the first two parts came to Barth in a dream, and followed the story of the Prodigal Son, with the way of the Son into the Far Country followed by his homecoming to the Father. In the first part the cross and resurrection confirm the true Godhead, and in the second part the true humanity, of Jesus Christ. These two parts were then given another perspective in the account of the prophetic office, and the result was the most serious articulation of the 'threefold office' of Christ in Christian history. Barth dealt with Christ as priest, king, and prophet and in each part refused to divorce 'person' and 'work', insisting, like Schleiermacher, that they have to be taken together. This is not the end of his Christology, however. Because Barth's interest is in the *totus Christus*, the accounts of human sin which accompany the three aspects of his Christology—the knowledge of reconciliation in justification, sanctification, and vocation; the gathering, upbuilding, and sending of the community; and the being of Christians in faith, hope, and love—all belong with the Christology. The first three volumes are, then, expounded in five great transects. It is vital, however, to realize that iv/4 was not an appendix but an intrinsic part of the whole. The practical and political implications

---

[30] KD iv/1, 712; CD, 637. Jüngel draws attention to this and maps out the shape of the whole of KD iv. Jüngel, *Barth*, 47. On the other hand Barth also remarked: 'I do not like the term "architecture" too much, for it connotes "building" or "system". Christian truth is like a globe, where every point points to the centre.' *Karl Barth's Table Talk*, ed. J. Godsey, Edinburgh, Oliver & Boyd, 1963, 13.

[31] Barth explained the relations of the sections in each part in terms of the intersection of vertical and horizontal lines, going back to the geometrical analogies he had favoured at the start of his career: Human sin gives us the horizontal line, and Christology the vertical. Justification, sanctification, and vocation represent the intersection of the horizontal by the vertical, whilst the doctrine of the Church, and of faith, hope, and love represent the horizontal line seen as intersected by the vertical. KD iv/1, 718–19; CD, 643.

which are everywhere latent in the first three volumes are spelled out here, but they do not add anything substantially new to the discussion.[32] This means that the account of the lordless powers in *The Christian Life* is indispensable to our understanding of the three completed volumes. If we excerpt the discussion of the *enhypostasia*, for example, and read it on its own apart from the ethics, as 'Barth's account of the incarnation', we will certainly misunderstand it. The doctrine of reconciliation *as a whole* is orientated to that 'clear knowledge, critique and overcoming of the regime of unrighteousness' which we find in *The Christian Life*.[33]

Berthold Klappert has also thrown light on the interrelation of the different parts of the doctrine of reconciliation in a study of the role of the resurrection within it.[34] Barth predicates the whole doctrine on the covenant, and this also applies to the resurrection. We cannot understand the resurrection, therefore, outside the covenant with Israel, and the inclusion of all human beings in its fulfilment in Christ. Earlier in the *Dogmatics* Barth had understood the resurrection in the light of the Exodus, and now it is set in the perspective of universal liberation.[35] Barth's reading of the priestly and messianic office of Christ in the light of the prophetic helps us to understand the fulfilment of the covenant in reconciliation as the founding promise of redemption. In IV/1 Barth sets out the humiliation of the Son of God as the history of the universal establishment of justice (Luther's theme of the justification of the godless); in IV/2 the exaltation of the Son of Man as the history of the universal gift of freedom (Calvin's reading of sanctification); in IV/3 the prophetic office deals with the corresponding liberation and redemption of all human beings and the world (the theme of the ecumenical movement: I would rather say, of the Blumhardts). Thus, justification and sanctification are the foundation and presupposition of liberation; liberation is the goal of justification and sanctification. In his understanding of reconciliation, Klappert finds, Barth sets 2 Corinthians 5.17 (the reconciliation of the world in the Messiah) and 2 Corinthians 5.19 (God's new world in the Messiah) back to back. The effect of this is to bring Barth's concern with what God does with Israel together with the liberative perspective of the coming new world of God. The Easter event as awakening

---

[32] In 1953 Berkouwer suggested that Barth could move in two directions: either to unqualified *apocatastasis*, or to the way of 'renewed reflection on the seriousness of the human decision which, according to the overwhelming testimony of Scripture, is associated with the kerygma that goes out to the world'. Berkouwer, *Triumph of Grace*, 290. It is clear that Barth took this second path, not, I believe, at Berkouwer's prompting, but as an expression of the logic of his theology as developed from 1916 on.

[33] So Plonz, *Herrenlosen Gewalten*, 321.

[34] B. Klappert, 'Die Rechts-, Freiheits und Befreiungsgeschichte Gottes mit dem Menschen', EVT 49 (1987), 460–78.

[35] So KD II/1, 19–20; CD, 19–20.

(*Auferweckung* iv/1) and raising (*Auferstehung* iv/2) is set on one side as the revelation of the fulfilment of the covenant, and the threefold parousia (iv/3), in which the 'battle history' of Christ mediates between first and final coming, is set on the other. From one point of view justification and sanctification can be regarded as the ground of liberation, and from another point liberation is the goal at which they aim. The doctrine of reconciliation is, therefore, a massive exposition of the claim that 'Jesus means freedom'.

CHRIST FOR US TODAY

'Who is Christ for us today?', Bonhoeffer had asked. Only when we have learned to speak in a secular fashion of God would Christ be no longer an object of religion, 'but something quite different, indeed and in truth the Lord of the world'. 'Since God in His deity is human,' Barth said in 1956, theological culture 'must occupy itself neither with God in Himself nor with man in himself but with man-encountering God and the God encountering man and with their dialogue and history'.[36] Christology, then, will be an exposition of this encounter, and here Barth makes his response to Bonhoeffer's question and challenge. He does so, however, through an exposition of the threefold office, which is an account of the person and work of Christ placed in the perspective of prophecy.[37] For many critics this confirmed the image of Barth as 'neo-orthodox': 'Barthianism managed to combine the dreariest conservative traditionalism with the same unseemly boastfulness about its conformity with recent trends that it had castigated in the liberals.'[38] A deeper analysis shows that Barth was attempting to respond to his context at a fundamental level. In his analysis of commodity fetishism Marx spoke of 'the magic of money' as 'the unmediated incarnation of all human work, in which that work is transubstantiated into value'.[39] Sabine Plonz makes the point that any Christology has to make clear the relationship between the mediation of Christ and what Marx reveals as the 'real' mediation between human beings—namely money. It has to make clear the relationship between the false transubstantiation of work into value, a sacrificial process in our society, and the death of an innocent man, the 'atonement'. It raises acutely the question of avoiding idolatry. Barth, who had already described capitalism as 'almost unequivocally demonic' explicitly addresses these issues in iv/4, but implicitly in the earlier volumes.[40]

[36] Barth, *Humanity of God*, 53.
[37] Barth felt that the priestly and royal work of Christ were 'exhaustive'. KD iv/3, 6; CD, 7.
[38] Barr, *Biblical Faith*, 117.
[39] K. Marx, *Capital*, i, Moscow, Progress, 1954, 133.
[40] Plonz, *Herrenlosen Gewalten*, 333. The description of capitalism is in KD iii/4, 610; CD, 531–2.

The Lord as Servant: The Priestly Work of Christ

Restoring Relationships

Feminist theology has increasingly sought to understand atonement in terms of the 'restoration of right relationships'.[41] An understanding on these lines provides the framework of Barth's account. As with the doctrine of creation the concept of covenant, which is to say committed relationship, is fundamental. At the deepest level the presupposition of reconciliation is the triune relationship. Reconciliation occurs when 'God allows the world and humanity to take part in the history of the inner life of His Godhead.'[42] Reconciliation is to be understood primarily as the 'confirmation and fulfilment of the covenant with human beings which is the free self realization of God's being in relation'.[43] Conversely, because the world participates in the being of God, God's being, which is God's history, 'is played out as world history'.[44] Unlike the account in I/2 Barth does not start with the pre-existent Logos but with the history of reconciliation, which he emphasizes is real history. With a glance at Bultmann he remarks—reconciliation *cannot* be understood as superhistorical or history-less truth.[45] What is effected in it is 'the restitution, the resumption of a fellowship which once existed but was then threatened by dissolution. It is the maintaining, restoring and upholding of that fellowship [*Gemeinschaft*] in face of an element which disturbs and disrupts and breaks it.'[46] We see that like his teacher, Anselm, Barth wishes to take sin seriously as *breach of relationship*. 'The work of reconciliation [*Versöhnung*—translated misleadingly here as 'atonement'] in Jesus Christ is the fulfilment of the union [*Vereinigung*] between God and human beings and between human beings themselves which was originally willed by God.'[47] Unlike Anselm, Barth does not understand the breach of relationship primarily in terms of an offence to God's honour or to God's law. In such an interpretation, Barth says, God appears as the Lawgiver or the offended party. At the very heart of Barth's account of reconciliation, by contrast, is the humility of God.

The Humility of God

It is the emphasis on the humility of God which marks off Barth's account of reconciliation not only from those of Christian tradition but also from the Anglo-Saxon debate shortly after Barth's death about 'the myth of God incarnate'. At issue there, as Herbert McCabe has rightly insisted, is primar-

---

[41] M. Grey, *Redeeming the Dream*, London, SPCK, 1989.
[42] KD IV/1, 236; CD, 215.
[43] B. Klappert, *Die Auferweckung der Gekreuzigten*, Neukirchener, 1971, 241.
[44] KD IV/1, 236; CD, 215.   [45] KD IV/1, 171; CD, 157.
[46] KD IV/1, 22; CD, 22.   [47] KD IV/1, 37; CD, 36.

ily our understanding of God.[48] Barth agrees. False gods, he maintains, are characterized by their otherworldliness, supernaturalness and otherness. These attributes are but a reflection of human pride and here we see how directly Barth is addressing Camus's *homo homini Deus*. For, 'God is not proud. In his high majesty, he is humble.'[49] 'We may believe that God can and must only be absolute in contrast to all that is relative, exalted in contrast to all that is lowly, active in contrast to all suffering, inviolable in contrast to all temptation, transcendent in contrast to all immanence, and therefore divine in contrast to everything human, in short that he can and must be only the "Wholly Other". But such beliefs are shown to be quite untenable and corrupt and pagan, by the fact that God does in fact be and do this in Jesus Christ.'[50] The humility of God is *itself* redemptive: 'It is the act of the humiliation of the Son of God *as such* which is the exaltation of the Son of Man, and in him of human essence.'[51] That which resists God in human beings wants 'a God or fate or Supreme Being which does not stoop to the being of man but is self-sufficient; and it wants this God as a supreme symbol for the self-resting and self moved sovereignty, autarchy and self sufficiency of human being'.[52] In contrast to this the humility of God, the *obedience* of the Son, deconstructs the entire notion of human self sufficiency, the reinstatement of Nietzschean human being which Barth clearly suspected in the language of 'man come of age'. What is redemptive about the incarnation is the revelation that 'self-moved sovereignty, autarchy and self sufficiency' is not divine, is, in fact, a demonic parody of the divine. In the light of Jesus Christ 'the empty loveless gods which are incapable of condescension and self-humiliation can be understood only as false gods'.[53] The rebel disclaims divinity, said Camus, in order to share in the struggles and destiny of all men.[54] God reveals the true nature of divinity, says Barth, for precisely the same reason—because what has passed for 'divinity' simply destroys us. Autarchy, self sufficiency and all the rest represent the refusal of relationship. The humility of God on the other hand reveals not the powerlessness of God—as in Bonhoeffer's 'only the powerless God can help'—but rather the nature of God's power, which is love in humility, the seeking and recreation of relation. The very possibility of this is grounded in God's triune relationality. We cannot avoid, says Barth, the astounding conclusion of a divine obedience. We know God as the one who rules and commands in majesty, and as the one who obeys in humility. 'God is God in these two modes of being which cannot be separated, which

---

[48] H. McCabe, *God Matters*, London, Chapman, 1987, 54 ff.
[49] KD IV/1, 173; CD, 159.   [50] KD IV/1, 203; CD, 186.
[51] KD IV/2, 111; CD, 100 (my italics).
[52] KD IV/3, 290; CD, 252.   [53] KD IV/1, 145; CD, 132.
[54] Camus, *The Rebel*, 270.

cannot be autonomous, but which cannot cease to be different. He is God only in these relationships and therefore not in a Godhead which does not take part in this history, in the relationships of its modes of being, which is neutral towards them.'[55] In Christ 'God himself humiliated Himself—not in any disloyalty but in a supreme loyalty to His divine being (revealing it in a way which marks it off from all other gods) . . . Jesus Christ is the reconciler of all people of all times and places by the fact that in him God is active and revealed as the One who in His freedom, in his divine majesty, so loves that in him the Lord became a servant . . . the servant of us all.'[56] Reconciliation, then, happens in this moment of humiliation, God's *Weg in die Fremde*, which challenges every idea of 'man come of age'.

'For Us'—Christ our Representative

What has happened in Jesus Christ? To put it in general terms, says Barth, 'there took place in him the mighty self intervention [*Selbsteinsatz*] of God for us human beings'.[57] Christ took our place. But he did so as our 'representative' [*Stellvertreter*]. The death of Christ is the judgement of death fulfilled on the Representative of all other people.[58] The logic of representation, as many have pointed out, is very different from that of substitution. The representative speaks for me, stands up for my interest. The 'pro nobis' is not that of a propitiatory or expiatory death but of the God who is for us in Christ, who dies to put a barrier on the road to our self deification. In understanding what Barth is saying we need to be careful not to be misled by the tendency of the English translation to fall into the language of substitution, the vehicle of a far less nuanced theology than Barth's.[59] Nevertheless, we must be clear that for Barth everything hangs on the 'for us'. 'Everything depends upon the fact that the Lord who became a servant . . . was and did all this for us . . . If the nail of this fourfold "for us" does not hold, everything else will be left hanging in the void as an anthropological or psychological or

---

[55] KD IV/1, 222; CD, 203.

[56] KD IV/1, 147; CD, 134.   [57] KD IV/1, 614; CD, 550.

[58] KD IV/1, 330; CD, 300. It is true that *Stellvertreter* can be translated as 'substitute' but its dominant meaning is as 'representative'.

[59] In the previous quotation, for example, *selbsteinsatz* is translated by 'substitution'. Arnold Come makes this point very strongly, speaking of a 'drastic misrepresentation' of Barth. *Barth's Dogmatics for Preachers*, London, SCM, 1963, 200–3. He points out that in the lead statement of Para. 59 *die vollbrachte Rechstat* is translated 'satisfaction'. But Barth goes out of his way to distance himself from traditional satisfaction theory, as I show below. Dorothee Sölle argues that Barth's account of representation is 'objective' and fails to include human beings. Dorothee Sölle, *Stellvertretung: Ein Kapitel Theologie nach dem 'Tode Gottes'*, 2nd impression, Stuttgart, Kreuz, 1965, 114 ff. Berthold Klappert objects, rightly in my view, that what Sölle cites as cases of Barth's 'objectification' refer to Christ taking our place as judge. Klappert, *Auferweckung*, 208–9.

sociological myth.'[60] Barth expounds this fourfold 'for us' in terms of Christ taking our place as Judge, taking our place as the judged, being judged in our place, and acting justly in our place. What we have here represents, in Bertold Klappert's words, 'a correction and deepening of traditional thinking about Christ as our Representative in the direction of a christological-personal account of representation'. Not only that, but a taking up and deepening of the Socinian critique of the way in which we are redeemed in that Barth understood perfectly well that a reconciliation which does not reach us is no reconciliation.[61]

According to the New Testament, Christ is the Judge of the world and of all people, but absolutely decisive here is that we are not speaking of the judge of the Western legal tradition, the judge invoked in the *Dies Irae* for example, but of the judge of the Hebrew tradition, whose task is to stand up for the oppressed, who is a redeemer and saviour. Judgement therefore is not a threat, the justification of all ruling class oppression, but *promise*. It is this above all in undermining the human desire to be our own and our neighbour's judge. 'Not all men commit all sins, but all men commit this sin which is the essence and root of all other sins.'[62] Man come of age, Camus's man with divine pretensions, is man who is sure of the right to sit in judgement. That Christ is our judge both puts an end to our dreams of divine likeness but also lifts from us the burden of always giving sentence. Because Jesus Christ is the Judge, and not myself, 'the whole of the evil responsibility which man has arrogantly taken to himself is taken from him'.[63] Redemption, therefore, is once again the attack on, or deconstruction of, human pretensions to the divine. But this applies also to the second 'for us'. God's act of solidarity means that 'It is no longer our affair to prosecute and represent this case.' 'What he in divine omnipotence did amongst us as one of us prevents us from being our own judges, from even wanting to be, from making that senseless attempt on the divine prerogative, from sinning in that way and making ourselves guilty . . . He is the man who entered that evil way, with the result that we are forced from it; it can be ours no longer.'[64] This was made possible by the fourth point, that Christ 'fulfilled all righteousness', which means that he repented freely where we maintain our innocence. It was in this way that he 'did what was sufficient'—Barth's drastic reinterpretation of 'satisfaction'. It is his 'fulfilled righteous deed' (*vollbrachte Rechtstat*) which does this.

If we are not to misunderstand Barth it is his exposition of the third 'pro nobis', that Christ is judged in our place, which we have to follow most

---

[60] KD IV/1, 300; CD, 273. [61] Klappert, *Auferweckung*, 207.
[62] KD IV/1, 242; CD, 220. [63] KD IV/1, 257; CD, 234. [64] KD IV/1, 260; CD, 236.

closely. Barth emphasizes that the *passion* of Christ is an *action* of God, an act of divine solidarity in created space and time. The key to understanding the passion is understanding *to whom* it happens rather than *what* happens.[65] What Barth is trying to do here, Klappert remarks, is to think the significance of the cross for the concept of God, 'through to the end'.[66] He rejects the Anselmian idea that Christ offered satisfaction to the wrath of God. This thought, he says, 'is quite foreign to the New Testament'.[67] All the same, the concept of punishment cannot be completely rejected or evaded. 'My turning from God is followed by God's annihilating turning from me. When it is resisted his love works itself out as 'death dealing wrath'.[68] Everything depends, however, on how this is understood. It can mean, and Barth appears to mean, that human hubris necessarily ends in death. The passion and death of Christ then both spell out what the consequences of human self deification are and attack this hubris. 'The very heart of the atonement is the overcoming of sin: sin in its character as the rebellion of man against God, and in its character as the ground of man's hopeless destiny in death.'[69] Understood like this we have the non-sacrificial account of death Sabine Plonz is looking for, to challenge the death dealing of the lordless powers.

Much atonement theology has presupposed the logic of retribution, which is that bad deeds must be paid for, but Barth eschews this logic. He rejected the idea that prisoners made expiation for their crimes, and according to him the necessity of Christ's death arose 'not out of any desire for vengeance and retribution on the part of God', but because of the radical nature of the divine love, which could "satisfy" [*genug tun*] itself only in the outworking of its wrath against the man of sin, 'only by killing him, extinguishing him, removing him'.[70] Barth is careful to point us to his reinterpretation of satisfaction. He makes clear that he wants no truck with propitiation, and there is no discussion of expiation either. It is not by suffering our punishment as such but 'in the deliverance of sinful man and sin itself to destruction, which he accomplished when he suffered our punishment' that Christ 'blocks' the source of our destruction. 'He has seen to it that we do not have to suffer what we ought to suffer; He has removed the accusation and condemnation and perdition which come to meet us; He has made them objectless; He has saved us from destruction and rescued us from eternal death.'[71] There are now two ways of approaching this. We can ask: why must suffering and death be involved?

---

[65] KD iv/1, 271; CD, 240. I am following Klappert here. *Auferweckung*, 216.
[66] Klappert, *Auferweckung*, 193.   [67] KD iv/1, 279; CD, 253.
[68] KD iv/1, 279; CD, 253.   [69] KD iv/1, 278; CD, 253.
[70] KD iv/1, 280; CD, 254. For his view of punishment for criminals see Busch, *Barth*, 442.
[71] KD iv/1, 279–80; CD, 254.

Then we have the logic of retribution and what is usually understood as 'substitutionary atonement'. Or, with Klappert, we can say: 'the uniqueness of the passion of Christ is the uniqueness of his person . . . the condescension of this person on the cross is the key to the interpretation of his passion'.[72] Why? Because it is the suffering and death of God which is the ultimate critique of all 'proud and inhuman gods'. God in humility takes our place and bears the consequences—damnation and death— which the attempt to be as gods brings with it. The 'object' of this damnation is removed because God makes Godself the object. The suffering and death of Christ make clear the terrible nature of sin, what its costs are—but also that the final cost is not going to be borne. Christ's pure life offering is, then, 'a superior act of divine defiance meeting our defiance'.[73]

Christ is our Representative both in the crucifixion and in the resurrection, which signifies God's acceptance of Christ's death. It represents the 'verdict of the Father' on Christ's work, 'the fulfilment and proclamation of God's decision concerning the event of the cross', the answer of the grace of God the Father to the humiliation of the Son.[74] To read the cross in the light of the resurrection is to read it in the light of a dynamic movement, of the presence of Christ to all history. The resurrection and crucifixion have a differentiated unity. Whilst not the same they must not be taken apart. 'There is no Crucified *in abstracto* . . . all theologies or pieties or exercises or aesthetics which centre on the cross . . . must be repudiated at once.'[75] The force of this is to critique all satisfaction oriented theologies. When the Word of the Cross is understood in the light of the resurrection, then, it is 'the disclosing and punishing of the sin which at its root consists in this obstinate ignoring of the truth that we do not need to help ourselves because God is for us and our cause is his cause'.[76] The positive intention of Christ's death is to turn human beings to God, to posit them afresh, to free them for the future.[77] This is a clear restatement of the central thrust of the previous section. In the light of the resurrection, the Word of the Cross is a promise of life and not a threat of death, a gospel which demands unconditional trust and total obedience.[78]

As opposed to Bultmann, Barth insists that the resurrection is a historical event, in the same way that the creation is a historical event, the kind of event for which he uses the category of saga. We would be guilty of a 'fundamental misunderstanding' if we thought that because the resurrection

[72] Klappert, *Auferweckung*, 217.   [73] KD iv/1, 308; CD, 280.
[74] KD iv/1, 340; CD, 309. KD iv/1, 345; CD, 313.
[75] KD iv/1, 380; CD, 344.   [76] KD iv/1, 383; CD, 347.
[77] KD iv/1, 342; CD, 310.   [78] KD iv/1, 384; CD, 347.

was not historical in the usual sense we could interpret it 'as though it had never happened at all, or not happened in time and space in the same way as the death of Jesus Christ'.[79] Bultmann's account, in Barth's view, amounts to 'a kind of parthenogenesis of faith without any external cause'.[80] The danger is also raised of a retreat from the body, back to an idealist reading of history, which is untrue to the God who engages with history and, as we have seen, may have reactionary political consequences.[81] Conversely, Barth understood the resurrection to have concrete political consequences. When Bishop Wurm asked him in 1947 whether he thought the Church should proceed against Bultmann the answer was a decided negative, partly on account of Bultmann's undoubted greatness as a New Testament scholar. But Barth also felt that: 'If Rudolf Bultmann were surrounded by a church which in its preaching and order, in its politics and relation to state and society, in its whole way of dealing with modern problems, were to put into practice even a little of its belief in the Risen Lord, then not only would it be practically immune against the heresies of the Bultmannian conclusions and theses but it would also have in reply to Bultmann the one argument which could perhaps cause him to abandon his basic position, with its tying of the gospel to a pagan ontology.'[82]

Barth also understands the resurrection as the 'first parousia' of Christ, and as such the removal of the barrier between Christ's life in time and the initiation of his life as the Lord of all times.[83] It is the overcoming of Lessing's problem of the 'foul wide gap' between the first century and the eighteenth or twenty-first. Because Christ is only the first fruits, the resurrection is the initiation of eschatological hope.

The eschatological perspective in which Christians see the Crucified and Resurrected and the alteration of their own situation in him is not the minus-sign of an anxious 'Not Yet', which has to be removed but the plus sign of an 'Already', in virtue of which the living Christ becomes greater to them and altogether great, in virtue of which they here and now recognise in him who is the first word and final word, in Him who is the subject and object of the basic act of God the subject and object of the consummating act of God.[84]

<hr/>

[79] KD IV/1, 370–1; CD, 336.

[80] KD IV/1, 374; CD, 339. If the New Testament community was really constituted by the kerygma then, he insists, a much more imposing place would be ascribed to its first bearers, the apostles, than is actually the case. KD IV/2, 179; CD, 160.

[81] See above p. 224–5.   [82] B–B (ET), 146.

[83] KD IV/1, 348; CD, 316.   [84] KD IV/1, 361; CD, 327.

The Servant as Lord: The Kingly (Messianic) Work of Christ

Incarnation as History

Many commentators have drawn attention to the 'actualistic' nature of Barth's thought, which is to say to the fact that act and event are his central ontological categories. It is in virtue of this that he is prepared to talk about God's 'history', and to cast providence within the terms of the ongoing history of God with creation. Here too, in the exposition of the doctrine of the incarnation, he insists that to read the incarnation as *history* is the fundamental contribution and difference he makes to the debate. To say 'Jesus Christ lives' is to say that the history of the incarnation takes place in the same way today as it did yesterday. 'It is the most up to date history of the moment.' 'When we say that Jesus Christ is in every age, we say that His history takes place in every age . . . This is the new form which we have given to Christology.'[85] It is because Christology is the unfolding of a drama that it is not 'obscure metaphysics'.[86] Here the importance of taking this exposition with what follows in IV/4 is at its greatest. The account of *enhypostasia* is not 'obscure metaphysics' because it issues in the attack on the lordless powers and in an address to human alienation which happens in and through the *totus Christus*. At the same time we have the reverse side of the teaching of IV/1. The humiliation of God, and the death of the Son of God on the cross, judged and redeemed proud and inhuman gods. But proud and inhuman gods are at the same time those miserable and self hating creatures whose 'vileness' we learn about in the contemporary novel. This creature needs to know about the glory of being human.

Barth was alerted to the danger of idolatry creeping in through Christology by his study of the *communicatio idiomatum* as it was developed by the Lutherans. This led him to believe that it contained the seed of the idea that the human essence as such is capable of divinization. His critique of this doctrine, therefore, becomes a critique of any kind of doctrine of the *übermensch*. 'If the supreme achievement of Christology, its final word, is the apotheosised flesh of Jesus Christ, omnipotent, omnipresent and omniscient, deserving of our worship, is it not merely a hard shell which conceals the sweet kernel of the divinity of humanity as a whole and as such?'[87] In place of this he puts an account of the communication of grace, in which there is a mutual participation of divine and human essence. Divine essence

---

[85] KD IV/2, 119; CD, 107. Barth dislikes Anselm's formula of the 'God man' because it obscures this historicity, as do attempts to represent Christ in art, and as did many older conceptions of God, which represented God as 'dead of sheer majesty'. KD IV/2, 128, 114, 93; CD, 115, 103, 85.

[86] KD IV/3, 154; CD, 136.   [87] KD IV/2, 89; CD, 82.

(*Wesen*) is 'the free love, the omnipotent mercy, the holy patience of the Father, Son and Holy Spirit'.[88] The human essence—that which makes a human being a human being as opposed to God, and angel, or an animal— is determined 'wholly and utterly, from the very outset and in every part, by the electing grace of God'.[89] This is not the deification of human essence. Christ is qualitatively different from other people, but in his *humanity*. For, 'It is genuinely human in the deepest sense to live by the electing grace of God addressed to all men.'[90] Because the human essence of the Son of God always remains human essence we have to talk of the humanity *of* God.[91] Alongside this critique of all false gods goes the corresponding exaltation of the human. In Christ 'our human essence is given a glory and exalted to a dignity and clothed with a majesty which the Son who assumed it and existed in it has in common with the Father and the Holy Spirit—the glory and dignity and majesty of the divine nature'.[92]

Is not Barth's account of the *enhypostasia* essentialist, and therefore abstract? It acquires this cast in the English translation through the use of the Latin *humanum* for Barth's *das Menschliche*.[93] Marquardt argues that Barth's intention was quite different. He highlights the category of possibility (*Möglichkeit*), of human potential. What is assumed is 'the concrete *possibility* of the existence of a human being, which will be like the *concrete* possibility of *all* human beings, in which realisation he, like us, will be our brother'.[94] On the one side this emphasis on the concrete guards against any mythologizing—it is with historical, concrete humanity that we have to do. But on the other side what is assumed is 'more than the individualised, abstract humanity of an individual existing for itself. Its reality and concreteness is its universal collective character, it is the humanity of the "human species" [*Gattung Mensch*]'.[95]

Hermann Diem has severely criticized Marquardt's reading of Barth at this point, charging him with having replaced the true Christological *enhypostasis* with an anthropological *humanitas*, so that we have a sort of left Hegelian version of the deification of humanity.[96] My understanding, however, is that Marquardt is arguing that the Word's assumption of *das Menschliche* is a way of speaking of God's radical solidarity with the whole of humankind, and conversely of the taking of the whole of humankind up into God. This is confirmed by Barth's later insistence

---

[88] KD iv/2, 94; CD, 86.   [89] KD iv/2, 96; CD, 88.
[90] KD iv/2, 98; CD, 89.   [91] KD iv/2, 78; CD, 72.
[92] KD iv/2, 111; CD, 100.
[93] KD iv/2, 51; CD, 48. In iii/2 *das Humane* is also translated by *humanum*.
[94] KD iv/2, 51; CD, 48 (emphasis Marquardt's).
[95] Marquardt, *Theologie*, 266.
[96] H. Diem, 'Karl Barth as Socialist' in Hunsinger, *Barth and Radical Politics*, 119–33; here p. 131.

that 'there is no Jesus existing exclusively for himself, and there is no sinful human being who is not affected and determined by his existence' because there is an 'ontological connection' between God and human beings.[97] In the light of the hypostatic union, in which the Son of God becomes the brother of all human beings, we can say that God and human beings are held together in inseparable unity but inseparable distinction. This is a political reading of Chalcedon which seems to me to be faithful to Barth's intentions.[98] Barth naturally recognized that *das Menschliche* can only be actualized in the form of actual individual human beings—but this applies also to Christ. The doctrine of the *enhypostasis* seeks to make this point.

It is the fact that we cannot have to do with God without having to do with Christ, and therefore our own human essence, which is the decisive objection to natural theology. In the ideas of natural religion, theology and law what is 'natural' is defined apart from Christ. But 'The antithesis to this "natural" is not in the first instance the concept of "revealed", but that of a human nature once and for all and definitively exalted in Jesus Christ, once and for all and definitively placed at the side of the Father and in fellowship with him.'[99]

The Messianic History of Jesus

Unlike the patristic tradition, Barth incorporates a detailed account of the New Testament material into his Christology. The purpose of this is not to give us an account of the 'historical Jesus' as such (he shared with Bultmann a complete disinterest in this quest), but to set out an account of Jesus' liberating messianic history.[100]

In I/1 Barth spoke of 'the Rabbi of Nazareth, historically so difficult to get information about . . . so easily a little commonplace alongside more than

---

[97] KD IV/2, 311; CD, 281.

[98] Cf. G. Hunsinger's comment: 'When Barth speaks of "humanity", he uses the term in a sense that is realist rather than idealist, social rather than individual, political rather than ontological . . . When he speaks of "the humanity of Jesus Christ" he is thinking of that humanity in the concrete, realist sense so that by implication the significance of Christ's humanity is equally realist and concrete: political, social, historical. At this point, it seems to me, Marquardt has interpreted Barth correctly.' *Barth and Radical Politics*, 137.

[99] KD IV/2, 112; CD, 101.

[100] Barth, *How I Changed my Mind*, 69. In relation to the story of the empty tomb Barth said in conversation: 'Historical proof would infringe on human freedom. Faith means "no crutches". Faith is sustained only by the renewal of the word of God, revelation.' *Table Talk*, 60. He also believed that the 'basic text' with which we are dealing is 'the fact created by the divine act of majesty . . . of revelation'. We cannot get 'behind' this, but have to accept it as a given. KD IV/2, 136–7; CD, 122–3. As Webster observes, 'This explains why Barth's account of our *knowledge* of Jesus Christ is so slight, indeed almost cavalier, in its handling of . . . history and hermeneutics.' Webster, *Barth's Ethics*, 87.

one other founder of a religion and even alongside many later representatives of his own "religion".[101] Here he begins with the converse, that Jesus was present 'in a way which could not fail in some sense to be seen or heard'.[102] Although he did not exercise divine authority or omnipotence he was nevertheless its 'full and direct witness'.[103] His act is above all his word, his preaching, the substance of which is 'the coming of the kingdom, the fulfilment of the lordship of God on earth, its concrete institution in direct contrast to all other lordships, the striking of the last hour for these dominions however long they may still persist'.[104] His acts had 'in their very structure, a conclusive character, so that negatively at least they were signs of a new thing that he proclaimed in his Word and introduced in his existence'. They were miraculous in the sense that they represented the irruption of 'an alien will and unknown power into what appeared to be self evident and inflexible normality'.[105] They are acts of power, but not the power of maximal freedom which can do what it wants. What is truly miraculous about them is that a new and astonishing light is cast on the human situation.[106] Above all they are acts in which human life is affirmed, for God's glory is threatened by human destruction.

As a human being Jesus exists analogously to the mode of existence of God and this constitutes his messianic existence. With God he is ignored and forgotten, with God he is decisively in favour of the weak and meek and lowly. 'In fellowship and conformity with this God who is poor in the world the kingly man Jesus is also poor.'[107] Following this is the 'pronouncedly revolutionary character' of his relationship to the orders of life in his society.[108] 'He did not oppose other "systems" to these . . . He simply revealed the limit and frontier of all these things.'[109] We do not know Christ if we do not know him as the partisan of the poor and as this revolutionary in whose teaching we can find critiques of the political order, the family, and the economic order.[110] Here Barth implicitly makes his riposte to the somewhat hysterical criticisms of opponents like Reinhold Niebuhr, who wanted

---

[101] KD I/1, 171; CD, 165.   [102] KD IV/2, 175; CD, 156.
[103] KD IV/2, 180; CD, 161.   [104] KD IV/2, 226; CD, 204.
[105] KD IV/2, 234; CD, 211.   [106] KD IV/2, 244; CD, 220.
[107] KD IV/2, 188; CD, 169. I prefer the term 'kingly' for *königlich* because of the associations of the term 'royal', at least for English readers.
[108] KD IV/2, 191; CD, 171.
[109] KD IV/2, 192; CD, 172. Marquardt notes that Barth does not characterize Jesus as a revolutionary but speaks rather christologically-eschatologically of the God who is found in solidarity with the poor in the depths, and who is thus the royal man. *Theologie*, 295–6.
[110] KD IV/2, 200; CD, 180. That we are called to follow the revolutionary royal man has the implication that 'it is not human beings in themselves, but the graced human being who is partisan and revolutionary. The "natural" man is precisely not this because he is the possessor and the one who has, the one who takes no risks. But the graced, free, human being in solidarity, and only him or her, is the revolutionary.' *Theologie*, 296.

to hear from him a condemnation of communism similar to his earlier opposition to fascism.[111] It is clear from the gospels, Barth maintains, that the right of God is in irreconcilable conflict with every human right; that the divine state is quite incompatible not merely with the wicked totalitarian state but with every conceivable human regime; that the new thing cannot be used to patch or fill the old. It is evident that *all* human order, whether capitalist or communist, is here betrayed 'into the proximity of a final and supreme menace'.[112] This applies very precisely to the increasingly affluent citizens of the 'never had it so good' society: the blessing promised to disciples, Barth warns, stands at 180 degrees to current ideas of happiness and good fortune. It does not promise us 'the good life' but that our being will be lit up in a new way by the kingdom of God.[113]

The final word, however, is not political or ethical, but a word about joy. It is because Protestantism has forgotten about grace that it has become a moralistic affair, lacking in joy. Jesus is not the image of a divine No but of a divine Yes to creation. God's wrath was encountered in Christ but only as the purifying power of his mercy, of his free, real, and active grace.

Resurrection and Human Freedom

The paragraph on the 'direction of the Son' in IV/2 corresponds structurally to the 'verdict of the Father' in IV/1.[114] Where in IV/1 resurrection represented God the Father's vindication of the humiliated Son of God, here the resurrection is understood as 'the definite and comprehensive and absolutely unequivocal exponent of the character of his being as revelation'.[115] The resurrection and ascension of Christ speak of the accomplished reconciliation of the world in its character as revelation. 'With the New Testament . . . and with the whole Church as it is orientated by it, we take our stand on the truth that the fact created by the divine act of majesty has also the character of revelation, that its ground of being is also its ground of cognition. It is for this reason that we know of this fact, and count on it, and take it as a presupposition.'[116] We cannot establish the 'how' of the resurrection. It takes place in 'sacred incomprehensibility'. The proper response to it is confession. 'We cannot try to go "behind" it, either behind the fact that it is given, or behind the way in which it is legitimate and possible for us to act in correspondence to this fact.'[117] Our response to the resurrection is to 'act in correspondence with this fact'. The kingly Man is the bringer of

---

[111] Barth's strongest criticism is expressed in the very forthright, not to say angry, article for *The Christian Century* in 1958, already cited.

[112] KD IV/2, 200; CD, 179.   [113] KD IV/2, 209; CD, 188.

[114] So Klappert, 'Rechts', 470, whose account I follow.

[115] KD IV/2, 150; CD, 134.   [116] KD IV/2, 136–7; CD, 122.

[117] KD IV/2, 138; CD, 123.

the messianic kingdom of freedom. In the resurrection this freedom becomes 'a stormy truth, reaching out to grasp all people'.[118] Through the Spirit it does in fact grasp us and gifts us a concrete and world altering freedom.[119]

At the end of the paragraph Barth sets out an account of the guidance (*Einweisung*), warning (*Zurechtweisung*) and instruction (*Unterweisung*) we are given in the use of our freedom. According to the first, the Spirit places us 'in a very definite freedom' which alarms, incites, and unsettles us precisely by setting us under our own law, the law of grace.[120] Under the second, Barth notes that this freedom cannot be misused, but only used or not used. The Holy Spirit 'champions freedom against unfreedom, obedience against disobedience, our life against death, the one possible thing against the many impossible'. As the fire which Jesus came to cast upon the earth, he causes real weal and woe.[121] Finally, 'in face of the instruction of the Holy Spirit there can only be the most concrete obedience'. The Spirit 'does not put the Christian at a point or in a position. He sets him on the way, on the march. And it is a forced march, in a movement which never ceases . . . He does not make him either a great or a little *beatus possidens*. He makes him a seeker . . . who has not yet apprehended, but wants to apprehend, because he is already apprehended.'[122]

The Light of Life: The Prophetic Work of Christ

Barth took the heading for his exposition of the prophetic office from Barmen, and that at once alerts us to what we can expect. In a move with which we are now familiar Barth reiterates that there is no way out of the *circulus virtuosus*. 'We have learned from the content of our presupposition and assertion, and only from its content, that because it is true it is legitimate and obligatory.'[123] It is a mistake, however, to read this in a narrowly epistemological way, for Barth understands the knowledge of revelation as a supremely world changing reality. Barth comes to the prophetic office through Feuerbach. It is not we who put Christ to the question, as Feuerbach thinks, but he who questions us and demands of us, concretely, action which corresponds to the illumination he brings. Indeed, the prophetic office of Christ can be understood 'only with reference to its origin and goal in praxis'.[124] Only praxis makes clear that Christ is in fact revealed to us.[125] It must, however, be revealed, for a mute and obscure god could

[118] KD IV/2, 334; CD, 300.   [119] KD IV/2, 339–40; CD, 304–5.
[120] KD IV/2, 405–7; CD, 363–4.   [121] KD IV/2, 410–14; CD, 367–70.
[122] KD IV/2, 416–22; CD, 372–7.   [123] KD IV/3, 95; CD, 86.
[124] KD IV/3, 87; CD, 79.   [125] Plonz, *Herrenlosen Gewalten*, 345.

only be an idol. It is precisely the eloquence and radiance of Christ's life and *act* which ensures that Christian theory can *only* be the theory of a definite praxis.

The praxis in view, however, is that of a community schooled in Scripture. Christ is 'the One . . . who makes himself visible in the documents of this whole historical nexus'.[126] Barth's concern is on the one hand to repudiate a knowledge of Christ through direct experience but on the other to insist that the community's picture of Christ is not arbitrary. 'It is he who lives, not the picture. But he himself lives only in the form which he has in the picture.'[127] The difference from Bultmann's understanding of Christ risen into the kerygma is that Barth insists that it is the resurrection which engendered Scripture in the first place. It is Scripture which is 'the fiery cloud and pillar which in every age precedes the community and all its members as an invariably authentic direction to the knowledge of its Lord'.[128] It is from Scripture that we learn how to witness to Christ with both the necessary humility and the necessary firmness. We have 'so to enter into the biblical mode of thought' that the self evidence of Christ makes its impact on us.[129]

In the main section on the prophetic work Barth is concerned first to distinguish Christ's work from that of the Old Testament prophets, and then to relate it to 'other true words' found outside the Christian revelation.

Christ and the Prophets

The question of Christ's difference from the prophets was always raised by liberal theology. The tradition which went back at least to Socinus, and which had a notable representative in Albert Schweitzer, tended to focus on the teaching *of* Christ rather than the teaching *about* him. But Christ is not simply a mouthpiece of the divine Logos, like the prophets, but *is* the divine Logos. As the word of enacted reconciliation, and as the unique mediator between God and humankind, he does not just address Israel, but *all people*. Where the prophets suffer from the contradiction between God and humankind, Christ bridges it.

The prophets of Israel, and the history of Israel, cannot, however, be put on a par with other truths and lights. The history of Israel in its totality and interconnexion is universal prophecy. In its totality it witnesses to reconciliation and has a mediatorial dimension. Thus the prophecy of the history of Israel in its unity 'is comparable to that of Jesus Christ in an unqualified sense which is not true of the testimonies of any individual prophets, even

---

[126] KD IV/3, 46–7; CD, 44.   [127] KD IV/3, 46; CD, 44.
[128] KD IV/3, 147; CD, 130.   [129] KD IV/3, 106; CD, 95–6.

the greatest of them'.[130] In this history the Messiah himself takes form so that its witness is his self witness.[131]

Eavesdropping on the World

Hendrik Kraemer's insistence at The World Missionary Conference at Tambaram in 1938 that Christ alone was the way to salvation caused a storm of indignation, and he was often (wrongly) accused of being 'Barthian'. In fact he had come to that view, which he later modified, independently. Whilst he was modifying his view, however, Barth maintained it. The 'free and friendly acceptance of many lights of life and words of God' was, in Barth's view, 'quite illegitimate and prohibited'.[132] On the lines of his treatment of religion in 1/2 Barth maintained that this was not an attempt to absolutize Christian subjectivity, the Church, or its tradition. 'It is a christological statement. It looks away from non-Christian and Christian alike to the One who sovereignly confronts and precedes both as *the* Prophet.'[133]

In support of such an 'exclusive' view Barth argued that the world of both Israel and the early Church was as pluralist as our own. In neither Testament is there acknowledgement of the truth of other systems of thought or religions. The Word which Christ is, Barth maintained, does not need to be completed by others. Citing Barmen, he repeats that Christ is the one Word of God whom we must trust and obey in life and death.

To say this, however, does not mean that there are not other words which are notable and other revelations which are real. Because the Risen Christ rules in the heights and the depths we have to be ready to 'eavesdrop in the world at large'.[134] We can expect to hear true words outside the Church, in which the community finds itself 'lightened, gladdened and encouraged in the execution of its own task'.[135] The uttering and receiving of such

[130] KD IV/3, 71; CD, 65.

[131] Barth restates a patristic doctrine in claiming that the difference between Old and New Testaments is that in the first the messianic dispensation is latent, whilst in the second it is patent. When we say 'Jesus Christ' we have in view the one prophet of the one covenant in its twofold form.

[132] KD IV/3, 97; CD, 88. H. Berkhof compares Calvin and Barth's use of the term *theatrum gloriae Dei* to Barth's great disadvantage, and Barth is said to regard the world 'merely' as the backdrop against which the action of Christ takes place. The passage in KD IV/3, 155 (CD, 137) is cited as evidence for this. The argument is set out in Macken, *Autonomy*, 71–2. However, this passage does not in the least reserve a Greek cyclic view of the world for creation and a Hebrew linear view for salvation history. On the contrary, 'histories are found in [creation] too', but continuity is what is important about it. This seems to me a not unfair account of what we mean by 'nature'. The negative of this passage is intended as the dialectical prelude to the affirmation which follows: the lights of creation are not extinguished nor their significance destroyed. KD 157; CD, 139.

[133] KD IV/3, 100; CD, 91.   [134] KD IV/3, 130; CD, 117.

[135] KD IV/3, 128; CD, 115.

words is part of the divine overruling, preservation, and reformation of the Church.[136] Barth considers the New Testament parables to be the proto-types of such words because in them we see the way in which the imagery of late Jewish apocalyptic and types or caricatures of everyday life are trans-formed to become 'real testimony to the real presence of God on earth'.[137] The criteria for discerning these parables are agreement with Scripture and the confessions of the Church, and the fruits to which such words give rise. Such words always function to lead us more deeply into the given world of the Bible. They differ from the Word of Scripture in that they are limited to a specific time and situation and their reception is not an affair of the whole community but only of part of it.[138] Amongst the 'parables of the kingdom' in the secular world Barth instances 'the sobriety of a scholarly or practical and everyday investigation of the true state of affairs . . . the disquiet, not to be stilled by any compromise, at the various disorders of personal life and of that of state and society . . . a humanity which does not ask or weigh too long with whom we are dealing in others, but in which we find a simple solidarity with them and unreservedly take up their case'.[139]

Even in his discussion of true words outside the Christian sphere, however, Barth continues to insist that he is not speaking of natural theol-ogy. Natural theology, which appeals to a knowledge of God 'given in and with the natural force of reason' does not speak of the triune God but about a Supreme Being, or about providence, and these understandings of God, and the views of humankind which go with them, do not commit us in the way in which revelation does.[140] The distinction between secular parables and natural theology is thinnest in his account of the creaturely world which, precisely because it is created by God, 'has also as such its own lights and truths and therefore its own speech and words'.[141] Barth wants to avoid any 'two kingdoms' thinking which might imply that there is any sphere of creaturely occurrence outwith God's rule. On the one hand Barth wants to say that 'As words of terrestrial being they are only terrestrial words . . . They are not . . . divine disclosures nor eternal truths.'[142] On the other hand the existence, rhythm, and contrariety of the created world constitute 'a summons and invitation to the active ordering and shaping of things, and therefore a step into freedom'.[143] The word of creation, however, lacks the binding character and irrevocable finality of the Word of God. We have to

---

[136] KD iv/3, 147; CD, 130.
[137] KD iv/3, 125–6; CD, 112–13.
[138] There is an illuminating discussion of the question of 'secular parables of the truth' in Hunsinger, *How to Read Barth*, Epilogue.
[139] KD iv/3, 140; CD, 125.   [140] KD iv/3, 131; CD, 117.
[141] KD iv/3, 157; CD, 139.   [142] KD iv/3, 160; CD, 141.
[143] KD iv/3, 166; CD, 147.

recognize the way that the truth of God both challenges the truth of the creature and also institutes and integrates it.

Jesus is Victor

In IV/3 and in the final fragments Barth returns to the Blumhardts, and their central affirmation that 'Jesus is Victor'. The wheel comes full circle and, once again faced with triumphant liberalism in all spheres, Barth understands Christ's work in terms of an ongoing conflict, a 'battle history'.

The immediate background to this section of the *Dogmatics* was the Hungarian uprising. Barth's refusal to speak out against communism led to hostility in which, as he wrote to his sons, 'I felt more isolated . . . than at any time since 1933 in Bonn and 1938–41 here in Basle. There was hateful witchhunting of the few Workers' Party people, and senseless clamour for the termination of Swiss neutrality . . . Even among the Christians everything seemed to be tottering.'[144]

Against this background he read the atonement as a *history* of the assault of light on darkness, a history of liberation. What is attacked is human self certainty—the certainty, for example, of standing up for the so called 'free world'. Christ takes the initiative in this attack; he is not passive. 'In this history we do not have an intrinsically right and beautiful and good truth modestly confronting a hostile and autarchic world . . . In it there is no recognition of an adult world [*mündigen Welt*] capable of affirming or rejecting its declaration . . . In it every opponent is first attacked.'[145] The history of reconciliation includes the establishment of those who witness to Christ. 'Salvation history is the history of the *totus Christus*, of the Head with the body and all the members. This *totus Christus* is *Christus victor*.'[146]

The 'battle history' of Jesus Christ is the account of how the *knowledge* of Christ assails the forces of darkness. Barth attacks the disparagement of knowledge in Western society. 'It is not the case that Christian knowledge can be regarded . . . as a mere acceptance or reflection, as mere thought, as mere conviction of perhaps a profound and even emotional nature.'[147] On the contrary, the 'constantly disclosing' Word of reconciliation speaks with clarity and urgency to 'real human beings' and to their central concerns. It is *as it is light, Word and truth* that reconciliation is historical in a distinctive and outstanding way.[148] Another way of putting this is to say that reconcili-

---

[144] Cited in Busch, *Barth*, 426.   [145] KD IV/3, 273; CD, 238.

[146] KD IV/3, 247; CD, 216.

[147] KD IV/3, 249; CD, 218. Hunsinger discusses this aspect of the knowledge of revelation in ch. 6 of *How to Read Barth*, esp. 160, 163.

[148] KD IV/3, 240; CD, 211.

ation, or atonement, occurs within the field of the war of ideologies which was the dominating political reality of the 1950s. For this very reason Barth argues that the struggle against the Word of reconciliation above all takes the form of world views, which function to keep the really urgent questions of human well being at a safe distance, and which operate on the level of principles rather than concrete reality. All of them seek to immunize, tame, and harness the Word. But the 'battle history' of the Word is the story of their deconstruction, which occurs not through moralism, but through affirmation. The Word of grace is not the Word of divine morality in conflict with human immorality. 'The history of Jesus Christ is the unmerited but unconditioned and unmistakeable Yes of God to man.'[149] What is set out in this history are neither utopian dreams nor practical programmes for the amelioration of the world but 'something incomparably more basic and helpful because quite simply far more true, namely, that the future has already begun'.[150] In this future we are free to let ourselves go and not to try and take ourselves into our own hands. With the eschatological perspective of the Bible, the gospel speaks of the present irruption of the future, 'of the advent of the new man here and now, of his peaceful and merry life in fellowship with the present, as it also speaks of the present passing of the old man'.[151]

It is in this section that Barth discusses C. G. Berkouwer's accusation that he teaches a 'triumph of grace' which took insufficient note of evil. He acknowledged that the phrase could have been used for this section, but he did not like it and felt that it did not say 'with sufficient acuteness what should be said at this point'.[152] He certainly believed, however, that the victory of Christ was not in doubt, and that this victory was a victory of *grace*—of divine affirmation and forgiveness over against all attempts to live by principles—but he never underestimated the conflict, as we shall see below.

MAN COME OF AGE?

It is part of the design of *Church Dogmatics* IV that the Christology cannot be separated from the account of sin, or the Church, or the individual. It is Christ who reveals the depths and dimensions of the human problem ('sin'). Knowledge of sin without Christ is impossible because human beings are 'crooked even in the knowledge of their crookedness'.[153] 'The Christian concept of sin is not to be gained in a vacuum, *remoto Christo*, but from the

---

[149] KD IV/3, 262; CD, 229.   [150] KD IV/3, 282; CD, 246.
[151] KD IV/3, 286; CD, 249.   [152] KD IV/3, 199; CD, 174.
[153] KD IV/1, 399; CD, 361.

Gospel to the extent that the Gospel itself, as the good news of human liberation by and for the free God, has also the character and form of the true Law of God.'[154] Once again what is at stake is that *abstraction*, principles, cannot help us, but only a concrete history. In Christ we have to do with 'no world of ideas' which we can play with for a while and then turn our back on, nor with a teacher whom we may grow beyond but with 'the archetype [*Urbild*] of every person, the true and living *lex aeterna*'.[155] Against our tendency to regard evil as an accidental and transitory determination of human being, Christ discloses our real situation 'by confessing himself one with sinners, by making their situation his own, by undertaking to represent their case before God'.[156] The remaining transects of the *Dogmatics*, then, sketch out two great movements: the destructive movement of 'man come of age' and the counter response evoked by revelation, the critique of modernity *and the affirmation of its deepest aspirations*. It is essential in understanding Barth to take the critique with the affirmation. He does not, in Luddite fashion, rail against modernity. On the contrary, he recognizes the importance of the demand for freedom and autonomy, for true rationality. His accounts of justification, sanctification, and vocation are concerned with this affirmation, and his doctrine of the Church with its realization.[157]

Bonhoeffer meant the phrase 'man come of age' positively. As we have seen, he praised Barth for his critique of religion and then, developing this quite differently from Barth, understood its implications to be that human beings finally had the chance to dispense with an immature understanding of God. Modernity cleared the way for the Church to address people in their strength rather than their weakness. Barth refers to *mündigkeit* (maturity, coming of age) at a number of points in the exposition of reconciliation, but his evaluation of it is very different. For him the idea of 'man come of age' is itself a symbol of everything that is wrong with modernity. Taking up the theme of secularization Barth comments: 'In the sphere of Christendom there are many who belong sociologically, by name and baptism, but who do not in fact belong, and practically speaking are blind and deaf heathen. There is a whole human world which, in relation to all religion, not to mention the Word of God, regards itself as still or once again "adult" [*mündig*—Barth uses the inverted commas], which obstinately believes itself

---

[154] KD IV/3, 426–7; CD, 369.

[155] KD IV/1, 445; CD, 402. *Und so ist dieser das ewige, brüderliche Urbild eines Jeden, der Mensch ist: er die wirkliche, die lebendige, die nicht in unser Herz und Gewissen beschlossene, sondern über uns beschließende lex aeterna.*

[156] KD IV/1, 448; CD, 404. This represents a radicalization of R. C. Moberly's idea that Christ repents in our place. *Atonement and Personality*, London, J. Murray, 1909.

[157] So Schellong: 'The negation is not Barth's only word. It serves a positive, in which the modern is taken up and transcended [*aufgehoben*].' 'Barth als Theologe', 74.

to have "come of age" [*sich selbst obstinat für mündig sein*], which means that it holds itself to be sovereign.'[158] The delusion of 'having come of age' is the characteristic delusion of modernity.[159] In his polemic against the sovereign, 'autonomous', human being for whom 'freedom' is the highest goal it is 'the bourgeois . . . individual, who through a lordly grasp on nature and his fellow human being, through possession and the effort to increase possessions exalts himself and seeks thus the guarantee of his freedom'.[160] This behaviour is effectively a form of idolatry, as Barth had noted in the first *Romans*: 'the deified human being fills the world with idols'.[161]

Barth certainly believed his analysis of sin to be an analysis of human being as such, his account of contemporary history to be valid for all history, but it is clear that it is decisively stamped by the critique of modernity, and especially of the capitalist society Barth knew, characterized by individualism, alienation, fragmentation, competition and the dominance of bourgeois values. Thus he addresses the person of the 'first, second and dreaded third world war' who saw either their vileness or divinity in existentialism, and whose vileness was depicted 'with striking honesty' in the contemporary novel.[162] He observed sharply that 'after all the individualism, criticism and scepticism' from which they had come his contemporaries could find nothing more sensible than life in the avowed friend–foe relationship of nations and classes and races and economic claims and interests. He singles out possessions, the assumption that violence is the way to resolve things, and the family as the areas for critique. Whilst the nuclear family was being valorized in his society Barth wrote: 'It is the concentration of neighbourly love on these persons which really means its denial. It is the indolent peace of a clannish warmth in relation to these persons, with its necessary implication of cold war against all others.'[163] And he attacks any semi-detached existence: 'To exist privately is to be a robber.'[164]

True and False Righteousness

The threefold analysis of Christ's person and work leads to a threefold analysis of human sin. The Lord who becomes a servant reveals human

---

[158] KD IV/3, 133; CD, 119. Macken translates: 'And there is . . . a whole human world which for one reason or another obstinately considers itself still or once again "of age" in relation to the Word of God, though scarcely in relation to all religion. And that means a human world which considers itself sovereign.' Macken, *Autonomy*, 67.

[159] So also in *Christliche Leben*, 365; ET, 214.

[160] Schellong, 'Barth als Theologe', 53.

[161] Ibid., 40 f.

[162] KD IV/1, 679; CD, 609; KD IV/1, 662; CD, 594.

[163] KD IV/2, 623; CD, 551.   [164] KD IV/1, 870; CD, 778.

'pride', the desire of human beings to be like God, to be lords, to be their own judge, and to be their own helper.[165] In each case pride consists in the attempt to do without God, to do for oneself that which God alone can do—in this case very much a critique of modernity. 'A man's god is that which is supreme for him. If he himself is supreme, then he is his own god.'[166] The third form of pride, the attempt to be our own helper, has the deepest form of concealment—the establishment of ethics. 'There begins the whole misery of the moral battle of everyone against everyone else, in which . . . we are always deceived about our friends as well as our enemies (and) the dreadful pagan saying is true that war is father of all things—the war which is always holy and righteous and necessary . . . the war of blood or the (in God's sight probably no less infamous and terrible) cold war.'[167]

In his account of the Fall Barth denies any 'ontological godlessness' to human beings. Nevertheless, the cross shows that a corruption which is 'both radical and total' is part of the 'voluntary and responsible life' of every one. This is the *Ursünde*, the 'original' sin in which there is 'a solidarity between the individual and all others, and therefore a unity of the whole of humankind in pride and the fall'.[168] Human history is characterized by both outstanding achievements and failures but 'the really outstanding thing beyond and in the antitheses is the all conquering monotony—the monotony of the pride in which man has obviously always lived to his own detriment and to that of his neighbour'.[169] The name 'Adam', as used in the biblical narrative, is the truth concerning us as it is known to God and told to us which forbids us to dream of any future state of historical perfection.[170]

The counter movement to human hubris, the desire to be like God, is justification, the realization of God's right 'in its relation to . . . man as wrongdoer'.[171] It has to be understood as a history, an *event* between God and human beings, in which Christ's history becomes our history. 'It is our true history (incomparably more direct and intimate than anything we

---

[165] The analysis is worked out through a step by step exegesis of Genesis 3.

[166] KD IV/1, 468; CD, 421. Barth makes the point through an exegesis of the story of the golden calf, where Aaron functions as 'the man of the national church' who accepts the *vox populi* as the *vox Dei* and acts accordingly. The relation of this form of sin to modernity is made clear in the second lecture of *The Knowledge of God and the Service of God*.

[167] KD IV/1, 501; CD, 451. Biggar comments that Barth means by 'ethics' here 'the subjective idealist conception of the making of moral judgements as an autarkic process, as a process in which the human subject is absolutely self determinative'. Biggar, *Hastening*, 7–8. He puts his finger on why Barth felt the need to oppose this later on in talking of 'the moral self-righteousness that lies at the root of social strife'. Ibid., 90. This was what Barth saw to be the failure of Ragaz's position, and why he sought an ethic in terms of grace and justification.

[168] KD IV/1, 561; CD, 504.   [169] KD IV/1, 566; CD, 507.

[170] KD IV/1, 570; CD, 511.   [171] KD IV/1, 614; CD, 550.

think we know as our history).'[172] Justification, in other words, is a way of talking about the ontology of grace, the fact that all reality exists as the outworking of God's affirmation and is sustained by the creative work of forgiveness.[173] It is above all, and concretely, knowledge of our pardon, 'the living Word of the living God in the present of every man', a form of realized eschatology.[174] Our pardon means that our sin is 'covered and overlooked, and despised and disparaged by God', and therefore not worthy of further consideration. Through it we are placed in a state of hope realized in faith. The justified person exists 'as she hopes from day to day and hour to hour, in the hope . . . for the solution of the riddle, the removal of the contradiction, the revelation of the mystery of her history in all those transitions which she continually has to make'.[175] She lives by the constant prevailing of the promised forgiveness of sins against the accusation from which she comes. Justification, thus construed, is a counter manifesto both to man come of age, and to Camus's rebel. As noted in Chapter 5, justification is at the heart of much of Barth's teaching about the relation of Church and society in the addresses he gave at the end of the war: 'Where the church is alive, she lives not by the law, which imprisons and judges human beings, but by the gospel, which absolves them and makes them free.'[176] This was the basis of his offer of friendship to the Germans, which was the doctrine of justification in action.[177]

True and False Freedom

If the humiliated Lord reveals our pride, the Exalted Son of Man reveals our sloth. It is not the sins of weakness but the sins of strength which matter, Bonhoeffer wrote to Bethge. 'In the genius, hubris . . . in the bourgeois, fear

---

[172] KD IV/1, 612; CD, 548. In the account of justification Barth uses the language of satisfaction less cautiously than he did in the account of the atonement. The negative side of justification is that Christ suffered for all people what they ought to suffer: their end as evildoers; their overthrow as the enemies of God; their extirpation in virtue of the superiority of the divine right over their wrong. To satisfy God's righteousness human beings would have to perish genuinely and finally—but then God's project would fail. Christ therefore suffers for us. Through his humility Christ fully satisfied the righteousness of God on its negative side, the side of wrath.

[173] Strictly *as the outworking of*. A problem with the term 'ontology' is that it suggests a static account of being, something which is impossible in Barth.

[174] KD IV/1, 640; CD, 573; KD IV/1, 668; CD, 598.

[175] KD IV/1, 672; CD, 602.

[176] 'Ein Wort an die Deutschen' (1945) in *Der Götze Wackelt*, 89.

[177] Thus Barth wrote to someone who objected to his assertion that all Germans were responsible for what happened: 'What I have tried to do with my thesis of "friendship nevertheless" is to punch a hole in the wall (between German and Swiss) . . . Observe that it is not unimportant that I have simply tried to place myself on the ground of the evangelical teaching of the *iustificatio impii*.' *Eine Schweizer Stimme*, 398.

of free responsibility.'[178] A month later he reflected: 'Is not the weakness of men more often more dangerous than deliberate malice? I mean such things as stupidity, lack of independence, forgetfulness, laziness, idleness, corruption, being easily led astray.'[179] Only in the light of Christ's exaltation is this dimension truly made known, our mediocrity exposed, our 'evil inaction', and our desire not to have our existence illuminated by God.[180] Barth asks whether the secularization and dehumanization of human life in society does not owe something to retreat into a private, which is to say a rapacious, Christianity. The equation of the private with the rapacious is a hallmark of his critique of the bourgeois condition. Such counterfeit Christianity 'cuts at the very root of the confidence and comfort and joy . . . in which we should live as Christians'.[181]

In what we must take as an allusion to Heidegger's account of human existence as care Barth understands this as a central form of sin which leads to the disintegration of society. 'Two or three or even millions of grains of sand, however tightly they may be momentarily compressed, can never make a rock. Anxious man is a mere grain of sand. Each individual has his own cares which others cannot share with him and which do not yield to any companionship or friendship or fellowship or union or brotherhood.'[182] The end result of all this is human misery, a 'bondage of the will' in which we fail to make use of our freedom. Sloth, we might say, is typically *petit bourgeois* sin of those who feel constrained, if not content, to limit their ambitions and who dare not explore their freedom. Barth calls Christians, on the other hand, not simply to have the courage to use their reason, but to use their solidarity, their friendship, their whole social imagination, in the service of the kingdom.

As human pride is met with justification, so sloth is met with sanctification.[183] Like justification, sanctification has to be understood as a history with universal import, having Christ at the centre. The existence of a sanctified group, the Church, is representative of the sanctification of all

---

[178] Bonhoeffer, *Letters and Papers*, 345.

[179] Ibid., 392.

[180] KD IV/2, 452; CD, 403. Again there are four dimensions to this which correspond to the discussion of human nature in III/2, and which amount to a critique of the semi-detached individual, living for him or herself, without God and without the neighbour. KD IV/2, 473–4; CD, 420–1; KD IV/2, 499; CD, 443.

[181] KD IV/2, 499; CD, 442.   [182] KD IV/2, 539; CD, 477.

[183] For the pietism which remained a major force in Protestantism, and with which Barth only began to reach an accommodation at this stage of his life, justification tended to be swallowed up by sanctification. Barth saw a variant of this problem in Bultmann and indeed felt that the most serious objection to Bultmann's theology was that faith in the redemption accomplished in Christ merges into the obedience of the sinner. The existential account of the atonement, he felt, failed to adore the mystery of God's free affirmation of the sinner. KD IV/2, 570; CD, 504.

human beings.[184] Sanctification, which happens only in and through the community, is the movement by which we receive direction from Christ through the Spirit and thus realize our freedom.

Barth challenges the fashionable equation of holiness with wholeness. The process of sanctification does not mean that we cease to be sinners, but we become *disturbed* sinners. 'As an undisturbed sinner he is always a covenant breaker, unreconciled with God and unusable by him. The better he succeeds in achieving inner harmony the less he can be reconciled with God and used by him.'[185] The saints are those who have the divine contradiction of their sinning written on their hearts. Sanctification, then, is about the *disturbance* of bourgeois complacency.

Concretely, sanctification involves the call to discipleship. In an oblique reference to von Balthasar's criticism, Barth notes that the call to discipleship binds us not to an idea of Christ, a Christology or a Christocentric system of thought, but to the living Lord. The command to follow Jesus is a summons to a first definite step, involving a right about turn, a complete break and a new beginning. 'It always involves the decision of a new day; the seizing of a new opportunity which was not present yesterday but is now given in and with the call of Jesus.'[186] The command is always unambiguous and always sets forth the kingdom drawn near, and therefore the true and definitive *break* in world history. To be Christian is to make clear this break in the human situation. It also means the corresponding action, 'works', marked by 'radical claimlessness . . . calm and resolution and vigour' and free humour.[187]

Like justification, discipleship is a call to conversion which is not a matter of one moment in our life, but forms the content and character of the whole.[188] The *vita christiana* in conversion is the event, act, and history in which at one and the same time human beings are still wholly the old man and already wholly the new, not in a static equipoise but in the whole turning from one to the other. Revelation, which is an invitation, is at the heart of the process because God does not compel us, for 'mere compulsion is basically evil and demonic'.[189] Rather, the power with which God meets us is that of a permission and ability. What liberates us is 'the truth, revealing itself to human beings, that God is for them'.[190]

True and False Witness

The third aspect of Barth's Christology, the account of Christ, the 'true Witness', leads to a trenchant account of the falsehood of human beings, in

[184] KD IV/2, 587; CD, 519.   [185] KD IV/2, 594; CD, 525.
[186] KD IV/2, 609; CD, 538.   [187] KD IV/2, 672; CD, 594.
[188] KD IV/2, 641; CD, 566.   [189] KD IV/2, 654; CD, 578.
[190] KD IV/2, 655; CD, 579.

which they oppose the light of election and reconciliation and seek to hide themselves from God, their fellows, and themselves. 'If pride and sloth are the works, falsehood is the word of the man of sin.'[191] To the extent that reconciliation is itself a work of revelation, falsehood is human 'counter revelation to the divine revelation of grace' and is therefore sin 'in its most highly developed form'.[192] It is Christ as Rejected, Judged, Despised, Bound, Impotent, Slain, and Crucified, the Christ whom Nietzsche so despised, who makes this clear. 'The denominator common to his Word in all its dimensions and contents, the one point of truth in all its declarations, is that it is the Word of the *suffering* Witness to the Truth.'[193]

> As the Word of this man, the Word of the crucified Jesus Christ is distinguished from all other human words as God's Word by the fact that it is spoken out of the great, conclusive and absolute silence in which all the words of all other men reach their end and limit, namely the silence of the death of this man. God alone as the only Lord of life and death can break this silence, and therefore speak out of this end and limit of all human words. For he alone is beyond this end and limit. If there is human speech out of and therefore in penetration of this silence, and therefore from this beyond, as such it can only be the speech of God. But the crucified, dead, and buried man Jesus Christ does speak. Those who hear him, hear God.[194]

Life without illusion was Camus's theme. Addressing the same question and the same generation Barth finds its possibility only in the crucified Christ, in whom we see the reflection of our own human reality divested of all illusion.

Human falsehood is a movement of evasion, which Barth in an important distinction characterizes as not primarily a moral but a spiritual phenomenon. Just because cultures where Christ is known are exposed 'to a relatively much stronger unsettlement and constriction' by the truth of God, falsehood is the specifically Christian form of sin.[195] Thus, much Christian theology and art is an attempt to evade the challenge of the cross, to replace the free God with the 'solemn, tranquillising and even soporific idea of God as the supreme being'.[196] The concealment characteristic of all sin is especially strong here. The liar does not deny the truth but confesses it with great emphasis and solemnity, but in so doing patronizes and domesticates it. 'The true and succulent lie always has something of the scent of the truth. In some manifestations of falsehood it is heavy with the truth in the form of truisms . . . a radiant aspect of righteousness and holiness, of wisdom, excellence and prudence, of zeal, austerity and energy.'[197] Given the back-

---

[191] KD iv/3, 430; CD, 373.   [192] KD iv/3, 432; CD, 374.
[193] KD iv/3, 451; CD, 391 (my italics).   [194] KD iv/3, 473–4; CD, 410–11.
[195] KD iv/3, 521; CD, 452.   [196] KD iv/3, 517; CD, 449.
[197] KD iv/3, 504; CD, 438.

ground here, we cannot fail to see the free world ideology which was used as a stick by Barth's opponents to beat him with. Paradigmatic of false witness is 'that gigantic maw of lying, the Press, which today, with its exaggeratedly bright or gloomy imparting of news, its interpretations, insinuations, commendations and calumniations in the service of a one-sided interest, at once the slave and master of public opinion is *the* word which is drummed into the ears of all of us every day.'[198]

The condemnation of human beings follows their falsehood. Abandoned to a false image, the human situation disintegrates in all its dimensions. Nevertheless, if the era *post Christum* is an era characterized by the lie, 'It is also and much more the sphere in which the manoeuvres of lying man are constantly disrupted and thwarted as by an invisible hand [*wie durch eine unsichtbare Hand*].'[199] The allusion to Adam Smith is unmistakeable. Over against the 'invisible hand' of the market, setting all into competition, ruling through advertising and the inducement of false desire, is the counter hand of God witnessing to the alternative truth of cooperation and true desire.

Barth discusses the counter movement to human falsehood in terms of vocation, the goal of which is 'the self giving of Christ to the Christian and the Christian to Christ' which produces a 'community of action' so that 'The cause of Christ, the relation of God to the world and the world to God, quite naturally and self evidently takes precedence in his life over all other concerns.'[200] Vocation arises from encounter with the living Jesus Christ and is 'no less than the Christmas mystery of the eternal Word of God in the flesh'.[201] This reading of vocation is a challenge to a fading Christendom. 'In adopting and championing this thesis we cut to the very quick . . . the Christian world and Western man.'[202] Why? Because the assumption has been that to be born in Europe is automatically to be 'born a Christian'. Barth is adamant that the Christendom period is over. There never was a real alignment between civilization, culture, and political power and the gospel, but the illusion of it has now passed, 'even in Spain'. Now we have to recognize that 'a person's being as a Christian is either grounded in her vocation or it is simply an illusion which seems beautiful perhaps in the after glow of a time vanished beyond recall'.[203] A Christian is one who is claimed by Christ as Lord but Christ's lordship is not a blind, brute power working

---

[198] KD iv/3, 521; CD, 452.

[199] KD iv/3, 547; CD, 475. The inevitable question arises as to whether this commits Barth to universalism. As in *Church Dogmatics* iii he refuses to take this for granted, but he does insist that we are 'surely commanded the more definitely to hope and pray for it'. KD iv/3, 550–1; CD, 478.

[200] KD iv/3, 681–7; CD, 594–9.   [201] KD iv/3, 599; CD, 521.

[202] KD iv/3, 602; CD, 523.   [203] KD iv/3, 604; CD, 525.

mechanically. Christ 'is not the rampaging numinous which strikes man unconditionally so that he can only be petrified and silent before it . . . He does not humiliate or insult man. He does not make him a mere spectator, let alone a puppet.'[204] Christ's power is the liberating power of his Word which is opposed to all compulsion and eliminates and discards it. It is the power of his prophecy, Word and promise, in which we are awakened to faith and obedience.

The essence of Christian vocation, Barth argues, is that God makes us his witnesses. Because genuine witness is emphatically counter cultural it brings us into conflict with the ruling powers: 'If . . . a person is not oppressed by his environment, if she has nothing serious to fear or to suffer at its hands, she has reason carefully to ask at least whether and how far she is genuinely Christian at all.'[205] In an obvious reference to his own experience throughout his life, Barth talks of the difficulties of swimming against the stream:

However great may be the solidarity which Christians feel and practise in relation to the world, their way can never be that of the world—and least of all that of the supposedly Christianised world . . . Sometimes they will be regarded as individualists and sometimes as collectivists. On the one hand they will be accused as authoritarians, on the other as free thinkers; on the one hand as pessimists, on the other as optimists; on the one hand as bourgeois, on the other as anarchists . . . Things generally accepted as self evident will never claim their absolute allegiance, even though they take on a Christian guise. Nor will they command their complete negation, so they can hardly count on the applause of the revolutionaries of their day.[206]

In an age of doctrinal tolerance Christian confession may be allowed but there will be all the less tolerance for the free decision and act of Christians. 'To this the reaction will be sour and bitter. It will be met with mistrust and repudiation, with suspicion and scorn, and even sometimes open indignation . . . Measures will be taken to silence or destroy it, or at least to render it innocuous.'[207]

To the believer vocation means a complex pattern of liberation, supremely realized in prayer, in which we are drawn out of solitariness into fellowship, delivered from the ocean of unlimited possibilities to the one necessity of Christ, and freed to rejoice in a true humanism, finding significance in the smallest details of human life. In other words, its consequence is the discovery of alternative patterns of living, which Barth considers to be the pattern of true freedom.

---

[204] KD iv/3, 607; CD, 528. [205] KD iv/3, 709; CD, 619.
[206] KD iv/2, 690; CD, 610. [207] KD iv/2, 690; CD, 610.

THE IMAGINED COMMUNITY

In face of the disintegration of capitalist society, with its false freedom and its fundamental antagonisms, Barth sketched out a picture of the Christian community as 'a preliminary outline of the whole human world justified in Christ', a vanguard movement.[208] In a world which had lost all sense of community Barth believed that what it meant to be community was to be lived out by Christians, first together and then individually. He emphasized this fact in his terminology, where he felt that the word 'Church' should be avoided as much as possible. 'At all events, this overshadowed and overburdened word should be immediately and consistently interpreted by the word "community".'[209] Called into being by the Holy Spirit, the Church exists as the paradigmatic imagined community for humankind.[210] By iv/3 Barth is speaking of a threefold form of the parousia, at the resurrection, in the work of the Holy Spirit, and in the second coming.[211] The second form of the parousia is the 'age of the Church', in which Christians are given a part in the contest of 'the Resurrected One, who is still on the way, still in conflict, still moving towards the goal which he has not yet reached'.[212]

The Free Community

As with every other part of his *Dogmatics*, so here, Barth abandons the distinctions between being and act, essence and existence. The Church's being is its act. 'Church *is* when it takes place that God lets certain people live as His servants, His friends, His children, the witnesses of the reconciliation of the world with Himself.'[213] The visibility of the Church is of the essence in virtue of its exemplary role within human society as a whole. On the other hand, it is not purely an earthly historical fellowship either, but has a third dimension, the creation of the Spirit. 'There is no direct identity between

[208] KD iv/1, 718; CD, 643. I am following Schellong, 'Barth als Theologe', 62–6.

[209] Barth, *Evangelical Theology*, 37.

[210] KD iv/1, 724; CD, 648. Michael Murrmann-Kahl has explored the impact of Barth's theology on the Church in the former East Germany. His conclusion is that, positively, Barth's rather idealized sketch of the true Church functioned as an immanent critique of socialism, exerting pressure to move from 'really existing socialism' to an improved socialism; but that, negatively, this normative strength was a weakness when it came to dealing with the church structures that actually existed. In 'Ein Prophet des wahren Sozialismus? Zur Rezeption Karl Barths in der ehemaligen DDR', *Zeitschrift für die Neuere Theologie geschichte* 1 (1994), 139–66; here, 166.

[211] KD iv/3, 337ff.; CD, 292ff.

[212] KD iv/3, 380; CD, 329.

[213] KD iv/1, 727; CD, 650. Barth omits the definite article.

what the community is and any confession, theology or cultus, any party, trend, group or movement in the being of the community.'[214] The community can never be other than an *église du désert*, a moving tabernacle. It exists eschatologically, in the time between the first parousia of Christ and the second, in a movement from direct vision to direct vision.[215] Barth even commits himself to the statement that 'human history was actually terminated' at the moment of the resurrection, so that the time which follows is properly called the end time. Our history is a postscript, 'but a real history', the purpose of which is the evocation of human response. God will not allow the consummation 'until His grace has found its correspondence in a voice of human thanks from the depths of the world reconciled with Himself . . . from the heart of His human creation'.[216]

The secret of the community's third dimension is its existence as the body of Christ. Barth's view that 'The community is the earthly-historical form of existence of Jesus Christ Himself' resembles the Roman Catholic doctrine of the Church but has to be taken alongside his equally strong criticisms and relativizations.[217] The body of Christ comes into being and acquires historical form as the Spirit 'realises subjectively' the election of Jesus Christ.[218]

What it means to say that the Church is the body of Christ Barth expounds by looking at the four *notae ecclesiae*, with an eye on a whole range of contemporary difficulties. Thus the exposition of the unity of the Church obviously relates to the question of ecumenical division. As far as Barth is concerned, the plurality of churches can only be understood with reference to geographically separated and therefore different congregations. 'Each community has its own locality, its own environment, tradition, language, etc. But in that locality, as established and appointed by the Lord of all the communities, it should be the one complete community.'[219] The scandal of division has to be addressed, but precisely through loyalty to particular traditions. Each individual church lives by the certainty and claim that it is the Church and by taking this seriously 'the unity of the Church is proclaimed in all its perverse plurality'.[220] Each church has to begin with its own penitence, with its own attempt to hear Christ. It is recognition that Christ is the unity of the Church, a true Christocentrism, which is the surest road to unity. Most tellingly, Barth denies that we can distinguish between Israel and the Christian Church. Israel and Church are related as promise and fulfilment, *terminus a quo* and *terminus ad quem*. Barth reiterates his view

---

[214] KD IV/1, 733; CD, 657. It is this dimension Barth finds missing from Schleiermacher and it is this which calls for belief *in* the Church.

[215] KD IV/1, 810; CD, 725. [216] KD IV/1, 824; CD, 737.

[217] KD IV/1, 738; CD, 661. [218] KD IV/1, 744; CD, 667.

[219] KD IV/1, 750; CD, 672. [220] KD IV/1, 761; CD, 681.

that there can be no Jewish missions. 'The decisive question is not what the Jewish Synagogue can be without Him, but what the Church is as long as it confronts an alien and hostile Israel.'[221]

The holiness and catholicity of the Church both signify its existence as a counter cultural reality. The holiness of the Church means its contradistinction to the surrounding world, for it is not a society on a par with others, even though it shares their sociologiocal dimensions. Similarly catholicity speaks of an essence which has never altered and cannot alter and which therefore cannot be identical with any local culture. 'Christians will always be Christians first, and only then members of a specific culture or state or class.'[222]

Against Roman Catholic attempts to locate apostolicity in the succession of bishops Barth maintains that it means being 'in the discipleship, in the school, under the normative authority, instruction and direction of the apostles'.[223] Apostolicity is identical in substance with the Scripture principle, and the apostolic community is that which hears the apostolic witness of the New Testament. It exists as an apostolic Church, therefore 'only as it exercises the ministry of a herald'.[224] But to exist as a herald is, of course, to witness to the new reality and the new world made known in Christ.

The individual is summoned to the community through the awakening power of the Holy Spirit, which calls her to faith. In faith, which is constituted by relationship to its object, human beings *cease to be in control, and just so do they realize their true freedom.*[225] There is a strong pull away from Christ but 'Whenever faith takes place in a person, it will always mean a swimming against this current—a counter movement which is not undertaken in her own reason and strength.'[226] In its negative form faith is an emptying, including an emptying of all the results of practices of self emptying. 'It begins at the point where all the works of man are at an end, including his quiescence and silence and anticipatory dying. Christian faith is the day whose dawning means the end of the mystical night.'[227] Positively, it is encounter with the living Jesus Christ, a being from and to him, an echo of his action.[228] Because we cannot have faith without our neighbours we are called to witness, the

---

[221] KD IV/1, 749; CD, 671.   [222] KD IV/1, 785; CD, 703.
[223] KD IV/1, 798; CD, 714.   [224] KD IV/1, 809; CD, 724.
[225] This section contains an incisive critique of Bultmann, whom Barth believed dissolved redemption into the event of faith, just as the Catholic doctrine of the Mass was the bloodless repetition of Calvary. Barth insists that faith is a response to the act of God in Christ. It is analogous to that, but is not to be identified with it. KD IV/1, 858; CD, 767. See also the important commentary of Klappert, *Auferweckung*, 251–72.
[226] KD IV/1, 833; CD, 745.   [227] KD IV/1, 702; CD, 629.
[228] KD IV/1, 707; CD, 633.

activity which constitutes Barth's concrete account of how revelation makes a difference in the world.

The School of Love

If justification leads to the gathering of the community, sanctification leads to its 'upbuilding'. This takes place in growth in numbers, but decisively in growth in depth—intensive, vertical, and spiritual growth—and to understand this we need the concept of the kingdom, the lordship of God established in the world. Christ is in the truest sense both the community and the kingdom. We cannot say that the community is the kingdom, but the kingdom is the community: 'As the kingdom of God itself is on the way from the first to the last revelation it is the community. As the kingdom or rule of God is engaged in this movement, it creates the sphere corresponding to it.'[229] The full significance of this only emerges in IV/4 where prayer for the kingdom is understood as prayer for the establishment of righteousness and peace here and now.[230] That there is a real identity between Christ, the kingdom of God, and the Church means that the community has an exemplary function within world history, for example in the way in which it structures itself on the law of service which is fundamental to the being of the Church.[231] The Church's orientation is that of an 'anarcho-socialist, decentralized, democratic group', whose existence creates 'repercussions and correspondences' in the world.[232] From the Church's deed and word 'those outside' need to learn 'that things can be different, not merely in heaven but on earth, not just some day but even now, than those to which they think they must confine themselves in the formation and administration of their law'.[233] The practical implications of this were spelled out by Barth in his letter to Gustav Heinemann in 1946 on the theme of rebuilding German society. The Church, he said, had to be rebuilt from the grassroots up, and Christians had to learn to practise democracy in their own sphere because 'the law under which they stand is the same law, *mutatis mutandis* under which alone the [German] people can recover'.[234]

The community's upbuilding is threatened from without by overt persecution or indifference and from within by the twin dangers of secularization and self glorification. By 'secularization' Barth means the bondage of the

---

[229] KD IV/2, 742; CD, 656.

[230] *Christliche Leben*, 410; ET, 240.

[231] KD IV/2, 784; CD, 692; KD IV/2, 820; CD, 723. Barth notes, though, that there is no question of the state adopting the Church's understanding of itself.

[232] H. Gollwitzer, 'The Kingdom of God and Socialism' in Hunsinger *Barth and Radical Politics*, 89.

[233] KD IV/2, 818; CD, 721.

[234] In Barth, *Der Götze Wackelt*, 99, quoted by Schellong, 'Barth als Theologe', 64.

Church to a particular ideology or culture or philosophy. It takes place 'when it wants to be the Church only for the world, the nation, culture or the State. . . . It then loses its specific importance and meaning'.[235] The mistake of self glorification, on the other hand, is for the Church to exalt itself above others, in which case what is erected is simply an idol. The remedy for these dangers is the recognition that, though savingly necessary, the Church is never an end in itself: 'the work of man which takes place in the true Church occasioned and fashioned by God is revealed as such only as it points beyond itself'.[236] The goal of its upbuilding is that the sanctification of all humanity as this has already taken place *de iure* in Christ may be revealed and lived out *de facto*. Living between the twofold parousia of Christ it represents this sanctification in a provisional though necessary way.

Called into the community, the individual has to learn there what it means to love. Already in his doctrine of creation Barth had qualified the distinction between *agape* and *eros* he had outlined in the second Romans commentary, a qualification made absolute by Nygren.[237] In Barth's view, whilst it is clear that it is only *agape* which liberates us, we do not have to insist on the antithesis between the two loves. *Agape* is grounded in God's Yes and as such is superior to *eros*, but precisely for this reason does not seek to eliminate it altogether.

Love is a free action, the spontaneous self giving of the one to the other just because the other is there and confronts us, an action which corresponds to the very being of God as this is made known in the covenant. 'In this act in which he willed to be and became ours, and we were to be and became his, God is the authoritative and powerful basis of the . . . human act corresponding to the act of God.'[238] As human beings we do in the form of a reflection or analogy what God does originally and properly, as a response to the Word spoken in the love of God. Because it is free the act of love is always new, unusual, and unexpected, and essentially involves joy. 'Love and joy have it in common . . . that neither of them is ordered or can be produced or practised to order. Both grow of themselves from God the Liberator, and from the occurrence of his act of liberation.'[239]

The object of love is in the first instance God. By the end of his career Barth had turned his back on the objections to expressions of love for Jesus which he had felt in his earlier years. 'Without love for God there is no obedience to God or love for one's neighbour. Without love for Jesus there is no discipleship.'[240] The person who loves God is no heaven storming idealist but

---

[235] KD IV/2, 756; CD, 668.
[236] KD IV/2, 698; CD, 617.
[237] Cf. KD III/2, 337 ff.; CD, 379 f.
[238] KD IV/2, 863; CD, 761.
[239] KD IV/2, 895; CD, 789.
[240] KD IV/2, 902; CD, 796.

nevertheless her interest is in the kingdom of God *on earth*. Love for God is unthinkable without love for the neighbour. The 'neighbour' is 'one who is loved apart from and side by side with God, but for the sake of the love of God'.[241] Christian love cannot be watered down into a universal love of humanity but is bound up, once again, with witness. Christians are 'God's witnesses to every person and to the whole world' and indeed to one another, and witness is their most fundamental act of love.[242]

Hope in the World

The third aspect of Christology situates both Christ and the community within the frame of world history. For Barth there is in the strict sense no secular or profane history.[243] Human history as a whole is the record both of the providence of God and of the confusion of human beings. Above and beyond these two is the Christian gospel that in Christ the grace of God was, is, and will be addressed to the world. Christ is the new reality of world history. This means that 'the twofold form of world history loses the appearance of autonomy and finality, the character of an irreconcilable contradiction and antithesis'.[244] The coming of the kingdom will be the final and definitive manifestation of what has already taken place in him. In virtue of Christ the Church can only be *for* human beings and cannot be 'anti', not even against individuals like Hitler. The act of God in Christ is a clear decision for the new human being and the new form of the world, and the community attests this in resolute decisions for and against. 'Whether by declaration or impressive silence, whether by partisanship or rejection of partisanship or even the formation of its own party, it will resolutely participate.'[245] It is always expected to do or refrain from doing specific things and in so doing changes world occurrence. Barth quotes von Weizsäcker, whose protest against nuclear weapons he shared: 'Resolves genuinely taken change the world.'[246] This relative alteration of the world is brought about by the erection of signs. 'No more than this is demanded. But this is unconditionally demanded.'[247]

Because the community is both wholly visible and invisible it exists in total dependence and total freedom in relation to its environment, in total

---

[241] KD iv/2, 911; CD, 803.   [242] KD iv/2, 924; CD, 814.

[243] KD iv/3, 787; CD, 687.   [244] KD iv/3, 816; CD, 713.

[245] KD iv/3, 823; CD, 719. Once again, I cannot follow Macken, and the other critics he cites, who believe that Barth does 'too little justice to the specific character and the subjectivity of the Church, to its relatively independent being, out of an anxiety that the glory of God might thereby be diminished'. Macken, *Autonomy*, 178. The whole thesis seems a perverse misconstrual of what Barth is about.

[246] KD iv/3, 823; CD, 719.   [247] KD iv/3, 824; CD, 720.

solidarity but also in critical distinction.[248] It exists for the world and indeed is the point in the world where the world may know itself in truth and reality. Solidarity with the world, 'unreserved participation in its situation', is therefore part of its essence.[249] Such solidarity involves, amongst other things, a tackling of social evils through diaconate and prophecy. 'The diaconate and the Christian community become dumb dogs, and their service a serving of ruling powers, if they are afraid to tackle at their social roots the evils by which they are confronted in detail.'[250] Prophecy, on the other hand, is action based on perception into the meaning of current events, relationships, and forms in their connection to the imminent kingdom of God. The community is called to a fellowship which establishes true human relationships across racial, cultural, and class boundaries. Such a fellowship is above all signified in baptism and the eucharist in which the divine fellowship 'is the prototype [Urbild], the meaning and the power of the visible and significatory action of the community and therefore of the unification of men therein attested'.[251]

God's great Yes in Christ is the community's cause—we remember here Barth's characterization of the contemporary novel, with its concentration on human vileness. The Church was to be counter cultural in this as well. Because it is a Yes to which we witness it has to be with 'an address of radiant content and cheerful manner'.[252] The community does justice to its task, which embraces believer and unbeliever alike, when it addresses people as creatures to be relieved, liberated, and cheered. 'The Christian community is either the place of this great anticipatory joy [Vorfreude] in relation to all people and creation or it is not the Christian community.'[253]

Within the community, and schooled by the community, the individual is called to hope, which is the answer to the question of the contradiction of Christian existence, to our existence as *simul iustus et peccator*, but also to the sense of the weakness of the Christian community. 'What can a few Christians or a pathetic group like the Christian community really accomplish with their scattered witness to Jesus Christ? What do these men really imagine or expect to accomplish in the great market, on the battle field or in the great prison or mad house which human life always seems to be?'[254] The answer is that we are given freedom to hope and to bear witness to the change in the human situation which Christ has actually effected.[255]

---

[248] In terms of its language and structure it is completely part of the surrounding world but its invisible truth remains. There is an analogy with the eucharist. The elements have the capacity to indicate and confirm the fellowship of the community with its Lord without ceasing to be what they are. KD iv / 3, 832; CD, 727.

[249] KD iv / 3, 884; CD, 773.   [250] KD iv / 3, 1023–4; CD, 893.
[251] KD iv / 3, 1034; CD, 901.   [252] KD iv / 3, 918; CD, 802.
[253] KD iv / 3, 929; CD, 812.   [254] KD iv / 3, 1053; CD, 918.
[255] KD iv / 1, 349; CD, 317.

The Christian hopes as a member of the community, rather than as an individual. She is a representative who keeps the watch apart from which God does not will world occurrence to proceed, but is also a representative of surrounding humanity. Hope is in Christ and yet penultimate hopes are of vital importance:

> If the sphere of the penultimate is left empty by pure hope of the ultimate, and is therefore made a place of hopelessness, there will exult and dance and triumph in it demons of the crassest because uncontrolled and undisciplined worldliness which has always proved to be the consequence of too rigidly eschatological versions of Christianity.[256]

As we move from present to future we therefore look also to penultimate developments. The corruptible and mortal cannot be a sphere of hopelessnesss. 'Just because the Christian hopes for the ultimate and definitive, she also hopes for the temporal and provisional. Just because she hopes with joy for the dawn of the great light, she hopes with provisional joy for the little lights.'[257]

In his teaching on the community, and the individual formed by it, Barth is sketching out something of what Bonhoeffer might have meant by 'religionless Christianity'. For the community is 'not called out of the world, but . . . is itself world . . . the world as rightly formed, the beginnings of a society freed for fellowship [*Brüderlichkeit*]. It is more profane than the "free" world peopled with idols and therefore unfree. Correspondingly the kingdom of God, to which the Church is aligned, is not the overcoming of the world but of the inhumanity of the world.'[258] Over against the egoistic rationalism of the modern concept of freedom Barth proposes a counterattack. 'The Church is the concrete place of this contestation and counterattack—not because the Church can bring reconciliation, but because it witnesses to the fact that reconciliation is realised by and through God for all people. And the Church has thus to witness by means of its entire existence.'[259] What this meant concretely was spelled out in the last fragments of Barth's *Dogmatics*.

THE CHRISTIAN AS REBEL

At the conclusion of the doctrine of creation Barth had set out an ethics of freedom. Of course freedom had also been his theme in the doctrine of reconciliation, and it was a particular concern as he turned to the ethics of

---

[256] KD IV/3, 1075–6; CD, 936
[257] KD IV/3, 1077; CD, 938.
[258] Schellong, 'Barth als Theologe', 64.
[259] Ibid., 65.

reconciliation. In the postscript to his Czech friend Hromadka's, *Gospel for Atheists*, published in July 1958, Barth reiterated his view that the Church could not be bound by any ideology, and that Christ died not only for those on the left, but also those on the right, capitalists, imperialists, and fascists. In his letter to Christians in East Germany, written a month later, his advice was above all not to howl with the wolves. It was tempting, therefore, to continue the ethics of freedom, but he felt at this point that this concept did not adequately capture the relation of command and obedience he wanted to describe. Setting aside the ideas of repentance, faith, thanksgiving, and faithfulness as alternatives he finally opted for an ethic of invocation, of calling upon God. This is, of course, rat poison for man come of age.

The gracious God is also the commanding God who 'is himself historical' and who 'among and with and for and to men . . . acts and speaks as himself man'.[260] The hour of God's rule has dawned in Christ, in whom we encounter 'the divine seizure and exercise of power'.[261] This divine action demands a corresponding human action and this is calling upon God. Barth understands the command 'Call upon me' to be the basic meaning of every divine command and 'invocation according to this command as the basic meaning of all human obedience'.[262] Such invocation is not just personal but a 'supremely social matter, publicly social, not to say political and even cosmic'.[263] Christians 'are not private people. They stand in public service'.[264] They do so, however, in a relationship of genuine encounter, the shape of which is prayer.

Accordingly, Barth proposed to develop the ethics of reconciliation as an exposition of the Lord's Prayer, and to deal with baptism in the prologue, referring to the foundation of the Christian life, and with the eucharist in the epilogue, referring to its renewal, as human actions corresponding to particular divine commands. What emerged, in the fragments we have, was a very distinctive theology of rebellion.

Baptism: Gift and Response

Only the section on baptism was revised for publication and here Barth ended his life, as he began it, with controversy, in calling for an end to infant baptism. Here we find no retreat into the quiet waters of church sacra-

---

[260] Barth, *Christliche Leben*, 18; ET, 13.   [261] Ibid., 21; ET, 15.

[262] Ibid., 69; ET, 44. Biggar comments: 'the concept of invocation serves . . . to bring eschatological yearning right into the heart of the Christian life . . . the eschatological dimension has spilled out from the epilogue into the centre of Christian life'. *Hastening*, 81. This is very finely said, but did it not happen in *Romans*?

[263] *Christliche Leben*, 154; ET, 95.   [264] Ibid., 33; ET, 23.

mental practice. Rather, it is in baptism that 'the critical-active impact of the understanding of the Church comes to expression in that baptism is established and interpreted in connection with the witness giving action of Christianity'.[265]

How does the kingdom of God come into a person's life? The answer is through baptism with the Holy Spirit. Through the Spirit we become open, seeing, hearing, and comprehending as to what has happened in Christ. 'The beginning of the Christian life takes place in a direct self-attestation and self-impartation of the living Jesus Christ, in his active Word of power which goes forth *hic et nunc* to specific people in the work of the Holy Spirit.'[266] This is a form of grace in which reconciliation is actually effected. It is the beginning of a new life in a distinctive fellow humanity although it always remains a beginning and is never self-sufficient or complete.

Spirit baptism does not exclude water baptism but, on the contrary, makes it possible and demands it. Water baptism, on the other hand, is the first step of faith, love, hope, and service. It is the human work of basic confession in which the Christian community is associated with those newly joining it and they with it. It can be regarded as a form of petition for the coming of the kingdom. As a response to the divine act and Word it cannot be performed in subjection to a controlling socio-logical mechanism but must always be 'a breaking of all rules, customs, sequences and arrangements'.[267] Obedience and hope are two terms for this one human action, which represents the decision to let God be our God.

After baptism we become personally co-responsible for the execution of the missionary command which constitutes the community. The purpose of mission is not primarily church growth but that an account should be given of the hope that is in us. In words which recall *Romans* Barth describes the Christian as 'More restless than the most restless, more urgent than the most urgent revolutionaries in his immediate or more distant circle', demanding the peace of the world.[268] Once we are baptized there can be no truce with the *status quo*. Baptism is a 'saving deed of hope' in Christ which consists in the fact that the baptizing community prays that Christ will be responsible for them. 'Prayer with hope in Jesus Christ means an end of all idle gaping, the strongest possible break with all neutrality or passivity, and a going to it with the freest resolution.'[269]

---

[265] Schellong, 'Barth als Theologe', 66. Later he writes: 'In my view KD IV/4, with the denial of infant baptism, is the test whether or not one has understood or has a clue about what it is that Barth is up to and what Barth intended, and which way it was he sought.' Ibid., 72. I agree. It implies a devastating comment on much Anglo-Saxon reception of Barth.

[266] KD IV/4, 35; CD, 31.   [267] KD IV/4, 145–6; CD, 133.

[268] KD IV/4, 221; CD, 201.   [269] KD IV/4, 230; CD, 209.

All this makes it plain why Barth had to refuse the possibility of infant baptism, which completely obscured its character as the human response to God's initiative. 'The Christian life cannot be inherited as blood, gifts, characteristics and inclinations are inherited. No Christian environment . . . can transfer this life to those who are in this environment. For these too, the Christian life can begin only on the basis of their own liberation by God, their own decision.'[270] Infant baptism, then, obscures the concrete process of liberation, the movement in which, as it were, we get into gear.

The Children and Their Father

In his account of baptism Barth insisted that human beings are taken seriously as independent creatures by God. They are not run down or overpowered but set on their own feet, addressed and treated as adults. Human liberation is effected 'wholly from without, from God', but is still truly *human* liberation. 'The history of Jesus Christ does not destroy a person's own history.' What has to be realized, Barth maintains, is that divine omnicausality is not the same as *sole* causality.[271] Because this is the case we can say both that action is truly ours, and that this is only the case as we are truly dependent on God our Father.

The opening words of the Lord's Prayer characterize the prayer as a whole as 'invocation of God'. Christian life is 'life in the vocative' and the name 'Father' is a *'locum tenens* for the vocative'.[272] The word characterizes God as a Thou who meets us 'in the incomparable seriousness of a friendliness which cannot be defeated by any indifference or even hostility on their part'.[273] With the permission which derives from Christ's own practice of prayer we call on God as God's children, who are never masters or virtuosos in prayer.

In invocation of God the Father everything depends on whether or not it is done in sheer need (not self won competence), in sheer readiness to learn . . . and in sheer helplessness . . . Christians who regard themselves as big and strong and rich . . . are not Christians at all.[274]

We recognize once again here Barth's attack on 'man come of age'.

God wills history, intercourse, and living dealings with his children, and this takes place in the invocation which is itself a gift of grace. Life as calling upon God is above all prayer for the Holy Spirit, *geistlich* (Spiritual) but not *geistig* (religious). It is a 'supremely social matter, publicly social, not to say political and cosmic'.[275] The Christian life structured around invocation is not 'a wonderful glass-bead game played for its own sake by a company of

---

[270] KD IV/4, 202; CD, 184.
[271] KD IV/4, 25; CD, 22.
[272] *Christliche Leben*, 79; ET, 51.
[273] Ibid., 92; ET, 59.
[274] Ibid., 127–8; ET, 79–80.
[275] Ibid., 154; ET, 95.

initiates in a quiet valley with no outward contacts'.[276] At the same time we are not to fret about public recognition of our activity.

In the nexus of human history as a whole, Christians in their special nature are not outsize figures, not prodigies . . . They are indispensable ordinary little people with the task of doing here or there, in this way or that, what is entrusted to them, namely, passing on the news of the mystery and miracle of the renewal of all things which has taken place in Jesus Christ and which in this last time of ours is moving toward its definitive manifestation.[277]

Christian invocation of God has the character of a serving function in the life of human society, of a contribution to world history that is indispensable as an antidote.[278] Invocation, finally, rests on the fact that the God revealed in Christ is not a self enclosed supreme being, who cannot be codetermined from outside, who is condemned to work alone, but 'a God who in overflowing grace has chosen and is free to have authentic and not just apparent dealings, intercourse and exchange with his children'.[279] It is not just human beings who correspond to God, but God corresponds to our invocation.[280]

The Struggle for Human Righteousness

Christians are people with a definite passion. 'In no circumstances . . . can they be cowards, blind worms, bored, boring, or commonplace.'[281] Their passion is for the honour of God, for the hallowing of God's name. There is both knowledge and ignorance of God in the world, the Church and the individual. It is the vacillation and darkness in all of these spheres which means that God's name needs to be sanctified. We pray for God to hallow God's name in 'a total and definitive action, whose force does not leave a little opposition and contradiction, but none at all'.[282] It is a victory of *light* over darkness that we look for. What happened in Christ had the power to raise 'an unmistakeable protest against the dishonouring of the name of God in our present'.[283] It leads us to act because 'the law of prayer is the law of action'.[284] Zeal for the honour of God means revolt. It calls us to rebellion and resistance (*Aufstand und Widerstand*) against the regime of vacillation—compromise with the lordless powers. It is a kind of resistance movement

---

[276] Ibid., 157; ET, 96.   [277] *Christliche Leben*, 159–60; ET, 98.

[278] Ibid., 165–6; ET, 101. Biggar notes that the fact that all we can do is to witness to the coming kingdom underscores the essential orientation of all Christian action toward the eschatological future. *Hastening*, 86.

[279] *Christliche Leben*, 169; ET, 103.   [280] KD IV/4, 117; CD, 106.

[281] *Christliche Leben*, 180; ET, 111. They are not, Barth notes, 'angry young men'.

[282] Ibid., 267; ET, 160.   [283] Ibid., 276; ET, 165.   [284] Ibid., 282; ET, 168.

which questions the reigning practice, brings to light its limits, strengthens nonconformity, issues a warning against collaboration and keeps alive the hope of liberation.[285] This nonconformist practice flows from allowing the real precedence of the Word of God in our lives. As this particular person, with my whole bundle of determinations I live, think, and act 'as, above all things, I hear the Word of God'.[286] All the steps I take are interim ones, but action of some sort is imperative. 'If the annex of action is missing, then the first petition (and with it the whole of the Lord's Prayer) becomes no more than idle chatter in his heart and on his lips.'[287]

Christians are summoned to revolt not against people, but *for* all humankind and therefore against the disorder which controls and poisons and disrupts all human relations and interconnections. It is a militant revolt against the lordless powers, the motors of society, the secret guarantee of our conventions, customs, habits, traditions, and institutions. 'Through mankind's fault, things are invisibly done without and above man, even above the human individual in all his uniqueness, by the host of absolutisms.'[288] These are 'the great impersonal absolutes in their astonishing wilfulness and autonomy'.[289] They are the 'principalities and powers' of the New Testament. The world picture of the New Testament, says Barth, may have been 'magical'. What is more important is that the people of the first century 'were less hindered than we are by the world picture of their contemporaries, which was also their own, from taking freely into account the strange reality and efficacy of the lordless powers'.[290] We know them in the form of political absolutisms, with their drive for empire. It was Hobbes who theorized this in *Leviathan*, a 'typical modern man, man-come-of-age, unencumbered by any world behind or above the present one'.[291] We know them as Mammon, which Barth desribes in terms very similar to Marx's theory of commodity fetishism: 'Money is a flexible but powerful instrument which, supposedly handled by man, in reality follows its own law. In a thousand ways it can establish some opinions and even convictions and suppress others. It can also create brutal facts . . . It can serve peace yet pursue the cold war even in the midst of peace. It can make ready for a bloody war and finally bring it about. It can bring provisional paradise here and the corresponding provisional hell there.'[292] There are ideologies, to whose presuppositions and sketches we ascribe a permanent and quasi-divine normativity so that we cease to have anything of our own to say. Finally (Barth does not claim that his list is exhaustive) there are 'chthonic forces'—Barth instances fashion, sport, pleasure, and the

[285] Ibid., 292–3; ET, 174.   [286] Ibid., 303; ET, 180.   [287] Ibid., 307; ET, 181.
[288] Ibid., 368; ET, 216.   [289] Ibid., 372; ET, 219.   [290] Ibid., 369; ET, 217.
[291] Ibid., 375; ET, 220.   [292] Ibid., 382; ET, 224. Cf Plonz, *Herrenlosen Gewalten*, 326.

obsession with speed—all expressions of the rule of capital, and forces of death.[293] 'Death' is not a metaphor: 'How can we fail to note the daily lists of traffic accidents and their victims, whose total numbers (in 1960, 65,000 in Europe) have already reached and even surpassed the number of those lost in war.'[294]

Over against the kingdom of human disorder stands the kingdom of divine order. The fact that Christians pray 'Your kingdom come' is a proof that God resists the torrent of human injustice and evil. Prayer for the coming of the kingdom is a call for human righteousness and order amidst disorder but it does not come as a continuance of our action. 'Those who know the reality of the kingdom, Christians, can never have anything to do with the arrogant and foolhardy enterprise of trying to bring in and build up by human hands a religious, cultic, moral or political kingdom of God on earth.'[295] Prayer for the coming kingdom is a strictly eschatological prayer and looks towards an act of God as the goal and end of all human history. Because Christ is known in his three 'times' this is not inconsistent with saying that it is Christ who is the kingdom. 'He is the mystery that cannot be imprisoned in any system of human conceptuality but can be revealed and known only in parables. He is God acting concretely within human history.'[296] Christians, then, wait and hasten toward the dawn of God's day. They wait by hastening, praying that justice be done. Though they cannot 'bring in the kingdom' they are claimed for action in the effort and struggle for human righteousness. 'They may and can and should rise up and accept responsibility to the utmost of their power for the doing of the little righteousness.'[297] Christian action will be 'kingdom like', which means that in all circumstances it takes place with a view to people, in address to people, and with the aim of helping people rather than in the interests of a particular cause. From the start Christians are 'humanists' whose especial task it is to bring people hope. 'To bid man hope, and thus to mediate to him the promise that he needs, is their task. Concern for this is their conflict.'[298]

JESUS MEANS FREEDOM

The doctrine of reconciliation, cut short as it is, probably by many hundreds of pages, is a huge tract which defies a cursory summary. We can see,

[293] That Webster finds humour here represents a failure to see the connection of the cthonic forces with capital. Barth emphasizes their seriousness. Webster, *Barth's Ethics*, 203: *Christliche Leben*, 390; ET, 228.

[294] *Christliche Leben*, 395; ET, 231.   [295] Ibid., 456; ET, 264.

[296] Ibid., 435–6; ET, 252.   [297] Ibid., 459; ET, 265.   [298] Ibid., 468; ET, 270.

though, that at every stage Barth is concerned for human freedom in critical response to the Enlightenment tradition's own preoccupation with this. Along with Adorno and Horkheimer he recognizes that in many respects the Enlightenment tradition has failed. It sought freedom but found hegemony. Christ, says Barth, has come to deliver us from the hegemony of the lord-less powers, to deliver us from the tyranny of all forms of totalitarianism, including the totalitarianism of the market, which in turn trades on the 'cthonic powers'. The revelation we have in Christ calls us to witness: the dynamic of the doctrine of reconciliation runs between these two concepts. This has nothing to do with what Gutiérrez characterizes as the 'typically Western' problem of how we can know God, which never troubled Barth for a moment.[299] Nor is it a gnostic construal of redemption. On the contrary, it is an understanding of reconciliation which is gracious—which invites but does not compel—and which involves human beings. Reconciliation is the work of the *totus Christus*. God chooses to involve human beings in the process. Christ in the Spirit empowers us to a life of resistance and revolt. A free life, according to Barth's picture, is a life of guerrilla warfare, the life of a resistance fighter, but in a spirit of joy, celebration, and thankfulness, and always *for* human beings and never against them. Would that Calvin had recognized the humanity of God, he said in 1956. 'His Geneva would then not have become such a gloomy affair. His letters could then not have contained so much bitterness.'[300] Freedom is *gifted* us. It does not put us in the situation of Hercules at the crossroads, like Camus's rebel, but rescues us from that situation.

It would be a strange freedom that would leave man neutral, able equally to choose, decide, and act rightly or wrongly! What kind of power would that be! Man becomes free and is free by choosing, deciding and determining himself in accordance with the freedom of God. The source of man's freedom is also its yardstick. Trying to escape from being in accord with God's own freedom is not human freedom.[301]

It is in the exercise of this freedom, Barth maintains, that we have a real possibility to escape hegemony.

---

[299] See G. Gutiérrez, *Essential Writings*, ed. J. B. Nickoloff, London, SCM, 1996, 35 ff.

[300] Barth, *Humanity of God*, 46.

[301] Barth, 'The Gift of Freedom' in *Humanity of God*, 73. The lecture was delivered in 1953.

7

Theology and Human Liberation

Truth predicts the eclipse of truth,
And in that eclipse it condemns man,
Whose self-love with its useful schools of thought,
Its pious camouflage of a God within,
Is always the cause of the shadow, the fall, the burial,
The smug rub of hands
Amid a reek of research.

. . .

We touched His crag of paradox
Though our tempestuous leader, now dead,
Who ploughed from Safenwil to show us greatness
In a God lonely, exiled, homeless in our sphere,
Since His footfall breeds guilt, stirs dread
Of a love fire-tongued, cleaving our sin,
Retrieving the soul from racial evolution,
Giving it grace to mortify,
In deeps or shallows, all projections of the divine.

Jack Clemo, 'On the Death of Karl Barth',
Selected Poems (Bloodaxe Books, 1988).

In July 1968, a month before the conference of Latin American bishops at Medellín, and five months before Karl Barth's death, Gustavo Gutiérrez outlined proposals for a 'theology of liberation'. He agreed with Barth and Anselm that theology was 'faith seeking understanding', and understood faith as commitment to God and human beings. 'If faith is a commitment to God and human beings, it is not possible to live in today's world without a commitment to the process of liberation.' Theology itself he understood as a second step, a reflection on this commitment.[1] Liberation theology emerged at a time of renewed hopes all over the world, both North and South, a time of protest against repression and enslavement of all sorts, and of faith in the project of revolution.

[1] Gutiérrez, *Essential Writings*, ed. J. Nickoloff, London, SCM, 1996, 24–5. Gutiérrez emphasized that what he was articulating was 'part of the very fabric of intellectual life' in Latin America in the 1960s.

Thirty years later Jorge Castaneda chronicles 'utopia unarmed', the collapse of the Latin American left throughout the continent, to some extent bound up with the end of 'really existing socialism' in Eastern Europe.[2] A sense of exhaustion in liberation theology seems to be part of this collapse.[3] It is not just the attack on the base communities by both right wing governments and conservative hierarchies which accounts for this, nor the expansion of 'apolitical' evangelical groups throughout the subcontinent. Rather, questions of substance attach to liberation theology similar to the reservations Barth felt about Ragaz and religious socialism in general.[4] In the attempt to be faithful to the God who takes the side of the lowly, liberation theology committed itself to the priority of praxis and the 'true Church of the poor', so that for some practitioners, at least, the poor themselves became the bearers of the gospel and theology became reflection on praxis in itself.[5] One can imagine how Barth would have reacted to such proposals: any theology which begins with human experience represents, in his view, a return to the fleshpots of Egypt because some kind of ideological captivity is certain to be involved. Yet Barth has some claim to be a liberation theologian before his time.[6]

At least a decade before liberation theology emerged Barth was speaking of God as 'the Liberator' and of Christ as 'partisan of the poor'. Appealing to the whole course of Barth's theology, from *Romans* onwards, Paul Lehman characterized Barth as a theologian of 'permanent revolution'.[7] He highlighted the role of revolution in a Christ centred history in *Romans*; Barth's emphasis on the freedom of God for human beings and of human beings for God in the Prolegomena; the priority of election over creation, people over things, of a chosen people over a random people, whose vocation among all peoples is the overcoming of history within history in the doctrine of election; the certainty of God and of God's human and humanizing presence in creation; co-humanity as the basic form of humanity in Barth's anthropology; the fact that the principalities and powers have no ultimacy but are finally instrumental to God's humanizing purposes in the account of providence; the way in which the law has the form of the gospel,

[2] J. Castaneda, *Utopia Unarmed*, New York, Knopf, 1993.
[3] I do not think this applies to the whole. In different ways E. Dussel and F. Hinkelammert express the radical ideology critique Barth strives to articulate.
[4] M. Bonino recognized this already in 1979. See, 'Historical Praxis and Christian Identity' in R. Gibellini (ed.), *Frontiers of Theology in Latin America*, Maryknoll, NY, Orbis, 1979, 263–72.
[5] Sabine Plonz, however, points out that the religion of the poor highlights a quite different picture of God to that of the ruling classes and to that extent is to be understood as an expression of cultural resistance to the dominant culture. *Herrenlosen Gewalten*, 349.
[6] Gutiérrez recognizes this. *The Power of the Poor in History*, London, SCM, 1983, 203.
[7] P. Lehman: 'Karl Barth, Theologian of Permanent Revolution', *Union Theological Seminary Review* 28/1 (1972).

so that patterns and structures of human relatedness in the world are never established in themselves and never self-justifying but instrumental to human fulfilment; the shattering of the inhumanity of man to man in reconciliation and the humiliation and exaltation of Christ as the prototype and prospect of what humanity is to be; and finally the existence of an experimental community in the world, called and sent as the spearhead of that shaping of all people into the human reality, fulfilment, and joy which God in Christ has begun. This article was begun before the publication of the final fragments, with the revolutionary light they cast on the whole doctrine of reconciliation and of the sacraments which would have completed Lehman's case.[8]

Peter Eicher has likewise argued that we have the outlines of a liberation theology in Barth, looking partly at Barth's understanding of social democracy as a parable of the kingdom in the Tambach lecture, a parable which both changes reality whilst at the same time keeping the difference between political action and God's action open, and partly at the implications of Barth's detailed exegesis of the story of the 'rich young ruler' in 1942.[9] The story illustrates the fundamental premiss of the doctrine of election, namely, God's eternal choice for our freedom, the way in which our election is bound up with our determination for our neighbours, and the need for our liberation from the bondage of Mammon as the essential presupposition of our fellow humanity. 'This theology of liberation has its sting in the liberation of the (economically, politically, socially and religiously) rich from the possessions with which they both imprison themselves and bring death to their fellow creatures.'[10] Eicher finds four main ways in which Barth contributes to liberation theology: the grounding of ethics in the doctrine of the God who loves in freedom; the witness of the Church in concrete political situations to the specific implications of God's liberating will in Christ; the call to the witnesses to liberation to follow the Lord who freely became poor; and our freeing from social ethical moralizing in the light of the doctrine of election. 'The fulfilment of our social duty simply becomes self evident in our being bound to the true Lord of History.'[11]

If it is true that there is a sense of exhaustion in liberation theology it could

---

[8] Noting that reformism thinks in terms of the permanence of the system, but revolutionary thinking of transcending the system Gollwitzer clearly sees Barth committed to a revolutionary theology. 'The Kingdom of God and Socialism' in Hunsinger, *Karl Barth and Radical Politics*, 92.

[9] P. Eicher, 'Gottes Wahl: Unsere Freiheit' in *Einwürfe*, ii, Munich, Kaiser, 1986, 215–36. The exegesis is to be found in KD II/2, 681–701; CD, 613–30. Of course Marquardt, Peter Winzeler, Sabine Plonz and others also illustrate in detail many ways in which Barth can be considered a theologian of liberation.

[10] Ibid., 231.

[11] Ibid., 233.

be, then, that there are resources in Barth's work on which those committed to human liberation can draw. I believe this to be the case, and I hope that the preceding exposition has demonstrated this. To put it in a nutshell, what Barth's contribution amounts to is this: *with the heart of the Christian tradition, Barth understands that only grace can bring liberation, but unlike the mainstream of that tradition his break with idealism led him to understand grace in its radical political consequences, in its consequences for the body and for the whole of human life.* In this final chapter I shall try to spell out the implications of this.

THE CENTRALITY OF FREEDOM

There are many ways in which the central thrust of Barth's theology can be construed, but if one placed Galatians 5.1, 'For freedom Christ has set us free', as the epigraph to the entire *Dogmatics* one would not go far wrong.[12] In the Prolegomena it is the freedom of God which stands as an absolute barrier to reducing Scripture to a system. In the doctrine of creation the out-working of the covenant is in terms of a fourfold fugal freedom, for God, for life, in fellowship, and in limitation. In the doctrine of reconciliation the account of justification, sanctification, and vocation are an account of true human freedom as opposed to the unfreedom of 'sin', which is always understood in terms of concrete practices and not abstractly. All of this rests on the understanding of God as 'the one who loves in freedom', to whom human beings must correspond. Of course, this is not to say that freedom is a 'master concept' in Barth—the last thing he would agree to! But with great rigour he attempts to map out what is entailed in really believing in the freedom of God, supremely revealed in the way of the Son of God into the far country. Freedom is central to Barth's theology because God is free. In a lecture in Germany in 1953 on Christian ethics, he chose to talk about 'the gift of freedom':

In the light of his revelation, God is free in word and deed; He is the source and measure of all freedom insofar as he is the Lord, choosing and determining himself first of all . . . This is not abstract freedom. Nor is it the freedom of aloof isolation . . . God's own freedom is trinitarian, embracing grace, thankfulness and peace. Only in this relational freedom is God sovereign, almighty, the Lord of all.[13]

Why is freedom so important, as opposed, for example, to peace or order, which are also divine attributes, and which the world also needs? Why is it

---

[12] This is assuming, of course, that Macken and the witnesses for the prosecution he summons are mistaken. Macken allows that 'Within the ontology of grace . . . and never apart from it, Barth affirms an autonomy of man.' *Autonomy*, 158. The question which Barth puts insistently is whether there is any other kind of real autonomy.

[13] Barth, *Humanity of God*, 68.

freedom which takes the place of the classical *aseitas* in his theology? The answer is that it is freedom which makes love possible. Barth's doctrine of God is an account of how, in and through all of the divine attributes, love and freedom mutually interpret one another. Because this is true for God, it is also true for us. Without freedom, love would be meaningless—but without love, what would life mean? When Barth describes God as 'the One who loves in freedom' he characterizes freedom in love and love in freedom as the heart of all reality. The task of human life, as we learn this in Christ, is to learn to love in freedom. To put this in a non-Barthian way, freedom is at the heart of life because only free beings can love, and 'love' is the best one-word account of the meaning and purpose of life that we have yet come up with. Barth prefers to say: Christ reveals the meaning and purpose of life, and he does this in a complex re-definition of love (which, for example, puts many questions against *eros*). 'Love', as this is made known to us in Christ, implies decision, commitment, responsibility, action. It implies politics. As such it is the very heart of human dignity. That the psalmist can exclaim, 'What a piece of work is man!', follows from our capacity to love in freedom.

EMBODIED FREEDOM

All Christian theology begins from the assumption that there are important ways in which human beings are unfree, but the 'bondage to sin and death' of which Paul talks has often been understood in a resolutely idealist way. Social and material conditions are not important: what counts is the freedom of the soul. Liberation theology, by contrast, begins with the insistence that it is illusory to talk of freedom where people are destroyed by poverty. Of course the poor also know how to love, and it might therefore be said, and has indeed often been said, that they are free in the truest sense. There is certainly something in this, but at the expense of missing the very heart of the Christian revelation. It is not just that life where the springs of joy are quenched by the struggle to survive, where survival itself is the last thing which can be taken for granted, is no life. Neither is it just the case that very profound questions about distributive justice are raised, and were raised by both Jesus and the prophets. What is missed is the role of the body in the economy of God. Human life is, not by accident, or lamentably, life in the body, and love is love in the body, for embodied creatures. Spirit is not apart from this but in and through it, as the hypostatic union and the resurrection make clear. We could not have a more emphatic affirmation of the body than we find in the core Christian story and its theological commentary. But the term 'the body' here refers not *just* to our physical nature but is also shorthand for realities like sanitation, shelter, clean water, bodily integrity (the right to freedom from fear of rape, torture, murder). The objection to idealist philosophies or theologies is that they ignore this simple truth, choosing to valorize the spiritual apart from the body. Barth appreciated the Hebrew Bible because there were so many tangible things in it. It made clear that 'the Gospel is not purely a spiritual thing . . . Rather, it is for soul and *body*, heaven and *earth*, inward and *outer* life . . . We must be concerned with the whole man: as a rational being, on the earth, with two feet planted here.'[14] Theologies which thus refuse the dualism of body and soul, are political theologies—they are theologies of liberation in the strong sense to which we have grown accustomed.

FREEDOM AND REVELATION

Barth's theology is a political theology in the first instance as a theology of revelation. Barth was not concerned with revelation only in his Prolegomena, in his account of the knowledge of God, but throughout, and not least in his account of the prophetic office of Christ. Throughout he makes clear that the revelation of the crucified God critiques all projected hegemonies. Barth's critique of religion, which so won Bonhoeffer's praise, is also political critique because the forces of death in our society and the rule of the idolatrous powers belong together, as he emphasized in the concluding lectures of the *Dogmatics*.[15] Understanding this point is the essential corrective to the perception that Barth's theology as a whole is a moral or practical theology.[16] If we stop there, and do not see the political dimension of revelation's attack on hegemony, we run the risk of understanding it within that middle class framework Barth attacked from beginning to end. (An important part of the story of the reception of Barth in Anglo-Saxon countries could be written in terms of the fact that English has no adequate translation for the term *bürgerlich*.) As a practical theology it is also a political theology—a theology with concrete political implications, which analyses and critiques economic and political realities *theologically*.[17] The unity of Barth's theology is 'theological existence today: the theological engagement which implies a political, the political engagement which implies a theological'.[18]

[14] Barth, *Table Talk*, 32 (Barth's emphasis).

[15] So Plonz, *Herrenlosen Gewalten*, 355. Cf. also her remark that 'The strength of his theology lies in the ideology critique directed at bourgeois society.' Ibid., 353.

[16] This is John Webster's thesis.

[17] Gollwitzer, however, feels that Barth limited himself too much to moral critique and did not undertake sufficient analysis. 'The Kingdom of God and Socialism' in Hunsinger, *Barth and Radical Politics*, 103. See further below.

[18] Marquardt, *Theologie*, 28. An American commentator who has seen the point is Joseph Bettis, in his account of Barth's 'socialist humanism'. He believes that Barth's mature theology,

Barth's theology is a political theology *as it is a theology of revelation*. This is missed in the Anglo-Saxon discussion because the Prolegomena are read in the light of an epistemological discussion quite irrelevant to Barth, and liv/3 is read in the context of dialogue with other religions.[19] When we read Barth in the perspective of liberation theology, however, the 'flying arrow of Barth's theology of revelation' appears quite different.[20] Liberation theology understands itself as deeply committed to conscientization, helping people to understand the structures which oppress them so that they can then act to change them. But this is how revelation functions in Barth. In the Church we find the place, in the midst of contemporary reality, where false ideas are seen through and rendered harmless, false hopes are limited, their unnecessary threats banned, and a word spoken which breathes frankness and wisdom, patience and resolution, responsibility and solidarity.[21] 'Revelation', an account of the significance of Jesus Christ for human history, is not esoteric knowledge, nor is it a 'controlling concept' which can feed philosophical debates about how we might or might not know God, but issues at every point in 'ethics'—the behaviour of human beings which corresponds with the liberating God. As the final fragments make clear, it issues in an analysis of the structures of oppression which calls us to resistance. The response to revelation is 'confession', 'witness'—not to the past, but to the action of the liberating God in present day history. Both in *Romans* and in the final volumes, the implication of revelation is revolution because it is the God who makes all things new who is revealed. 'Theology which knows what it is about is theology of revolution, far from all fashionable trends and the decline into the "journalism of revolution" . . . it is *necessarily* theology of revolution, and does not need to become something else tomorrow, or the day after tomorrow. And it is then necessarily, as a theology of the One who takes the side of the poor, itself partisan, socially conscious, and class conscious.'[22]

Part of the reason that Barth developed a theology of revelation is that he realized sometime around 1915 that to be truly liberative theology cannot tie itself to one political programme, especially not that of a 'Christian'

'as it is expressed in the *Church Dogmatics*, leads directly, inevitably and necessarily to radical political ethics'. 'Political Theology and Social Ethics' in Hunsinger, *Barth and Radical Politics*, 161.

[19] Thus James Barr objects to Barth's making revelation a 'controlling concept' that the question whether God exists or not, and how we define knowledge of God over against the knowledge of other sciences, are contemporary questions which are of no interest to the biblical writers. *Old and New*, 89. But of course they are of very little interest to Barth either, as the Anselm book set out to make clear.

[20] The phrase is Marquardt's. *Theologie*, 246.

[21] 'Die Christlichen Kirchen und Die Heutige Wirklichkeit' (1946) in *Der Götze Wackelt*, 103.

[22] Marquardt, *Theologie*, 296.

political party, his absolute *bête noir*.[23] He was sure that theology would always be on the left, on the side of the weak and the oppressed, but he saw death—because the end of freedom—in theology becoming 'court chaplain' to either legitimist or revolutionary movements. In his last major publication he reaffirmed what he had said at Tambach, which so upset the religious socialists. The Word, he said

> is not the proclamation of some sort of principle, a new moral and political programme, or a better ideology. But what is involved and meant by that Word is rather and immediately the woe and the salvation which are eternal *and thus also temporal*, heavenly *and for this reason also earthly* . . . woe and salvation to the poor rigid Communists and woe and salvation to the still poorer (because still more rigid) anti-Communists.[24]

What was essential, in his view, was that the Christian community always manifest solidarity with the oppressed. Out of that solidarity comes the attempt to tackle social evils in detail.[25] How this is done raises an important challenge on the part of liberation theology to Barth's ethics. Alan Brews observes that hearing the Word of God in what Barth calls the borderline (*Grenzfall*) situation demands social analysis. Barth always assumes this, but never emphasizes the need for it or provides viable models for it. But for the liberation theologian 'the whole of life is a *Grenzfall* situation. The *Grenzfall* for the contextual theologian is the norm . . . There is no way around analysis. It is imperative that theologians search for tools to aid them in the analysis of the context of Christian praxis.'[26] In fact Barth's practice in Safenwil, where he read the *Textilarbeiter* and compiled several 'thick notebooks' on the industrial situation shows that he understood the need for analysis very well, and I believe we can learn what his response to this objection would be. Naturally, he would say, you have to have analysis. The important thing is to bring that together with your reading of Scripture and your theology, just as you read newspaper and Bible alongside one another for preaching. But analysis is not itself part of the theological task, and in order to maintain theology's ideological-critical role, must not be allowed to become so.[27]

---

[23] 'a supposedly "Christian" party is in principle an abomination to me, especially when it is in power'. *Late Friendship*, 19.

[24] Barth, *Evangelical Theology*, 79.

[25] KD IV/3, 1023–4; CD, 893.

[26] A. Brews, 'Theology and Violence' in Villa Vicencio, *On Reading Barth*, 88.

[27] Nigel Biggar calls attention to a distinction in Barth's thought between 'theological' and 'Christian' ethics where the 'actual handling of the problems of human life' is distinguished from the elaboration of basic principles. *Hastening*, 159, referring to the discussion in KD II/2. This also accounts for the lack of analysis in the *Dogmatics*.

Commenting on the difficulty of distinguishing between dogmatics and political ethics Schellong remarks: 'Barth expected no answer about meaning from the gospel; rather, he heard

FREEDOM AS FULLNESS OF LIFE

That theology might contribute, at least modestly, to political liberation, is amply demonstrated by the theology which supported the union struggles in Safenwil, and which found expression at Barmen. Both liberation theology and the theology of at least the early Barth give the lie to the vulgar Marxist contention that religion is *necessarily* a distraction from the task of political change—though Barth's lifelong polemic against religion is his version of precisely this critique. With this, however, theology's task has by no means ended. I do not want to say that it has 'just begun', which might imply an idealist relativizing of the body creeping in by the back door. However, since theology is essentially concerned with the exploration of what the dimensions of 'life in all its fullness' might be, it cannot stop at the minimum conditions for an adequate human life. Recognizing that both love and freedom are profound mysteries, all theology sets out to explore these mysteries and to prevent any premature closure—which is why, on the night that he died, Barth was working on a lecture on 'Breaking Out, Turning Around, Confession' (*Aufbrechen—Umkehren—Bekenntnis*).[28] That the task of exploring the dimensions of love and freedom knows no end is what is meant by the word 'God'. That the exploration is not aimless but has shape and direction is signified, for Christian theology, by the name 'Jesus Christ'. Barth's theology, like any worthwhile theology, is an extended account of what life in all its fullness means. It shares with liberation theology the concern both to radicalize *and to relativize* the significance of the 'political' narrowly construed. The reality of freedom and love *include* the political and the economic, and cannot be articulated without it, but they are not exhausted by it. It is the God who is *love* who is, as Barth said, 'God the Liberator' (*Gott der Befreier*).[29]

What, then, are the dimensions of a theology which truly contributes to fullness of life? In the first place such a theology can only exist in profound resonance with human culture as a whole. The depth of Barth's reading, his deep and rich acquaintance with European literature, art, and music tends to emerge only on the margins, in his letters, and records of conversations, but it has its theological correlate in his Christology, which grounds a solidarity with the whole human world and affirms a 'humanism of God', and in his eschatology, where art and humour (and Marlene Dietrich as well as

---

it speaking of the powers that transform the world.' 'On Reading Karl Barth from the Left' in *Barth and Radical Politics*, 156.

[28] Hunsinger notes that Barth was 'more concerned to prevent premature closure, when the biblical witness did not warrant closure, than to achieve orderly conceptual outcomes'. *How to Read Barth*, 34.

[29] KD IV/1, 895; CD, 789.

Mozart!) had their place.[30] It is in his account of anthropology, predicated on analogies with Christ, that we have Barth's praise for the *humanität* of classical Greece:

A certain agitation among theologians in the past few decades against Greek culture has not been a good thing. With their emphasis on eros the Greeks understood that human being [*der Mensch*] is a free, open hearted, willing, spontaneous, cheerful, bright and social being . . . How these Greeks knew how to see themselves as human beings, to speak with one another, to live together in freedom, as friends, as teachers and scholars, and above all as citizens . . . The *agape* of the Christian would not be what it claims to be if it remained hidden to the transparency of Greek *eros*; when a person schooled in Hellenic culture encounters the Christian, he should feel a sense of solidarity to the very depths of his erotic being.[31]

One of the greatest losses we have in Barth's work is not simply the failure to complete the *Dogmatics* but the projected lecture on Goethe for his course on the nineteenth century, which he never took up after the war.[32] Barth's theology is a *humanist* theology in the sense that it is primarily affirmative of human endeavour, and not carping, accusatory, and nay-saying. His political word was always a word of promise.[33] What drew Barth to Carl Zuckmayer was the 'never failing compassion' with which he viewed human darkness, corruption, and misery. 'Mephistopheles is absent.'[34] The same was true of Barth's theology—the demons and the lordless powers are not Mephistopheles. 'On the basis of the eternal will of God we have to think of *every human being*, even the oddest, most villainous or miserable, as one to whom Jesus Christ is Brother and God is Father, and we have to deal with

[30] See above, ch. 3. Cf. R. J. Palma, *Karl Barth's Theology of Culture: The Freedom of Culture for the Praise of God*, Allison Park, Pa., Pickwick, 1983. Palma believes Barth did not take culture seriously enough (p. 82). The evidence is, rather, that he lived it passionately and deeply and that it would probably have received extended treatment later on in the *Dogmatics* as part of humankind's 'answer' to God the redeemer. Schellong sees that Barth's love of Mozart is not an incidental, biographical matter but has consequences for Barth's theology. 'Reading Barth from the Left' in Hunsinger, *Barth and Radical Politics*, 39. Also Hunsinger, *How to Read Barth*, 28. Apart from being a Mozart devotee, Barth was also an enthusiastic filmgoer, and especially liked Marlene Dietrich, whom he wanted to give a place 'probably in eschatology' where in the Münster lectures he dealt with art. Busch, *Barth*, 312; Barth, *Ethics*, 506–12.

[31] KD III/2, 340–3; CD, 282–5. I have used Edward Oakes's splendid translation of the last sentence, and he also draws attention to the importance of Barth's use of *humanität* and the difficulty of translating it. In *Theology of Barth*, 118 von Balthasar cites the text very partially, omitting Barth's severe negatives. We can also note here Barth's insistence on the necessary openness of Christians to non-Christians. 'We are constrained to an absolute openness to all other human beings, without exception.' KD IV/3, 566; CD, 493.

[32] Schellong agrees, describing it as 'the most grievous gap' in Barth's work. His interest, of course, is in what we would have learned there of Barth's attitude to modernity. 'Reading Barth from the Left' in Hunsinger, *Barth and Radical Politics*, 42.

[33] Marquardt, *Theologie*, 65.

[34] *Late Friendship*, 8.

him on this assumption . . . It is identical with the practical acknowledgement of his human rights and his human dignity.'[35]

Another way of saying this is that a theology which serves fullness of life
must be a theology of joy. Joy may not be constitutive of freedom in the way
that love is, but it is a dismal freedom, and a very curious love, which knows
no joy.

> Love and joy have it in common . . . that neither of them is ordered or can be pro-
> duced or practised to order. Both grow of themselves from God the Liberator, and
> from the occurrence of his act of liberation. And the one is the infallible criterion of
> the other.[36]

Barth liked to tease his German audiences with his disparaging remarks
about Beethoven in comparison to Mozart. In the same lecture on 'The
Gift of Freedom', quoted above, he remarked: 'There is an abundance
of serious, pious, learned and ingenious theological undertaking. But
lacking the sky-light and hence serenity, the theologian remains a gloomy
visitor upon this earth of darkness . . . whose teachings compare with
the sombre music of Beethoven or Brahms!'[37] 'Mozart's centre', he
wrote in 1956, 'is not like that of the great theologian Schleiermacher,
identical with balance, neutralization and finally indifference. What
happens in this centre is rather a splendid annulment of balance, a turn
in the strength of which the light rises and the shadow winks but
does not disappear; happiness outdistances sorrow without extinguishing
it and the "Yes" rings stronger than the existing "No" . . . One can never
perceive equilibrium, and for that reason uncertainty or doubt, in Mozart's
music.'[38] Not only the triumph of the Yes over the No, but also the 'splendid
annulment of balance' is what we find in Barth's theology, the hallmark of
its joy.[39]

For Barth the connection between freedom and joy, like that between
love and joy, was self evident:

---

[35] Barth, *Humanity of God*, 50. Cf. also 'Brechen und Bauen' in *Der Götze Wackelt*, 119.

[36] KD iv/2, 895; CD, 789.   [37] Barth, *Humanity of God*, 87.

[38] Barth, 'Mozart's Freedom' in *Wolfgang Amadeus Mozart*, Grand Rapids, Eerdmans, 1986,
55. One could read the whole lecture as an account of what Barth was striving for in his theology. K. Sonderegger makes something like this point in her article 'On Style in Karl Barth', *SJT*
45 (1992), 65 ff. 'To read Barth carefully, at length, is to be caught up in a drama of light and
shadow, of figures in chiaro-scuro, of exposition inflamed by passion and twists of irony and
compassion. The drama is drawn in master strokes and no critique can encompass them or
domesticate them' (p. 65).

[39] Cf. also Bonhoeffer's remarks about Barth's *hilaritas*—confidence in his own work, bold-
ness, and defiance of the world and of popular opinion, steadfast certainty that in his work he
was showing the world something good, and high spirited self confidence. Bonhoeffer, *Letters
and Papers*, 229.

Freedom is *being joyful.* Freedom is the great gift, totally unmerited and wondrous beyond understanding. It awakens the receiver to true selfhood and new life. It is a gift from *God,* from the source of all goodness, an ever-new token of his faithfulness and mercy . . . Through this gift man who was irretrievably separated and alienated from God is called into discipleship. This is why freedom is joy![40]

The sense of freedom and joy in Barth's theology is nowhere clearer than in the most beautiful of his short books, *Evangelical Theology,* which is certainly the best introduction to his work. He characterizes theology as a modest and in an exemplary way free science which 'joyfully respects the mystery of the freedom of its object'.[41] The source of this joy is the resurrection of Christ which for Barth is a prohibition of despair, a license to hope, the archetype of all good surprises. It informs the grimmest of situations and all political struggle.[42] As the archetype of surprises the resurrection is also the archetype of those miracles which reveal the richness and comprehensiveness of the divine ordering of things and which constantly surprise us.[43] Hunsinger rightly points out that mystery and miracle are intrinsic to Barth's understanding of the reality of God's engagement with the world, so that we live in a world in which we are continually 'surprised by joy'.[44]

The sense of wonder and astonishment which runs through the *Dogmatics,* and which grows stronger as the need for polemics fades into the background after 1942, is likewise part of this joy and part of a truly liberative theology. 'A quite specific astonishment stands at the beginning of every theological perception, inquiry, and thought . . . This astonishment is indispensable if theology is to exist and be perpetually renewed as a modest, free, critical and happy science.'[45] Such wonder made sure that the common was always uncommon and the strange was never domesticated.

Theology which stands in the service of fullness of life will also be generous, affirmative, radiant with the gospel (the word 'radiant' occurs with increasing frequency in Barth's later theology). It will, in short, be a theology of grace, and it is no accident that Barth's two greatest forerunners as theologians of freedom are Augustine and Luther. All three understand that moralism is destructive of human life. All three at some stage in their careers spoke sharp, angry, and quite unjustified 'No's to their opponents, but 'Yes' was the overwhelming content of their gospel, and this is

---

[40] Barth, *Humanity of God,* 75.   [41] Barth, *Evangelical Theology,* 9.

[42] A humble but very fine commentary on this is the testimony of the work of Fr Rogelio Ponseele, who ministered to the FMLN in El Salvador. *Death and Life in Morazán,* London, CIIR, 1989.

[43] KD IV/2, 165; CD, 147; KD III/3, 182; CD, 161.

[44] Hunsinger, *How to Read Barth,* 189 ff.   [45] Barth, *Evangelical Theology,* 64.

perhaps more true of Barth than it is of either Augustine or Luther. 'The content of God's Word is his free, undeserved Yes to the whole human race, in spite of all human unreasonableness and corruption.'[46] God does not turn towards human beings, he wrote, without an inexorably sharp 'No', and thus theology must also speak this 'No', but Christ has taken this 'No' upon himself.

What takes place in God's humanity is, since it includes that 'No' in itself, the affirmation of man . . . moral earnestness is a praiseworthy thing and the gift of penetrating and perhaps witty analysis of the times . . . is a fine gift. But the task of bringing the gospel to light is more urgent than manifesting that earnestness and bringing this gift into play. He to whom this *positive* task is not absolutely the supreme task, who first of all wants to shout at, bewilder, or laugh at men on account of their folly and malice, had better remain silent altogether.[47]

It is at least worth noting that part of the context of Barth's 'No' to Brunner was the latter's enthusiasm for Moral Rearmament, an enthusiasm which led to a dreadful evening when, to the embarrassment of all, Brunner engineered Barth's attendance at an Oxford Group Meeting.[48] Moralism brought out in both Augustine and Barth their most intransigent and ungracious 'No'. Barth's lifelong hostility to principles, world views and 'isms' of all sorts is likewise bound up with the perception that they are a form of moralism, that they preach that human beings can redeem themselves by their own efforts.

CHRIST AND FREEDOM

Barth is much clearer than Augustine in insisting that the grace which affirmed human beings was neither a power nor a principle, but a name. 'The last word I have to say whether as a theologian or as a political animal [*Politiker*],' he said in his final radio interview, 'is not a concept like "grace" but a name: Jesus Christ. *He* is grace, and *he* is the final thing, beyond the world, the Church and also beyond theology. We cannot capture him, but we have to do with him, and what I have sought to do in my long life is . . . to highlight this name and say: *there . . .!*'[49]

There are a number of ways in which we can understand this insistence. One is that the 'name' resists systematization, and reduction to a few principles. It calls for constant re-narration, in a storytelling which is self involving. Again, that the last word is a 'name' speaks of a reality which redeems

[46] Barth, *Evangelical Theology*, 79.
[47] Barth, *Humanity of God*, 58–9.
[48] This was in 1933. Hart, *Barth versus Brunner*, 145.
[49] Barth, *Letzte Zeugnisse*, 30–1.

us by constantly de-centring us through the life of prayer and gratitude.[50] David Ford has said finely that the *Dogmatics* 'is primarily a spirituality of knowledge, a knowledge which has endless personal and practical implications, but which is first of all knowledge of a person distinct from ourselves who is portrayed in the Bible'. It is, in fact, 'an ascesis of truth'.[51] What Barth's *theology* makes clear is the role *spirituality* (a word Barth himself rarely uses) plays in our redemption: marked by Barth's constant return to prayer, his insistence that theology cannot be done without it, and his understanding of Christian life as life in gratitude, as response to the grace which is Christ. Barth opposes the 'name' to principles and world views because these become hypostases for individual, community, or national positions which can then be used to sanctify destruction. Of course, the name of Christ has been used in the same way, but Barth would object that here we are dealing with a living Lord who constantly shatters our certainty about him.

FREEDOM AND DIFFICULTY

A theology in the service of fullness of life will be unafraid of what today are called 'aporia'—the perplexities and difficulties which a facile theology simply 'solves'.[52] Barth, says Jüngel, 'sought paths that stood up to aporia. For this reason his thought, his knowledge, became above all aporetic'.[53] This is true, but it is true not just because Barth was an extremely complex thinker, but because he was always concerned to relate his theology to the world in which he lived. It was this concern which forced him to the dialectical thinking of the second *Romans*. Barth frequently draws attention to the necessary brokenness of theological thought. Since through God alone can God be known theological talk must of necessity time and again grow silent. 'This growing silent, this lack of consistency, openness, the uncompletedness of Barth's theological thought, this denial of concepts, is the starting point for the category of praxis *inside* theology . . . Theology is no closed theory which is realized in praxis or as praxis.'[54]

---

[50] That the gospel de-centres us and deconstructs taken for granted positions is a real point of connection between Barth and some postmodern theory. So W. Lowe, 'Barth as Critic of Dualism', *SJT* 41 (1988), 377 ff.; and much more fully G. Ward, *Barth, Derrida and the Language of Theology*, Cambridge, Cambridge University Press, 1995.

[51] D. Ford, *Barth and God's Story: Biblical Narrative and the Theological Method of Karl Barth in the 'Church Dogmatics'*, Frankfurt, Lang, 1985, 168.

[52] Speaking in 1947 Barth said we needed a new Leibniz who would help us to see the world affirmatively, but without the superficiality, dullness (*Fadheit*) and cheapness of Leibniz. 'Brechen und Bauen' in *Der Götze Wackelt*, 112. Clearly he understood it as his own vocation.

[53] Jüngel, *Barth*, 69.   [54] Marquardt, *Theologie*, 196.

If I am right about the sense of exhaustion in liberation theology this may be because it has been insufficiently 'aporetic', and because its practical engagement has not been sufficiently reflected in 'dialectical' thinking. Barth's determination to stay with the difficulty is evidenced by his frequent rethinkings and rewritings, his refusal to solve the difficulty by recourse to existentialism, to hermeneutics, or even a 'Christ principle'. A theology which is insufficiently 'aporetic' in this way will be marked by superficiality, and sometimes by dishonesty—the claim that Christianity has 'the answer for everything'. It has no staying power because its addressees sooner or later discover they are being fobbed off, either because such a theology fails to illuminate the depths and complexities of experience, or because it too cheaply evades the hard issues of evil, injustice, and suffering. C. G. Berkouwer, and much more sharply Gustaf Wingren, accused Barth of something like the latter.[55] Barth responded: 'Is there any sharper discrimination of evil or warning against it, any stronger recognition of its sinister character, than that which is pronounced . . . in the existence of Jesus as Victor?'[56] It is undeniable that the note of victory in Barth's theology borders on triumphalism, but his counter question has to be weighed, as to what is entailed in confessing Christ as Victor and whether 'doubt is so attractive . . . it must always be regarded as justifiable'.[57]

Superficiality in theology is usually bound up with rationalism of one sort or another—and one of Barth's crucial insights is to see the connection between pietism and rationalism. Those who find in Barth a master system clearly find his theology rationalistic, but there is no point where Barth's theology has the predictability of a system, where we know from the premisses what the conclusions will be. The unattractive, and ultimately impossible thing about systems, is that they impose too neat a structure on the untidiness and messiness of reality, not to mention on the freedom of God. They are free of surprises. Tillich's generous remark that Barth at least strove hard not to become his own pupil calls attention to the many surprises in the *Dogmatics*. It is not just the outright changes of mind, as on baptism, nor the later realization of misguided emphases which Barth draws attention to in his 'Table talk', but the constant freshness of the treatment of each locus, the many sidedness, which continues to generate discussion which is developing in many directions. A theology which serves the fullness of life must be fecund, and there is every indication that this is profoundly true of Barth's. This is because his theology is, and continues to be, full of surprises.

---

[55] Berkouwer, *Triumph of Grace*; G. Wingren, *Theology in Conflict*, Edinburgh, Oliver & Boyd, 1958.

[56] KD IV/3, 203; CD, 177. Barth sets out his response in detail at KD 198–206; CD, 173–80.

[57] KD IV/3, 201; CD, 176.

An aporetic theology is a theology which does not solve everything, but which constantly raises fresh questions and fresh difficulties. 'Despite its monumental nature,' says Michael Weinrich, 'Barth's theology remains far more a question than an answer.'[58] A refusal to give up questioning marks Barth's attitude to all the greatest of his predecessors. This is particularly true of his relation to Schleiermacher. Just a few months before his death he writes:

The door is in fact not latched. I am actually to the present day not finished with him. Not even with regard to his point of view. As I have understood him up to now, I have supposed and continued to suppose that I must take a completely different tack from those who follow him. I am certain of my course and of my point of view. I am, however, not so certain of them that I can confidently say that my 'Yes' necessarily implies a 'No' to Schleiermacher's point of view. For have I indeed understood him correctly? Could he not perhaps be understood differently so that I would not have to reject his theology, but might rather be joyfully conscious of proceeding in fundamental agreement with him?[59]

I think we find in Barth's lifelong admiration for Calvin as a teacher a similar refusal to believe that he himself has the answers. In the 1922 lectures he insisted that the great thing about Calvin was that you learned from him and passed on. Speaking in 1964 on the 400th anniversary of Calvin's death, Barth said 'Calvinistic orthodoxy . . . was and is a contradiction in terms.'

You could and can still today only go to Calvin's school and learn from him. And because he wanted to direct his congregation, and with himself also his hearers and readers, to the school of the Holy Scriptures, the limits of his greatness and also the weaknesses of his strength had to and have to become visible and become serious problems in the instruction to be had from him.[60]

Exactly the same, I believe, applies to Barth, and was intended so to do.

FREEDOM AND IMAGINATION

In 1967, in a comparison of the early work of Barth and Bultmann, James Smart spoke of 'the divided mind of modern theology'.[61] Thirty years on, the division is obviously just as deep. We have noted at a number of points James Barr's contempt for what he calls 'The countless pages of wearisome, inept, and futile exegesis' in the *Church Dogmatics*, which

[58] Eicher and Weinrich, *Der Gute Widerspruch*, 76.
[59] Barth, *Theology of Schleiermacher*, 274–5.
[60] Barth, *Fragments Grave and Gay*, 108.
[61] J. Smart, *The Divided Mind of Modern Theology*, Philadelphia, Westminster, 1967.

stem from the fact that Barth's theology was 'at bottom a dogmatic-philosophical system, in which the biblical exegetical foundation . . . was logically incidental'.[62]

Now what counts as wearisome, inept, and futile obviously varies very markedly, for writers and theologians as various as George Steiner, John Updike, David Ford, and Katherine Sonderegger clearly do not find it so, and for myself I would prefer to say humorous, often tendentious, always provocative, and full of profound insights.

These two readings—alienating, systematizing, totalitarian on the one side, liberating, freely responsive and modest on the other—can obviously only be mediated by the extended argument of critical reception. There is, after all, still an ongoing argument about Augustine, Aquinas, and Schleiermacher, let alone Barth! One of the points at issue, however, and it was at issue from Barth's first *Romans* on, is the role of imagination in theology, which is what Barth had in mind, I believe, in speaking of his preference for the old doctrine of inspiration in the preface to the first *Romans*. The sternly admonishing finger which is wagged at Barth's exegesis is presumably wagged in the interests of truth. Here is someone who claims to be exegeting a text but who in fact is reading into it more or less what he likes. The point is important because truth is integral to freedom: 'The truth shall make you free.' No truth, no genuine freedom. But is Barth's manner of reading Scripture hostile to truth? David Ford has argued that Barth's scriptural exegesis prefigures much of what today we understand as a literary reading of Scripture.[63] Barth arrives at his doctrines by following the scriptural narrative, by treating the Bible, in Kelsey's term, as 'a vast, loosely structured non fictional novel'.

Narrative is taken to be the authoritative aspect of scripture; it is authoritative in so far as it functions as the occasion for encounter with an agent in history, viz. the risen Lord. Hence we may say that scripture is taken to have the logical force of stories that render a character, that offer an identity description of an agent. Scripture does this by means of certain formal features of the writing, certain patterns in the narrated sequences of intentions and actions. It is to these patterns that the theologian appeals to authorize his proposals.[64]

To use Scripture like this gives priority to imagination as opposed, say, to using the texts to reconstruct as accurately as possible what people in the ancient past may have thought. Barth's critics complain that his exegesis of Genesis 1.26, for example, could not possibly be what the original authors

[62] Barr, *Biblical Faith*, 203, 131. Amongst a number of protests at Barr's treatment of Barth, see A. Thistleton, 'Barr on Barth and Natural Theology: A Plea for Hermeneutics in Historical Theology', *SJT* 47 (1994), 519 ff.

[63] Ford, *Barth and God's Story*, esp. chs 3 and 4.

[64] D. Kelsey, *The Uses of Scripture in Recent Theology*, London, SCM, 1975, 48.

intended and therefore does violence to the text.[65] On one level this objection is sound, but on another level is there not something of the woodenness of the letter as opposed to the freedom of the Spirit here? Barth approaches the diverse documents of Scripture as essentially an inspired, and therefore inspiring, stimulus for our imagination. That they are *theopneustos* does not mean that the reader can play fast and loose with them, but it does mean, first, that a unity across this diversity is presupposed, and secondly that a whole variety of readings, which may be playful and in earnest at the same time, and which often choose to stay with the surface of the text, are in order. This is partly because no reading is final: every reading constitutes only a *consilium* for others to take note of. They are a challenge but not a command.[66] Such exegeses are part of *church* dogmatics—that is, part of an extended and ongoing conversation and argument which circles round the text. It is the conversation which provides the control:

> In every century the Church has had to find out anew the meaning of Scripture. The task remains. We must trust that the Holy Spirit will lead us into all truth. We have no pope in Protestantism, but we do have *secondary* criteria. Sound exegesis will be done *within the communion of saints.* The Bible is given to the community of the Church. Tradition helps us toward sound exegesis, and tradition includes the whole history of the Church (including the nineteenth century!).[67]

When Barth defined dogmatic method as 'openness to new truth' such openness has much to do with the degree of imagination with which we are prepared to approach the text. He opposed wooden historicist readings of Scripture, and lamented the 'ridiculous and middle class habit of the modern Western mind which is supremely phantastic in its chronic lack of imaginative phantasy, and hopes to rid itself of its complexes through suppression'.[68] The pre-historical sphere, he maintained, is accessible to our imaginations though not to our perception. 'The human possibility of knowing is not exhausted by the ability to perceive and comprehend. Imagination, too, belongs no less legitimately in its way to the human possibility of knowing. A man without imagination is more of an invalid than one who

---

[65] See the apoplectic comments in Barr, *Biblical Faith*, 160–1. Nigel Biggar emphasizes the role of narrative in Barth's ethics. To the objection that Scripture cannot be reduced to *one* narrative, but contains an irreducible plurality he replies that there remains a meta story of God's pursuit of his creatures' salvation. *Hastening*, 103–4. Of course it can then be argued that Christian readings do violence to the Old Testament.

[66] KD I/2, 961; CD, 859. On this question see S. Sykes, 'Barth on the Centre of Theology' in *Barth Methods*, 17–54.

[67] *Table Talk*, 97. The conversation of the Church is also the way ethics works for Barth. See the account of the necessity for admonition. KD III/4, 8; CD, 9. As Biggar puts it, the Church is 'a school for the formation of moral character'. *Hastening*, 127. See the whole discussion of character, and the response to Hauerwas's criticisms, 127–45.

[68] KD III/1, 87; CD, 81.

lacks a leg . . . In principle each of us is capable of divination and poetry, or at least capable of receiving their products.'[69]

In his exegesis Barth keeps an eye on historical critical work but does not allow it to act as a final arbiter for understanding.[70] Instead, he prioritizes imagination.[71] The 'truth' of his readings, then, is more like the 'truth' of a picture, or a piece of music. To take one of his favourite artists, Botticelli, what would it mean to speak of the 'truth' of *Primavera* or *The Birth of Venus*? The indignant observation: 'Botticelli clearly did not understand the human body—everything is out of proportion. Send him back to the anatomy class!' would only bring ridicule on the critic, though it is true that as representations Botticelli's figures have their proportions all wrong. To such a critic we would have to say: 'Botticelli was trying to do something quite different. He offers us a deeper understanding of the human body than an "accurate" representation could do.' Something of the same applies to Barth's biblical exegeses, especially when they are set alongside many conventional commentaries, which ultimately say nothing illuminating about the text at all.[72] This priority of imagination in his exegesis is part of his attempt not 'to compete with the Holy Spirit and unduly restrict his operation' in the reading of Scripture.[73]

The imagination of Barth's exegesis of Scripture is part of the vivid imagination, the ability to see a question from many different angles, of his theology as a whole. The importance of this is that imagination is a crucial dimension of human freedom, of any struggle for liberation. The goal of political struggle is, said Marx, the liberation of the imagination, but imagination is required for liberation struggle in the first place.[74] Barth's theology, because it draws on Scripture in the way that it does, 'funds our imaginations', opens up the perspectives of liberative practice.[75]

---

[69] KD III/1, 99; CD, 91.

[70] For a very fine plea for the importance of historical critical work which recognizes that allegory is involved in much of that, and which is responsive to narrative and literary readings, see Chris Rowland, 'An Open Letter to Frances Watson', *SJT* 48/4 (1995), 507–17.

[71] That Barth prioritizes imagination does not mean, on the other hand, that for him Scripture was non-cognitive and non-informative. As George Hunsinger emphasizes, Barth's exegesis was directed against both literalism and expressivism. 'At the heart of Barth's differences from expressivism lay his rejection of the premiss that images and metaphors when applied to God cannot strictly and properly be true.' Hunsinger, 'Beyond Literalism and Expressivism: Karl Barth's Hermeneutical Realism', *Modern Theology* 3/3 (1987), 213 ff. Also, *How to Read Barth*, 44 f.

[72] Cf., for example, Barth's 'wild' exegesis of Leviticus 14 in KD II/2, 394 ff.; CD, 357 ff. with that of Martin Noth, a scholar Barth respected. Barth reads it as 'obviously' dealing with election and rejection, which it obviously is not, but how stimulating is his reading over against Noth's!

[73] *Kerygma and Myth*, II, 127.

[74] K. Marx, *The German Ideology*, Moscow, Progress, 1976, 47.

[75] The phrase is Walter Brueggemann's, *The Bible and Postmodern Imagination*, London, SCM, 1993.

GOING BEYOND BARTH

Christian theology, as Lessing made so uncomfortably clear at the end of the eighteenth century, is strapped between the universal and the particular. Throughout this study we have sought to understand Barth's theology as accompanying its context, but this raises the question of how relevant it is beyond that context. 'Theology is a progressive and continuous understanding, which is variable to a certain extent. If it were merely the understanding of abstract truth, this would not be true.'[76] This is Gutiérrez, but it could equally be Karl Barth. Barth himself insisted that different contexts required different theologies. Thus on his American trip in 1962 he urged his hosts to develop a 'specific American theology' as a theology of freedom. The Statue of Liberty, he said, needed a good deal of demythologization. A true theology of freedom should be for that freedom 'to which the Son frees us, and which as his gift, is the one real human freedom—My last question for this evening is this: Will such a specific American theology arise? I hope so.'[77]

A similar response was evoked in the summer of 1968 by a then unknown Japanese theologian, Kosuke Koyama, who had just taken over the editorship of the *South East Asian Journal of Theology*. An issue of this journal was to be devoted to Barth, and he was asked for a contribution. His reply is illuminating not just for the question of going beyond Barth, but for his understanding of theology as a whole. A Christian pursues good theology, Barth maintained, when they seriously dwell *bei die Sache*, and, with equal courage and humility, diligent work and straightforward prayer recognize and confess the first commandment, and secondly when they pursue their work with joy and humour. 'No morose theologians! No boring theology!' But he was more interested in their work. 'In my life I have spoken many words. But now they are spoken. Now it is your turn.' First he urged them to respond to the burning problems of their own context, their own ruling-ideologies and 'realities', responsibly and concretely, not as Western or Barthian theologians but as joyful *South Asian* Christians. 'You must be this in the gifted and permitted *freedom* which we find where the Spirit of the Lord is' '(2 Corinthians 3.17)'. But then, with an eye on the emergence of regional or sectional theologies, he emphasized that there is one Spirit, one Lord, and one God, which needs to be recognized in the one Church and the establishment of peace on earth far better than has been the case in Europe.[78]

---

[76] Gutiérrez, *Essential Writings*, 24.   [77] Barth, *How I Changed my Mind*, 79.

[78] 'No boring theology! A Letter from Karl Barth', *South East Asian Journal of Theology* 2 (Autumn 1969), 3. Now reprinted in Barth, *Offene Briefe*. It is the very last of all Barth's open letters.

'Now it is your turn': Barth joins that part of the tradition which can no longer answer back but, like Augustine, Luther, Schleiermacher, and all the other theologians he invoked in his lectures on the nineteenth century, he is amongst those who 'are not dead, but live'. As they were a vital part of his context, so is he of ours. 'The common action of hearing and receiving', Barth wrote, 'is partly contemporary . . . but to a much greater extent it is non contemporary: it takes place among those who belonged to an earlier and those who belonged to a later age in the Church, between the present age and those who preceded it'.[79]

To claim that Barth's theology has something to contribute to the process of human liberation is not to deny that there are many aspects of his work which need modification or even a completely fresh ground, or aspects which are far from liberative.[80] It is clear that if there is the shadow of imperfection on all human work, then it lies more heavily on theology than elsewhere—precisely in view of its attempt to speak of 'that than which a greater cannot be conceived'—and the greater the theology the deeper the shadow. We can instance Augustine on sexuality, or the use of force against heretics, or Aquinas and Calvin's elision of divine foreknowledge and predestination. There are undoubted shadows in Barth's work. One thinks above all of his very ambiguous account of Israel, the quite unsustainable position on the subordination of women, and the position on homosexuality. Unlike Macken and the critics he summons I do not believe his position on freedom to constitute such a shadow. On the contrary, I agree with Eicher and others that Barth understands and sets out a picture of what constitutes true human freedom.[81]

Despite the shadows, therefore, I believe that Barth's work from first to last makes a profound contribution to human liberation. It does this, of course, in the many-sidedness of its approach to *die Sache*, Jesus Christ, from which springs its depth and its spirituality, and in its ability to generate questions. It is liberative, however, especially in its hostility to abstraction and its concern for the concrete. In this connection the role that the Blumhardts play in Barth's theology from his first commentary on Romans to the final

---

[79] KD I/2, 655; CD, 588.

[80] Amongst areas where we need to go beyond Barth there is, of course, the area of eschatology which he did not live to finish, there is wide recognition of the unsatisfactory nature of his doctrine of the Trinity, there are wide ranging questions about how satisfactory his pressing of the analogy of relations is in his anthropology, questions about how far he does justice to the seriousness of human history with his insistence on the 'game like character' of human achievement, and the question of his adequacy in coping with an aggressively pluralist society. That Barth felt unease about the latter is indicated by his final remarks about Schleiermacher, and the possibility of a theology of the Holy Spirit.

[81] Cf. also W. Krötke, 'Gott und Mensch als "Partner" ', *ZTK* (1986).

fragments is of crucial importance. Christoph Blumhardt's secret, Barth wrote, in 1919, 'was his endless movement between hurrying and waiting, between lively participation in the fullness of what is and astonished inner waiting for that which seeks to be through the power from on high . . . The unique element, and I say it quite deliberately, the prophetic, in Blumhardt's message and mission consists in the way in which the hurrying and the waiting, the worldly and the divine, the present and the coming, again and again met, were united, supplemented one another, sought and found one another.'[82] Blumhardt was a man who 'believed in God and believed also in human beings, and because he believed in human beings believed also in the renewal of the world'. Each step requires the other, and the culmination of the logic is the renewal of the world. 'The renewal of the world is the bracket of the God–human relationship.'[83]

Barth returned to Blumhardt in liv/3, and then again in the final fragments. In these Barth wrote: 'When the two Blumhardts did not speak of the kingdom indirectly . . . but directly . . . they pronounced the name of Jesus . . . Very naively, but with axiomatic certainty, they were thinking of the reality of the risen and living Jesus himself, acting and speaking as a distinctive factor no less actual today than yesterday.'[84] This was their interest rather than the God–man of early Christology or the Jesus of history of their contemporaries, and this was true for Barth too. The Christ of the *Dogmatics* is the *risen* Christ: the details of the hypostatic union are only designed to help us see how this is the case. Those who believe in the resurrection cannot be idle, acquiesce in human unrighteousness and disorder, 'in the mortal imperilling of life, freedom, peace and joy on earth under the lordship of the lordless powers . . . to adjust themselves . . . to the status quo; to establish themselves on this; and perhaps with gloomy sceptical speculation to find comfort in the thought that until God's final and decisive intervention, the course of events will necesarily be not only as bad as previously but increasingly worse'. Taking up the the Blumhardts' motto Barth insists that they '*wait* and *hasten* toward the dawn of God's day, the appearing of his righteousness . . . They not only wait but also hasten. They wait by hastening . . . Aiming at God's kingdom, established on its coming and not on the status quo, they do not just look toward it but run toward it as fast as their feet will carry them.'[85]

Christians are established on the coming kingdom, and not on the status quo. 'Although theology is no enemy to mankind,' Barth said in his 1962 lectures, his swansong, 'at its core it is a critical, in fact a revolutionary affair,

[82] Barth, 'Past and Future' in *The Beginnings of Dialectical Theology*, ed. J. Moltmann, 45.
[83] Marquardt, *Theologie*, 186.   [84] Barth, *Christliche Leben*, 448; ET, 259.
[85] Ibid., 456; ET, 263.

because as long as it has not been shackled, its theme is the new man in the new cosmos.'[86] The beginning of his distinctive theological journey was the perception that the theology he had learned was so shackled, and he sought strenuously to avoid this fate by swimming against the stream in the changing situation of the five decades of his active theological life. In Peter Eicher's phrase, his theology constituted a good, liberating, and helpful contradiction opposed to the destructive contradictions of the day.[87] It is against hegemony, and understands Christian life as a constant struggle against hegemony. But it is against hegemony because it understands the vividness, joy, celebration, and forgivenness of human life as this is promised us in Christ. It is the gospel of freedom for life. As such it constitutes an invitation to us to respond, theologically, to our own context, for freedom, in faith in the God of life.

[86] Barth, *Evangelical Theology*, 119.
[87] P. Eicher and M. Weinrich, *Der gute Widerspruch*, Neukirchen, Patmos, 1986, 27–8.

Appendix: Barth's Work in Context

History	Culture
1909 Austria annexes Bosnia Bethmann Hollweg German chancellor	Matisse: *The Dance* Mahler: Ninth Symphony Gide: *Strait is the Gate* T. Mann: *Königliche Hoheit*
1910 Revolution in Portugal Japan annexes Korea Revolt in Albania	Stravinsky: *The Firebird* Kandinsky: *Concerning the Spiritual in Art* Wedekind: *Schloss Wetterstein*
1911 Italy declares war on Turkey German warship at Agadir Assassination of Russian premier Kaiser demands Germany's 'Place in the sun'	Heym: *Der ewige Tag* Strauss: *Der Rosenkavalier* Blue Rider group in Munich
1912 Arms race between Germany and Britain War between Turkey and Balkan states Titanic sinks	Picasso: *The Violin* Strauss: *Ariadne auf Naxos* Hauptmann: *Atlantis*
1913 Balkan wars Poincaré president of France	Stravinsky: *The Rite of Spring* T. Mann: *Death in Venice* Shaw: *Pygmalion* Kellermann: *Der Tunnel*
1914 August: First World War Battles of Mons, Marne, Ypres	Kokoschka: *The Vortex* Conrad: *Chance* Braque: *Music* Stravinsky: *Le Rossignol*
1915 Battles of Ypres, Loos, and Gallipoli Sinking of *Lusitania*	Holst: *The Planets* Picasso: *The Harlequin* Einstein discovers Theory of Relativity
1916 Battles of Verdun, Somme, and Marne Easter Rising in Ireland	Matisse: *The Three Sisters* Dada starts in Zürich Brod: The Redemption of Tycho Brahe
1917 Russian revolution Battles of Arras, Passchendale, and Cambrai Spartacist League founded Starvation in Germany	Prokofiev: Classical Symphony Beckmann: *Woman Taken in Adultery* Feuchtwanger: *Jud süss*
1918 End of First World War Abdication of Kaiser Revolution in Berlin General strike in Switzerland	Pirandello: *Six Characters in Search of an Author* Beckmann: *Die Nacht* H. Mann: *Der Untertan*

Barth's life	Barth's publications	Other publications	
Barth 25 years old Pastor in Geneva	*Modern Theology and Work for the Kingdom of God* *What shall we do?*	Harnack: *Acts of the Apostles* James: *A Pluralistic Universe*	1909
Lecture on 'Faith and History'		Hilferding: *Finance Capital* Drews: *The Christ Myth* Kutter: *Sie Müssen* (2nd edn) Natorp: *General Psychology*	1910
Pastor in Safenwil Engaged to Nelly Hoffmann	*Jesus Christ and the Social Question*	Natorp: *People's Culture and Personality* Troeltsch: *Significance of Historicity of Jesus for Faith*	1911
Death of Barth's father	*Christian Faith and History*	Troeltsch: *The Social Teachings of the Christian Churches* Jung: *Theory of Psychoanalysis* Vaihinger: *The Philosophy of As If*	1912
Barth married		Husserl: *Ideas Toward a Pure Phenomenology* Unamono: *The Tragic Sense of Life* Freud: *Totem and Taboo*	1913
Birth of Barth's first child, Franziska Decision to break with liberal theology	*Faith in the Personal God*	Schlatter: *Christian Ethics*	1914
Joins SPD Markus born Meeting with Christoph Blumhardt	Address: 'The War, Socialism and Christendom'	Scheler: *Essays* Cohen: *The Concept of Religion in the System of Philosophy*	1915
Begins work on *Romans* Involvement with unions in Safenwill	Address: 'The Righteousness of God: The Strange New World of the Bible'	Buber: *The Spirit of Judaism* Lukacs: *Theory of the Novel* Soderblom: *The Becoming of Christian Faith*	1916
Christoph born	*Seek God and You Shall Live* (with Thurneysen)	Freud: *Introduction to Psychoanalysis* Jung: *The Unconscious* Gogarten: 'Religion Weither?'	1917
Romans finished		Bloch: *Vom Geist der Utopie* Spengler: *The Decline of the West* Natorp: *The German Soul*	1918

	History	Culture
1919	Peace of Versaille: Reparations Liebknecht and Luxemburg murdered	Manuel de Falla: *Three Cornered Hat* Gropius forms Bauhaus Hesse: *Demian*
1920	League of Nations founded Violent demonstrations in Germany End of civil war in Russia	Modigliani: *Reclining Nude* Kaiser: *Gas II* Kraus: *The Last Days of Mankind*
1921	French troops occupy the Rhine SA begin to terrorize opponents	Klee: *The Fish* Prokofiev: *The Love of Three Oranges* 'Neue Sachlichkeit' exhibition
1922	German currency collapses W. Rathenau assassinated Soviet Union formed	Miro: *The Farm* Eliot: *The Waste Land* Brecht: *Baal* Joyce: *Ulysses*
1923	French invasion of Ruhr Hitler putsch in Bavaria fails Stresemann German chancellor	Broadcasting starts in Germany Rilke: *Duino Elegies* Le Corbusier: *Towards a New Architecture*
1924	Mussolini's main rival murdered New Reichsmark introduced Death of Lenin	Puccini's *Turandot* T. Mann: *The Magic Mountain* Schnitzler: *Fräulein Else*
1925	Von Hindenberg becomes president Locarno treaty: French troops withdraw	Berg: *Wozzeck* Eisenstein: *Battleship Potemkin* Kafka: *The Trial* H. Mann: *The Chief*
1926	Germany joins League of Nations Trotsky expelled from Politburo Hitler Youth founded	Chagall: *Lovers' Bouquet* Kafka: *The Castle* Gide: *The Counterfeiters*
1927	Germany joins International Court of the Hague Allies withdraw from Germany	Hesse: *Steppenwolf* Brecht: *Hauspostille* Kafka: *America*
1928	Kellogg-Briand peace pact Fascists extend power in Italy First Soviet five year plan	Brecht and Weill: *Threepenny Opera* Hauptmann: *Till Eulenspiegel* George: *Das neue Reich*

Barth's life	Barth's publications	Other publications	
Tambach lecture	*Romans* 1st edition *Past and Future: Nauman and Blumhardt*	Overbeck: *Christendom and Culture* Dintzer: *The Sin against the Blood* Wernle: *Calvin*	1919
Rewriting *Romans*	*Biblical Questions, Insights and Vistas* *Unanswered Questions in Contemporary Theology*	Weber: *Economy and Society* Mauthner: *Atheism in the West* Gogarten: *Between the Times* Bultmann: *Religion and Culture*	1920
Moves to Göttingen in October Matthias born		Wittgenstein: *Tractatus* Thurneysen: *Dostoevsky* Gogarten: *The Need of Absoluteness*	1921
Calvin lectures Founding of *Zwischen den Zeiten*	*Romans* 2nd edition *Basic Questions of Christian Social Ethics* *The Word of God as the Task of Theology*	Gogarten: *Against Romantic Theology* Buber: *I and Thou* Gilson: *Thomism*	1922
Schleiermacher lectures	*The Need and Promise of Christian Preaching* *The problem of Ethics in the Present* Exchange with Harnack	Holl: *Collected Essays: Luther* Schlatter: *Christian Dogma* Lukacs: *History and Class Consciousness* Thurneysen: *Socialism and Christianity*	1923
Meets C. von Kirschbaum Dogmatics lectures	*Come Holy Spirit* *The Resurrection of the Dead* *The Word of God and Theology*	Thurneysen: *Scripture and Revelation* Gogarten: *Historicism* Brunner: *Mysticism and the Word*	1924
Moves to Münster Hans Jakob born	*Principles of Dogmatics According to Herrmann* *Desirability and Possibility of a General Reformed Creed*	Troeltsch: *Glaubenslehre* Hitler: *Mein Kampf* pt i Buber and Rosenzweig: *Translation of Torah* Herrmann: *Dogmatics*	1925
Lectures on nineteenth century	*Church and Culture*	Hitler: *Mein Kampf* pt ii de Chardin: *Le Milieu divin* Bultmann: *Jesus*	1926
Lectures on ethics	*Philippians* *Keeping the Commandments* Prolegomena to *Christian Dogmatics*	Heidegger: *Sein und Zeit* Thurneysen: *The Word of God and the Church* Althaus: *The Gospel and Life* Adam: *The Essence of Catholicism*	1927
C. von Kirschbaum becomes Barth's assistant	*Theology and Church* *The Word of God and the Word of Man* *Roman Catholicism as a Question to the Protestant Church*	Benjamin: *On the Origins of German Tragedy* Pius XI: *Mortalium Animus* Bergson: *La Pensée et le mourant*	1928

History	Culture
1929 World economic collapse Death of Stresemann Hitler appoints Himmler 'Reichsfuhrer SS'	Remarque: *All Quiet on the Western Front* Döblin: *Berlin Alexanderplatz* Sternberg: *Der blaue Engel*
1930 Great Depression Nazis win one-third of seats in Reichstag	Musil: *The Man without Qualities* Simenon: *Pietr le letton*
1931 Revolution in Spain Japan invades Manchuria Fall of Spanish monarchy	Zuckmayer: *The Captain of Kopenick* Brecht and Weill: *Mahagonny*
1932 6 million unemployed in Germany Hindenberg re-elected president Papen government	Bauhaus closed by Nazis Huxley: *Brave New World* Fallada: *Little Man, What Now?*
1933 Hitler becomes chancellor Reichstag fire Trade unions suppressed Concordat with Vatican German church established Banning of SPD	Matisse: *The Dance* Strauss: *Arabella* Book burning in Germany T. Mann: *Joseph and his Brothers*
1934 Hindenburg dies: Hitler assumes full power Röhm purge Barmen confession	Scott Fitzgerald: *Tender is the Night* Benn: *Art and Power* Zweig: *Erasmus of Rotterdam*
1935 Conscription introduced in Germany Jews deprived of citizenship Versailles Treaty repudiated Italy invades Abyssinia	Eliot: *Murder in the Cathedral* Zweig: *The Masterbuilders* Epstein: *Ecce Homo*
1936 Berlin Olympics Germany occupies demilitarized Rhineland Spanish civil war	Prokofiev: *Peter and the Wolf* Cannetti: *Auto da fé* Bernanos: *Diary of a Country Priest*
1937 Britain and France agree on appeasement Airship Hindenberg destroyed	Picasso: *Guernica* Degenerate art exhibition in Munich
1938 9 November: Kristallnacht Austria occupied Sudetenland occupied	Isherwood: *Goodbye to Berlin* Eisenstein: *Alexander Nevsky* Sartre: *La Nausée*
1939 Outbreak of Second World War Pius XII becomes Pope	Joyce: *Finnegan's Wake* Steinbeck: *The Grapes of Wrath* T. Mann: *Lottee in Weimar*

Barth's life	Barth's publications	Other publications	
Adds eighteenth century lectures	*Fate and Idea in Theology* *The Doctrine of the Sacraments*	Mannheim: *Ideology and Utopia* Cassirer: *Philosophy of Symbolic Forms* Althaus: *Outlines of Dogmatics* Wobbermin: *Principles of Evangelical Theology*	1929
Moves to Bonn	*The Holy Spirit and the Christian Life* *Theology and Contemporary Man* *Quousque tandem?*	Brunner: *God and Man* Nygren: *Agape and Eros* Rosenberg: *The Myth of the Twentieth Century*	1930
Joins SPD Dehn Affair Meets Bonhoeffer	*Anselm* *The Need of the Evangelical Church* *Work as a Problem of Theological Ethics*	Jaspers: *The Spiritual Situation of the Time* Heim: *Faith and Thinking* Wobbermin: *The Word of God and Evangelical Faith*	1931
Lectures on theology and mission Seminars on Calvin	*Church Dogmatics* I/1	Curtius: *German Spirit in Danger* Brunner: *The Divine Imperative* Jaspers: *Philosophy*	1932
Lecture: 'The First Commandment as a Political Axiom' Farewell to *Zwischen den Zeiten* Meets Niemöller	*Theologische Existenz Heute!* *Abschied* from *Zwischen den Zeiten*	Tillich: *The Socialist Decision* Bultmann: *Faith and Understanding* Bonhoeffer: *Creation and Fall* Niebuhr: *Moral Man and Immoral Society*	1933
November: suspended from teaching Barmen	*Nein!*	Vischer: *The Christian Witness of the Old Testament* Picard: *The Flight from God* Temple: *Nature, Man and God*	1934
Expelled from Germany Moves to Basle	*Credo* *God's Search for Man*	Eichrodt: *Theology of the Old Testament* Buri: *The Significance of New Testament Eschatology* Peterson: *The Book of Angels*	1935
Continuing church struggle from Switzerland	*God's Election of Grace*	Benjamin: *Art in an Age of Mechanical Reproduction*	1936
Church Dogmatics I/2 completed Gifford Lectures	*Justification and Justice*	Brunner: *Man in Revolt* Balthasar: *Apocalypse of the German Soul*	1937
Lectures on the church struggle in Oxford and Birmingham Letter to Hromadka	*Church Dogmatics* I/2 *The Knowledge of God and the Service of God*	Lukacs: *The Young Hegel* Lubac: *The Social Aspects of Dogma* Huizinga: *Homo Ludens*	1938
Working on *Church Dogmatics* II/2 Lectures in Holland, France,	*Church Dogmatics* II/1 *The Faith of the Church* *The Sovereignty of the Word*	Rahner: *Spirit in the World* Brunner: *The Divine Imperative* Rougemont: *Love in the West*	1939

History	Culture
1940	Germany occupies France, Norway, Denmark, Holland, and Belgium Battle of Britain Dunkirk	Chaplin: *The Great Dictator* Stravinsky: Symphony in C Major Goes: *The Neighbour*
1941	Germany invades Russia Japan bombs Pearl Harbour USA enters the war 'Final Solution' begins	Shostakovitch: Leningrad Symphony Ehrenberg: *The Fall of Paris* Sayers: *The Mind of the Maker*
1942	Japan invades Burma Battle of El Alamein Battle of Stalingrad	Eliot: *Little Gidding* Heym: *Der Fall Glasenapp*
1943	German army surrenders at Stalingrad Allies invade Italy Heavy air attacks on German cities	Shostakovitch: Eighth Symphony Moore: *Madonna and Child* Hesse: *The Glass Bead Game*
1944	D-Day Arnhem and German counteroffensive in the Ardennes Assassination attempt on Hitler fails	Sutherland: *Christ on the Cross* Zweig: *The World of Yesterday* Genet: *Notre Dame des Fleurs*
1945	8 May Germany surrenders 6 August Hiroshima	Orwell: *Animal Farm* Britten: *Peter Grimes* Sartre: *Roads to Freedom*
1946	United Nations established Churchill's 'Iron Curtain' speech Nuremberg trials	Chagall: *Cow with Umbrella* Beauvoir: *All Men are Mortal* Zuckmayer: *The Devil's General*
1947	India, Burma, and Sri Lanka become independent	Anne Frank's Diary T. Mann: *Doctor Faustus* Frisch: *Santa Cruz*
1948	Cold War begins Berlin air lift Gandhi assassinated Foundation of Israel	Mailer: *The Naked and the Dead* Greene: *The Heart of the Matter* Celan: *Der Sand aus den Urnen*
1949	NATO formed German Democratic Republic formed Vatican announces excommunication for those who preach or practise communism	Böll: *The Train Was On Time* Orwell: *1984* Brecht's: *Mother Courage* in Berlin
1950	McCarthy Committee starts witch-hunt USSR develop atom bomb Korean War begins Assumption of Mary proclaimed	Anouilh: *La Répétition* Cocteau: *Orphée* Chagall: *King David*

Barth's life	Barth's publications	Other publications	
Barth called up Urges resistance to Germany	*La Confession de la Foi de l'Eglise*	Mannheim: *Man and Society* Maury: *Election and Grace* Ayer: *The Foundations of Empirical Knowledge*	1940
Barth's mother dies Reprimanded for political intervention Death of Matthias	*A Short Commentary on Romans* *In the Name of Almighty God*	Bultmann: *The Scope of Demythologizing* Gilson: *God and Philosophy* Niebuhr: *Nature and Duty of Man*	1941
BBC broadcasts lead to a university reprimand	*Church Dogmatics* ii/2 *Letter to an American Churchman*	Balthasar: *Presence et Pensée* Merleau-Ponty: *The Structure of Behaviour* Fromm: *The Fear of Freedom*	1942
Reconcilation with Ragaz	*The Church's Teaching on Baptism*	Sartre: *Being and Nothingness* Cullmann: *The First Christian Confessions of Faith* Werner: *Religious Content of Existentialism*	1943
Urging friendship for Germany Member of Committee for a Free Germany	*Jesus und das Volk*	Adorno and Horkheimer: *Dialectic of Enlightenment*	1944
First return visit to Germany Lecture in Stuttgart	*A Swiss Voice* *Church Dogmatics* iii/1 *A Word to the Germans*	Kümmel: *Promise and Fulfilment* Lubac: *The Discovery of God* Sartre: *Existentialism is Humanism*	1945
Lectures in Bonn	'The Christian Community and the Civil Community' *The Christian Church and Present Day Reality*	Cullmann: *Christ and Time* Brunner: *Dogmatik* i Auerbach: *Mimesis*	1946
Lectures in Bonn Participation in ecumenical meeting in Bossey	*Nineteenth Century Protestant Theology* *Dogmatics in Outline* *Brechen und Bauen*	Jeremias: *The Parables of Jesus* Heuss: *Deutsche Gestalten* Jaspers: *The Question of Guilt*	1947
Participation in WCC Assembly in Amsterdam Visit to Hungary	*Church Dogmatics* iii/2 *A Hungarian Journey*	*Kerygma and Myth* i Bultmann: *Theology of the New Testament* i Brunner: *Christianity and Civilization*	1948
Discussion for 'a new humanism'	*The Church between East and West*	Buber: *Tales of the Hasidim* Beauvoir: *The Second Sex* Tillich: *Shaking of the Foundations*	1949
Seminars on Catholicism and Calvin Barth attacked in Bern Great Council	*Church Dogmatics* iii/3 *Fear Not!*	Brunner: *The Christian Doctrine of Creation and Redemption* Noth: *History of Israel* Congar: *True and False*	1950

	History	Culture
1951	Korean War continues Spy scandal in Britain	Picasso: *Massacre in Korea* Böll: Where were you Adam? Britten: *Billy Budd* Camus: *The Rebel*
1952	Eisenhower elected President in USA August: 16,000 escape from East to West Berlin	Stravinsky: *Babel* Beckett: *Waiting for Godot* Frank: *Links wo das Herz ist*
1953	Death of Stalin Korean War ends USSR explodes H-bomb Failed revolt in GDR	Durrenmatt: *An Angel Comes to Babylon* Stockhausen: *Electronic Study* Remarque: *A Time to Live and a Time to Die*
1954	Occupation of West Germany ended McCarthyism finally condemned Algerian war begins Evanston Conference of WCC	Chagall: *The Red Roofs* Schoenberg: *Moses and Aron* Golding: *Lord of the Files*
1955	Warsaw pact created Germany joins NATO	Dali: *The Lord's Supper* Nabokov: *Lolita* Tippett: *Midsummer Marriage*
1956	Suez crisis Invasion of Hungary Castro lands in Cuba	Bicentenary of Mozart's birth Camus: *The Fall* Durrenmatt: *Der Besuch der alten Dame*
1957	Eisenhower begins second term Sputnik Appeal against nuclear weapons by leading scientists Common Market founded	Bernstein: *West Side Story* Osborne: *The Entertainer*
1958	Khruschev becomes leader in USSR John XXIII becomes Pope	M. von der Rohe: Segram Building Pasternak: *Doctor Zhivago* Moore: *Reclining Figure*
1959	Castro liberates Cuba Algerian crisis Cyprus becomes a republic	Poulenc: *La Voix Humaine* Greene: *Our Man in Havana* Fellini: *La Dolce Vita* Grass: *The Tin Drum*
1960	Macmillan's 'Wind of Change' speech Sharpeville Brezhnev President of USSR Kennedy President of USA	Shirer: *The Rise and Fall of the Third Reich* Sartre: *Critique of Dialectical Reason* Bolt: *A Man for All Seasons*
1961	Berlin Wall built Eichmann arrested and tried in Jerusalem First man in space	Heller: *Catch 22* Fellini: *Boccacio 70* Grass: *Cat and Mouse*
1962	USA establishes a military command in Vietnam Cuban missile crisis Vatican II begins	Britten: *War Requiem* Solzhenitzyn: *One Day in the Life of Ivan Denisovitch* Albee: *Who's Afraid of Virginia Woolf*

Barth's life	Barth's publications	Other publications	
Demythologizing controversy Seminar on Schleiermacher	*Church Dogmatics* III / 4	Bonhoeffer: *Letters and Papers from Prison* Brunner: *The Misunderstanding of the Church* Balthasar: *K. Barth*	1951
Barth awarded Royal Service Medal for the Cause of Freedom Meeting with Bultmann	*Christ and Adam* *Rudolf Bultmann: An Attempt to Understand Him*	*Kerygma and Myth* ii Niebuhr: *Christ and Culture* Buber: *The Hassidic Message*	1952
Participates in preparatory meeting for Evanston Lectures in Germany	*Church Dogmatics* IV / 1 Letter to L. Zaisser	Jung: *Answer to Job* Wittgenstein: *Investigations* Heidegger: *Introduction to Metaphysics*	1953
Intervention on German rearmament	*Against the Stream* *Volkstrauertag*	Berkouwer: *The Triumph of Grace* Bloch: *Principle of Hope* i and ii Jonas: *Gnosis*	1954
Finishes *Church Dogmatics* IV / 2	*Church Dogmatics* IV / 2 *The Order of the Community*	Marcuse: *Eros and Civilisation* Diem: *Theology as Church Science* Schweizer: *Lordship and Discipleship*	1955
Barth 70 years old Death of Pierre Maury and Artur Frey	*The Humanity of God* *Mozart*	Buri: *Reason and Revelation* Miskotte: *When the Gods are Silent* Bornkamm: *Jesus of Nazareth*	1956
Lectures on 'The Individual in Modern Times'		Küng: *Justification* Rad: *The Theology of the Old Testament* Tillich: *Systematic Theology* ii	1957
Intervention on nuclear weapons Seminar on Tillich	*Letter to an East German Pastor*	Wolf: *Barmen* Hromadka: *Gospel for Atheists* Arendt: *The Human Condition*	1958
Lectures on the ethics of reconciliation Meeting with pietists	*Church Dogmatics* IV / 3.1 *Deliverance to the Captives*	Bloch: *Hope* iii Balthasar: *Theology of History* Fuchs: *The Hermeneutical Problem*	1959
Meeting with Billy Graham	*Church Dogmatics* IV / 3.2 *Philosophy and Theology* *The Possibility of a Liberal Theology Today*	Canetti: *Crowds and Power* Brunner: *Doctrine of the Church* Gadamer: *Truth and Method*	1960
Seminars on final sections of *The Christian Life*	*Ein Gespräch in der Brudergemeinde*	Balthasar: *Herrlichkeit* i Kreck: *Die Zukunft des Gekommenen*	1961
Final Semesters in Basle	*Evangelical Theology*	Jungel: *Paul and Jesus* Trilhaas: *Dogmatics* Buri: *Human Beings and Grace*	1962

Select Bibliography

PRIMARY WORKS

Kirchliche Dogmatik, 13 vols., Munich, Kaiser, 1932; then Zürich, Evangelischer Verlag, 1938–1965

Gesamtausgabe: all published by Theologischer Verlag, Zürich (in order of publication)

Karl Barth–Rudolf Bultmann Briefwechsel 1911–1966, ed. B. Jaspert, 1971
Ethik I (1928/30), ed. D. Braun, 1973
K. Barth–E. Thurneysen Briefwechsel 1913–1921, ed. E. Thurneysen, 1973
K. Barth–E. Thurneysen Briefwechsel 1921–1930, ed. E. Thurneysen, 1974
Briefe: 1961–1968, ed. J. Fangmeier and H. Stoevesandt, 1975
Erklärung des Johannes Evangeliums (1925/6), ed. W. Fürst, 1976
Das christliche Leben (1959–61), ed. H. Drewes and E. Jungel, 1976
Die Theologie Schleiermachers, ed. D. Ritschl, 1978
Ethik II, ed. D. Braun, 1978
Die christliche Dogmatik im Entwurf, ed. G. Sauter, 1982
Offene Briefe 1945–1968, ed. D. Koch, 1984
Der Römerbrief, 1st edn, ed. H. Schmidt, 1985
Unterricht in der christlichen Religion, i: *Prolegomena* (1924), ed. H. Reiffen, 1985; ii: *Die Lehre von Gott/Die Lehre vom Menschen* (1924/5), ed. H. Stoevesandt, 1990; (ET, *The Göttingen Dogmatics*)
Vorträge und kleinere Arbeiten, 1922–1925, ed. H. Finze, 1990
Vorträge und kleinere Arbeiten, 1905–1909, ed. H. Drewes and H. Stoevesandt, 1992
Die Theologie Calvins (1922), ed. A. Reinstädtler and H. Scholl, 1993
Vorträge und kleinere Arbeiten, 1909–1914, ed. H. Drewes and H. Stoevesandt, 1993
Vorträge und kleinere Arbeiten, 1925–1930, ed. H. Schmidt, 1994

Other:

Das Wort Gottes und die Theologie, Munich, Kaiser, 1925
Die Auferstehung der Toten, Munich, Kaiser, 1926
Suchet Gott, so werdet ihr leben!, Munich, Kaiser, 1928 (with E. Thurneysen)
Erklärung des Philipperbriefes, Munich, Kaiser, 1928
Die Theologie und die Kirche, Munich, Kaiser, 1928
Der Römerbrief, 2nd edn (1922), Munich, Kaiser, 1929
Nein! Antwort an Emil Brunner, Munich, Kaiser, 1934
Credo, Munich, Kaiser, 1935
Eine Schweizer Stimme 1938–1945, Zürich, Theologischer Verlag, 1945
Christliche Gemeinde im Wechsel der Staatsordnungen: Dokumente Einer Ungarreise, 1948, Zürich, Evangelischer Verlag, 1948

Theologische Fragen und Antworten, Gesammelte Vorträge, Zürich, Zollikon, 1957
Karl Barth zum Kirchenkampf, Beteilung—Mahnung—Zuspruch, Theologische Existenz Heute (New Series), Munich, Kaiser, 1956
Fides Quaerens Intellectum, 2nd edn, Zürich, Evangelischer Verlag, 1958
Der Götze Wackelt, ed. K. Kupisch, Zürich, Theologischer Verlag, 1961
'No boring theology! A Letter from Karl Barth', *South East Asian Journal of Theology* 2 (Autumn 1969)
Letzte Zeugnisse, Zürich, Evangelischer Verlag, 1969
How I Changed my Mind, Edinburgh, St Andrew Press, 1969
Gottes Freiheit für den Menschen, Berlin, Evangelischer Verlag, 1970
Anfänge der dialektischen Theologie, ed. J. Moltmann: i, Munich, Kaiser, 1962; ii, Munich, Kaiser, 1963
Karl Barth–Martin Rade: Ein Briefwechsel, ed. C. Schwöbel, Gütersloh, Gütersloher Verlagshaus Gerd Mohn, 1981
Klarung- Wirkung-Aufbruch, Berlin, Union, 1986
Karl Barth–H. Miskotte Briefwechsel 1924–1968, Zürich, Theologischer Verlag, 1991

ENGLISH TRANSLATIONS
(in chronological order of publication)

Church Dogmatics, ed. G. W. Bromiley and T. F. Torrance, Edinburgh, T. & T. Clark, 1956–77
The Resurrection of the Dead, tr. H. Stenning, London, Hodder & Stoughton, 1933
Come Holy Spirit: Sermons by K. Barth and E. Thurneysen, Edinburgh, T. & T. Clark, 1934
The Word of God and the Word of Man (ET of *Das Wort Gottes und die Theologie*), tr. D. Horton, London, Hodder & Stoughton, 1935
The Church and the Churches, London, J. Clarke, n.d.
Credo, tr. J. McNab, London, Hodder & Stoughton, 1936
The Knowledge of God and the Service of God, tr. J. Haire and I. Henderson, London, Hodder & Stoughton, 1938
The Holy Ghost and the Christian Life, tr. R. Birch Hoyle, London, F. Muller, 1938
A Letter to Great Britain from Switzerland, London, Sheldon, 1941
The Church and the War, New York, Macmillan, 1944
Natural Theology, tr. P. Fraenkel, London, Bles, 1946
A Shorter Commentary on Romans, tr. D. van daalen, London, SCM, 1959
Anselm: Fides Quaerens Intellectum, tr. J. Robertson, London, SCM, 1960
The Faith of the Church, tr. G. Vahanian, London, Fontana, 1960
'Rudolf Bultmann:—An Attempt to Understand Him' in *Kerygma and Myth*, ed. R. Fuller, London, SPCK, 1960
Dogmatics in Outline, tr. G. Thomson, London, SCM, 1960
Deliverance to the Captives, tr. M. Wieser, London, SCM, 1961
Theology and Church (ET of *Die Theologie und die Kirche*), tr. L. Pettibone Smith, London, SCM, 1962
The Epistle to the Philippians, tr. J. Leitch, London, SCM, 1962

Karl Barth's Table Talk, ed. J. Godsey, Edinburgh, Oliver & Boyd, 1963

Christ and Adam: Man and Humanity in Romans 5, tr. T. Smail, Edinburgh, Oliver & Boyd, 1963

Evangelical Theology, Edinburgh, T. & T. Clark, 1963

Revolutionary Theology in the Making: Barth–Thurneysen Correspondence, 1914–1925, tr. J. Smart, London, Epworth, 1964

God Here and Now: Religious Perspectives, tr. P. van Buren, London, Routledge & Kegan Paul, 1964

Prayer and Preaching, London, SCM, 1964

Against the Stream: Shorter Post-War Writings, London, SCM, 1964

The Heidelberg Catechism for Today, tr. S. Guthrie, London, Epworth, 1964

The Humanity of God, tr. J. Thomas and T. Wieser, London, Collins, 1967

Call for God: New Sermons from Basel Prison, London, SCM, 1967

Community, State, and Church, Gloucester, Mass., Smith, 1968

Ad Limina Apostolorum, tr. K. Crim, Edinburgh, St Andrew Press, 1968

Fragments Grave and Gay, tr. E. Mosbacher, London, Fontana, 1971

Protestant Theology in the Nineteenth Century: Its Background and History, tr. B. Cozens and J. Bowden, London, SCM, 1972

Revelation and Theology: An Analysis of the Barth–Harnack Correspondence of 1923, ed. H. M. Rumscheidt, London, Cambridge University Press, 1972

Ethics (ET of *Ethik* I and II), tr. G. W. Bromiley, Edinburgh, T. & T. Clark, 1981

Karl Barth–R. Bultmann Letters 1922–1966, tr. G. W. Bromiley, Grand Rapids, Eerdmans, 1981

Letters 1961–1968, tr. G. W. Bromiley, Edinburgh, T. & T. Clark, 1981

The Christian Life, tr. G. W. Bromiley, Grand Rapids, Eerdmans, 1981

A Late Friendship: The Letters of Karl Barth and Carl Zuckmayer, tr. G. W. Bromiley, Grand Rapids, Eerdmans, 1982

The Theology of Schleiermacher, tr. G. W. Bromiley, Edinburgh, T. & T. Clark, 1982

Wolfgang Amadens Mozart, tr. C. Pott, Grand Rapids, Eerdmans, 1986

Witness to the Word (ET of commentary on John 1), tr. G. W. Bromiley, Grand Rapids, Eerdmans, 1986

The Göttingen Dogmatics: Instruction in the Christian Religion, vol. I, tr. G. W. Bromiley, Grand Rapids, Eerdmans, 1991 (ET of *Unterricht in der christlichen Religion*)

The Theology of John Calvin, tr. G. W. Bromiley, Grand Rapids, Eerdmans, 1995

SECONDARY WORKS

ADORNO, T., and HORKHEIMER, M., *Dialectic of Enlightenment*, London, Verso, 1973

BALTHASAR, HANS URS VON, *The Theology of Karl Barth: Exposition and Interpretation*, tr. E. Oakes, San Francisco, Ignatius, 1992

BARR, J. *The Semantics of Biblical Language*, Oxford, Oxford University Press, 1961

—— *Old and New in Interpretation*, London, SCM, 1966

—— *The Bible in the Modern World*, London, SCM, 1973

—— *Biblical Faith and Natural Theology*, Oxford, Clarendon, 1993

BEINTKER, M., 'Der Römerbrief von 1919' in G. Sauter (ed.), *Verkündigung und Forschung: Beihefte zu 'Evangelische Theologie' 2 (1985)* Munich, Kaiser, 1987

—— *Die Dialektik in der 'dialektischen Theologie' Karl Barths*, Munich, Kaiser, 1987

BENJAMIN, W., *Illuminations*, tr. H. Zohn, London, Fontana, 1968

BERKOUWER, G., *The Triumph of Grace in the Theology of Karl Barth*, London, Paternoster, 1956

BETTIS, J., 'Is Barth a Universalist?', *SJT* 20 (1967)

—— 'Barth's Rejection of Natural Theology and the Hermeneutical Problem', *SJT* 22 (1969)

BIGGAR, N., *The Hastening that Waits: Karl Barth's Ethics*, Oxford, Clarendon, 1993

BIGGAR, N. (ed.), *Reckoning with Barth*, London and Oxford, Mowbray, 1988

BLASER, K., *Combats- Idées- Reprises: Karl Barth 1886–1986*, Freiburg, Lang, 1987

BOCK, P., *Signs of the Kingdom: A Ragaz Reader*, Grand Rapids, Eerdmans, 1984

BONHOEFFER, D., *Letters and Papers from Prison*, 3rd edn, London, SCM, 1967

BONINO, M., 'Historical Praxis and Christian Identity' in R. Gibellini (ed.), *Frontiers of Theology in Latin America*, Maryknoll, NY, Orbis, 1979

BUESS, E., and MATTMÜLLER, M., *Prophetischer Socialismus: Blumhardt—Ragaz—Barth*, Freiburg, Exodus, 1986

BULLIVANT, K. (ed.), *Culture and Society in the Weimar Republic*, Manchester, Manchester University Press, 1977

BULLOCK, A., *Hitler: A Study in Tyranny*, Harmondsworth, Penguin, 1990

BULTMANN, R., 'The New Testament and Mythology' in *Kerygma and Myth*, tr. R. Fuller, London, SPCK, 1960

BURGSMÜLLER, A., and WETH, R., (eds), *Die Barmer Theologische Erklärung*, Neukirchen, 1983

BUSCH, E., *Karl Barth: His Life from Letters and Autobiographical Texts*, tr. J. Bowden, London, SCM, 1976

—— *Glaubensheiterkeit*, Neukirchen, 1986

CAMUS, A., *The Rebel*, tr. A. Bower, Harmondsworth, Penguin, 1962

CASTAÑEDA, J., *Utopia Unarmed*, New York, Knopf, 1993

COMAROFF, J. and J., *Of Revelation and Revolution: Christianity, Colonialism and Consciousness in South Africa*, Chicago, University of Chicago Press, 1991.

COME, A., *Barth's Dogmatics for Preachers*, London, SCM, 1963

CORT, J., *Christian Socialism*, New York, Orbis, 1988

CRAIG, G., *Germany 1866–1945*, Oxford, Clarendon, 1978

DIEM, H., 'Karl Barth as Socialist' in G. Hunsinger (ed.), *Karl Barth and Radical Politics*, Philadelphia, Westminster, 1976

EBERLE, M., *World War I and the Weimar Artists*, New Haven and London, Yale University Press, 1985

EICHER, P., *Einwürfe*, Munich, Kaiser, 1986

EICHER, P., and WEINRICH, M., *Der gute Widerspruch*, Neukirchen, Patmos, 1986

EYCK, E., *A History of the Weimar Republic* (2 vols.), London, Oxford University Press, 1964

FIDDES, P., 'The Status of Woman in the Thought of Karl Barth' in J. M. Soskice (ed.), *After Eve*, London, Collins, 1990

FISHER, S., *Revelatory Positivism?: Barth's Earliest Theology and the Marburg School*, Oxford, Oxford University Press, 1988

FORD, D., *Barth and God's Story*, 2nd edn, Frankfurt am Main, Lang, 1985

FRYKBERG, E., 'The Child as Solution: The Problem of the Superordinate–Subordinate Ordering of the Male–Female Relation in Barth's Theology,' *SJT* 47 (1994)

GAY, P. *Weimar Culture: The Outsider as Insider*, Harmondsworth, Penguin, 1974

GEGENHEIMER, R. (ed.), *Porträt eines Theologen*, Stuttgart, Radius, 1970

GOGARTEN, F., *Gericht oder Skepsis?*, Jena, Diedrichs, 1937

GRAMSCI, A., *Selections from the Prison Notebooks*, New York, International Publishers, 1971

GREEN, C., *Karl Barth: Theologian of Freedom*, London, Collins, 1989

GREY, M., *Redeeming the Dream*, London, SPCK, 1989

GUNTON, C., *Becoming and Being*, Oxford, Oxford University Press, 1978

GUTIÉRREZ, G., *The Power of the Poor in History*, London, SCM, 1983

——*Essential Writings*, ed. J. B. Nickoloff, London, SCM, 1996

HAMER, J., *Karl Barth*, tr. D. Maruca, London, Sands, 1962

HÄRLE, W., *Sein und Gnade: Die Ontologie in Karl Barths Kirchlicher Dogmatik*, Berlin, de Gruyter, 1975

HART, J. W., *Karl Barth versus Emil Brunner: The Formation and Dissolution of a Theological Alliance 1916–1936*, Unpublished D.Phil thesis, Oxford, 1993

HEIBER, H., *The Weimar Republic*, tr. W. Yuill, Oxford, Blackwell, 1993

HOBSBAWM, E., *Age of Extremes*, London, Abacus, 1994

HOFFMANN, P., *The History of the German Resistance*, tr. R. Barry, Massachusetts, MIT Press, 1979

HOOD, R., *Contemporary Political Orders and Christ*, Allison Park, Pa., Pickwick, 1985

HUNSINGER, G., *How to Read Karl Barth*, Oxford, Oxford University Press, 1991

HUNSINGER, G. (ed.), *Karl Barth and Radical Politics*, Philadelphia, Westminster, 1976

Jacob, M., '. . . noch einmal mit dem Anfang anfangen', *EvT* 32 (1972)

JENSON, R., *God after God*, Bobbs Merrill, Indianapolis, 1969

JÜNGEL, E., *The Doctrine of the Trinity*, Edinburgh, Scottish Academic Press, 1976

——*Karl Barth: A Theological Legacy*, tr. G. Paul, Philadelphia, Westminster, 1986

KELSEY, D., *The Uses of Scripture in Recent Theology*, London, SCM, 1975

KERR, F., *Immortal Longings: Versions of Transcending Humanity*, London, SPCK, 1997

Kerygma and Myth: A Theological Debate, ed. H. W. Bartsch: i, London, SPCK, 1960; ii, London, SPCK, 1962

KIRSCHBAUM, C. VON, *The Question of Woman*, ed. E. Jackson, Grand Rapids, Eerdmans, 1996

KLAPPERT, B., *Die Auferweckung des Gekreuzigten* (1971), 3rd impression, Neukirchener, 1981

——*Israel und die Kirche*, Munich, Kaiser, 1979

——'Die Rechts-, Freiheits und Befreiungsgeschichte Gottes mit dem Menschen', *EvT* 49 (1987)

KNIESCHE, T. W., and BROCKMANN, S., (eds), *Dancing on the Volcano: Essays on the Culture of the Weimar Republic*, Columbia, Camden, 1994

KNITTER, P., *No Other Name?*, London, SCM, 1985

KÖBLER, R., *Schattenarbeit*, Cologne, Pahl-Rugenstein, 1987

KOLB, E., *The Weimar Republic*, London, Unwin, 1988

KRAFT, D., 'Israel in der Theologie Karl Barths', *Communio Viatorum* 27 / 1–2 (1984)

KUTTER, H., *Sie Müssen*, Jena, 1910

LAQUEUR, W., *Europe in our Time: A History 1945–1992*, Harmondsworth, Penguin, 1992

LEHMAN, P., 'Karl Barth as Theologian of Permanent Revolution', *Union Theological Seminary Review* 28/1 (1972)

LEUBA, J. L., 'Le problème de l'église chez Karl Barth', *Verbum Caro* 1/1 (1947)

LOVIN, R., *Christian Faith and Public Choices: The Social Ethics of Barth, Brunner and Bonhoeffer*, Philadelphia, Fortress, 1984

McCABE, H., *God Matters*, London, Chapman, 1987

McCORMACK, B. L., *Karl Barth's Critically Realistic Dialectical Theology: Its Genesis and Development 1909–1936*, Oxford, Clarendon, 1995

MACKEN, J., *The Autonomy Theme in the Church Dogmatics: Karl Barth and his Critics*, Cambridge, Cambridge University Press, 1990

MANN, G., *The History of Germany since 1789*, tr. M. Jackson, London, Chatto & Windus, 1968

MARQUARDT, F. W., *Die entdeckung des Judentums für die christliche Theologie: Israel in Denken Karl Barths*, Munich, Kaiser, 1967

——*Der Christ in der Gesellschaft 1919–1979*, Munich, Kaiser, 1980

——*Theologie und Sozialismus: Das Beispiel Karl Barths*, 3rd edn, Munich, Kaiser, 1985

MARSHALL, B., *Christology in Conflict*, Oxford, Blackwell, 1987

MARX, K., *Capital*, i, Moscow, Progress, 1954

MARX, K., and ENGELS, F., *Correspondence 1846–1895*, London, Lawrence, 1934

——*Collected Works*, Moscow, Progress, 1975

MATHENY, P., *Dogmatics and Ethics*, Frankfurt, Lang, 1990

MOLTMANN, J. (ed.), *Anfänge der dialektischen Theologie*, Munich, Kaiser, 1977

O'GRADY, C., *The Church in the Theology of Karl Barth*, London, Chapman, 1968

——*The Church in Catholic Theology*, London, Chapman, 1969

PACHTER, H. M., *Modern Germany: A Social, Cultural and Political History*, Boulder, Col., Westview, 1978

PALMA, R., *Karl Barth's Theology of Culture*, Allison Park, Pa., Pickwick, 1983

PLONZ, S., *Die herrenlosen Gewalten: Eine Relektüre Karl Barths in befreiungstheologischer Perspektive*, Mainz, Grünewald, 1995

PUGH, J., *The Anselmic Shift: Christology and Method in Karl Barth's Theology*, Frankfurt, Lang, 1990

ROBERTS, R. H., *A Theology on its Way?: Essays on Karl Barth*, Edinburgh, T. & T. Clark, 1991

ROSATO, P., *The Spirit as Lord*, Edinburgh, T. & T. Clark, 1981

RUMSCHEIDT, H. M. (ed.), *Karl Barth in Re-View*, Pittsburgh, Pickwick, 1981

RUMSCHEIDT, H. M. (ed.), *Footnotes to a Theology: The Karl Barth Colloquium 1972*, Ontario, Corporation for the Publication of Academic Studies in Religion in Canada, 1974

SAUTER, G. (ed.), *Verkündigung und Forschung*: Beihefte zu 'Evangelische Theologie', Munich, Kaiser, 1985

SCHELLONG, D., 'Karl Barth als Theologe der Neuzeit' in *Karl Barth und die Neuzeit, Theologische Existenz Heute* (New Series), Munich, Kaiser, 1985

SCHOLDER, K., *The Churches and the Third Reich*, i: *1918–1934*, tr. J. Bowden, London, SCM, 1987; ii: *The Year of Disillusionment 1934*, tr. J. Bowden, London, SCM, 1988

——*A Requiem for Hitler, and Other New Perspectives on the German Church Struggle*, London, SCM, 1989

SELZ, P., *Beckmann*, London, Abbeville, 1996

SMART, J. D., *The Divided Mind of Modern Theology: Karl Barth and Rudolf Bultmann 1908–1933*, Philadelphia, Westminster, 1967

SONDEREGGER, K., 'On Style in Karl Barth', *SJT* 45 (1992)

STICKLEBERGER, H. E., *Ipsa assumptione creatur: Orthodox Christologie und weltliche Existenz in der 'Kirchlichen Dogmatik' Karl Barths*, Bern, Peter Lang, 1979

STOEVESANDT, H., '"Von kirchenpolitik zur Kirche!" Zur Entstehunggeschichte von K. Barth's Schrift "Theologische Existenz Heute!",' *ZTK* 76 (1979)

SYKES, S., (ed.), *Karl Barth: Centenary Essays*, Cambridge, Cambridge University Press, 1989

——*Karl Barth: Studies of his Theological Methods*, Oxford, Clarendon, 1979

THOMPSON, J., *Christ in Perspective: Christological Perspectives in the Theology of Karl Barth*, Edinburgh, St Andrew Press, 1978

——*The Holy Spirit in the Theology of Karl Barth*, Allison Park, Pa., Pickwick, 1991

THURNEYSEN, E., 'Theologie und Sozialismus' in den Briefen seiner Frühzeit, Zürich, Theologischer Verlag, 1973

TORRANCE, T. F., *Karl Barth: An Introduction to his Early Theology*, London, SCM, 1963

——*Karl Barth: Biblical and Evangelical Theologian*, Edinburgh, T. & T. Clark, 1990

VILLA-VICENCIO, V., (ed.), *On Reading Karl Barth in South Africa*, Grand Rapids, Eerdmans, 1988

WARD, G., *Barth, Derrida and the Language of Theology*, Cambridge, Cambridge University Press, 1995

WEBB, S. H., *Refiguring Theology: The Rhetoric of Karl Barth*, Albany, State University of New York Press, 1991

WEBSTER, J., *Barth's Ethics of Reconciliation*, Cambridge, Cambridge University Press, 1995

WEST, A., *Deadly Innocence*, London, Mowbray, 1995

WIGGERSHAUS, R., *The Frankfurt School*, tr. M. Robertson, Cambridge, Polity, 1994

WILLIAMS, RAYMOND, *Marxism and Literature*, Oxford, Oxford University Press, 1977

WILLIAMS, ROWAN, 'Barth, War and the State' in N. Biggar (ed.), *Reckoning with Barth*, London and Oxford, Mowbray, 1988

WINGREN, G., *Theology in Conflict*, Edinburgh, Oliver & Boyd, 1958

WINZELER, P., *Widerstehende Theologie: Karl Barth 1920–35* Stuttgart, Alektor, 1982

WYSCHOGROD, M., 'Why Was and Is the Theology of Karl Barth of Interest to a Jewish Theologian?' in H. M. Rumscheidt (ed.), *Footnotes to a Theology: The Karl Barth Colloquium 1972*, Ontario, Corporation for the Publication of Academic Studies in Religion in Canada, 1974

Index

Printed in the United Kingdom by
Lightning Source UK Ltd., Milton Keynes
136767UK00002B/91/A